LATER MEDIEVAL METAPHYSICS

Medieval Philosophy
TEXTS AND STUDIES

Later Medieval Metaphysics

Ontology, Language, and Logic

Edited by
CHARLES BOLYARD
and RONDO KEELE

Fordham University Press • New York • 2013

Fordham University Press has no responsibility
for the persistence or accuracy of URLs for
external or third-party Internet websites referred
to in this publication and does not guarantee that
any content on such websites is, or will remain,
accurate or appropriate.

Fordham University Press also publishes its books
in a variety of electronic formats. Some content
that appears in print may not be available in
electronic books.

Library of Congress Cataloging-in-Publication Data
Later medieval metaphysics : ontology, language,
and logic / edited by Charles Bolyard and Rondo
Keele. — First edition.
    p. cm. — (Medieval philosophy)
  Includes bibliographical references (p.   ) and
index.
    ISBN 978-0-8232-4472-0 (cloth : alk. paper)—
    ISBN 978-0-8232-4473-7 (pbk. : alk. paper)
    1. Metaphysics—Early works to 1800.
I. Bolyard, Charles, editor. II. Keele, Rondo,
1968– , editor.
    BD111.L28 2013
    110—dc23

                                    2012036566

Printed in the United States of America
15 14 13   5 4 3 2 1
First edition

This volume is dedicated to Paul Vincent Spade, Emeritus Professor of Philosophy at Indiana University. Professor Spade spent his entire academic career at Indiana, after having earned an A.B. from Wabash College, a Licentiate of Mediaeval Studies from the Pontifical Institute of Mediaeval Studies in Toronto, and a Ph.D. from the University of Toronto.

Professor Spade's scholarly work focuses primarily on medieval logic and semantic theory, especially during the fourteenth century. Figures such as Walter Burley, William of Ockham, and Thomas Bradwardine are frequent subjects of his research, but he has published on a wide range of topics and thinkers. Over the course of his career, he has authored or edited 10 books, and just shy of 100 scholarly articles, shorter translations, and shorter critical editions. In addition, he has written numerous reviews and made freely available a large number of translations, critical editions, and classroom lecture materials. He is an innovator in the use of the internet as a means of disseminating philosophical material, having won awards for his Medieval Logic and Philosophy web page, and having served for many years as a member of the editorial board of the online *Stanford Encyclopedia of Philosophy*.

For those lucky enough to have been his students, Professor Spade is best remembered for his masterful teaching. His lectures showed great philosophical depth and technical detail, all while being delivered in his trademarked quirky and entertaining style. Lucid expositions of the most recondite doctrines were sprinkled with strange tidbits of "lore and gossip," as he put it, about the philosophers under discussion. One learned not only the intricacies of supposition theory, for example, but also how death by quill pen could end an otherwise promising career. Thankfully, the storyteller himself has not yet shared that fate.

Paul Vincent Spade is a teacher, scholar, jazz connoisseur, and a true lover of wisdom. And though he would deny it if asked, he is a giant upon whose shoulders many stand. May this volume of essays stand as a witness to their gratitude.

CONTENTS

Acknowledgments   *xi*

Introduction   1
Charles Bolyard and Rondo Keele

PART I   ESSENCE, EXISTENCE, AND THE NATURE
OF METAPHYSICS

1   Duns Scotus on Metaphysics as the Science
of First Entity   11
Rega Wood

2   Aquinas vs. Buridan on Essence and Existence   30
Gyula Klima

PART II   FORM AND MATTER

3   The Form of Corporeity and Potential and Aptitudinal
Being in Dietrich von Freiberg's Defense of the Doctrine
of the Unity of Substantial Form   47
Brian Francis Conolly

4   Accidents in Scotus's *Metaphysics* Commentary   84
Charles Bolyard

PART III   UNIVERSALS

5   Avicenna Latinus on the Ontology of Types
and Tokens   103
Martin Tweedale

6   Universal Thinking as Process: The Metaphysics
of Change and Identity in John Buridan's
Intellectio Theory   137
Jack Zupko

PART IV   LANGUAGE, LOGIC, AND METAPHYSICS

7   Can God Know More? A Case Study in Later Medieval
    Discussions of Propositions   161
    Susan Brower-Toland

8   The Power of Medieval Logic   188
    Terence Parsons

9   Iteration and Infinite Regress in Walter Chatton's
    Metaphysics   206
    Rondo Keele

10 Analogy and Metaphor from Thomas Aquinas to Duns
    Scotus and Walter Burley   223
    E. Jennifer Ashworth

    Notes   249
    List of Contributors   301
    Index   303

ACKNOWLEDGMENTS

The contributors wish to acknowledge their debt to the work of Paul Vincent Spade, whose lucid, entertaining, and pioneering scholarship in medieval metaphysics was the inspiration for the plan of this volume. Each essay owes some portion of its range, ideas, and insights to the fact that we have had his work to build on.

We wish to thank our anonymous reviewers for their helpful suggestions and comments. The editorial and production teams at Fordham University Press and Westchester Publishing Services have been indispensible as well. In particular, we would like to thank Helen Tartar, Thomas Lay, Eric Newman, and Kathleen Sweeney at Fordham, and Lyndee Stalter and Paul Vincent at Westchester. Their patience as they worked with us on this project is noteworthy, and their assistance has been greatly appreciated.

Introduction

CHARLES BOLYARD AND RONDO KEELE

Medieval metaphysics and modern-day metaphysics share much common ground; many issues of concern to medieval metaphysicians would be quite familiar to those who find themselves in a present-day metaphysics seminar. These earlier philosophers worried about the nature of change, the fundamental structure of reality (and of the entities within that reality), identity, time, and so on. It is easy to look past this fact, however, because of the fundamental ontology they adhered to: for them, God, angels, and miracles were entities and phenomena that had to fit into their metaphysical systems. Just as contemporary metaphysicians work with the ontology of modern science, so too the medievals worked within their theological ontologies. Though this book's intended audience is primarily specialists in or students of medieval philosophy, helping contemporary nonmedievalist philosophers see past these initial differences in language, terminology, and context is a secondary aim.

In this volume, we concentrate in particular on some intricate and fascinating discussions that took place in metaphysics during the Later Middle Ages, centering on some thirteenth- and fourteenth-century debates in the Christian West. These discussions drew heavily from the twelfth-century rediscovery of the full Aristotelian corpus and the Islamic and Jewish philosophical works that were translated alongside it. Though we touch on only a few of the many thinkers who considered these issues, our aim is to give the reader insights into some of the most central metaphysical discussions in which they engaged.

Perhaps unsurprisingly, medieval philosophers divided their enquiries along different lines than we do today. For most of them (John Buridan is a notable exception here), theological studies were their main focus, and their philosophy is usually found under the cover of seemingly unrelated discussions of such topics as, for example, the nature of the transubstantiation. In addition to this entanglement, medieval metaphysics is often continuous with medieval discussions of logic, language, and epistemology. While some elements of these philosophers' works are unquestionably "pure" treatments of metaphysical problems, most are not. And to ignore these mixed treatments is to ignore much of what is important in medieval metaphysics. Given these realities, we have not attempted to rid our investigations of their contextual trappings; our readers should not be surprised to find the discussions leading in directions that would be unanticipated from our volume's title alone.

So what else is distinctive about later medieval metaphysics? In order to begin to untangle the mass of arguments and positions that is medieval philosophy, it's best to begin with a rough and admittedly oversimplifying formula. Let's start with the following (paraphrased) claim by Paul Vincent Spade, and work from there:

> In order to understand Medieval Philosophy generally, one need only achieve a thorough grounding in Ancient Greek and Neoplatonic Philosophy, mix in the doctrine of contingent creation, and turn the crank. Medieval accounts of the nature of the soul, God, free will, and change easily follow.[1]

Now we can expand on this. The single most important influence on the metaphysical thought of the Later Middle Ages was Aristotle. Plato was well known, yet only a few of his works were translated into Latin; most medievals knew of Plato through only one of his dialogues (roughly half of the *Timaeus*), and through multiple secondary accounts given by earlier philosophers such as Augustine, Cicero, or the commentators who attempted to reconcile Neoplatonism and Aristotelian philosophy. Evidence of this focus on Aristotle is seen especially in the terminology in use: substance, accident, matter, and form are commonly referred to (though often quite differently understood) by nearly everyone who wrote during the period; references to Platonic Forms occur, but they often show only the vaguest familiarity with Plato's discussions and arguments. In any case, despite Aristotle's strong influence, his positions were sometimes rejected outright—for example, regarding the immortality of the soul, or as seen in William of Ockham's famous reduction of the number of Aristotle's categories from ten to two—and they were almost always modified or developed to a significant degree.

Another obvious influence was Christian theology. Though theological doctrine, then as now, was developing alongside the philosophy with which it interacted, there were some claims that had a particularly strong impact on later medieval thought. First, the Christian notion of a perfect, freely creating God was definitely not something found in Aristotle. Second, divine omnipotence (which easily follows from God's perfection) was a central position emphasized by philosophers from the late thirteenth-century onward. These claims led, for example, to the view that if God can do anything, the world and everything in it are thoroughly contingent in nature. Third, the doctrine of the Trinity, which attempts to find a place between tritheism and the absolute unity and simplicity of God, was highly influential on metaphysical debates; maintaining that God is simultaneously three and one required considerable metaphysical dexterity. Other doctrines naturally played a role in the discussions of the period, many of them not envisioned by, or out-and-out in contradiction to, Aristotle himself.

Finally, Jewish and Islamic thought played a key role in the development of Christian philosophy. Ibn-Sina (Avicenna to the Latins) examined the notions of essence and existence in some detail; Ibn-Rushd (or Averroes) was particularly well known for his explanations of Aristotle's account of the soul. Most importantly, however, these thinkers laid significant groundwork for ways in which Ancient Greek metaphysics, especially as seen in Plato and Aristotle, is compatible with the Abrahamic religions. Augustine had done much to bring Platonic thought into philosophical and theological play for the later medievals, and Islamic and Jewish thinkers performed the same role as regards Aristotelian philosophy. Especially as one approaches the Later Middle Ages, the arguments become denser, the terminology becomes more specialized, and the philosophy becomes ever more interesting as it moves farther and farther from these Greek roots.

As will be seen in the essays that follow, medievals held widely divergent views on a number of issues; attempts to define a shared scholastic view on any given question are usually as misguided as the medievals' attempts to discover a similarly shared Platonic/Aristotle synthetic position. Did any medievals seriously question God's existence in their works? Not really. Were any of them idealists in any strong sense? Perhaps, but at best there were only a few. Beyond this basic agreement, however, you will find some who are realists about universals, and some who are nominalists. Some philosophers take great pains to discover what exactly it is that individuates substances, while others treat the issue as a (mere) brute fact. Thomas Aquinas, John Duns Scotus, and Ockham may be the best-known philosophers of the Later Middle Ages, but it would be a serious misunderstanding to think either that they are fundamentally in agreement on most metaphysical issues, or if they do happen to be in agreement on any particular point, that their shared view exhausts the possibilities worked out by their medieval contemporaries. There is no One Voice that can characterize the thought of the Middle Ages with any degree of historical accuracy.

Our volume is organized topically. The first section, "Essence, Existence, and the Nature of Metaphysics," consists of two essays. Rega Wood investigates Scotus (1265–1308) and what exactly he takes the proper subject of metaphysics to be. Is it God, being (or entity) in general, or is it something else? In the background of Scotus's account lie concerns about the nature of metaphysics generally: What exactly is its place among the sciences? Is it subordinate to any of them (theology, for example), or is it something that stands on its own? Furthermore, what counts as good metaphysical reasoning? Must it be deductively certain? Wood explains how different answers to these questions may be found in different works of Scotus, and from these scattered treatments, she pieces together an account of Scotus's mature position.

Gyula Klima's article focuses on the nature of essence and existence in creatures—that is, in created entities. More specifically, he looks at Aquinas (1224–74) and his intriguing account of these fundamental notions from *On Being and Essence*. He then defends Aquinas against a few important objections, one by Anthony Kenny in his recent work *Aquinas on Being*, and the other by the medieval arts master Buridan (1295–1361). The discussion ranges widely over issues in epistemology, language, and metaphysics proper.

Next, we investigate the relation between "Form and Matter." Brian Francis Conolly covers form and matter in humans, as discussed by Dietrich von Freiberg (1250–1310). Do humans have many substantial forms (rationality, animality, corporeity), or is there only one that encompasses all of them? At death, does one's corpse still retain the same substantial form(s) it had before, while living? In investigating numerous arguments given by Dietrich and his opponents, including those of Aquinas and Giles of Rome (1243/7–1316), Conolly explores issues concerning personal identity, change, and unity.

Charles Bolyard discusses a special type of form: the accident (e.g., one's post-holiday body shape). He focuses on Scotus's account of accidents in his commentary on Aristotle's *Metaphysics*. Whereas Aristotle emphasizes an accident's dependence upon the subject in which it inheres, Scotus's account is notable for giving accidents increased independence and ontological heft. This raises a host of questions: How can an accident and its subject be a unity in any strong sense? Does knowing an accident entail knowing its subject? Can an accident exist without a subject at all?

Our next topic concerns two contributors to the great medieval debate over the existence and nature of "Universals." First, Martin Tweedale gives us some important background to later medieval discussions by exploring the type/token distinction in Avicenna (980–1037), who was incredibly influential on such thinkers as Aquinas and Scotus. Tweedale explains how Avicenna seeks to find a middle position between monism and idealism. Monism, as understood here, is the view that there is no fundamental distinction between, for example, any two humans. Idealism, on the other hand, is the view that one's being human is ultimately mind-dependent. As Tweedale argues, Avicenna escapes both monism and idealism by holding that universality is an accident: humanity is not *in itself* a universal, though it can function that way in the correct circumstances.

Second, Jack Zupko's essay reveals an interesting similarity between Ockham (1285–1347) and the Parisian arts master Buridan: the advancement of an *intellectio*-theory of universal cognition. Ockham's adoption of this theory under pressure from Walter Chatton (1285–1343) seems to have had no direct influence on Buridan's support of the same theory, according to which one's concept of things denoted by general terms is identical with one's thinking of those things generally. In his detailed and well-documented exposition, Zupko shows how Buridan actually held two versions of the theory, an early one which—although quite promising—he abandoned without modification or explanation, and a mature theory which resembles in many respects that adopted by Ockham and Chatton. As Zupko shows, however, both theories are consistent with Buridan's nominalism on universals.

The final topic in our collection, "Language, Logic, and Metaphysics," should prove of interest not only to specialists, but also to modern analytic philosophers interested in viewing the logical sophistication of these late medieval theologians in action, especially in their implications for subtopics important to metaphysics as it is often construed today, including philosophy of mind, ontological commitment, and philosophy of language.

First, Susan Brower-Toland radically revises the landscape of a central, well-studied debate in Ockham scholarship, the question of how and to what extent Ockham disagreed with his contemporaries about the objects of propositional attitudes. By clarifying the positions of Ockham, Chatton, and Robert Holcot (1290–1349) on the role played by objects of propositional attitude relations, she shows how these three thinkers, previously assumed by almost all scholars to be at odds, are actually talking past one another in virtue of their distinct conceptions and aims. If correct, Brower-Toland's discovery of this will completely reshape our understanding of these vital Oxford debates in philosophy of mind.

Next, Terence Parsons conducts a focused and compact survey of medieval Aristotelian logic with a special eye toward gauging its adequacy compared with modern predicate calculus. For example, he inquires into its utility for certain tasks we recognize as important today, such as the formulation of relational logic and its proof theory, and the treatment of mathematical claims in the Peano axioms. Parsons finds the rich system of medieval logicians remarkably adequate to all these needs, save only for a failure in relation to Peano's fourth postulate, and the statement of transitivity of ">." After some analysis he makes the source of the failure clear: in the absence of a theory of anaphoric pronouns, such as are represented by quantifiers and bound variables today, no general statements of those important principles of Peano arithmetic can be given. Nevertheless, it is the successes rather than the failures of their systems which will challenge modern preconceptions and most surprise the reader.

Rondo Keele makes a foray into what he calls "applied logic," investigating a complex argument strategy employed against Ockham by his greatest contemporary opponent, Chatton. Chatton conceives a two-part strategy which attempts to force a kind of iteration of conceptual analysis, together with an infinite explanatory regress, in order to establish that one particular philosophical analysis is ultimately dependent on another. Chatton uses this strategy against Ockham in order to show that the latter's reductionist metaphysics depends ultimately upon a deeper level of realist assumptions that he can neither evade nor explain away. Keele then shows how, earlier in his career, Chatton found himself on the receiving end of this same strategy, defending his own highly original solution to the problem of future contingents from the very iteration-regress attack he would subsequently use on Ockham. Keele concludes with an examination of Chatton's attempts to avoid the consequences of his own strategy, and draws some connections between this argument strategy and modal collapse in modern logics.

Finally, Jennifer Ashworth gives a survey account of the interrelations of three extremely important notions that were constantly employed in many forms of argumentation in metaphysics: analogy, metaphor, and equivocation. In particular, Ashworth explores a crucial change in the concept of analogy that occurred from Aquinas to Scotus to Walter Burley (1274–1344). Since Scotus's concerns with analogy and equivocation on the concept of being are at the very heart of his metaphysics, Ashworth's essay ends with a translation from Scotus's commentary on Aristotle's *Categories*, making this important text available to nonspecialists and bolstering her exposition of the change itself.

Our approach has not been a comprehensive one; rather we have sought to bring the reader the very latest research on this rich and relatively under-studied era of philosophical thought. For broader background and overviews of the metaphysical debates of the period, see especially Kretzmann, Kenny, and Pinborg's *The Cambridge History of Later Medieval Philosophy* (Cambridge, 1982), McGrade's *The Cambridge Companion to Medieval Philosophy* (Cambridge, 2003), Spade's idiosyncratic yet highly readable *A Survey of Mediaeval Philosophy, Version 2.0* (online at http://pvspade.com/Logic/docs/Survey%202%20Interim.pdf), and, most recently, Pasnau's two-volume *The Cambridge History of Medieval Philosophy* (Cambridge, 2010). Gracia and Noone's encyclopedia-style *A Companion to Philosophy in the Middle Ages* (Blackwell, 2003) is also an excellent source for introducing the thought of the most important philosophers of the period.

I ESSENCE, EXISTENCE, AND THE NATURE OF METAPHYSICS

1

Duns Scotus on Metaphysics as the Science of First Entity

REGA WOOD

Among Paul Vincent Spade's many distinguished contributions to research in the history of philosophy is a study of "The Unity of Science according to Peter Auriol." As Spade notes, Aureol considers nine previous opinions, including "two (!) of Duns Scotus." Moreover, Aureol may be mistaken in his evaluation of Scotus's views.[1] Alas, disagreement is one hallmark of Scotus studies, and those disagreements are about fundamental questions. The two that will concern us here are: What is the subject of the science of metaphysics and how is it unified?

These are fundamental issues since Aristotelians call metaphysics "first philosophy" because it validates the first principles and concepts assumed in the special sciences of physics, psychology, etc. And the unity of its subject is vital to the success of its demonstrations, since the virtual inclusion of the truths of a science in its subject is the hallmark of a science that shows why things are as they are. Indeed, true science is distinguished from mere proof precisely on this basis. True *propter quid* science or demonstration proceeds from a cause and conveys understanding of the principles of things, while *quia* proofs start from an effect and can only show that something is the case, not why this is so.[2] Surprisingly, for Scotus, the subject of metaphysics is neither specifically nor generically unified and cannot, therefore, provide true understanding of all its conclusions, as we shall see below.

Prior to establishing the grounds for its unity, of course, we must answer the question what is its subject according to Scotus. Three classic answers were offered. Avicenna held that the subject of metaphysics was *ens qua ens*. Aristotle himself may have held that its subject was substance as such, but Averroes claimed that it was more specifically first substance—that is, the independent substance that is ontologically prior to all other substances.

As we shall see below, Scotus entertained all three possibilities. In this paper, I will argue that there is good reason to believe he ultimately decided for the last option[3] and concluded that metaphysics was a *quia* science whose subject was first entity—that is, the independent entity that is ontologically prior to all other entities. I shall base these claims on a study of the first question of his *Questions on Aristotle's Metaphysics*,[4] which presents what I argue is Scotus's mature, perhaps indeed his final, position on the subject of metaphysics.

Changes in Scotus's Position

I hold with Dominique Demange that there are two redactions of this question, the first of which antedates the *Ordinatio*, and the second of which postdates even the *Reportata Parisiensia*, a late work. In the first, Scotus holds that substance is the subject of a *propter quid* science of metaphysics;[5] in the second he maintains that first entity is the subject of a *quia* science of metaphysics. The second redaction, which from now on I will call M2 and contrast with M1, also holds that part of the metaphysics of first entity is a *propter quid* science whose subject is entity *qua* entity—a science which I will henceforth refer to as the "science of entity" in order to avoid repeating the reduplicative phrase.[6]

Here I am going to assume that Demange and I have successfully argued for this conclusion and turn my attention to the relation between the doubts stated at the end of M2 and the prologue to Scotus's *Reportata Parisiensia*, citing the version of the *Reportata* known as 1A which is much like the text of the *Additiones Magnae* compiled by William Alnwick. I will refer to 1A's prologue as the 'Paris prologue.'[7]

My aim will be to show how much the two discussions have in common and try to explain why Scotus changed his mind. So let me start by stating three theses on the subject of metaphysics defended by Scotus at one time or another. I will state them in the terms employed by Demange, but number them in the order we think Scotus first defended them:[8]

+ Theory 1: The primary subject of metaphysics is substance = M1.
+ Theory 2: The primary subject of metaphysics is the concept of being.
+ Theory 3: The primary subject of metaphysics is first being = M2.

Demange and I agree that the third theory (M2) is more fully developed than, and basically compatible with, the second. But though we two agree, most of our distinguished predecessors disagree. This is probably because if you accept our interpretation, you need to disregard categorical statements to the contrary from the Paris prologue, a late work.

Now no one is much worried about the statements Scotus makes in his logical works and in M1 that being cannot be the subject of metaphysics,[9] because it is an equivocal concept, and, of course, only fallacious inferences can be based on propositions in which terms are used ambiguously. But without a doubt this belief lies behind the claim in M1 that substance is the subject of metaphysics.

Correspondingly, we hold that just as the claim that substance is the subject of metaphysics was given up when Scotus demonstrated to his satisfaction that entity was univocal, so too when Scotus showed to his satisfaction that entity could not be the subject of metaphysics as a whole, he abandoned his earlier denial that God could be the subject of metaphysics. In so doing, Scotus also gave up the theory according to which the general science of metaphysics is a *propter quid* science, but retained the claim that there is a *propter quid* metaphysics of entity, though it is only part of metaphysics.

Assuming that we are generally right, I turn now to some reflections on the costs and benefits of M2, with special reference to the relation of the Paris prologue to the Doubts stated at the end of M2.

The Costs of M2's Solution

One of the most obvious costs of M2's solution is that Scotus cannot maintain that metaphysics *is* a demonstrative science, though he can say that it *includes* a demonstrative science.

What does Scotus gain in all this? M2 has three important advantages:

+ It does not suppose that metaphysics is organized as a search for knowledge of the most minimal and imperfect of beings, mere entity (M2 123, pp. 57–58).
+ It affirms with Aristotle that the aim of metaphysics is felicity.[10]
+ It offers new support for the claim that metaphysics is first philosophy, since it is the science that deals with the primary entity on

which all others depend[11] and the first aspect (*ratio*) under which
entities can be considered.

What about us? What would we gain, and what we would have to give
up? It would be nice to find that Scotus's most influential discussion of the
topic was also one he endorsed. But, alas, M2 may state its conclusions only
provisionally, since though M1 explicitly addresses the question, "What is
the proper subject of Metaphysics?," M2 asks a more limited question (M2
130, p. 60): "How could God be the subject of metaphysics?"

So one cost for us is that we could not be sure to what extent Scotus
endorses the claim that God or first entity is the subject of general metaphysics. Another problem is that we would face a situation in which the
principal statement of Scotus's views on the subject of metaphysics is
found in a work for which we have a text that is unsatisfactory in many
respects. Apart from the occasional sentence that makes no sense and the
unanswered objections,[12] it is not entirely clear what paragraphs comprise
M2, since we cannot simply assign all the later additions (*additiones*)
to M2.[13]

The core of M2 comes from paragraphs 110–63 (pp. 53–72) which is a
single addition, that some manuscripts begin earlier at 97 (p. 49). Paragraphs
97–103 (pp. 49–51) are a series of objections against M1, and paragraphs
104–9 (pp. 51–53) are self-described as pertaining equally to M1 and M2,
so there is little doubt that paragraphs 97–163 belong as a whole to M2.

Similarly, the first addition (paras. 32–33, pp. 28–29) is a revised response
to Averroes that is explicitly referenced by M2, and so it, too, must be included in M2.[14] The third addition (paras. 44–57, pp. 32–35) also belongs to
M2, since it revises the reply to Averroes' claims about separated substances
in accordance with M2 and may be referenced in M2 (M2 129, p. 59). But
though Demange and I agree on this point, the reader should note that it
includes a passage in which Scotus seems to identify himself with the position stated at M1.[15]

There is, however, there is at least one addition that does not seem to
belong to M2, namely the second addition found in paragraph 41, which
strengthens an objection to positing first entity as the subject of metaphysics.[16] And there is a longer passage about which we cannot be sure.[17] On my
view, then, M1 is 1–31, 34–40, 42–43, 58–78, and 84–96; M2 is 32–33, 44–57,
and 97–163; and we do not know about paragraphs 41, 79–83.

Another problem is that we might find ourselves in the situation where the chronology was entirely unclear. Demange has apparently shown that M2 is later than the first question of book VI of Scotus's *Metaphysics*, and it is also true that it must be after at least some parts of book I, question 8.[18] But is not so clear that we can show that M2 must date from after the Paris prologue.[19] One problem is that although it is clear that M1 denies that entity is univocal, it is by no means certain that M2 affirms that thesis. And few Scotists would be entirely comfortable with a Scotus who was uncommitted on that point, since as Ludger Honnefelder points out, for Scotus even the principle of bivalence fails if entity is not univocal.[20] Nevertheless, *pace* Demange,[21] though M2 must assume univocity in support of the claim that the science of entity is part of the science of first entity, nonetheless Scotus states his univocity thesis only hypothetically in M2.

Does M2 Offer a Solution Scotus Could Endorse?

An Assessment Plan: Central to the decision about whether M2 represents Scotus's considered opinion is its relation to the Paris prologue. As Demange correctly points out, M2 presents sophisticated responses to many of the arguments stated in the Paris prologue.[22] Does that mean that M2 is after the Paris prologue and reflects a more mature position? Since this is not obvious, I will examine the doubts (*dubitationes*) with which M2 ends and ask to what extent Scotus's responses to them are adequate to the problems that prompted the Paris prologue's rejection of first entity as the subject of metaphysics. Finally, I will look to other indications from the Paris prologue on the question whether Scotus might find the balance of costs and benefits characteristic of M2 acceptable.

At the outset, we should note that it is clear from the Paris prologue,[23] as well as from M2, that 'first entity' is the only plausible alternative to 'entity' as the subject of metaphysics. The Paris prologue rejects the former suggestion on account of several problems.

+ Paris problem 1: A *propter quid* science of first entity exceeds our intellectual capacity and cannot naturally be acquired.
+ Paris problem 2: The *quia* science that demonstrates God's existence is physics, and it would be absurd to suggest that physics is prior to metaphysics.

✦ Paris problem 3: There is only one science of God—theology, not
metaphysics.

✦ Paris problem 4: Metaphysics is about entity, which is a science that
can reach the conclusions that concern us.

✦ Paris problem 5: First entity cannot be the topic of a speculative
science.

M2 concedes the first problem: a metaphysics of first entity cannot be a
propter quid science for human beings. The second problem does not militate
against M2, since, like the Paris prologue, M2 allows that though both physics and metaphysics show the existence of God, metaphysics does so in accordance with a concept more proper to God.[24] Discussing the third problem
would require that we understand M2's position on the proper relation
between theology and metaphysics. That is an interesting subject,[25] and it
is considered in M2's Doubt 6, but I am not going to consider it here, since
it is hard to understand what Doubt 6 has to say on the subject. Instead, I
will turn to M2's replies to objections that suggest that the subject of metaphysics must be entity, 'entity as entity'. Then I will look at problems with
'first entity' as the subject of a science.

If I can show that M2 adequately replies to these objections, then I will
maintain that rehabilitating it may be worth the cost.

First Objection: Metaphysics Is about Entity

So let's start with Scotus's reply to Thomas Aquinas, to himself in the Paris
prologue,[26] and to other contemporaries, who would surely say to him: "It
is fine to maintain that knowledge of the first entity is the *aim* of metaphysics, but mistaken to maintain that it is its *subject*."

M2 takes up this objection in Doubts 1, 3, and 5. Indeed, the very first
argument in support of Doubt 1 is also stated in the Paris prologue.[27] The
absolute concept 'entity,' is prior to the relative concept 'first entity,' so the
science of entity is prior to and more certain than the science of first entity.
M2 replies by claiming that though the science of entity is prior by origin,
it is not prior in our intention—that is, though we must acquire it first, it is
not our primary object in doing metaphysics. And similarly, M2 would be
entitled to appeal to the Paris prologue in support of its claim that though

entity is the first object of intellect, it is not its essential (*per se*) object, only God (and thus, first entity) is.[28]

Doubt 3 explains in what sense the subject of a science can be its end—namely, science aims at perfect knowledge of its subject.

Doubt 5 shows that entity cannot be the principal subject of metaphysics, even if we grant that entity is univocal, such that it could serve as the subject genus studied by metaphysics. For a genus can serve as the subject of a science only if it is equally concerned with all members of the genus, not (as in the case of metaphysics) when we are primarily concerned with a single species. Unlike those who seek knowledge of generically unified sciences, we study metaphysics primarily in order to learn about first entity (M2 153, p. 68).

Can a similar distinction be found in the Paris prologue? Yes, indeed. The Paris prologue makes the same distinction in explaining what are the requirements of a first subject in any science.[29] Assuming as his contemporaries did that the relation of the objects of our faculties parallels the relation of the subject of a science to the habit acquired,[30] the Paris prologue distinguishes between the objects of different faculties: all colors are equally the objects of our vision and so its science is generically unified; but the primary and only adequate object of God's intellect is God, which means that God's theology is specifically unified.

Now it is true that the Paris prologue goes on to explain that the proper subject of theology virtually contains all truths of the science of theology—that is, they can be demonstrated from the concept of God as God, which is not a claim M2 could make about its subject. However, since M2 gives up the claim that human metaphysics as a whole is a demonstrative *propter quid* science, with a real definition of the essential nature of its subject, there is no reason to suppose that the concept of first entity as understood by human metaphysicians virtually contains the science. Nonetheless, M2 concludes that since metaphysics is not equally concerned with all objects but principally with first entity, and its truths are organized in a search for knowledge of first entity, first entity must be its subject.[31]

What is the relation of metaphysics to the science of entity? M2 claims that the science of entity is a part of the science of first entity. It claims that a science of metaphysics that did not include first entity would be like a grammar that dealt with nouns and verbs, but not sentences (M2 141, pp. 64–65).

And probably Scotus would expect us to grant that if first entity is part of the subject of metaphysics, then it must be its principal part. So M2 responds to the Paris problems by claiming that a science of entity, though a necessary part of the science, is an incomplete metaphysics, knowledge of whose subject is not pursued for its own sake (M2 141, pp. 64–65; M2 153, p. 68).

Second Objection: First Entity Cannot Be the Subject of Science

Nonetheless, Paris problem 5, poses a potentially fatal objection to M2. According to the Paris prologue,[32] one reason first entity cannot be the subject of the science of metaphysics is that we do not immediately comprehend it. Before we can comprehend it, we must show that 'first' and 'entity' are compatible concepts. And M2's Doubt 6 adds that if this requirement did not obtain, a contradiction in terms, such as 'inanimate animal', could be posited as the subject of a science. Therefore, since a science presupposes the existence of its subject, rather than showing the nonrepugnance of its parts, first entity cannot be the subject of a science (M2 155, p. 69).[33]

In general M2's Doubts consider obstacles to positing first entity (FE) as the subject of metaphysics similar to the problems posed by the Paris prologue and also add to them:

+ Obstacle 1: FE cannot be the subject of a first science (cf. Ord. 3.165, pp. 108–09).
+ Obstacle 2: FE is not perceptible (D1.2, D2, RP 1A 3.1, 191, p. 60; AM 3.1, p. 20b).
+ Obstacle 3: FE is an accidentally apprehended *ratio* or essence (M2 D6 154, D2 reply).
+ Obstacle 4: FE posits nothing in its nature, but only a relation to the knower (D2 reply).
+ Obstacle 5: FE is not a general subject (M2 D6).
+ Obstacle 6: FE has no distinct predicates (M2 D1.2).
+ Obstacle 7: FE does not act necessarily (M2 D1.3).

The last three obstacles can be disregarded in my view, because though there are some problems with M2's handling of them, these very same obstacles militate against the subject Scotus proposes for theology, God as God.[34]

Presumably, then, Scotus is satisfied that he can handle them satisfactorily, though M2 does maintain that metaphysics, unlike theology, is a general science (M2 D1.142, p. 65; D6.155, 158).

The first four obstacles are more difficult, though it does seem that the first two could be handled easily, since M2 does not maintain that human metaphysics is a first science if by that we mean a demonstrative science. Rather metaphysics is an *a posteriori, quia* science, and the subject of a *quia* science need not be immediately evident or accessible to sense. Moreover, as M2 points out, a *quia* science requires only a nominal, not a real, definition of its subject (M2 132, 136, pp. 60, 63). So these obstacles do not militate against a *quia* science of first entity.

This is not quite the reply M2 offers in response to these problems, and it probably would not suffice for obstacles 3 and 4 which pertain to first entity's accidental, non-quidditative character. Also there are some textual problems with Doubts 2 and 6.

So I will turn now to the textual problems, starting with Doubt 2. Here the problem is that in response to the question, "How could first entity be the subject of metaphysics?," M2, as it currently stands, states that first entity is not naturally knowable (M2 145, p. 65).[35] However, this is no reply at all, but rather an objection to positing first entity as the subject of a science. Such a reply would, in effect, repeat the first problem stated in the Paris prologue on the grounds that first entity is neither sensible nor immediately evident.[36] Moreover, the arguments in favor of the reply do not support the conclusion that first entity is not naturally knowable. So something is wrong with the text.

Doubt 2 offers five arguments in support of its reply, so we ought to be able to determine what the intended reply is by seeing what conclusion those arguments justify. Unfortunately for this strategy, the conclusions justified differ. However, the last three of the five can be seen as arguments that first entity is not a subject of physics, or natural philosophy properly speaking. That would be a relevant response to one of the principal concerns of M2, the same concern reflected in Paris problem 2—namely, to describe how physics and metaphysics differ in their treatment of first cause or first entity.

So I have adopted the hypothesis that M2's response to Doubt 2 explains why first entity is the subject of metaphysics rather than physics. I suggest that rather than reading "non est ratio naturaliter cognoscibilis," we should read "non est ratio a naturali cognoscibilis"—'First entity is not knowable by the naturalist', rather than 'First entity is not naturally knowable.'[37]

The last argument for Doubt 2's reply *(five,* "Nec etiam") explains that though the naturalist demonstrates the existence of first entity, he does so only accidentally, insofar as it happens that first entity is the end of motion. Argument *four* ("Tum") states that first entity posits no nature but only a relation to the knower, so it will support the reply by concluding that first entity is not the subject of a science of nature such as physics. *Three* ("Tum") holds that first entity is a concept common to all sciences, and hence not specific to physics, but appropriate to the most general science. *Two* ("Tum") indicates that first entity pertains to the mode of a science, which is not established in but presupposed by a science, and I am at a loss to explain its relevance. *One* ("Tum") holds that first entity is apprehended accidentally, just as similarly the object of physics is not body as such but rather body in motion. So I suggest that we are intended to infer that first entity is the object of metaphysics rather than physics, or at least no more the object of physics than metaphysics.

My general view, then, is that Doubt 2 is meant to show that first entity is properly the subject of metaphysics rather than physics. However it is possible that Doubt 2 is more generally raising an objection against first entity as the subject of a science. And that certainly is a central objection against positing first entity as the subject of metaphysics, one that is forcefully stated in the Paris prologue. So we will turn to it next, as we consider Doubt 6, which is centrally concerned with that objection.

Doubt 6 objects against a science of first entity that nothing can be demonstrated of first entity from entity, since first entity is a particular. This objection concludes by making the same point as Doubt 1—namely, that the science of the transcendental passions of entity, such as unity, is prior to the science of first entity, but on different grounds—namely, that the universal is prior to the particular.

Doubt 6 replies by claiming that the this same science deals with both the universal and the particular. Moreover, it suggests two methods for demonstrating the existence of first entity, from the notions of order and primacy (M2 158, p. 70). It concludes by saying that the science of metaphysics demonstrates the passions of entity, such as one and true, first and second, and (most of all) first entity. The aim of metaphysics is not to seek knowledge of God as God but rather knowledge of entity in its highest degree, and therefore first entity is its subject. Human metaphysics seeks to know what is naturally knowable about first entity, and everything naturally knowable about first entity is a transcendental. It is true that what first occurs to, and is best known by, our intellects is common entity rather than first entity, but common entity is not what our intellects primarily seek to know. Their naturally achievable end is the proof of primacy which is the consummation of the science of metaphysics. It is this knowledge or wisdom that constitutes the felicity described as the metaphysical act of knowing in *Ethics* 10 (M2 160, p. 71; 123, p. 57).[38] So M2 shows that first entity not only can be, but must be, the subject of metaphysics, since metaphysics is about entity in its highest degree, not mere common entity.

Other Considerations in Support of M2's Solution

If we now turn back to the Paris prologue, we will see that Scotus was perennially concerned with the objection that Aristotle had described metaphysical knowledge as felicity.[39] We see, too, that despite the limitations on what it can show, M2's metaphysics meets all the criteria for a science stated by the Paris prologue, except that it is not demonstrative. It is certain,[40] necessary, and discursive.[41] First entity (FE) also meets most of the requirements for the subject of a science:[42]

+ Requirement (1): FE specifies the subject.
+ Requirement (2): FE dignifies the science.
+ Requirement (3): Its attributes are predicated of it.
+ Requirement (4): Its properties are considered in the science.

True, FE fails to meet two requirements:

+ Requirement (5): FE is not the first object considered by the science that occurs to the intellect.
+ Requirement (6): FE cannot be the subject of the principles of the science, since our demonstrations do not begin with comprehension of its nature, but rather seek to prove conclusions about its nature from our knowledge of common entity.

But as we saw, M2 responds that requirement (5) does not apply to metaphysics, since in this case, the first object the intellect encounters is not the subject that organizes the science. Similarly, requirement (6) pertains to *propter quid* sciences, and M2 holds that metaphysics is a *quia* science.

And finally, M2 follows the pattern set by the Paris prologue. Just as the Paris prologue makes the paradigm of theology be God's theology, however distant our capacity is from God's, so M2 makes God's metaphysics the paradigm of metaphysics. Of course, we cannot acquire God's metaphysics; ours is only a *quia* aggregate of habits. However, limited though human metaphysics' conclusions regarding first entity may be, our transcendental science of metaphysics allows us science of some of the same conclusions as God's. Like God's metaphysics, our metaphysics is about entities as they are attributed to God, and if this were not so, it would not be first philosophy (M2 134–35, pp. 61–62).

The extent to which the Paris prologue and M2 agree is striking. They both hold:

+ Thesis 1: *Propter quid* knowledge of God cannot naturally be acquired.
+ Thesis 2: *Propter quid* science of entity is possible.
+ Thesis 3: *Quia* science of first entity is naturally possible.
+ Thesis 4: Generic sciences are equally concerned with all the things they consider.
+ Thesis 5: Entity is the first object of intellect, and God is its *per se* object.

Indeed, the Paris prologue suggests that many truths can be deduced *a posteriori* in *quia* proofs regarding God.[43] The Paris prologue and M2 may even agree about human felicity. M2 presents metaphysics as the felicity described by the philosophers, and the Paris prologue agrees. True, the Paris prologue holds that metaphysics only counts as felicity in a qualified sense, since it is not based on intuiting God,[44] but nothing to the contrary is stated in M2. So the Paris prologue and M2 appear to agree on another thesis:

+ Thesis 6: Metaphysics is the felicity described by the philosophers— which, however, is not felicity absolutely speaking, the felicity achieved by the blessed.

Of course, they do not agree about everything. The Paris prologue and M2 disagree entirely about whether our science of metaphysics has the same subject as God's metaphysics, since, as the Paris prologue repeatedly claims, there is only one science of God—namely, theology.[45] It is tempting to suggest that the Paris prologue must mean to qualify this conclusion in some way, since it allows that many things can be proved with certainty about God by philosophers.[46] But it does not explicitly do so. Moreover, we should note that M2 and the Paris prologue also disagree about whether such proofs pertain, strictly speaking, to metaphysics. The Paris prologue holds they pertain only qualifiedly to metaphysics.[47]

On the whole, the comparison with the Paris prologue suggests that M2 represents a substantial change in position with, however, many persistent commitments and shared views. And though the text of M2 is messy and difficult, it does not seem possible that it antedates the Paris prologue. For M2 responds thoughtfully to the objections the Paris prologue poses for it as we have seen,[48] and the converse is not the case. So if, despite appearances, the Paris prologue were the last presentation of Scotus's views, it could only be at best a partial statement, since it does not address the question: What is God's metaphysics?, and it does not take into account objections M2 states cogently.

Perhaps the most important of these unconsidered objections rests on the minimality of the concept of entity. The Paris prologue does not consider the claim that entity, a concept deliberately chosen for its minimality, cannot contain God, since knowledge of the less perfect cannot virtually contain knowledge of the more perfect, and knowledge of entity is the most imperfect of knowledge (M2 123, pp. 57–58). Rather the Paris prologue unreflectively asserts that God as God is contained in entity as a common object.[49] For M2, by contrast, though in a sense entity is the first object of the intellect, that sense is limited to priority of origin (M2 140, p. 64). Indeed, it seems that for M2 the fact that entity is an imperfect object is one principal motive for a change in position.

The Unity of Metaphysics as First Philosophy

The last consideration that indicates the advantages of M2 arises in part from the disagreement with which we began—namely, about the unity of science. As Spade has pointed out,[50] Peter Aureol criticized Scotus because he allowed for generically unified sciences, and it is generally agreed that Scotus does do just that. Indeed, Demange argues that for Scotus metaphysics itself is generically unified.[51] But given that the subject of metaphysics is a unique single thing and not a genus (M2 153, p. 68), one would expect it rather to be a specifically unified science. Surprisingly, however, it appears that general metaphysics may be neither specifically nor generically unified according to M2.

M2 seems to claim that the general metaphysics possible for us in this lifetime is simply an aggregate of habits unified in virtue of their relation to the single subject to which all the objects it considers are attributable. It is not entirely clear how this aggregate is unified, except that it is one in virtue of its subject (una ex unitate subiecti). But despite what may be its rather minimal unity, general metaphysics is the only first science possible for us. For only general metaphysics allows us to know entities in accordance with the first aspect under which they can be considered—namely, as attributes reducible to first entity (M2 134, p. 61). To show how M2 reaches this conclusion I will do two things:

+ First, I will show how M2's views on the unity of the science (or rather the sciences) of metaphysics are part of its defense of Averroes and his interpretation of *Metaphysics* 4.
+ Second, I will interpret M2's statements on the sciences of metaphysics.

One major of advantage of M2's solution is that it allows Scotus to follow Averroes in affirming *Metaphysics* 4.2.1003b17–18: "Everywhere science deals chiefly with that which is primary, and on which the other things depend." As stated in M1, this authority supports the claim that substance is the subject of metaphysics; substance must be the subject, since God cannot be. God cannot be the subject of a *propter quid* science (M1 18, p. 21; M1 64–65, p. 37), since (a) nothing can be demonstrated as a cause of God and (b) God has no distinct attributes, being absolutely simple.

In rehabilitating the claim that first entity, a separate substance, is the subject of metaphysics (M2 115, p. 55), M2 gives up the claim that metaphysics is a *propter quid* science as noted. In so doing, M2 also gives up the claim that as *we* understand it the subject of metaphysics virtually includes the conclusions that comprise the science. This radical step removes some obstacles as we have seen, but the problem remains that you cannot have a science in which attributes are demonstrated of a subject if that subject has no distinct attributes. This problem M2 solves by claiming that conceptual distinction suffices, specifically natural priority.

The passage in which M2 defends Averroes' claim that attributes can be predicated of first entity in a scientific demonstration is complicated, and I will be suggesting some emendations to the text as I interpret it (M2 131, p. 60). After reminding his readers of Averroes' arguments as stated at M1 (25–26, p. 25) and the attributes under consideration—God's being unmovable and perpetual, for example—M2 adverts to its own additional, supplementary defense of Averroes (*secundum illam additionem quae superius posita*) quoting it in part. Here I will cite a slightly revised version of the text, using mention marks differently and making a minor change in edition indicated by italics.[52]

> Si enim prius naturaliter et aliud potest esse medium sciendi posterius naturaliter et aliud, hoc non est in quantum hoc 'aliud', quia hoc accidit, sed in quantum hoc, sicut est aliud, *est* [*cod.* DEFM] ita prius naturaliter et prius notum secundum se, et illud posterius. Sed ita est invenire in proprietatibus vel attributis divinis, igitur etc. (M2 32, p. 28)

Despite the labored prose, the point seems simple enough: suppose the medium in a demonstration is previous to something else that needs to be shown. What is important is not that the medium is other—indeed, Scotus here claims that that is, or could be, adventitious. Rather what is important is that the medium is naturally prior, and what needs to be shown is posterior. This point is partly repeated in the main body of M2. Again at least the punctuation should be changed and a textual change also seems helpful:

> [S]i prius naturaliter et aliud potest esse medium sciendi posterius, medium sciendi posterius naturaliter et aliud, hoc non est in quantum 'aliud', quia hoc accidit, sed in quantum hoc *est prius naturaliter et illud posterius* [*cod.* B2 DEF], ut ibi patet. (M2 131, p. 60)

This argument is one of two preliminaries to M2's answer to the question what is God's metaphysics and what kind of metaphysics is possible for us, for angels, and for the blessed. It bears on God's metaphysics and the *propter quid* habit of general metaphysics that is not possible for us. By contrast, the other preliminary, M2's distinction between science as a habit and science as an aggregate, seems chiefly concerned to carve out a space for human metaphysicians in this life, albeit a limited one.

In making the distinction between metaphysics as a unified habit and as an aggregate of many conclusions bearing some relation to each other, M2 (131, p. 60) appeals explicitly to an earlier(!) discussion in book VI. Unfortunately, this reference cannot be verified. We, the editors, cite VI.1.812, but that cannot be right. In this passage (812) Scotus rejects an opinion on the grounds that it would make geometry a mere aggregate of habits rather than a unified scientific habit.[53] But M2 is concerned to defend metaphysics as a science that aggregates habits and appeals to an analogy with geometry. So this cannot be the intended referent.

Demange appeals more plausibly to a passage that Scotus canceled. Since it was replaced by another according to Mauritius, we printed it in an appendix. Worse, that canceled passage describes grades of unified habits, not aggregates. It describes generically unified sciences and appeals to the virtual inclusion of *per se* attributes in a subject whose real definition we presumably can know. But M2 seeks to justify metaphysics as an aggregate and holds that in this life we cannot really understand the subject of metaphysics, but can have only a nominal definition of it (M2 136, p. 63). So this also does not seem to be what is intended.[54]

Somewhat more likely would be a reference to VI.1.39–42.[55] This passage describes a minimally unified habit based on a remote genus. But again Scotus appeals to virtual containment and makes the distinction in support of entity as the subject of metaphysics. What is more M2 explicitly says that the metaphysics it defines is unified by its subject, first entity (M2 134, p. 61), which is, of course, singular and maximally united. So it seems that this also cannot be the referent.

Given the difficulties of referring to book VI, I will look instead at an earlier statement in M2 itself at paragraph 103 (pp. 50–51). Of course, this cannot be a reference to book VI unless this is a movable bit of the text that originated there. But paragraph 103 does have the advantage of being relevant; indeed it, or something very like it, is assumed by the paragraph 131. Paragraph 103 concludes that if science does not have to be unified in the manner prescribed the *Posterior analytics,* and we distinguish other different kinds of sciences, God can be the subject of metaphysics, just as he is the subject of theology. God could be the subject of such a science, even if (counterfactually) none of God's attributes could be shown to pertain to him.

Prior to stating this conclusion, paragraph 103 distinguishes between the subject of a science properly speaking and an aggregate [science] conveyed by cognition of many knowable things, simple and complex, principles as well as conclusions. The subject of an aggregate science may either be (a) something common to all the subjects of the proper scientific conclusions subsumed in it, or (b) something primary to which all the other things considered in the science are attributed (M2 103, p. 51).

Unfortunately, paragraph 103 explains the distinction exclusively in terms of the disjunct that does not immediately concern us—the common subject stipulated in (a), using an example taken from geometry. Suppose, M2 says, there is a science of geometry (1) that demonstrates of shape-in-general all its attributes and also a geometry (2) that demonstrates of the species of shape all their attributes. Geometry (2) would be subalternate to geometry (1). And though no attribute of shape-in-general would be demonstrated in geometry (2), its subject would be shape-in-general, because only shape-in-general would be common to everything considered in geometry (2). In like manner, "if this distinction is good," paragraph 103 concludes that God could be the subject of metaphysics, just as he is the subject of theology, because all "the other things depend" on him as the simply first being (*Metaphysics* 4.2.1003b17–18).

Here the claim is that metaphysics as a science of first entity would have to be an aggregate of demonstrations concerning knowable things insofar as they can be attributed to, or reduced to, first entity. This conclusion and the distinction between science as habit and science as aggregate seem to be the basis for M2's principal reply in paragraph 131 to the question: How can God be the subject of metaphysics? Based on the distinction explained in paragraph 103, paragraph 131 goes on to enumerate four different metaphysics of God or first being, one of which is further subdivided. The first two are sciences strictly speaking—that is, science as a habit:

1   There is a *propter quid* science that is a habit in which God's attributes are demonstrated of God in accordance with Averroes' opinion (M2 131, p. 60).

2   There is a *quia* science that demonstrates conclusions about God
from effects that could not exist without God (M2 132, pp. 60–62).

The next three sciences (3, 4a & 4b) are aggregates, and concerning
these sciences M2 tells us something about whether and for whom they
are possible:

3   An aggregate of science 1 and science 2 would be the most unified of
its kind—if it existed.

4   An aggregate of many conclusions and principles about God and the
other things that can be attributed to him as that which is primary—
that is, as first entity.

Science 4 is unified by the unity of its subject, not as the habitual
sciences are unified, but insofar as it is the subject to which everything else is attributed. Though created entity is univocal under the
aspect of first being (*sub ratione primi entis*), it can also be considered
as it is attributed to first entity. Thus the first consideration of all
entities is insofar as they are attributed to first entity, not to substance. And therefore if metaphysics is to be the first science, it must
pertain to all things considered in this respect.

4a   Science 4a derives knowledge of creatures from knowledge of God. It
is possible for angels who exist for long enough to think discursively
and perhaps also for the blessed. It is not, however, possible for us,
since our cognition comes from the senses and does not supply
essential or quidditative knowledge of God. God himself also
does not have science 4a, since his metaphysics is not acquired
discursively.

4b   Science 4b derives knowledge of God from knowledge of creatures,
and that is how human metaphysicians now have science. It is a *quia*
science that considers God as its primary subject and every other
entity insofar as it is attributed to the first entity. It is *quia* science,
since it neither supposes that God exists, nor starts from knowledge
of first entity.

So metaphysics in this life is unified only as an aggregate, though its
subject is maximally unified. But despite this limitation, it is the only first

science possible for us, since entity must be considered first in relation to the primary entity on which all other entities depend.

Conclusion

I hope to have persuaded you that a plausible case can be made that M2 states Scotus's mature position on the subject of metaphysics, since the subject of M2's metaphysics supremely dignifies the science. Unlike the science of entity, its subject is not the most imperfect of beings, but rather the primary being, first entity, to which all other entities can be reduced. The pursuit of the knowledge of this subject, and only this subject, counts as true felicity. Also unlike the science of entity, the science of first entity has the same subject as God's metaphysics. It is first science not only because its subject is first entity, but also because this is the first aspect under which all other entities are known. And though it is not a *propter quid* science it includes a *propter quid* science.

The evolution of Scotus's views from the Paris prologue to M2 is a change we can understand. Scotus has gone from reasoning that because metaphysics is a *propter quid* science, its subject cannot be God, to inferring that because metaphysics must be about God, human metaphysics is an *a posteriori, quia* science. And Scotus has done so for precisely the reason the Paris prologue would lead you to expect: because the human intellect has a natural inclination that cannot be satisfied with any object less than first entity,[56] it cannot be contented by entity. Human metaphysics principally considers entity for the sake of knowledge of first entity, and to the extent that it succeeds it achieves wisdom or natural felicity (M2 116–17, p. 56; cf. M2 123, pp. 57–58). So it may, indeed, be that M2 states Scotus's considered judgment about the subject of the science of metaphysics, or at least that it is closer to his final position than the Paris prologue.

2

Aquinas vs. Buridan on Essence and Existence

GYULA KLIMA

In this essay I will argue that although Anthony Kenny's objections to Aquinas's *intellectus essentiae* argument for the real distinction of essence and existence in creatures are quite easily answerable in terms of a proper reconstruction of the argument, the argument thus reconstructed is still open to an objection offered by the John Buridan in his *Questions on Aristotle's Metaphysics*. The discussion of how Aquinas could handle Buridan's objection will show that the conflict between their judgments concerning the validity of the argument rests on a fundamental difference between Aquinas's and Buridan's conceptions of how our concepts latch onto things in the world.

Kenny on the Intellectus Essentiae *Argument*

Aquinas's famous *intellectus essentiae* argument in his *De Ente et Essentia* is taken by many commentators to be one of his most serious attempts to prove his metaphysical thesis of the real distinction of essence and existence in creatures. Others would claim that this argument is only a part of a larger argument, which as a whole intends to prove the real distinction of essence and existence in creatures and the identity thereof in God. In any case, that interpretational issue aside, the *intellectus essentiae* argument in itself can quite justifiably be taken to be an intriguing attempt to prove the real distinction between essence and existence at least in *some* more obvious cases, which then can be regarded as the starting point of the larger argument for the entire thesis. The larger argument would then seek to establish that *if* essence and existence are identical in some case, *then* they can be identical only in a *unique* case, namely, in the case of God, from which it follows that essence and existence must be distinct in *all* other cases, namely, in all creatures.

In this essay, however, leaving the rest of the argument aside, I will confine my discussion to the piece of reasoning embodied in the following lines in Aquinas's text:

> Whatever is not included in the understanding of an essence or quiddity is coming to it from outside, entering into composition with the essence; for no essence can be understood without its parts. But every essence can be understood without knowing about its existence, for I can understand what a man or a phoenix is, and not know whether it actually exists in the nature of things. Therefore, it is clear that existence is distinct from essence, unless, perhaps, there is a thing whose quiddity is its own existence.[1]

In his controversial book, *Aquinas on Being*,[2] Kenny launched a two-pronged attack against Aquinas's argument.

On the first prong, he tried to establish that if Aquinas in this argument was talking about existence in the sense of "specific existence," expressed by the Fregean existential quantifier, then he was either talking nonsense or essence and existence are distinct both in God and in creatures. Kenny's reasoning is based on the idea that Aquinas's argument can plausibly be understood as claiming in its premises that while we know, for instance, what is meant by the word "phoenix," namely, a mythical bird that sometimes bursts out in flames and is later reborn from its ashes, we just do not know if there is such a thing, that is, we do not know if the word is true of something. Indeed, we actually know that the word "phoenix" is not true of anything, for nothing is a phoenix, which is precisely the Fregean quantificational interpretation of the notion of existence. However, as Kenny correctly concludes, on this interpretation Aquinas's argument would either amount to nonsense or it would prove too much. For on this understanding of the notion of existence, the thesis of the real identity of God's essence and existence would amount to something like the ungrammatical gibberish: "God's essence is ∃." On the other hand, if we assume that the argument is not nonsensical and works, then it must work in the same way for the term "God" as it does for the term "phoenix." But then the argument proves too much, for then, in the same way, we know what the term "God" means, but we do not know whether it is true of anything, for we do not know whether there is a God. Thus, if this is what the distinction of essence and existence means, then they are distinct in God just as well as they are in creatures.

On the other prong of his attack Kenny argues that if Aquinas was talking about existence in the sense of "individual being," meaning actuality, corresponding to the Fregean notion of *Wirklichkeit*, then essence and existence are identical both in God and in creatures. For then we have to say that just as for God to be actual is for Him to be God, so for a dog, say, Fido, to be actual is for Fido to be a dog. Therefore, if *this* is what the identity of essence and existence means, then Fido's essence is just as identical with his existence as God's essence is with His existence.

Thus, Kenny concludes, either way, the *intellectus essentiae* argument fails to establish Aquinas's desired conclusion. However, as I have argued in detail elsewhere,[3] Kenny's argument fails on several counts.

In the first place, Aquinas simply does not have a notion equivalent to the Fregean notion of an existential quantifier. In fact, a notion that would come closest to this notion in Aquinas's conceptual arsenal would be regarded by him not as a concept of existence, but as a *signum quantitatis*, namely, a *signum particulare*, the syncategorematic concept expressed by the Latin terms "quidam," "aliquid," or their equivalents, which render a proposition to which they are prefixed a particular, as opposed to a universal, singular or indefinite proposition (as in, "Quidam homo est animal" = "Some man is an animal," as opposed to "Every man is an animal," "Socrates is an animal," or "A man is an animal," respectively). In any case, Kenny's reason for holding that Aquinas would have to use in his argument the notion of specific existence, and, correspondingly, the notion of *nominal* as opposed to *real* essence,[4] is his unjustified assumption that Aquinas would take a phoenix by definition to be a fictitious bird as we do. However, from his argument, as well as from the parallel text of his *Commentary on the Sentences* (2SN, d. 3, q. 1, a. 1, co.), it is quite clear that Aquinas uses this example as the illustration of a real, but ephemeral, natural phenomenon, like a lunar eclipse or a rainbow, the essence of which we could know perfectly well in terms of a scientific definition without knowing whether this kind of thing actually exists at the present time. So, Kenny's objection definitely fails on the first prong, on account of simply missing Aquinas's point in the argument, taking it to deal with nominal, rather than real, essences, and operating with a notion of existence that is alien to Aquinas's thought.

But Kenny's objection fails on its second prong as well, even if the interpretation it involves is somewhat closer to Aquinas's original intention. For Kenny bases his objection on the false assumption that the distinctness of essence and existence would have to mean that it is possible to have one without the other. And so, he argues, since it is impossible to have a dog's existence without its essence—for a dog cannot be without being a dog—essence and existence would have to be the same also in the case of this creature. However, this assumption is obviously false: for it is clearly possible to have distinct, yet necessarily co-occurring items in reality. For example, it is clear that the triangularity of any particular triangle (its having three angles) is not the same as its trilaterality (its having three sides), unless sides and angles are the same items. But it is also clear that one cannot have a particular triangularity without a particular trilaterality. So, we have two really distinct items here, which are nevertheless inseparable in reality. Again, this particular material form, say, the substantial form of this particular block of wood, cannot exist without the matter it informs, and the matter it informs cannot exist (at least on Aquinas's conception), without this form actually informing it (since for both of them to be is nothing but for this particular block of wood to be). Still, Aquinas would take this form and this matter to be really distinct items in reality, since they are precisely those mutually exclusive, nonoverlapping, essential parts of the substance of this block of wood into which it has to be analyzed in Aristotle's hylomorphist metaphysics. Therefore, *pace* Kenny, real distinction does not have to mean real separability, which finishes off the other prong of his attack.

Reconstructing the Argument

Accordingly, to avoid the misunderstandings involved in Kenny's criticism, we have to understand the argument as dealing with real, individualized, essences, and arguing for their real, mind-independent distinction from real, individual acts of existence at least in those cases in which we have knowledge of the essence without knowing whether it is actually present in any actually existing individual. Therefore, taking "c" to be any arbitrarily chosen thing whose nature is known but whose existence is not known, the gist of the argument may be reconstructed as follows:

1. The nature of c is known.
2. The existence of c is not known.
3. Therefore, the nature of c is not the existence of c.

In fact, if we name the individualized nature of "c" by the proper name "n," and its individualized act of existence by the proper name "e." then this argument may be regarded as an instance of the following valid argument form of predicate logic:

1. Kn
2. ~Ke

---

3. e ≠ n

Accordingly, in this reconstruction, the argument is certainly immune to Kenny's criticism; indeed, it may appear to be absolutely uncontroversial. However, Buridan attacked the argument precisely in this reconstruction, on account of the logical peculiarities of the intentional verb it involves.

Buridan's Criticism

Buridan takes on Aquinas's argument in his *Questions on Aristotle's Metaphysics*. In the first place, in the following passage he reconstructs the argument precisely in the way I presented it above, as an objection to his own position, which he is going to answer after his own determination of the issue:

> I can have scientific knowledge of roses or thunder, and yet I may not know whether there is a rose or whether there is thunder. Therefore, if one of these is known and the other is unknown to me, then it follows that the one is not the same as the other.[5]

It is noteworthy in this reconstruction that Buridan is absolutely clear on the point of the argument Kenny missed, namely, that it is to prove the thesis of real distinction concerning the real essences of scientifically known but ephemeral natural phenomena, whose actual existence may not be known at any given time despite our scientific knowledge of their nature.

Buridan's criticism is based on the well-known phenomenon of the breakdown of the principle of the substitutivity of identicals in intentional contexts. It is easy to see this point, if we consider that the validity of Aquinas's argument as reconstructed above requires that its premises together with the negation of the conclusion should form an inconsistent set of propositions. Indeed, if the principle of the substitutivity of identicals is valid, then from the negation of the conclusion, which would claim the identity of existence and essence, we could promptly derive a contradiction, proving the requisite inconsistency. However, if this principle is not valid, then the contradiction is not derivable, which invalidates the original argument. Accordingly, Buridan starts his response to Aquinas's argument as he reconstructed it by making two important claims: first, that essence and existence differ in their concepts; second, that for this reason the argument as stated is a *non sequitur*:

> For the sake of answering the objections it seems that we should say in this question that essence and existence differ in their concepts. For the name "rose" and this name or expression "that a rose exists" are imposed from different concepts. Therefore, when it is said that I think of a rose, while I do not think that it exists, this I concede. But from this it does not follow that, therefore, the existence of a rose[6] differs from the rose; what follows is only that it is according to different concepts or on different accounts that the rose is thought of in terms of the name "rose" and the expression "that a rose exists."[7]

However, besides simply claiming the invalidity of the argument, Buridan also provides an explanation why it has to be invalid with an intentional verb:

> Here you need to know that we recognize, know, or understand things according to determinate and distinct concepts, and we can understand a thing according to one concept and ignore it according to another; therefore, the terms following such verbs as "understand" or "know" appellate [i.e., obliquely refer to] the concepts according to which they were imposed [to signify], but they do not so appellate their concepts when they precede these verbs. It is for this reason that you have it from Aristotle that this consequence is not valid: "I know Coriscus, and Coriscus is the one approaching; therefore, I know the one approaching." And this is because to know the one approaching is to know the thing according to the concept according to which it is called the one approaching. Now, although I know Coriscus, it does not follow, even if he is the one approaching, that I recognize him under the concept according to which I know him to be approaching. But this would be a valid expository syllogism: "Coriscus I

know; and Coriscus is the one approaching; therefore, the one approaching I know." Therefore, the situation is similar in the case under consideration: I understand a rose, but I do not understand a rose to exist, although a rose to exist I understand. The same applies to the other case: I concede that I have scientific knowledge about roses and thunder in terms of several conclusions, yet I do not have scientific knowledge about roses or thunder in terms of the conclusion that a rose or thunder exists.[8]

Buridan's criticism, as can be seen, is based on his celebrated theory of *appellatio rationis*, the theory according to which intentional verbs and their participles make their grammatical direct objects following them *appellate*, that is, obliquely refer to, their concepts. Indeed, if we make this oblique reference explicit, then the proposed argument will obviously be invalid. For then, using Buridan's example, the premises and the conclusion would have to be reformulated in the following way:

1'. I know the essence of a rose *qua* the essence of that rose.
2'. I do not know the existence of that rose *qua* the existence of that rose.
3'. Therefore, the existence of that rose is not the same as the essence of that rose.

That this argument is not valid is clear from the fact that from its premises and the negation of its conclusion we cannot derive a contradiction. For if we assume that the existence of that rose *is* the same as the essence of that rose, then from the two premises we can only conclude either that the existence of that rose I know *qua* the essence of that rose, or that the essence of that rose I do not know *qua* the existence of that rose, but either of these is clearly compatible with the other premise, namely, that I do not know the existence of that rose *qua* the existence of that rose or that I know the essence of that rose *qua* the essence of that rose.

To see that it is quite possible that the existence of that rose (which is the same as the essence of that rose) I know *qua* the essence of that rose while I do not know the existence of that rose *qua* the existence of that rose, we should just consider the perfectly analogous example from Aristotle, according to which it is quite possible that the one approaching (who is Coriscus) I know *qua* Coriscus, but I do not know the one approaching *qua* the one approaching (for I see him from afar and I do not recognize that he is Coriscus, which is the relevant sense of "knowing" in this context).

Thus, it seems that as long as we can know the same item *qua* some essence, but not *qua* some act of existence, it is quite possible for us to know the essence of a certain thing without knowing whether it exists or not, despite the fact that its essence and existence are the same. Therefore, Aquinas's argument fails to establish its desired conclusion, the real distinction of the essence and existence of a thing on the basis of the fact that we may know its essence without knowing its existence.

A Thomistic Response to Buridan's Criticism, and Its Implications

But this does not have to be the end of the story for Aquinas. In fact, if we take a closer look at Aquinas's actual formulation of the argument, we have to notice something that is entirely neglected in the version of it criticized by Buridan, namely, Aquinas's talking about "parts of the essence" without which it cannot be understood. What can he possibly mean by this? And what is the relevance of this to the validity of his argument?

Since according to Aquinas the essence or quiddity of a thing is what is signified in it by its quidditative definition[9] and the essence of a thing in and of itself is not a conglomerate of several distinct items, by "the parts of its essence," he means whatever is signified precisely by the parts of the quidditative definition of the thing.[10] In fact, since on his interpretation the definition is not primarily a linguistic expression, but an *intention*, that is, a concept of the mind expressed by the corresponding linguistic expression rendering this expression meaningful, we can say that on Aquinas's conception having scientific, quidditative knowledge about a thing is having in mind its quidditative concept, expressible by a scientific, quidditative definition. In this context, therefore, we need to distinguish between merely having some (no matter how vague and confused) concept of a thing, resulting from the mind's first, spontaneous abstractive act, and having its quidditative concept, which is a clear and distinct, articulate, concept, resulting from scientific inquiry into the nature of the thing.[11] Having this sort of quidditative concept, therefore, means clearly knowing its implications: for instance, if I have the clear and distinct quidditative knowledge of diamonds as being tetrahedrally crystallized pieces of carbon, then on account of having that concept, as well as the concept of electric conductivity, I know just as well that diamonds are poor conductors (as opposed, say, to graphite).

Now what does all this mean concerning the validity of Aquinas's argument and its Buridanian criticism? Concerning Buridan's criticism we should note that the breakdown of the substitutivity of identicals on account of the appellation of concepts in intentional contexts is conditioned on the *logical independence* of the appellated concepts in terms of which one and the same thing is conceived, known or understood. This is why it is possible for me to know, for example, my father, and not to know the man approaching, even if the man approaching is actually my father. For I may certainly have the recognition of him in terms of the concept whereby I conceive of him as my father, while lacking the recognition of him insofar as I merely cognize him as the man approaching (insofar as "having the recognition" of this person would mean being able to give an adequate answer to a question asking about the identity of this person). But this is so because the two acts of cognition in question *are logically independent*, whence I may perfectly well have the one without the other.

However, if the appellated concepts or acts of cognition *are not logically independent*, whence I cannot have the one without the other, then the situation is radically different. For instance, suppose I have perfect quidditative knowledge of all things moving toward me as such. Therefore, anything that moves toward me I know precisely insofar as it moves toward me. But I also know that anything that moves toward me approaches and anything that approaches moves toward me. Thus, it cannot be the case that I know the thing moving toward me insofar as it is moving toward me and I don't know the same thing insofar as it is approaching. And this is because the concepts appellated by the phrases "the thing moving toward me" and "the thing approaching" are logically equivalent; indeed, they are the same.

Or consider another, perhaps more intuitive example. If I have the scientific concept of a rainbow, say, as being the refraction of light on water suspended in air, then I cannot know a rainbow *qua* rainbow, without knowing it at the same time *qua* the refraction of light on water suspended in air. To be sure, before forming the scientific concept, I can certainly have some vague and confused knowledge of it as some colorful arch in the sky, without knowing it *qua* the refraction of light on water suspended in air. However, once I have formed its quidditative concept, I cannot have knowledge of the same thing without knowing the implications of its quidditative concept.

But then the situation would have to be similar with the notions of essence and existence, provided we are talking about the clear and distinct scientific understanding of a thing's essence, which involves having the articulate, quidditative concept of the thing, and knowing its logical implications. For in this situation, if the existence of the thing were the same as the essence of the thing, or, using Aquinas's phrase, it were "a part of" the essence of the thing, then this would mean that having the quidditative cognition of the thing would entail also having its cognition in terms of its existence: that is to say, we could not have its quidditative knowledge without knowing that it exists. Indeed, this is precisely what Aquinas hypothetically concedes in the conclusion of his argument:

> Therefore, it is clear that existence is distinct from essence, unless, perhaps, there is a thing whose quiddity is its own existence.

That is to say, if there *is* a thing whose essence and existence are the same, then having a clear and distinct cognition of the thing's essence would immediately give us the knowledge that the thing exists, which is the exact reason why Aquinas would say that although God's existence is self-evident *in itself*, that is, it would be knowable *a priori* by anyone with a clear and distinct cognition of divine essence, still, it is not self-evident *to us*, namely, human beings in our natural state, for in this state we just cannot have the clear and distinct cognition of divine essence that would allow us to realize the self-evident character of His existence.[12]

But then, how come Buridan didn't realize this point when he formulated his objection? Didn't he notice the possibility of the logical dependency of the appellated concepts that would again render Aquinas's argument valid?

Without going into much detail, I would suggest in conclusion that the answer to these questions is that on Buridan's conception of how our essential concepts latch onto things in the world, our concept of the quiddity of a contingently existing thing *always* has to be distinct and logically independent from our concept of the existence of that thing even if the thing in reality is both its own essence and its own existence. For on Buridan's conception the quidditative definition of a certain specific kind of things signifies these things absolutely, whether they are past, present, future, or merely possible, while in the context of a present tense proposition it supposits only for the presently existing ones, if there are any. The term "exists," on the other hand, supposits only for presently existing things. Therefore, if the kind of thing in question merely contingently exists, then there is no way for us to know on the basis of simply comprehending the definition of this kind of thing whether even a single thing of this kind falls under term "exist" right now, that is, whether it actually exists.

The picture, however, is radically different with Aquinas's conception. For Aquinas, our specific quidditative concept of a thing grasps precisely that *formal content* in the thing that essentially "shapes" the thing into the kind of thing it is. (A good illustration of what this *formal content* is would be the genetic code of a biological species determining the essential features of the kind of organism pertaining to that species, or the configuration of the nuclei of elemental atoms describable in terms of their atomic number, determining their electron-configuration and thereby their essential chemical features.) Therefore, if this formal content involves the existence of the thing, then it is impossible to form this quidditative concept of any single thing of this kind without at the same time forming the concept of its existence and conceiving of it as existent and thereby knowing that it exists.

For Buridan, on the other hand, concept formation does not consist in this sort of mental grasping of a formal content. It is merely the formation of an indifferent mental representation of a certain kind of things, the content of which is nothing but those things themselves, regardless of whether they actually exist or not. But it is quite obvious that one could form a concept of this sort without forming the concept of the existence of any single thing of this kind. Thus, it appears that in view of Buridan's objection formulated on the basis of *his* conception of the mental representation of essence and existence, the issue of the validity of Aquinas's argument in the last analysis turns on *Aquinas's own* conception of mental representation. For the ultimate question is, whether Aquinas's conception can support the claim that if essence and existence were in general the same, then their concepts could not be logically independently formed in our minds, and thus we could not have the scientific knowledge of essences of things without knowing, on that account, the existence of these things, that is to say, knowing their essence, we would have to know that they exist.

A Final Objection and Reply

Perhaps, the best way to explicate this last claim is to answer on Aquinas's behalf one final objection.[13] For on this understanding of Aquinas's position, one may still raise the following objection: Can I plausibly assume that I can have scientific knowledge of a certain kind of thing without knowing whether any singular thing of that kind exists at the moment, *without also assuming that the essence and existence of any singular thing of that kind are really distinct items in reality?* If not, then the argument, implicitly assuming its own conclusion, is clearly question-begging.

In response, it would seem we might just ask back: Do we acquire scientific knowledge of the essence of ununoctium by learning that it is an element of atomic number 118? One can certainly raise this question and answer it affirmatively without even thinking about the issue of whether there are any presently existing samples of this very unstable element in any lab on earth (let alone in any uncharted parts of the physical universe). However, based on this affirmation, and then reflecting on the issue that we have no idea whether any atoms of this element are in existence right now, one can, without further ado, accept the generalized premise that one can know the essence of a certain kind of thing without knowing its existence.

But relying on Buridan's objection one might retort at once that I could claim to have scientific knowledge of the essence of ununoctium only if I knew its actual existence, provided its essence and existence were in fact the same. I may simply (mistakenly) think that I know its essence on the basis of this definition, but in fact this is a very imperfect form of knowledge of that essence, not explicating *everything* it involves, whence I claim to have knowledge of essence without knowing existence simply on the basis of having a rather lax criterion for scientific knowledge, which, however, by stricter criteria, would have to contain the knowledge of the existence of the thing, if the essence and existence of the thing are in fact the same. So, I can assume that I know the essence of the thing without its existence only by *presuming* the conclusion, which still leaves the argument begging the question.

In answering this retort, we must not forget that the charge of question-begging (*petitio principii*) is the charge of an informal, epistemic fallacy (i.e., the argument is not claimed to be invalid or unsound): according to this charge, one cannot plausibly assume the premises without assuming the conclusion, that is, the knowledge of the premises cannot be obtained without a previous knowledge of the conclusion (or something known to be equivalent to it). So, a defender of an argument so accused should be able to point out independent, plausible grounds for the acceptability of the premises.

That is precisely what I attempted in the first paragraph of this section, with reference to ununoctium. But the retort, as I summarized it in the second paragraph of this section above, seems to undermine this attempt by claiming that as long as I do not know whether essence and existence are not the same, I cannot claim to have scientific knowledge of the essence of something without knowing its existence, which may just not be explicated in the rather incomplete knowledge of the essence I have in terms of the formulaic quidditative definition of the thing in question.

However, this objection is based on a very, indeed, as I will argue, unreasonably strong interpretation of what is required for the scientific knowledge of the essence of something. For let us not forget that for Aquinas the essence of something is whatever it is that its specific quidditative definition signifies in it. So, if I have the specific quidditative definition of the thing, I do have scientific knowledge of this essence (as opposed to the confused, prescientific knowledge I may have on the basis of knowing some generic and typical accidental attributes of that kind of thing), and this may still not involve the existence of the thing.

Nevertheless, the objector might still claim that I do not have a sufficiently clear and distinct knowledge of this essence until I know *everything* its essence involves, that is, *all* the essential attributes the thing has by virtue of having this essence, whereas a quidditative definition merely provides us explicitly with two specifying attributes (genus and specific difference, plus the more generic attributes implied by these higher up on the Porphyrian tree); and so, it may well be possible that existence is also among these essential attributes, just like any other essential attribute not explicated by the simple, formulaic definition. Do we really understand, for instance, *everything* that is essentially involved in having a rational nature? If not, then it may well be the case that existence is one of those things, but we claim to ignore it, simply because it is not explicated by the definition.

But it is at this point that the unreasonably strong requirement for the scientific knowledge of essence becomes explicit. The retort in this form assumes that we can have scientific knowledge of essence only if we are able to explicate *a priori all* the essential attributes a thing has by virtue of having that essence. But this is an unreasonably strong requirement, for scientific knowledge of specific essences certainly does not require *a priori*, logical omniscience (i.e., the claim that if x's having F implies its having G, then if I know that x is an F, then I know that x is a G; for then by knowing the axioms

I would have to know all conclusions of any axiomatic deductive science, which is simply not the case). Thus, I certainly can have scientific knowledge of some essence without knowing *all* attributes a thing must have by virtue of having that essence. Furthermore, and more importantly, I do not have to know *all* essential attributes of a thing (i.e., attributes the thing has by virtue of having its essence) in order to know of some attribute that it is *not* one of its essential attributes in this strict sense (just like I do not have to know every place on earth in order to know that something is nowhere on this earth, because I know that it is, say, on the moon). But then, I can certainly know the essence of the thing in terms of its scientific, quidditative definition, by virtue of which I know *a priori* that every singular thing that had, has, will have, or can have that essence had, has, will have, or can have the attributes explicitly or implicitly involved in that definition (even if I may not explicitly *know all* the attributes involved in that definition in this way). However, at the same time, I know that simply by virtue of knowing the essence of all these singulars in terms of their quidditative definition I do not know of any of them *a priori* whether they actually exist; I can only learn about their actual existence *a posteriori*. Therefore, even if I may not explicitly know all essential attributes of the thing *a priori* (while I do know some, namely, at least those explicated in the definition and those implications of this definition that I am aware of), I know that their existence is not one of them; that is to say, I do have scientific knowledge of the essence of this kind of thing, but I do not have this knowledge of the existence of any single thing of that kind by virtue of having this knowledge. However, on the basis of this understanding of what is and what is not involved in the scientific understanding of the essence of a thing one can plausibly concede to know scientifically what a certain kind of thing is and not to know whether any instance of that kind of thing actually exists without presuming, or even thinking about, the issue of the real distinction of essence and existence. Therefore, Aquinas's argument proves this, without begging the question.

Perhaps, one question still remains concerning the demonstrative force of Aquinas's argument. If it can be "saved" from Buridan's criticism only with appealing to Aquinas's own interpretation of the notion of essence as it is described in his own conceptual framework, whereas Buridan's criticism seems to be justified in *his* conceptual framework, does this mean that there is no absolute answer to the question whether the essence and existence of at least some creatures are really distinct? In other words, do we have to make our answer relative to the conceptual framework of each author, thereby somehow trivializing both their disagreement and the metaphysical point of the thesis itself?

I would briefly reply that we do have to make our answer concerning the validity of Aquinas's argument relative to the conceptual framework in which it is evaluated, but this still will not trivialize the issue. For even if we have to say that Aquinas's argument is demonstrative in his own conceptual framework, but not in Buridan's, this does not mean that their disagreement is something as trivial as a mere verbal disagreement. For in the case of mere verbal disagreement, the parties can easily resolve their apparent disagreement by simply "relabeling" the concepts *they both share*, but simply expressed by different terms. However, with the disagreement between Aquinas and Buridan, the case is just the reverse: they share the same words in the same language to express their own, rather different concepts of essence and existence, fitting into radically different conceptual frameworks, based on their very different conceptions of how our concepts latch onto things in reality.

Thus, if *we* want to deliver judgment on the demonstrative force of the argument without talking past Aquinas, but also taking into account the historically accumulated different conceptual frameworks in which it can still be competently evaluated, then we should evaluate not only the argument itself, and not only relative to this or that conceptual framework, but we should also evaluate those frameworks themselves. However, that is a rather different ball game, requiring the consideration of overall consistency, explanatory force, and comprehensiveness of entire systems of thought in a conceptual framework that accommodates them all, in the sense of making all their claims and arguments at least *logically commensurable* with each other.

II FORM AND MATTER

3

The Form of Corporeity and Potential and Aptitudinal Being in Dietrich von Freiberg's Defense of the Doctrine of the Unity of Substantial Form

BRIAN FRANCIS CONOLLY

Dietrich von Freiberg, O.P., was active in the late thirteenth and early four-teenth centuries.[1] He is probably best known for his work on the optics of the rainbow,[2] one of the most remarkable achievements of late medieval empirical science.[3] He has also gained some attention for his distinctive theory of the intellect, especially for the extent to which he draws upon Proclus' *Elements of Theology*.[4] In addition to his demonstrable interest in, and appropriation of Proclusian Neoplatonism, Dietrich's surviving writings show him also to be a very capable and knowledgeable Aristotelian thinker, deeply immersed in the philosophical controversies that were being discussed toward the end of the thirteenth century at the University of Paris.[5]

In the discussion to follow, I shall consider Dietrich's contribution to one of the most important of these controversies, namely, the question of the unity or plurality (or perhaps more precisely, simplicity or complexity) of substantial form, especially with respect to the substantial form of the hu-man being. The unity (or simplicity) of substantial form is among the most distinctive philosophical doctrines of Thomas Aquinas. The doctrine main-tains that the substantial form is not a complex structure, but consists instead in a simple and integral unity—the rational soul—which is sufficient to account for the various substantial perfections (e.g., nutrition, sensitivity, etc., roughly corresponding to the Tree of Porphyry). These substantial per-fections are attributed to the various substructures of a *complex* soul in the competing theory. (For the sake of convenience, this latter, competing theory will be referred to as that of the "pluralists.") This latter position holds, contrary to Aquinas, that the human substantial form is indeed a unity, but a complex one, the complex structure of which becomes most apparent through an analysis of its progress through generation: the lower substructures, for example, the vegetative soul, serve as subject for the higher substructures, for example, the sensitive soul, that arrive later in the course of generation. The end result again is a unity, but one in which this complex structure of its generation is in some manner preserved, typically understood by comparison to such processes as aggregation or lamination.[6]

While Dietrich, somewhat unusually for a Dominican thinker of this period, did not always defend Aquinas's doctrines (his opposition to Aquinas's theory of the separability of accidents is a well-known case in point[7]), with respect to the doctrine of the unity or simplicity of substantial form, Dietrich shows himself to be both an ardent and capable defender of the doctrine—without, however, compromising his own originality and independence as a thinker. This is perhaps most evident in Dietrich's treatment of what might be regarded as the most serious objection to the doctrine of the unity of substantial form, namely, that the doctrine is not capable of accounting for the numerical identity of the living and the dead body of Christ. The objection maintains that inasmuch as death entails the separation of the rational soul from the body, what is left behind—the corpse—cannot be said to be specifically, and therefore much less numerically, the same as the living body. This in general is not a problem, except however in the case of the body of Christ, where there is good scriptural authority, and theological need, to maintain that the living and dead body of Christ are numerically the same. The pluralists, with their theory of the complex or laminate structure of the human substantial form, can maintain that what remains after the departure of the rational soul is a body informed by specifically and numerically the same form of corporeity that was present in the living body, underlying as subject all the higher substantial perfections, including the now departed rational soul. Furthermore, this is the case not only with respect to the body of Christ, but also for all human beings. Defenders of the doctrine of the unity of substantial form in man must therefore show either that a special case can be made for the body of Christ, or else provide an account of numerical identity, peculiar to substantial corruption, which dispenses with strict specific identity as a necessary condition for numerical identity. Aquinas, and many Dominican defenders of the doctrine, took for the former path; Dietrich, as we shall see, attempts the latter.

The discussion will proceed as follows. After briefly discussing Aquinas's own attempt to respond to the objection of the numerical identity of the living and dead body of Christ, and a typical pluralist reply (from the Franciscan Richard Middleton) purporting to show the inadequacy of that solution, I shall first discuss Dietrich's sharp criticism of the pluralist position. This will be done by focusing upon his arguments that attempt to show that the pluralist position, in effect, results in *too much* identity between the living and the dead body, and is therefore unable to account for important differences between the living body and the corpse. I shall then consider Dietrich's alternative account of generation and corruption, which describes the various successive stages not by means of positive, independent terms (e.g., "embryo," or "corpse"), but in terms of privation and form, with "form" in this context understood as the perfected form in act (e.g., the adult human being), which is the culmination of the process of generation. The prior stages of generation (and the subsequent stages of corruption) are to be understood primarily and essentially as *privations* of this perfected form in act, and thus understood properly and primarily only in reference to the perfected form in act. This will lead to an important and original conceptual innovation by Dietrich, namely "aptitudinal being," which properly describes how, for example, the corpse, is what it is only by reference to the fully perfected form in act that is the end result of the process of generation. Aptitudinal being is analogous to "potential being," which aptly characterizes a being in the process of generation, for example, the embryo, which is, correlatively, what it is only by reference, again, to the fully perfected form in act that is the end result of the process of generation. I shall then provide a brief account of the conditions Dietrich sets out as necessary for a being to be arranged under a genus, and show that given these conditions, neither potential beings nor aptitudinal beings, strictly speaking, belong to a genus, although they are, he claims, *reducible* to the genus of the fully perfected form in act to which they implicitly refer. These considerations will lead to, first, a further serious criticism of the plurarlist position, namely, that it cannot account for the irreversible ordering that characterizes generation and corruption in nature. Second, these considerations also point us toward Dietrich's own solution to the problem of the numerical identity of the living and the dead body of Christ within the constraints imposed by the doctrine of the unity or simplicity of substantial form. His solution will be in effect to weaken the requirement of specific identity as the necessary condition for numerical identity to the requirement of only "being reducible to the same genus." The aptitudinal being of the corpse, he will in effect argue, is *reducible* to the same genus as the living human being, and this, he will argue, will prove to be sufficient to account for the numerical identity of the living and dead body, not only of Christ but of any man.

Theological Problems for the Doctrine of the Unity of Substantial Form in Man

The opponents of the doctrine of the unity of substantial form maintain that the theory runs into particular difficulty with a number of fundamental theological doctrines.[8] In particular, the theory runs into trouble with the peculiarities of Christ's death and resurrection. The primary difficulty for the theory, in this regard, is that it appears to be unable to account for the numerical identity of the living and the dead body of Christ. This is because,

> if the soul is the form of the *living* body, then there is a form of the *dead* body other than the soul, or the body of the dead one will not be a body. But no intelligent person posits that the dead body is not a body, because sense and reason contradicts it. Wherefore, the form in the body of Christ lying in the tomb will be other than <the form> in the body of Christ sitting at the Last Supper. But what differs in form also differs in number. Therefore it follows that the body lying in the tomb and developing in the womb of the Virgin or suffering on the cross are numerically distinct, which every Catholic repudiates as heretical.[9]

The problem for the proponents of the unity of the substantial form stems from two assumptions on their part. First, the correlate to the theory of the unity of substantial form is a theory that generation and corruption are kinds of motion or change that proceed through a succession of forms. On this theory, in the course of generation, upon the arrival of the succeeding and perfecting form, the previous form of the thing being generated is annihilated and completely replaced by the succeeding form. For example, in the generation of a man, upon the arrival of the rational soul—typically understood as occurring at some time during fetal development in the womb—the sensitive soul is completely replaced by the rational soul. It is not the case that the rational soul is merely superadded to the form or forms that the embryo might already have, for instance, the vegetative and sensitive souls. Rather, these are replaced completely by the rational soul.[10]

Events follow a similar course in corruption, according to the proponents of the theory of the succession of forms. At death, when the rational soul, which is to say the substantial form of the man, separates from the body (or more precisely, the matter), a new substantial form, namely, that of a corpse, completely replaces it. Nothing of the rational soul remains behind. That is, it is not the case that only the intellective soul separates, and the vegetative or sensitive soul, or at the very least the substantial form of human corporeity, remains behind, thereby providing the corpse with a substantial form. Rather, the entire substantial form is replaced.

In other words, it is not the case that at each stage in the process of generation a new form is added to what is already there, so that the substantial form of man or of any generated being at any given stage in the process of generation is in some manner the aggregate or conglomerate of all the previously existing forms since the start of the process of generation. Neither is corruption understood in terms of the successive removal of such forms, a peeling away of layers, as it were, or the subtraction of parts, down to the elementary forms. Rather, in the succession of forms theory, each new form at any given stage in the process of generation or corruption completely replaces the previous form, which in its turn, had likewise completely replaced the form it succeeded.

The second assumption that leads to the problem for the proponents of the unity of substantial form, is that, with Aristotle, they maintain that dead flesh is called "flesh" only equivocally.[11] That is to say, the substantial form of the living human body, which is to say, the rational soul, is at least *specifically* distinct from the substantial form of the dead body.[12] The problem of *numerical identity* follows swiftly: where there is not *specific* identity, there cannot be *numerical* identity.

Such problems are easily avoided by the proponents of the theory of the plurality of forms, since they think that generation is, by contrast, a more aggregative or at least cumulative kind of motion or change, wherein succeeding forms are in some manner added to previously existing forms in the course of generation (sometimes but not always seen as a progressive *aggregation* of forms[13]), while the more perfect forms are successively subtracted from the being during the course of its corruption. Hence, for them, death and the consequent corruption of the human being begins when the rational soul separates from the body. But this does not precipitate the arrival of a new and different substantial form, namely, that of the corpse. Rather, the dead body is constituted as such by the remaining forms that were left behind when the rational soul separated. Chief among these is the form of corporeity, which is *specifically* and *numerically* the same form in the dead body as it was in the living body. Hence, the numerical identity of the living and the dead body of Christ is accounted for by the form of corporeity that remains after the soul separated. An important consequence of this view is that such numerical identity holds not only for the living and dead body of Christ, but for that of any other man.

The contrasting accounts of generation and corruption help to clarify the metaphysical differences between the two views which can sometimes seem rather unclear, inasmuch as even the pluralists maintain that there is at least some *unity* to the substantial form. But the differences between the two positions are such that the competing metaphysics must be able to account for the contrasting physics. That is, the theory of the plurality of substantial form in man accounts for a theory of human generation in terms of addition, aggregation, or lamination, whereas the theory of the unity of substantial form is consistent with the theory of generation by the succession of forms. Thus, even though metaphysics considers the generated being apart from its generation and motion, the generated being must have an internal metaphysical structure that is consistent with the manner of its generation.

It can therefore be seen that the theory of the plurality of forms maintains that a substance is constituted by a series of layers of substantial forms, each layer or each member in the series corresponding to a stage in the substance's generation. The overall structural unity (necessary in order that we have *one being* and not several) of this series of forms is typically accounted for by the potentiality that each lower layer or prior member in the series has for the reception of its immediate successor.

The rational soul, on this view, therefore does not conjoin with matter immediately; rather its immediate subject is the composite, the "laminate substance" that has for its ultimate form the human sensitive soul; which in turn, has for its immediate subject that laminate substance that has for its ultimate form the human vegetative soul, and so on, down to the substance that is composed of prime matter and the human form of corporeity. Now it must be a *human* sensitive soul, and likewise for the others, in order that such a form or soul can be distinguished from that of any other kind of animal, such as a horse or a dog. The crucial difference is that the human sensitive soul is in potency to the rational soul; whereas the sensitive soul of a dog is not.

On this view, then, the rational soul, considered in itself, does not carry within itself sensitivity, vegetativity, corporeity, etc. Rather, there are distinct forms for each of these powers or perfections even if they are ultimately arranged under or subsumed by the rational soul, inasmuch as it is the ultimate substantial form for the human being. By contrast, on Aquinas's theory, the human rational soul does indeed contain within itself all these powers and perfections, and is conjoined *immediately* to prime matter.[14]

Responses to the Problem

Proponents of the theory of the unity of substantial form offered a number of responses to this problem. Before examining Dietrich's response, it would be worthwhile to take a brief look at other attempts to solve the problem on behalf of the doctrine of the unity of substantial form.

The "standard" response to the problem is to account for the numerical identity of the living and the dead body of Christ by reference to Christ's divinity. Such a response appears to have been first formulated by Aquinas himself in 1271, in his *Quodlibet* IV, q. 5, "Whether the body of Christ on the cross and in the tomb are one in number?"

> Whatever are one and the same in their supposit, or hypostasis, are one and the same in number. But the body of Christ lying in the tomb and hanging from the cross is one and the same in supposit or hypostasis. For the hypostasis that is the Word of God was never separated from his body. Therefore, the body of Christ hanging from the cross and lying in the tomb is one and the same in number.[15]

This became the standard response to the objection, in that it was adopted by many Dominicans and other defenders of the doctrine of the unity of substantial form, including Giles of Lessines.[16] It is important to note that Aquinas thus makes the living and dead body of Christ a special case. That is, it is not the case generally that there is numerical identity between the living and dead body of any man whatever. Rather it is only Christ's divinity that permits such identity between the living and dead body of Christ.

Aquinas's solution asserts, with good reason and sound scriptural authority, that the hypostasis (Christ's Godhead) was never separated from his body, even though the soul was separated (at Christ's death) and even though the soul is otherwise understood to be the medium whereby the hypostasis is united with the body.[17] The details of Aquinas's solution need not detain us here, but it does need to be emphasized that in Aquinas's view, the identity of the living and dead body of Christ is a special case, wherein, uniquely, numerical identity is preserved. It appeals to this "extra feature" of the person of Christ (not available to be appealed to in the case of any other human being) which can thus account for the identity of the living and dead body of Christ and incidentally also explain why such identity cannot be accounted for in other men.[18]

Yet such a move did not satisfy the Franciscans and the pluralists generally, who in any case can treat the numerical identity of the living and dead body of Christ not as a special case, but merely as an instance of what holds for all men generally. A particularly clear exposition of what Franciscan thinkers thought unsatisfactory about Aquinas's solution can be found neatly expressed by Richard Middleton:

> But perhaps you say that the body remains the same body in number because of the identity of the supposit. Against this, I argue as follows: Because of the identity of that thing which does not belong to the essence of the body, the body cannot remain the same in number, if the principle of the essence of the body does not remain the same. Now the supposit in Christ did not belong to the quiddity of the body. Therefore, the body would not remain the same in number because of the identity of that supposit, unless the principle of the essence of the body insofar as it is a body remained the same in number. Therefore, since the principles of the essence of the body are matter and the form whereby the body is a body, it would be necessary that after the separation of the intellective <soul> there remained a form giving being to the body insofar as it is a body, which would be the same in the dead <body> and in the living <body>; and so your solution is no <solution>.[19]

Similar reasoning can be found in the works of John Peckham, Peter John Olivi, Gonsalvus of Spain, and William de la Mare.[20]

In other words, Aquinas's solution fails, according to Middleton, because the supposit or hypostasis is not what makes the body of Christ to be a body.

Hence even if (or even *though*, as the case may be) the supposit remains united to the body, under Aquinas's theory, this appears not to be sufficient for numerical identity because it cannot even account for specific identity. Aquinas appears to acknowledge as much when he explains the second sense of *simpliciter* in *ST* III, q. 50 art. 5, according to which the living and the dead body of Christ are not the same:

> In another way "simply" is the same as "altogether" or "totally": in which sense the body of Christ, dead and alive, was not "simply" the same identically, because it was not "totally" the same, since life is of the essence of a living body; for it is an essential and not an accidental predicate: hence it follows that a body which ceases to be living does not remain totally the same.[21]

Aquinas's position therefore appears to be that the identity of the supposit and its unity with the body is sufficient to supercede questions about specific identity between the living and the dead body of Christ. That is, the question of the specific identity of the living and dead body of Christ as the necessary condition for the numerical identity of the same does not even arise because that numerical identity is already sufficiently accounted for by the identity of the supposit and its unity with the body.[22]

Hence, it becomes clear that Middleton's objection is to point out that this solution does not preserve the numerical identity of the body of Christ, *insofar as it is a body*, since the supposit is not what makes the body to be a body. That is, one can grant the numerical identity of the supposit, and its unity with the living body and the dead body, but this is not sufficient to account for the numerical identity of the body *insofar as it is a body*. It is, by extension, tacitly at least, also a rejection of the notion that the special case of Christ's divinity can be appealed to in defending the doctrine of the unity or simplicity of the substantial form against this objection.

We shall see momentarily how Dietrich takes up the cause of the doctrine of the unity of simplicity of substantial form at precisely this point. In addition to showing precisely why the pluralist position fails in general, Dietrich will argue that the numerical identity of the living and dead body of Christ can be accounted for without making any special appeal to the divinity of Christ. Rather, he will argue that such identity holds between the living and dead body of any man whatever.

Dietrich's Destruction of the Pluralist Position as Entailing Too Much *Identity between Living and Dead Body*

Dietrich discusses (and defends) at some length the doctrine of the unity of substantial form in his treatise *De origine rerum praedicamentalium*.[23] In addition, he discusses the problem of the numerical identity of the living and dead body of Christ in his treatise *De corpore Christi in mortuo*.[24] The former appears to date from the 1280s, and the latter may be based upon a disputed question that Dietrich conducted at the University of Paris.[25]

Dietrich's defense of the doctrine of the unity of substantial form begins by showing the insufficiency of the pluralist position. Tacitly granting that the pluralist position does indeed account for the numerical identity of living and dead body, his arguments attempt to destroy the pluralist position by showing that it in fact leads to *too much* identity between the living and dead body. Consequently, his argument runs, the pluralist position cannot account for (i) the living body's receptiveness of the rational soul and the dead body's lack of such receptiveness and (ii) the irreversible ordering of the processes of generation and corruption.[26]

In this section, we shall focus upon the first point. Here Dietrich is concerned primarily with the relation between body and soul on the pluralist theory. Dietrich will first argue that the living body cannot be what it is by the same form of corporeity whereby the dead body is what it is. Such identity is impossible, Dietrich argues, because the living body has a relation to the soul that the dead body does not, namely, the living body is *in potency* to the soul, whereas the dead body is not. In other words, the living body is receptive of, subject for, and made a living body in act by the soul, but the dead body neither is nor can be receptive of and subject for the soul, and consequently, is not and cannot be made a living body in act by the soul.

In particular, and, it appears, with a specific version of the pluralist theory in mind, Dietrich argues that this distinction between living body and dead body holds regardless of whether or not the body is conjoined to the soul through the medium of certain accidental dispositions. This is an important consideration because Dietrich discusses at some length a view wherein the specific and numerical identity of the form of corporeity whereby the living body is what it is and whereby the dead body is what it is is maintained, while their distinction with respect to their relations to the soul is accounted for in terms of the *harmony* or *temperament* of the body, which is a *disposi-*

tion of the body that is nevertheless considered to be *accidental* to body as such.

The question of whether any accidental dispositions in general intervene between body and soul figured prominently in the dispute over the unity or simplicity of substantial form in man. Aquinas addresses the question at some length in several works, notably, *ST* I, q. 76, art. 6, *On Spiritual Creatures*, art. 3, and *Questions on the Soul*, q. 9.[27] Aquinas argues that there would be no problem with such dispositions mediating the union of body and soul if soul were related or united to body as mover to thing moved. Since, however, the soul and body are correctly to be understood as being united as form to matter, there can therefore be no such mediating forms or dispositions, accidental or otherwise. Rather, soul must be united to body immediately.

In the course of his discussion of the problem, Aquinas considers a number of diverse candidates for these mediating accidental dispositions and rejects them all. These include such things as the powers of the soul, the phantasms in the imaginative faculty, the elemental powers hot, cold, wet, and dry, and the properties of the mixed body. Dietrich is similarly interested in rejecting the notion of any accidental dispositions mediating the union of body and soul. Yet Dietrich's discussion provides an interesting development of Aquinas's arguments precisely insofar as Dietrich considers the harmony or temperament of the body as the disposition accidental to the body as such which mediates the union of body and soul. It is also the presence or absence of this harmony or temperament—Dietrich's unnamed adversary argues—that distinguishes the living body from the dead body without compromising the specific or numerical identity of the form of corporeity whereby both the living body and the dead are numerically the same body.

Without knowing who the author of this argument is, it is of course difficult to appreciate its force; in particular, it is difficult to determine the source or motivation of this line of reasoning. However, one may guess that it stems from or is at least suggested by Aristotle's *De anima* I, 4 (412a) where the Philosopher says that the soul is the first perfection of the *organized* body, as if such *organization* were understood to imply a certain harmony or temperament of a body which otherwise in itself is indifferent to such harmony or temperament. That is, regardless of whether there is such organization, harmony or temperament, the body is still a body; but only with such organization or harmony can the body be united with the soul.[28]

Dietrich' s strategy, then is (i) first to argue that when *no* accidental disposition (whether it be harmony, temperament or anything else) is understood to mediate between body and soul, absurd consequences follow with respect to the relation between soul and body, largely because the dead body will be seen to be in the same relation to the soul as is the living body, viz., *in potency* to the soul. Dietrich then argues (ii) second, in effect, that if there were such an accidental disposition as harmony or temperament mediating between body and soul, as if introduced precisely in response to objection (i) above, such an accidental disposition could not serve to distinguish the living body from the dead body without at the same time compromising the specific and numerical identity of the form of corporeity whereby the living body and the dead body each is supposed to be a body. In other words, any attempt to respond to the first argument by appealing to mediating accidents to account for the *differences* between the living and dead body will be seen to undermine the pluralist attempt to account for numerical identity of the living and the dead body.

The Body Considered in Potency to the Soul Essentially

To say that the living body is conjoined to the soul *immediately*, without any intervening accidental disposition, and to maintain also that the body is related to soul as matter to form and therefore is *in potency* to the soul as matter is in potency to its form, implies that the body is in potency to soul *essentially*, that is, by its very essence. But if it is the form of corporeity whereby the body is what it is and hence, whereby it is in potency to the soul, then several absurd consequences follow if it is further maintained that the *dead* body is what it is by specifically and numerically the same form of corporeity. Thus, in *De origine rerum praedicamentalium*, Dietrich argues that

> it happens that matter and form in a *per se* being, that is, a substance, are united to each other without the mediation of any accidental disposition that would be the medium of formal union. Therefore, *if* in the generation of an animal the body were in potency *essentially* in its relation to the form of the soul to be introduced by the agent through the same substantial form of flesh by which flesh is flesh after death, not by the mediation of an *accidental* disposition that would be the formal medium between body and soul, but by its *essence, then,* since the same form remains that

was before, it follows that the body exists in the same relation to the form as before. Therefore, given the proximity of the agent, it will be possible for dead animals to resurrect; indeed, it would therefore be *necessary* that they sometimes do resurrect. <For> otherwise, some potency that befits the thing according to species will be totally pointless. But nature does not allow that.[29]

The trouble for the proponents of the pluralist position, then, is that the dead body is thus in precisely the same potential disposition in relation to the soul as the living body was, because it is specifically and numerically the same form of corporeity that makes both the living body and the dead body to be what they are. Consequently, the dead body just as much as the living body is in potency to the soul—is receptive of and can be the subject for the soul—by its very essence. But if the dead body has a natural and essential potency to be conjoined with a soul, it follows that it is possible, *by nature*, for a dead body to be resurrected, again, *by nature*. Furthermore, Dietrich points out, because there are no superfluous potencies in nature, it will therefore be *necessary* that bodies sometimes are resurrected *naturally*. That of course, is absurd, especially in the case of the human body, whose resurrection is to be accomplished only *miraculously*.

We find a similar argument in Dietrich's *De corpore Christi in mortuo*. Dietrich there again focuses upon the relation of the body to the soul, and again draws an absurd consequence from the assumption that it is specifically and numerically the same form of corporeity that informs both the living and the dead body. Thus,

> if the body, with the soul circumscribed, were through that substantial form <of corporeity> in the last disposition to the rational soul in the course of generation, and this final disposition is necessary and does not reject <its> act, a man by his nature would therefore never die.[30]

Thus, whereas before, the proponents of a numerically the same form of corporeity could give no reason for why a dead body should not *resurrect* naturally, that is, why a dead body should not be naturally reunited with a soul, here they run into the problem of explaining why the body should ever be separated from the soul in the first place. For the body, by its very essence, stands in a necessary relation to the soul. Hence, the soul cannot be separated from the body without destroying the very essence of the body.

But the proponents of the pluralist position insist that this is not the case; that is, they insist that upon the separation of the soul from the body, the essence of the body is *not* destroyed. But in that case, the body still stands in a necessary relation to the soul, which relation the body has by its very essence. But this is just to say that the soul *is not*, indeed, *cannot* be separated from the body. That is, a man cannot die.

With such absurd conseqences as these it would be difficult for the proponents of the pluralist position to maintain that the body is in potency to the soul essentially. The alternatives left open to the proponents of a form of corporeity, therefore, are either (i) to assert that the body is *not* in potency to the soul as matter is to form or (ii) to affirm that the body is in potency to the soul but that this potency stems not from the very essence of the body but from some disposition *accidental* to the body as such, but which makes possible a union of body and soul as matter and form. The former completely alters the dynamics of the discussion, in that it requires the relation of body and soul to be considered in terms other than the relation between matter and form, and understood in terms of, for instance, the relation between mover and thing moved, as Aquinas points out.[31] The latter, as Dietrich now proceeds to argue, while indeed providing some reason for adequately *distinguishing* the living from the dead body, nevertheless cannot do so while preserving numerical identity of the living and the dead body.

Harmony or Temperament of the Body as an Accidental Disposition Mediating the Union of Body and Soul

Dietrich now considers the view wherein the form of corporeity in itself is not sufficient for the reception of the soul. Rather, on this view there is also needed a certain harmony or temperament of the body, only by the presence of which is the body made receptive of the soul and can be a subject for the soul. On this view, this harmony or temperament is understood to be a disposition of the body that is *accidental* to the body as such. It is the presence and absence of this harmony or temperament that accounts for the radically important distinction between the living body and the dead regarding their respective relations to the soul (as if in response to the above objection), while at the same time supposedly preserving the specific and numerical identity of the form whereby the living body and the dead body are numerically the same body. Hence, as Dietrich explains, according to this view,

although the same substantial form remains in the flesh after death that
was in life, nevertheless, the same temperament and harmony of the flesh
does not remain, according to which it is possible, indeed, <according to
which> it would be necessary, for the soul to exist in it through the course
of generation.[32]

In other words, although specifically and numerically the same form of
corporeity still informs both the living body and the dead body, it is not the
form of corporeity as such that makes the body to be receptive of and subject
for the soul; rather it is a certain temperament and harmony of the flesh or
body that makes the body to be receptive of the soul. And it is this temperament and harmony that is destroyed when the soul separates from the body,
while the form of corporeity itself remains unchanged. Thus, the pluralist
can argue, the soul *can be* separated from the body *without* destroying the
essence of the body, and the dead body *cannot* naturally be rejoined with
the soul, even though the same form of corporeity that was in the living
body persists in the dead body. For the dead body does not possess the necessary harmony or temperament whereby it could be receptive of the soul.

Dietrich's argument against this position is complex. It is, effectively, to
argue that even if the harmony or temperament of the body is understood
to be the medium whereby the union of body and soul is possible, there can
be no transformation in this harmony to such an extent that the body could
no longer be the subject for the soul without the essence of the body itself
also being transformed, that is, without there also being some change to the
form of corporeity itself such that its numerical identity between living and
dead body would not be preserved. That is, any transformation affecting the
harmony to such an extent that the body cannot be the subject of the soul
necessitates a transformation in the very essence of the body itself. Therefore,
it is impossible that there be such a transformation in the harmony without
also compromising the numerical and specific identity of the form of corporeity whereby both the living body and the dead body each is a body. The
consequence of this is that such accidental dispositions as harmony or temperament of the living body cannot account for the distinction between the
living body from the dead body.

Dietrich proceeds by considering where precisely in the living body this
harmony resides, and offers what is meant to be an exhaustive list of alternatives. The harmony in question must either (i) reside in the substantial

form of corporeity itself, or (ii) it must characterize the *relation* of the substantial form of corporeity to its proper and immediate subject, or (iii) it must reside in some manner in the proper and immediate subject of that form.[33] Now, with respect to (i), Dietrich argues, the harmony in question cannot reside in the substantial form of corporeity itself, since substantial forms are simple, whereas *harmony* implies a certain proportion several different things owe to each other.[34] With respect to (ii), Dietrich points out that the harmony that characterizes the relation between the substantial form of corporeity and its proper subject cannot be the harmony that is between the *soul* and *its* proper subject, namely, *the body*. For the former harmony, that is, that between the substantial form of corporeity and *its* proper subject, is *not* transformed after death, since the pluralist maintains that it is specifically and numerically the same body, that is, the same union of the same substantial form of corporeity with the same proper subject. The latter harmony, that is, that between the body and the soul, by contrast, *is* transformed. Indeed, according to the pluralist, it is destroyed.

Therefore, since the harmony in question (i) cannot be in just the substantial form of corporeity and since (ii) it cannot be that harmony which characterizes the relation of the substantial form of corporeity with its proper subject, it follows that the harmony whereby the union of body and soul is possible and the presence or absence of which therefore distinguishes the living body from the dead body, without, however, compromising their specific and numerical identity, must reside in the subject for the form of corporeity.[35]

The pluralist, Dietrich thus argues, must therefore claim that the difference between the living body and the dead is ultimately due to a transformation in the harmony that resides in the subject for the form of corporeity: the presence of such harmony in the subject for the form of corporeity is what makes possible the union of body and soul; the absence of such harmony in the subject for the form of corporeity renders such union impossible. The problem with such a view, Dietrich appears to be arguing, is that it is not the proper subject for the form of corporeity, but the form of corporeity itself which accounts for the ability of the *composite* (of the form and corporeity and its proper subject) to be receptive of and subject of the rational soul. On the pluralist theory, the subject for the form of corporeity remains as the subject for the same form of corporeity despite the changes internal to the subject. But since, again, it is not its subject, but the form of corporeity itself which accounts for the receptivity of the composite subject, and since the same form of corporeity remains, any changes in its subject that do not affect its ability to be subject for the same form of corporeity therefore do not and cannot affect the ability of the *composite* to serve as subject for the rational soul. Hence the composite must be in potency to the soul as much after any such transformation in this harmony as before. In other words, any transformation of the harmony among the things that are the proper subject for the form of corporeity which does not affect the composition of the form of flesh and its proper subject also does not affect this composite from serving as proper subject of the soul. Consequently, any such transformation of harmony does not account for the distinction between living and the dead body if it is assumed that the form of corporeity whereby the living body and the dead body are each a body is specifically and numerically the same. This is so regardless of whether such harmony is thought to be *essential* or *accidental* to those things that are the proper subject for the form of corporeity.[36]

It appears, then, that the pluralists can provide no way of accounting for the fact that the living body is in potency to the soul while the dead body is not, while at the same time preserving the specific and numerical identity of that form of corporeity whereby the living body and the dead body each are a body and therefore the same body. This is so regardless of whether they try to account for this potency to the soul in terms of something *essential* or *accidental* to the living body.[37] In other words, by insisting upon the specific and numerical identity of the form of corporeity of the living body and the dead body, without, however, adequately accounting for the living body being in potency to the soul and the dead body not being in such potency, the pluralist has not, in effect, sufficiently distinguished between the living body and the dead body, which is to say, between life and death.

Irreversible Ordering and Aptitudinal Form

In the previous section, we have examined Dietrich's arguments against the pluralists that focus upon there being too much identity between living and dead body on their account. In particular, we have considered his efforts to show that the pluralist account of the numerical identity of the living and the dead body fails, by focusing upon the pluralists' inability to provide an intelligible account of how what is supposedly specifically and numerically the same body can yet have a completely different relation to the soul *before* death as compared to *after* death: prior to death, the body is in potency to, is receptive of and subject for the soul; after death it is and can be none of these. On the contrary, Dietrich has argued, this difference between the living body and the dead body regarding their respective relations to the soul is *essential* and therefore it will not be possible to account for the *numerical* identity between the two by reference to a "form of corporeity" shared by the living body and the dead body.

This is not meant to rule out the possibility of numerical identity altogether, however. Rather, Dietrich's argument has been that numerical identity cannot be accounted for by a form of corporeity shared in common by the living body and the dead body, simply because there is no such form shared in common by the two. Dietrich's own solution, we shall see, accounts for the numerical identity of the living body and the dead without relying upon any reference to a form supposedly shared in common by the living body and the dead body.

In the present section, we shall consider the way in which Dietrich reframes the problem by providing an alternative—but solidly Aristotelian—account of generation and corruption. This account will shift the concern from a sequence or series of forms all *positively* considered—for example, embryo, adult human being, corpse—to a consideration of these same moments in the process strictly in terms of privation and form, with the focus upon the *form intended by nature*, whereat the process of generation is culminated; the other moments in the process are to be considered primarily and essentially privatively, that is, as *privations* of this form. In addition, we shall consider briefly Dietrich's theory concerning the conditions whereby an entity can be ordered in or arranged under a genus, and his arguments for why neither the human embryo nor the corpse can be so arranged. These two considerations will lead to, first, an additional argument against the pluralist position, namely, that it cannot account for the *irreversible ordering* of the process of generation and corruption, and second, to Dietrich's own solution to the problem of the numerical identity of the living and the dead body of Christ.

Privative Opposition and Substantial Change in Nature

Regardless of whether we have been considering the pluralist or Thomistic models of generation and corruption, we have so far been discussing the generation of the human being in terms of a sequence or series of forms, each of which is considered positively, and wherein, on the pluralist model, the successive forms are added to, in some manner, the composite of the previous forms in the sequence, *without* replacing them. Schematically, this sequence could be represented as follows: A, A+B, A+B+C, etc. Alternatively, on the Thomistic model, each successive form completely replaces its predecessor. Schematically, such a sequence would appear as A, B, C, etc., where each letter represents one of the forms in the sequence, such as *corporeity*, *vegetative soul, sensitive soul*, up until the *rational soul*, which is the last substantial form to arrive and which completes or perfects the generation of the human being. The corruption of the human being, which is to say, the death of a human being, is seen in a correlative manner, this time however, on the pluralist model, a substantial form is *subtracted* from the composite or complex at each stage in the sequence, or, on the Thomistic model, substantial forms again successively replace one another.[38]

Dietrich argues, however, that these processes should *not* be understood or regarded as a sequence of forms, each of which is understood positively; rather, these processes should each be considered strictly in terms of just *one* form and its privations, diversely considered. That is, instead of understanding generation in terms of the sequence of several forms A, B, C, etc.—whether successively added or successively replaced—up to the arrival of the rational soul, which completes the generation of the human being, Dietrich wants to understand generation and corruption strictly each in terms of a change involving the form *man* understood as that whereat the process of generation is culminated, and the *privation* of that form. Thus, schematically, generation is to be understood in terms of the sequence ¬A, A; corruption is to be understood in terms of the sequence A, ¬A.[39] It is important to note that the *privation* here is not to be understood as absolute privation, as if the sequence went from prime matter completely devoid of form, to the composite of prime matter and substantial form. Rather, as will be come clear, Dietrich has in mind here *privative forms*, that is, forms that are to be understood primarily and essentially in terms of the privation of the form that is the culmination and terminus of the process of generation.

Substantial change in nature is of course more complicated than to be thought of simply in terms of the opposition between a form and its privation. There is after all not *one* process of change to consider, but *two*, namely, generation *and* corruption. Hence, the *privation* that characterizes, for example, the *embryo* in relation to *man*, is quite distinct from the *privation* that distinguishes the *corpse* from the *living body*. In the first place, a being *in potency* such as an embryo, though *lacking* the form is nevertheless moving toward the form, for example, *man*, whereas a being in the course of corruption not only *lacks* form but is as it were moving *away* from form and perfection.

Such differences between the privation characteristic of the being in the process of generation (i.e., being in potency) and the privation of the being in the process of corruption lead Dietrich to distinguish *aptitudinal being* as a *third* mode of being, in addition to *potential being* and *actual being*.[40] Actual being is the mode of being of a thing at the completion and culmination of the course of generation. That is, it is the mode of being of the perfected thing, for instance the adult human being, which is what the process of generation aims at. Both *potential being*, which is the mode of being of a thing in the course of generation, prior to the completion and culmination of that process, and aptitudinal being, which is the mode of being of a thing in the course of corruption, are characterized by privation in relation to actual being, which in the present context again means for Dietrich the culmination of the process of generation. Potential and aptitudinal being each *lacks* that which is possessed by actual being, namely, the form perfected in act, albeit, again, in rather different ways.

Now Dietrich calls aptitudinal being such because, while lacking the form and in no way *in potency* to the form, that which has aptitudinal being nevertheless is something that otherwise *ought* to have the form, just as, for example, a blind eye, while lacking in sight and not in potency to have sight, nevertheless, in some manner, *ought* to be seeing, *ought* to have sight. Similarly, and significantly, a corpse, while not possessing life and not in potency to be living, nevertheless *ought* to be living.[41] A glass eye or a bronze statue of Socrates, by contrast, do not have this "aptitude" for *sight* and *life* respectively.

This notion of aptitudinal being has a solid foundation in Aristotle, who in *Metaphysics* V distinguishes such aptitudinal being as one of the meanings of "privation," namely, as

not having something which a thing, either itself or its genus, should by nature have. For example, in *one* sense a blind man is said to be deprived of sight, but in *another* sense a mole is said to be so deprived.[42]

That *being in potency* should be aptly characterized as a privative mode of being in relation to actual being is perhaps less apparent. However, any being that is *in potency* lacks precisely that to which it is in potency, otherwise it would not be *in potency*, but in act. Thus, the embryo, being in potency to the perfected form that is the adult human being, lacks that perfection or completion which characterizes the culmination of the process of generation. In other words, the being in potency is deprived precisely of the form that it is moving toward in the process of generation. Hence, the embryo, at any point in the process of generation, is to be understood in terms of the *privation* of the perfected form that is the culmination of the process of generation. Potency and act, as Dietrich understands these terms in the present context, thus distinguish different stages in the course of generation: *act* indicates the completion and culmination of the course of generation, for example, the adult human being; *potency* characterizes any of those stages in the course of generation prior to that completion of that course, for example, the embryo, the infant, etc. Any of these prior, potential, stages are thus also characterized as *privative* because they lack precisely that completion and fulfillment of the course of generation which is manifest in the being in act.[43]

Now Dietrich does not think that this is merely one way of understanding the processes of generation and corruption, as if it were equally valid to understand generation in terms of a series of distinct substantial forms all understood positively in their own right; or if it were a clever way, for polemical ends, of viewing the process of generation which is really and essentially such a sequence or series of distinct forms, each of which is to be positively understood. There does appear to be some merit to this latter view, since, after all, the embryo, at any give stage in the course of generation is *a being*, and as such it must have some form; indeed, a form in act, even if it is still in potency to some further form. Hence, a pluralist might argue, this is precisely why it is necessary to distinguish and understand in a positive manner the form of corporeity, the vegetative soul, the sensitive soul, etc. That is, it is by each such substantial form that the embryo is a being in act at the corresponding stage in the course of generation, even if it is still in potency to the rational soul.

But Dietrich argues against such a view. That is, he argues, in effect, that the embryo, for example, is to be understood *primarily* and *per se* as a stage in the process of generation and thus in terms of the *privation* of the perfect form of the adult human being that is culmination of the process of generation. That it can be understood by some form considered positively at any given stage in the process of generation is *accidental* to the embryo. For the embryo, Dietrich argues, is not an end in itself intended by nature. Rather, it is *the man*—that is, the adult human being, in relation to which the embryo is in potency, that is intended by nature. Hence, it is primarily and essentially only in reference to the ultimate form of the process of generation that the being in potency is to be understood. That is, the embryo as such is what it is primarily and essentially by reference to the *man*; only secondarily and *per accidens* is it an "embryo," positively considered. In the case of the generation of man, this means that the embryo is to be understood properly, primarily and essentially, only in reference to the complete and perfected form of man; and its relation to this ultimate form in the course of human generation is characterized by *privation*. It lacks precisely that form in relation to which it is in potency. It would not be in potency to something it already possessed. Indeed, because any being intermediate in the process of generation would not be something intended by nature as an end, however positively one wishes to characterizes such a form, such positive characterization is *accidental* to the being in potency.

Conditions for Being Ordered in or Arranged under a Genus, and the Priority of Form

That a being in potency is what it is, that is, "receives the determination of its being," only from that form to which it is in potency, is discussed at some length by Dietrich in chapter 3 of his *De origine rerum praedicamentalium*. Therein Dietrich establishes the conditions by which alone a being can be ordered within or arranged under a real genus of being; failure to meet all of these conditions excludes a being from being ordered within a real genus. The conditions that a being must meet are (i) that it be a *being of nature* or that it *imply* a being of nature in some manner;[44] (ii) that it be *complete in the ultimate perfection* that is suitable for it according to its proper *ratio* and mode of its essence, that is, in having its species;[45] and (iii) it is necessary for it to participate the one *ratio* that is to be common to all the members of genus.[46] It is on the grounds of the failure to meet the first of these conditions that such things as *things of reason*,[47] *post-predicamentals*,[48] and *properties*[49] are all excluded from being coordinated within a real genus. It because they fail to meet the third of these conditions that the *separated intelligences*[50] and the *first principle of all things*[51] are excluded from being coordinated within a genus. We need not delay over Dietrich's arguments here.

The second condition, however, must be examined in some detail, since it causes problems for *incomplete beings*, a class which includes beings in potency in the process of generation, among other things.[52] Now the reason that a being must have complete being according to the *ratio* of its species is because

> the *ratio* of being, which is distinguished according to diverse genera, is the first and most formal of all intentions, as was said, by which a thing first formally differs from nothing. This is only according to the complete act of its quiddity and essence, as will be explained below. The reason for this completion and perfection in any such being is that it be a being simply and absolutely. Now such is what simply and absolutely was intended by nature, and there are such things, each of which has its entity and completion according to species absolutely and according to itself, not by accident.[53]

That a thing "first formally differs from nothing, only according to the complete act of its quiddity and essence" is discussed in chapter 4 of *De origine rerum praedicamentalium*. Dietrich therein rejects the notion of *being in potency* understood as an intermediate between being and nonbeing or nothing. It is in the context of this question that we find Dietrich's lengthy refutation of the doctrine of the plurality of substantial form in man, which is presented as an objection to Dietrich's own view that a being differs from nothing only by its complete act of specific being. That is, the pluralists claim, according to Dietrich, that a being in potency can differ from nothing by some form other than the ultimate form in the course of generation, by which a thing would have its complete act of specific being. These "other" forms just are the intermediate forms that a being in potency allegedly passes through, as it were, in the process of its generation to the complete act of the culminating form. That a being first differs from nothing only by the complete act of its specific being—even when it is still in the process of generation and therefore has not yet attained that complete form—to some extent thus depends upon Dietrich's refutation of the doctrine of the plurality of forms.

In any event, Dietrich, however, does not think that such incomplete beings as are beings in potency should be completely excluded from the coordination within a genus. Rather, he allows that they can be, and it appears ought to be, *reduced* to the same genus as the complete beings to which they are in potency:

> Now similarly, just as was said concerning the *principles of beings*, so it is also concerning *incomplete beings*, as are embryos and similar things that are in the process of generation. For they are led back to the same genus as the complete beings, not because of the substantial form that they eventually will have (since it does not constitute a complete being in nature), nor is it something *per se* intended by nature; rather, <they are led back to the same genus as the complete beings> insofar as matter participates something of the act and *ratio* of the ultimate form that is the end of generation. And because the ultimate form, according to this participation, is only under potential being (which cannot be found in nature without any act), it follows that nature finds the form of the embryo, under which matter stands in the interim, until it is made in the last disposition, which is a necessity, so that it is made under the act of the form absolutely intended; and then the form of the embryo ceases.[54]

The reason why such intermediate forms do not suffice for the coordination in a genus of a being is that such forms are not intended as ends *per se* by nature. Rather, only the complete act of form is so intended.

> For the evidence of this it is to be considered, that, as was said, a being ordinable in a genus absolutely and through itself is a complete being according to species. The reason for the completion consists in this, that it is a being *per se* in having its substantial form by a *per se* agent in relation to some end intended *per se* by nature. Now I call "end" that which belongs to the internal end, which is the proper operation of the thing, which is sometimes found in nature because of the perfection of the operating thing, as in complete beings, as in animals and similar things.[55]

Now the point of all this is to establish that Dietrich is not without justification for reorienting our understanding of the process of generation in the manner that he has, namely, in strict terms of form and its privation, for example, in terms of ¬A and A, as it were, which privation is implied by being in potency. For it is only in reference to the complete act of form that the being in potency is what it is. But, again, the being in potency refers to the form inasmuch as it is a privation of that form.

It is similarly so with regard to the process of corruption. That is, instead of regarding the process of corruption in terms of the sequence of forms, positively considered, that is, for example, the sequence wherein matter is informed first by the substantial form of man, and then by the substantial form of the corpse, Dietrich again insists that the corpse has being and is what it is only by its privative relation to the substantial form of man. Hence, instead of the sequence A, B, where A is the substantial form of man, and B the substantial form of the corpse, we have the sequence A, ¬A.

For in such change, by which a living thing becomes dead, or wine becomes vinegar, according to the intention of nature the corruption of "life" and the corruption of "wine" is more principal and intended through itself by nature. More principal, I say, than the generation of a substantial form of "death" or of "vinegar." Thus privation of the form of "life," whereat the corruption of life terminates, is essentially and principally intended by nature. However, a substantial form of "death" is found accidentally. For this form of "death" is introduced accidentally, namely, by way of corruption, which in such change is principal and essential [*per se*], and essentially and principally it is terminated at privation, which is the principle and essential terminus of such change. The generation of the substantial form, however, is by accident. And this is what the Philosopher says in VIII *Metaphysics*, where he says that "life" is not the matter of "death" nor "wine" of "vinegar," nor does matter essentially receive the form of "death" or of "vinegar," but accidentally, according to the course of the corruption of the animal and of the wine. Therefore, since in such change by which from a living thing a dead thing is made, the corruption of the form of life is essential and more principal than the introduction of a substantial form of death, it follows that the privation of the form of the animal in a dead animal, according to the intention of nature, is essential and more principal than a substantial form of death. Therefore, a dead animal is to be reduced to the genus of a category through such privation moreso than—indeed, absolutely—through a substantial form, which exists in it then. Thus, the dead animal will be in the genus of animated things, not in the genus of inanimate things. For such privation through itself follows in the subject of the substantial form, and it is there in place of the substantial form; and through itself it takes <its> meaning [*rationem*] from the substantial form itself, which it deprives, and is found in such deprived being through itself, whereas a substantial form of death <is found> by accident, according to what was said above.[56]

From such considerations it becomes clear that the privative opposition between living and dead body appears to preclude the possibility of there being a shared form, which was the main point of the arguments considered in the previous section. Nevertheless, although there are important differences between the privation that characterizes potential being and the privation that characterizes aptitudinal being, Dietrich's further criticism of the pluralist position, and his own solution to the problem will turn on the notion that both of these modes of being are primarily and essentially characterized as privative modes of being.

The Irreversible Ordering of Privatively Opposed Forms in Nature

It is not enough for Dietrich's argument against the form of corporeity that it be established that the living and the dead body are privatively opposed to each other, so that the presence of one implies the absence of the other. In addition, Dietrich establishes that these privative opposites occur in nature according to a certain irreversible ordering. Dietrich acknowledges, however, that not all privatively opposed forms occur in this manner. He must therefore distinguish between two modes of privative opposition that can be found in change in nature. The first mode is characterized by the *nonordered reciprocal* reception by matter of form and its privation. This mode characterizes the manner in which the elements change back and forth into one another.

> One of these <modes> is found in the reciprocal reception of either of them, namely, of form and of privation, in the same subject, as when matter that stands under the form of air generates fire, and again, the form of fire falls under privation in the generation of air according to a certain reciprocation. Now the cause of this reciprocation is that matter is in the same relation to either form, namely, air and fire, and there is required for the generation of either of the forms only its privation in a common subject, as the Philosopher says in VIII *Metaphysics*.[57]

In terms of privative opposition, such substantial change is characterized, according to Dietrich, by an unordered, reciprocal reception in matter of privatively opposed forms. That is, when air changes into fire, the air that is to be changed into fire is, prior to the change, also non-fire; and conversely, the fire that is to be changed back into air is also non-air prior to the change. Dietrich explains that for the reception of any of these substantial forms by matter, all that is required in matter is that there be the privation of the form. That is, in order for matter to receive the form of fire, all that matter needs is the privation of fire, which is implied in the *ratio* of any of the other elements. Thus, matter informed by air is at once informed, as it were, by non-fire. Now it is because each of the elementary substantial forms implies in its *ratio* the privation of any of the others that such change can be understood in terms of the successive reception of privatively opposed forms; but because the elements change back and forth into one another, this successive reception of forms is *unordered*.

It is somewhat more complicated with respect to the "higher" substantial forms of complex substances. For unlike the elementary forms, the higher substantial forms—for example, the substantial forms of mixed bodies and of besouled beings, do *not* change back and forth into each other. Rather, there is found in nature a precise ordering of the change between form and its privation.

But the other mode of privative opposition that is found in the privative changing of opposites in the same subject, consists in this, that the privative common subject of the opposites does not receive both of such opposites in a reciprocal manner (as was said in the mode just mentioned), but according to a certain order by which it successively receives either form, namely, that <according to> which there follows privation in the subject. For example, the form of life or the form of sight or the form of wine, and the form under which stands the privated being [*ens privatum*], because without a substantial form it cannot exist, for example, death, blindness, vinegar. Now the subject or matter does not receive the form of death unless it surrenders [*prae-cesserit*] the form of life, nor does it receive the form of vinegar, unless it surrenders the form of wine, as the Philosopher says in VIII *Metaphysics*. There is, therefore, a different mode in receiving successively some forms in a common subject, as was said.[58]

In other words, it is not the case, as in the elements, that the corruption of one form is as much the generation of another, as the corruption of air is as much the generation of fire. Rather, the generation or corruption of one form assumes priority over the corruption or generation of the other.

> Now since generation is terminated at being and form, whereas corruption is terminated at non-being and privation, it is to be considered, that, in such change by which the subject receives a form and its opposite privation, if, with respect to the intention of nature, the generation of the form introduced is more principal than the corruption of a form already existing in the thing, then the form introduced by generation was principally intended by nature. The privation, however (where the corruption of a pre-existing form is terminated), co-exists with the generated form by accident.[59]

For example, the generation of wine takes priority over of the corruption of grape juice; and the corruption of wine takes priority over the generation of vinegar. This is because in order for matter to receive, for example, "vinegar," that is, the privation of "wine," there is required, in addition to the arrival of the form of "vinegar," *that the matter had formerly possessed the substantial form of wine*, and that the substantial form of wine departs, as it were, with the arrival of the form "vinegar," which implies its privation.[60]

Dietrich thus distinguishes the second mode of privative opposition found in change in nature as consisting of *ordered, nonreciprocal* reception by matter of form and its privation; in particular, reception by matter of the privated form in the process of corruption must be preceded by the presence in matter of the perfected form in act.

The Substantial Form of the Dead Body Cannot Have Been in the Living Body

With this somewhat lengthy discussion of Dietrich's reframing of the way in which we look at the processes of substantial change in nature, we can now examine how he uses the ordered, non-reciprocal privative opposition of the living and the dead body to argue against the pluralist position that maintains that the numerical identity of the living and the dead body is achieved through numerically the same form of corporeity, shared by both the living and the dead body. Dietrich argues, in effect, that such a notion preserves neither the privative opposition between the living and the dead nor the irreversible ordering of the living and the dead.

And so, with respect to the second mode, in the path of corruption, matter does not receive the substantial form under which a privated being stands, unless a habit or form in the matter precedes <the privation>. The privation of <the habit or form> takes place [*reliquitur*] by means of a substantial form in matter after the corruption of the being. For example, the form of a dead animal and the form of vinegar, which are privated beings in an irreversible order, do not exist in matter unless the form of animal and the form of wine, <respectively,> precede <them> in the matter. The reason for this is the subjective nature of the being that has to be disposed in an essential order, which <order> is also *per se*. Now I say "order *per se*" with respect to the form and its opposite privation, insofar as the privation is the terminus of the corruption of form and includes the corruption in its *ratio*; not however, with respect to the substantial form of the dead animal, which is found accidentally in nature, as was said above.[61] Hence the Philosopher says in VIII *Metaphysics*, that a dead thing is made from a living thing not as from matter, but as night is made from day. He suggests by this that such order is accidental [*innuens per hoc huiusmodi ordinis acciden-talitatem*]. Now the prior effective cause of such an essential order is the determined and proper and natural period of the thing, which, according to its natural succession in the irreversible order, causes this succession. Therefore, as the Philosopher says in the same place, a return from a dead thing to a living thing or from vinegar to wine does not happen unless one arrives at the prime matter of either. Therefore, it is clear that the form of flesh of the dead animal was never in matter before the corruption of the animal.[62]

In other words, "soul and body" cannot be privatively opposed to "body" if "body" is univocal in each case. For the presence of "soul and body" does *not* imply the absence of "body"; indeed, quite the contrary. But this is precisely what would be required for the privative opposition between the living body and the dead body. And again, since the change from the living body to the dead body is understood to be corruption, and since corruption is a kind of change in nature, the principles of which are form and privation, it is necessary that the living body and the dead body be privatively opposed.

Note that this is not an argument against the doctrine of the plurality of forms in and of itself. Such a doctrine could be made consistent with the perspective on change that Dietrich is presenting here. In fact, Dietrich's argument could be seen as one in which it is granted that there is a form of corporeity in the living body in some manner distinct from the soul. Rather, this is an argument only against the notion that the numerical identity of the living and the dead body could be accounted for by the form of corporeity. That is, it is an argument only against the notion that "corporeity" is the numerically and specifically the same in the living body and in the dead the body.

Dietrich's opponents might respond, however, that their theory does indeed preserve both the privative opposition between and the irreversible ordering of the living and the dead body. For Dietrich understands form—whether simple or complex—as that which informs prime matter whereas his opponents may be said to understand form as the rational soul, and matter as body, that is, the human body apart from the soul. Hence the living body and the dead body are privatively opposed. For whereas the living body implies the *presence* of soul, the dead body implies its *absence*. In other words, "body" can be privatively opposed to "body and soul" inasmuch as "body" is also "*not* body-and-soul." Hence, it appears that the privative opposition between living and dead body, necessary for corruption, *is* preserved.

Such a response, however, betrays—from Dietrich's perspective, at least—a fundamental misunderstanding of the metaphysics of substantial change in nature, as well as a misconception of just what the problem is. For the corpse is not prime matter; it has some substantial form. Likewise, the human body conjoined to the soul is not prime matter. Rather, it, too, has some substantial form. The question is whether the substantial form of the body conjoined to the soul is the same as the substantial form of the corpse. Dietrich argues that it cannot be. This is because of the ordering of form and its privation in the process of corruption. The substantial form of the corrupted being cannot inform matter unless it is preceded by the perfect form, which perfect form must also have departed, as it were, prior to the information of matter by the posterior form. Hence, if "body" is the substantial form of the corpse, it cannot be present unless the "body" whereby the matter of the living body is informed has departed. Hence, they cannot be the same.

Dietrich has thus argued these two points against the pluralist account of, or solution to, the problem of the numerical identity of the living and the dead body. Accounting for this, as the pluralists do, by a numerically identical form of corporeity shared by and informing both the living body and the dead body, results in (i) too much identity—to the extent that the living and the dead body cannot be distinguished from each other, insofar as, on this view, the dead body should be as receptive of the rational soul as is the living body; and (ii) a failure to be able to account for the irreversible non-reciprocal order of generation and corruption.

It remains to consider Dietrich's own solution to the problem of the numerical identity of the living and the dead body of Christ.

Dietrich's Solution

Dietrich's solution rests upon the comparison between the privation that is found conjoined to potentiality in the generation of form and the privation that is found conjoined to "aptitude" in the corruption of form. To the extent that one accepts the numerical identity of that which is in the process of generation is coming to be and will be the perfect form in act, so should one accept, Dietrich will argue, the numerical identity of the perfect form in act and that which once was that form in act but is now in the process of corruption.

Dietrich does not merely assume, however, that there is numerical identity of that which in the process of generation is a privative potency and the complete form in act which is the terminus of generation. On the contrary, he offers no less than two arguments. First, Dietrich draws upon the authority of Aristotle and Averroes.

Therefore, just as in the process of generation a being in potency and then, with generation completed, a being in act, are reduced to the same genus; and not only to the same genus but to the same species; and not only this, but the same thing in number, according to the Philosopher[63] in VIII *Metaphysics*, where he says that when a being in potency becomes a being in act through generation, it does not become something else. Rather, <it is> the same thing that it was before, as an animal in potency becomes numerically the same animal in act—for such generation, according to the

Commentator,[64] does not bestow *multitude* by generation, but *perfection*.[65]

Second, Dietrich considers *potency* and *act* insofar as they are *modes* of being, which do not diversify the essence of a thing. Rather, throughout the process of generation there is but one and the same essence throughout, up to and including the complete form in act, at which generation is culminated and completed.

> <T>he privation that is adjoined to potency when the thing is a being in potency, does not deprive the essence or form of the thing to be generated, but only its act. Otherwise, it would not be a being in potency, the meaning of which is that such potentiality is founded upon the same essence that is then made in act. For the being in potency and then the being in act is the same thing according to the mode of the subject, which is subjected to the contraries. For otherwise there would be only disparity between the terms of generation—that from which and that to which—so that generation would also be impossible.[66]

It is important for Dietrich's solution to emphasize here that the very meaning of the term *generation* implies some underlying identity; otherwise there would be, as he says, only "disparity," which would not be sufficient for "generation" to be a kind of change. Rather, without this underlying identity there would instead be a mere concatenation of appearances.

As we have seen, it is a somewhat unusual sense of "potency" than is typical in discussions of late medieval metaphysics. For Dietrich is using "potency" and "act" to distinguish different stages in the course of generation—"act" indicating the completion of that course, for example, in the adult human being, while "potency" indicates those stages in the course prior to the completion and fulfillment of the course of generation, where further development is still to come, for example, infancy, childhood, etc. Such senses of "potency" and "act" are to be distinguished from their more typical meanings having to do with the composition of material entities, viz., with what is receptive of form, and form, respectively. Thus, the embryo or infant is "in potency" with respect to the adult human being in a manner completely different than the way that prime matter is in potency with respect to form, or the way in which the elements are in potency with respect to the mixed body constituted out of them.[67]

Granting thus the numerical identity between the being in potency and the being in act, Dietrich's argument for the numerical identity between the being in act and the being in the process of corruption ultimately depends upon the strength of the comparison between the potential being of the thing in the process of generation and the "aptitudinal" being of the thing in the process of corruption. The comparison turns on the consideration that in either case there is a privation related to form in an irreversible order. For on the basis of this comparison, Dietrich draws a similar conclusion regarding the numerical identity of the form in act and the "aptitudinally privated form," which occurs in the process of corruption.

> It is similar with respect to the privation that is adjoined to the aptitude in the deprived being, because it is founded upon the same essence in which also the act which is deprived, differing only according to hence and thence [*hinc inde*]. Otherwise, there would be only disparity between those terms, living and dead, so that a dead animal could be no more said to be apt by nature to live than a stone.[68]

One might object that the deprivation characteristic of the dead body differs from the deprivation that characterizes the being in potency in relation to the perfected form in act to such an extent as to make the meaning of *deprivation*, upon which Dietrich's solution turns, equivocal. For the being in potency, although deprived of the perfected form in act, is nevertheless *living* and thus in possession of a soul; whereas the dead body is not only deprived of the perfected form in act—even allowing for differences in the manner of deprivation—but also is not *living* and without a soul.

Yet Dietrich's point is that the dead body is what it is only by reference to, or in relation to, the perfected form in act, just as is the being in potency. Without this reference, the corpse would not be distinguishable from a stone. But of course the stone and the corpse do differ very significantly in kind, and the significance of this difference is accounted for by the reference to the perfected form in act, which reference the corpse has but the stone does not. Similarly for the being in potency—it is what it is only, primarily and essentially by its relation to the perfected form in act. It is understood as an intermediate stage in the course of generation that is intended by nature to arrive at the perfected form in act. At some point, as the corpse corrupts ever further, it will cease to be what it is by reference to the perfected form in act that once was. At that point what remains is instead more properly called the elements or simply and more aptly "dust." Likewise for the being in potency: at some point in the course of generation that from which the being comes to be is more aptly characterized not in relation to the perfected form in act, but as something else, for example, sperm or ovum.[69]

With these considerations, we are finally in a position to consider Dietrich's own solution to the problem of the numerical identity of the living and the dead body. Dietrich does indeed maintain that they are numerically identical, not just in the case of the body of Christ, but for all men. Such numerical identity is established on the grounds that (i) the numerical identity of the being in potency and the being in act is not questioned; (ii) that *potential* being and *aptitudinal* being are both primarily and essentially privative modes of being, and neither is ordinable under a genus, but which nevertheless are what they are because of their relation to the perfected form in act, and are therefore *reduced to* the same species as the perfected form in act, for example, the adult human being; and (iii) that there is therefore sufficiently strong analogy between *potential* being and *aptitudinal* being so that given the numerical identity between *potential* and *actual* being, there must also be numerical identity between *aptitudinal* and *actual* being.

In this way Dietrich is able to give some reasonable account of the numerical identity of the living and the dead body while at the same time avoiding those problems that he attributes to the pluralist position. That is, his solution leaves room and indeed gives some account of the important differences between the living and the dead body, and is also consistent with the irreversible, ordered, nonreciprocal change that characterizes generation and corruption.

Homonymy

It might appear, however, that Dietrich's solution itself still leaves too much identity, despite its advantages over the pluralist position in this respect. For the Philosopher famously maintains that "dead flesh is flesh only equivocally."[70] This equivocity would appear to exclude the possibility of any numerical identity between living and dead body. Since Dietrich has argued, however, that they are indeed numerically the same, and are reduced to the same species, it appears that Dietrich is speaking contrary to Aristotle.

This problem is not addressed in *De corpore Christi in mortuo*, but finds a detailed, if brief, treatment in *De origine rerum praedicamentalium*, chapter 3. There Dietrich explains that

> by the things just said, it is clear that it is agreeably and soundly conceded that the body of a dead animal is the same as that of the living animal, even though according to the philosophers it is conceded and it is true that dead flesh is flesh only equivocally, nor is it the same thing that was before. This is indeed true, if the substantial form of dead flesh is considered according to itself and not according to the meaning of the aforesaid reduction, which is extracted from the intention of nature constituting such beings. The same analogy with respect to difference is found in organs and limbs, such as in the eye and in the hand, and in similar things, insofar as they are constituted in their powers in the living body but are privated of them in the dead <body>, according to the Philosopher. Hence, a dead animal is not to be posited in the genus of inanimate bodies, as some imagine, but is reduced to the genus of animal, as Augustine shows generally concerning all privated beings in Book V *The Trinity*. For the meaning of *inanimate* and of the privation implied by it are one thing, insofar as with *animated* it divides the genus that is *body*; however, the meaning of *dead animal* and the privation implied by it is something else. For privation and form, insofar as these differences divide a genus, are not found according to their succession of each other in a subject according to nature, but only insofar as some one thing is to be distinguished into many, before nature falls into the first division by which beings are distinguished from each other; whereas the privation that the dead animal implies, and its opposite form are of the latter mode, as is clear.[71]

In other words, by considering the dead body apart from its relation to that form whereby what is now a dead body was once a living body, dead flesh and living flesh are indeed said equivocally. However, this does not affect the notion that dead flesh and living flesh are reduced to the same genus and even the same species. For, again, the form and privation which distinguish the living body and the dead body is not the form and privation—or better, the possession and privation, whereby a genus is divided into distinct species, that is, by the possession and privation of a specific difference.

Concluding Remark

There is still something unsatisfactory in Dietrich's solution, in that the result is surely a rather attenuated sense of numerical identity. He has in effect distinguished a sense of numerical identity that is grounded upon being "reduced to the same species" from that numerical identity grounded upon strict specific identity. Furthermore, his solution depends upon a rather tenuous analogy: just as the being in potency in the course of generation (e.g., the embryo) is numerically the same as the perfected adult human being, so is the corpse and the body of the living human being numerically the same, because in either case the being in potency and the aptitudinal being are reduced to the same species as the being in act, all by virtue of numerically the same perfected form in act, intended by nature and the terminus and culmination of the process of generation. The embryo is not yet perfected, although it is what it is by the reference to the perfected form to which it is directed in the course of generation. The corpse is what once was perfected, but is no longer; yet it, too, is what it is by reference to that whereby it was once perfected.

This is perhaps not the strong numerical identity that is sought for; but it no less a numerical identity than the solution proposed by the pluralists allows for. For surely there is a significant distinction (overlooked by the pluralists) between a body informed by the form of corporeity merely in potency to receive the soul (even granting them this with respect to the corpse) and the body informed by the form of corporeity further perfected by the rational soul and thus no longer possessing this (essential) potency. There may be therefore an even more attenuated sense of *specific* identity here in the pluralist theory, even if the sense of numerical identity appears superficially stronger (indeed, even if ultimately incoherent, as Dietrich has argued.)

On the other hand, we cannot ask for *specific* identity because the corpse, strictly speaking, does not belong to a species. As Dietrich has argued, it cannot be arranged or ordered under a species or genus because it is not a form intended by nature. Therefore, however attenuated a sense of numerical identity Dietrich's theory leaves us with—and it is attenuated only because it is not grounded upon strict specific identity, but upon "being reduced to the same genus or species"—it is the best we can hope for in the circumstances. To insist upon strict specific identity, and thus upon a much stronger sense of numerical identity, as the Franciscan pluralists thinkers do—apart from the problems associated with placing a corpse or an embryo in a genus or species in the first place—results in too much identity, and the consequent absurdities with respect to the processes of generation and corruption, as Dietrich has argued. At the very least, then, Dietrich must be given credit for reframing the problem in such a way that along with the various distinctions he introduces, he provides a plausible account of an homonymous numerical identity that the solution to the problem seems to require.

4

Accidents in Scotus's *Metaphysics* Commentary

CHARLES BOLYARD

Despite a historical bias toward considering primarily the substance of things, accidental features play an important and often ignored role in medieval philosophy. First, and most obviously, in typical cases a complete description of an item requires not only that one specify its substance—for example, its humanity—but also its accidents (being tall, sitting, etc.). Second, many medieval theories of universals rely in an important way on accidents, either in a constitutive or epistemic sense (see, e.g., Boethius's account of individuation from his *Theological Tractates*, or William of Champeaux's early theory of universals).[1] Third, insofar as theological considerations bear on philosophical concerns, we find medieval metaphysicians explaining the Eucharist in terms of a basic substance/accident ontology: for many medievals, this event is the only one in which the accidents can remain when the underlying substance is replaced. And finally, medieval accounts of cognition often explain sensation as a taking on of the accidental forms of things by the cognizer.

In short, without an adequate account of accidents and accidental predication, most medieval theories of metaphysics, epistemology, and theology are significantly incomplete. In this essay, I will examine John Duns Scotus's account of accidents, as seen in his *Questions on the Metaphysics of Aristotle* (hereafter QM).[2] As Giorgio Pini notes, Scotus's interest in the metaphysics of accidents "lies at the centre of his philosophical reflection and runs through his works both in Oxford and in Paris."[3] Though Pini relegates Scotus's QM discussion of accidents to a preliminary and inferior stage of his developing views on the subject, I find that even if this is so, there is still much that is worth further investigation there. I concentrate in particular on Scotus's primary discussions of accidents, in I.9, V.7, VI.2, VII.1–4, and VIII.1–3. I will begin by briefly presenting the accounts of accidents offered by Aristotle and Porphyry. After this, I will explore Scotus's account of accidents from the *QM*. It is my contention that though many of Scotus's arguments and positions are philosophically interesting, it is in his appeal to the natural world in this context that Scotus stands apart. In doing this, he presents a theory that is less ad hoc than those of his contemporaries: the ontological independence of accidents is asserted both in Eucharistic contexts and in the context of natural phenomena such as sound and light transmission. Furthermore, once his picture of accidents becomes evident, it is also clear how this, when coupled with the post-1277 emphasis on God's omnipotence, adds to the increased epistemological unease of the time: the specter of skepticism. Though Scotus addresses this unease in some of his later discussions in the context of divine illumination, especially as represented in the thought of Henry of Ghent, he does not directly address it in the *QM*.

Aristotle and Porphyry

The term "accident" (συμβεβηκός) is used throughout the Aristotelian corpus, but not consistently. The most significant discussions occur in the *Categories, Metaphysics,* and *Topics.* Though a thorough investigation of the proper interpretation of Aristotle on accidents is not within the scope of this paper, a sense of his position can be gleaned by looking briefly at the main accounts he offers.[4] In the *Categories,* Aristotle doesn't use the term itself in any thoroughgoing manner, but his explanation of the way that some items are "in" others was clearly taken to be an explanation of one of the most important aspects of accidents by those who read him in the Middle Ages. In *Categories* 2 (1ª24–25), for example, he explains that "by in a subject, I mean what is in something, not as a part, and cannot exist separately from what it is in."[5] This *dependency* of the nine nonsubstantial categories on the primary category, substance, was taken to be a fundamental characteristic of accidents.

The account of accidents given in the *Topics* emphasizes not their dependency, but rather their *nonnecessity.* As Aristotle explains,

> An accident is something which . . . [is] neither a definition nor a property nor a genus—yet belongs to the thing; and something which may either belong or not belong to any one and the self-same thing, as (e.g.) being seated may belong or not belong to some self-same thing. Likewise also

whiteness; for there is nothing to prevent the same thing being at one time white and at another not white. Of the definitions of accident the second . . . is sufficient of itself to tell us the essential nature of the thing in question. (*Topics* I.5, 102^{b}4–14)

This contingent attachment to any particular substance is thus taken to be fundamental to what an accident is.

Finally, the account of accidents offered in *Metaphysics* V.30 (1025^{a}14–34) emphasizes the *causal* nature of accidents. Here, Aristotle explains that there are two types of accidents, the first being more akin to the sorts of items addressed in the *Topics* and *Categories*. As he says here in the *Metaphysics*,

> We call an accident that which attaches to something and can be truly asserted, but neither of necessity nor usually, e.g. if one in digging a hole for a plant found treasure. This—the finding of treasure—happens by accident . . . Therefore there is no definite cause for an accident, but a chance cause, i.e. an indefinite one . . . The accident has happened or exists, –not in virtue of itself, however, but of something else . . . 'Accident' has also another meaning, i.e. what attaches to each thing in virtue of itself but is not in its substance, as having its angles equal to two right angles attaches to the triangle. And accidents of this sort may be eternal, but no accident of the other sort is.

We are thus left with three distinct ways of understanding Aristotle's accidents—as dependent entities, as nonnecessary entities, and as items with "chance causes." In an important piece of recent scholarship critical of what he calls the "doctrine" of accidents, Theodor Ebert explores the apparent inconsistencies in the various accounts of accidents given by Aristotle. As Ebert says,

> even where tradition has surrounded a doctrine of Aristotle's with the halo of an established and venerable truth, we should not shrink from looking for the cracks in the wall . . . Asking them anew may be more in the spirit of Aristotle than sticking to the dogmas of Aristotelianism.[6]

Ebert lays the blame for this false concretization of Aristotle's view squarely at the feet of Porphyry (and perhaps Alexander of Aphrodisias, whose commentaries on Aristotle apparently influenced Porphyry). The relevant text may be found in Porphyry's *Isagoge*:

Accident is what comes and goes without the destruction of the substrate. It is divided into two kinds. One kind of accident is separable and the other is inseparable. Thus sleeping is a separable accident, whereas being black is an inseparable accident of the crow and the Ethiopian . . . They also define accident as follows: accident is what admits of belonging or not belonging to the same thing, or what is neither a genus nor a difference nor a species nor a property, but always has its reality in a substrate.[7]

This account appears to take elements from both the *Topics* and *Metaphysics*, and as Ebert argues, it glosses over some of the inconsistencies in Aristotle's views. Ebert hints that the medievals and early moderns simply followed Porphyry's lead on this point.

While it is true that Porphyry was highly influential in framing the medievals' understanding of accidents, as Ebert suggests, it is not also the case that they blindly followed Porphyry, as this exploration of Scotus's views on the subject will show.

Scotus

Scotus's basic view of an accident (*accidens*) is analogous to his view of substantial form. While substantial form is something that primarily inheres in matter, thus forming a unity we call a substance, so too accidental form primarily inheres in substance. Though the general tendency among medievals is to treat accidents as something of a fundamentally different sort than substances, Scotus's view makes the difference between accidents and substances more a matter of degree than of kind: for him, all entities have being, or in the language of the medievals, being is univocal for substances and accidents.

Despite this difference, Scotus adheres to the commonly held distinction between absolute accidents and relational accidents. Instances of absolute accidents (e.g., whiteness) apply properly only to one individual substance, while instances of relational accidents apply properly to at least two individual substances at the same time (e.g., the relational accident of paternity applies to both a father and his son).[8] Relational accidents will be discussed only in passing here, and the primary focus will be placed on absolute accidents.

The general drift of the varied accounts of (primarily absolute) accidents given by Scotus in the *QM* is first to give accidents more autonomy, thus weakening their dependence;[9] second, to explore and expand their causal function, both in terms of what acts upon them, as well as how they can act upon others; and third, to introduce a more complex epistemological role for accidents than Aristotle offers. Each of these aspects of his view will be addressed in turn.

Metaphysical Aspects of Scotistic Accidents

First, Scotus signals his desire to give accidents a more robust ontological status when he analogizes the relation between accidental form and substance to the relation between substantial form and matter. Aristotle's view amounts to the claim—to borrow a phrase from Augustine's discussion of time—that an accident "tends toward non-existence."[10] But Scotus moves in another direction. As he says, "it is difficult to assign a manifest difference between the dependence of a perishable form upon matter from that of an accident upon its subject."[11] This analogy expresses itself in many ways. First, Scotus argues than an accident can continue to exist even if the underlying subject changes. This occurs most notably during the Eucharist, says Scotus, when bread and wine become the body and blood of Christ:

> What is really the same does not [both] remain and perish; also the exist-ing accident remains whereas the first inherence [in the subject] does not. Otherwise, if it remained . . . the subject was previously denominated by its accident and was called 'quantified bread' and after transubstantiation it would still be called bread . . . [But this] is false.[12]

In the same section, he also hints that the separability of soul (*qua* substantial form) from matter has an important lesson to teach us regarding accidents. As he says, "this difficulty is common to all united things whose components are able to exist apart, such as the soul and the body in man . . ."[13] In fact, Scotus explicitly argues that at least in one other case—that of sound—an accident can naturally exist without inhering in any subject whatsoever.[14] As he says,

> it seems that it was not the intention of the Philosopher to deny all entity formally (*entitatem formaliter*) to accidents except the entity of the sub-

stance in which it actually exists. The Philosopher in *Physics* IV assumes that there is sound in some space and he asks whether this space is empty, and he replies that if a body can be received in a space, it is empty; if it cannot, then it is not empty. Assuming, therefore, that an accident could not exist without a subject, contradictories would be simultaneously true, namely, that there be a body, and there is no body there. The natural entity of these [accidents] is through substance; they can [however] exist without substance [but] with an aptitude for a subject (*tamen possunt actualiter esse sine eo cum aptitudine ad subiectum*) . . . [T]he propositions of the Philosopher can be taken to mean that no [accident] can exist without an aptitude to a subject . . .[15]

While it is true that such accidents retain their directedness or, as he puts it, "aptitude for a subject," they need not actually inhere in those substances.[16]

With this increased independence of accidents comes an emphasis on the accidents' internal simplicity, perhaps in deference to the medieval commonplace that being and unity are convertible terms—i.e., that everything, insofar as it exists, is one; and vice versa. He treats of this issue in detail in article 1 of question 8 of the *QM*. Here, Scotus argues that in most cases, accidents do not have parts.[17] He appeals to a familiar principle:

> Paucity must always be assumed when through it the appearances are saved, according to the view of the Philosopher in Book I of the *Physics* . . . And therefore, the assumption of a plurality ought always to state some manifest necessity because of which that many are postulated; but nothing appears in accidents because of which one would have to assume they are composed of two essential parts.[18]

Though his position is qualified to some degree, the general thrust is to make accidents tend toward unity and simplicity. His main justification for his positions comes in his responses to a number of objections, four of which will be discussed here.

The first objection concerns the relationship between *simplicity* and *change*: simple forms, since they are uncompounded and nonmaterial, are by their nature imperishable, while accidents seem to be perishable.[19] Scotus responds by again analogizing the accident/subject relation to the substantial form/matter relation. As he argues, as in substantial generation, what is changed is the matter; so too in the accidental, what is changed is the subject. And thus the composite from it and the accidental form is able to be generated there *per se* and corrupted *per se*.[20]

In short, Scotus says that it is really the *compound* formed by the accident and the subject that is perishable. One should notice, however, that he doesn't directly answer the objection, since he is silent on the question of whether the accidental form *in itself* is eternal. Later in the text, however, he does assert that since an accident is "compatible with another without which it does not exist naturally," one would not say that the accident is incorruptible.[21] But even granting this point, Scotus still leaves open the possibility that some particular accident might be eternal, perhaps due to God's supernatural power.

The second objection concerns the linkage between *perfection* and *simplicity*. Since simplicity goes hand in hand with perfection, and since (by hypothesis) accidents are simple and substances are compound, it follows that accidents are by their nature more perfect than substances.[22] Scotus responds here by pointing out that the principle should be applied differently to the divine and to the mundane:

In perishable things generally speaking, the more simple is more imperfect ... because such a nature cannot tolerate as much actuality with its simplicity ... and generally that which can be actualized in more ways is the more perfect.[23]

The core of Scotus's response is his belief that in the natural world, the more complex organism is the more perfect one. And thus the complexity of a substance counts *toward* its perfection, rather than against it. Scotus does not follow the consequences of this view to any significant degree, but if he did, it appears that by this argument, wherein the ability to be actualized in more ways is the mark of greater perfection, matter itself—insofar as it is pure potentiality—would be the highest extent of natural perfection.

The third objection is also concerned with an accident's perfection. Rather than focusing on simplicity, however, this objection deals with *causation*: since something caused is more imperfect than its cause, and since accidents cause changes in their subjects, it follows that accidents are more perfect than their subjects.[24] In response, Scotus proposes what might be called an "additive" principle of perfection. As he puts it:

> With dependent things, it can well be the case that the dependent is more perfect which depends upon more [causes], from each of which causes it receives some of its perfection.[25]

In other words, if this view is correct and if it can be generalized, proofs of God's existence of the sort Descartes gives in his *Meditations* would be suspect, since the perfection in the idea of God could seemingly be gained through a plurality of other items that are not fully perfect in themselves: a number of imperfect ideas, it seems, could be used to create an idea of a God with all perfections.

The fourth and final objection to be considered here concerns itself with a few Boethian claims. According to Boethius, a simple form cannot be the subject of an accident, but some accidents themselves have accidents. Hence, accidents cannot be simple forms. He gives the examples of "a line that is straight and a curved line; a number that is even or uneven; or motion that is slow or fast."[26]

Scotus's response to this objection is unclear, but a possible reading of it is as follows.[27] Just as a *substantial* form—which in itself is simple—is susceptible to modification by an accident that inheres in the substantial-form-when-enmattered compound, so too an *accidental*-form-when-enmattered can be modified by the compound in which it inheres.

This interpretation is not without problems, however, for if this is truly what Scotus means, it seems more correct to say that the *substance itself*—that in which both the initial accident and the modifying accident inhere—is modified, not the first accident that inheres in it. If so, then accidents would not have accidents, which Scotus apparently wants to allow. It's unclear why he would not accept accidents that admit of accidents, especially given that he allows for nonsimple accidents in other cases.

In any case, it *is* clear that since Scotus wants to reify accidents to a fuller degree, and despite the fact that he is content to limit the perfection of accidents, he feels compelled to defend their unity.

Given all of this, as Berthold Wald points out, the important question for Scotus is to explain how two fundamentally distinct, independently existing entities—namely, a substance and its accident—can in any significant way be considered a unity when joined together.[28] More light can be shed on this by exploring the ways in which the two interact.

The second aspect of Scotus's position—the *causal* questions of whether and how accidents might act in concert with other accidents to give variations in intensity to their subjects—is, to judge by the amount of ink spilled, Scotus's main concern in the *QM*.[29] Heat, for example, is an "additive" accident, in the sense that more heat can be added to a substance with previous accidental forms of heat, without necessitating a wholesale replacement of the previous accident of heat.[30]

This additive nature fits nicely with his discussion of whether two accidents of the same species can exist in the same subject at the same time.[31] Scotus's basic answer to this question is a qualified yes: in some cases, this can occur.[32] Scotus can best be understood here, as in the previous discussion, by exploring his responses to objections.

The first objection concerns *unity*: "The unity of a thing and its entity stem from the same source. But the subject is the cause of the entity of its accident; therefore, of its unity; therefore, if the subject is one, so too is the accident."[33] Thus, according to this objection, a subject can have only one accident of a given species. Scotus replies by saying that the term "unity" is equivocal. He offers three types of unity—formal, material, and efficient—and shows why each is insufficient to support the objection.

If *formal* unity of subject and accident is meant, then "to understand an accident numerically one apart from a subject that has its own unity would be a contradiction, and even God could not separate the accident from its subject."[34] In other words, formal unity is too tight a restriction on any *single* accident's independence—an independence which is certainly required for the Eucharist and for the transmission of sound—and thus it cannot be used to restrict a subject to having a single accident of a species. Also, Scotus asks us to imagine such a unity of accident and subject in a case in which the subject changes from being white, to being black, and then back to being white again. According to Scotus, since "these whitenesses would be numerically one . . . the same numerical thing will naturally be frequently regenerated and repeatedly perish."[35] In other words, if we insist on such a formal unity of accident and subject, change (at least beyond the inherence of the original accident) is impossible. Finally, Scotus argues that such formal unity leads to causal problems: if we assume (following Aristotle) that "the subject is the cause of its accident," and furthermore hold that the subject and accident are formally one, then that one thing would cause itself.[36]

Given these problems with formal unity, Scotus next explores whether *efficient* unity—that is, a causal situation in which the cause and effect are united insofar as they are part of the same efficiently causal event—might support the objection. Here, Scotus says, we do not have any reason to limit ourselves to one effect of a causal event: a single efficient cause can produce effects that differ only numerically.[37]

Last, if we take unity to be a *material* unity of subject and accident—that is, that they share the same matter—Scotus thinks we cannot interpret this to mean that everything sharing the same matter is numerically one. He holds this view because changes of the sort mentioned above—namely, from white to black—would be impossible; the whiteness and blackness would be one with each other. As he puts it, in such a case, "contraries would be one numerically."[38]

The second objection to Scotus's view attempts to point to a problem with *multiplicity*. Matter is in potency to form in general, but not to any particular form. If this weren't the case, so the objection goes, then there would be "infinite potencies in matter," which likens matter too much to God.[39] And if matter is thus in potency only to form in general, any particular form of a species it receives exhausts that potentiality, with no room for other forms of that type.

Scotus sees no problem with allowing an infinite number of particular potentialities.[40] Returning to an earlier example—that of black-white-black change—Scotus offers two possible explanations.[41] First, if there is a potency to whiteness initially, which is then filled by the accident of whiteness, then further change back to that particular whiteness is impossible, since a whiteness that is numerically the same cannot come back into existence after having previously ceased to exist.[42] Thus, we're left with the second explanation, which is Scotus's view: in such a case, there are multiple potencies for whiteness in the substance all along.

Here, Scotus is trying to show that even when we think of simple cases of accidental change—cases in which only one accident of a species exists at a time in the subject—we are forced to admit multiple potencies, on pain of contradiction. Thus, why not allow multiple potencies of the same species to be filled at the same time? A problem for Scotus, however, is to explain why potencies cannot return after being fulfilled. Why is it the case that movement can only be from potentiality to act, and not vice versa? Is a restriction to one-way change required for other aspects of his metaphysics?

Scotus also defends the multiplicity of accidents by reference to the phenomenon of light and the nature of relations in nn. 65–70. First, he says, consider the case of one object being illuminated by two candles. On Scotus's view, the resultant illumination is "more intense than either of the two" individual candle illuminations.[43] As he goes on to explain later,

> it is necessary that the species be in proportion to the object; namely, as representing the object, it should not be more intense than what such an object is apt by nature to produce. For a more intense species would represent proportionately a more intense object.[44]

Given this, then, any time we have an "additive" accident situation—as in the case of two candles illuminating a single object—we must have two accidents at work at the same time. He explains later that in cases such as this, multiple sensible species can create a single, unified sight (or vision) without themselves being visible to the perceiver as distinct species.[45] Similarly, he says that "one species in the phantasm or memory suffices to imagine all [accidental inherences of this sort] that are specifically the same."[46] That is, moving up a cognitive level, from the level of sense to the level of phantasm or memory, does not eliminate the possibility of having the same one–many relationship between the item of which one is aware and the distinct items that go toward making up that item of awareness.

Thus even if the light bathing the object appears to be uniform (and so is not clearly separable visually into its component species), its overall increased illumination shows that the first accidental inherence of light did not prevent the addition of the second accidental inherence. As he says later, light is particularly odd, for it is "continually generated . . . there are as many of the same species [as the light produces]; indeed, there is an infinity of such."[47] In short, lighted objects simultaneously have an infinite number of accidental inherences of light, since the object is being bombarded by a stream of light-species, on Scotus's account. Perceptual distinguishability is not a requirement for the existence of multiple instances of a given accident type.

Second, Scotus uses relations to defend his view. As he puts it, when a particular father has a particular son, paternity in that father to this son has a unity greater than specific unity ... But the only paternity that is greater than specific is particular paternity, namely, just this paternity ... Through this paternity, however, a father is not related to all his sons, because if this son is destroyed, so too is this paternity.[48]

As Scotus goes on to explain, the father has one paternity per child, all of which are of the same species.[49]

So what is of particular interest in Scotus's account of accidents? First, it is not the influences of the Eucharistic sacrament on his metaphysics. Though the influence is large, other theologians such as Aquinas and Ockham held the doctrine to play just as large a role for their theories as it did for Scotus's. Second, it is not simply Scotus's insistence on the increased ontological independence of accidents, since again other thinkers of the period share his view. Instead, Scotus's *QM* account of accidents is notable because it gains such a large degree of support from natural phenomena—sound, light, and optics, most notably. His theory is not ad hoc in the way Aquinas's can appear to be. It is part of a comprehensive account of the world, both natural and supernatural.

Epistemological Aspects of Scotistic Accidents

This brings us to the third important aspect of Scotus's position on accidents: his account of whether and how accidents can be sensed, cognized, or known. His concerns can be divided into two main areas. First, he worries that despite some of Aristotle's claims to the contrary, Aristotelian science apparently requires that one have scientific knowledge of accidents. Second, Scotus wants to clarify exactly how the cognitive process works vis-à-vis accidents and their subjects.

Scotus addresses the former worry in terms of "subalternate" or subordinate sciences—that is, sciences such as optics and music that employ as some of their principles conclusions drawn from other, purer sciences (e.g., metaphysics, physics, or mathematics). Scotus tells us that subalternate sciences cannot be known without admitting the knowledge of accidents, since "the subalternate only adds an accidental difference to the subject of the higher science."[50] If such a science is to have any significant unity at all, and is not merely an "aggregation" of items, one must grant that this accidental difference is central to the science.[51] These theoretical commitments, of course, are contingent upon actually accepting these subalternate sciences as being sciences. Scotus, however, never gives any indication that he doesn't treat them as such, especially given his frequent references to the sciences of music and optics.

The latter worry—which centers on the role of accidents in the cognitive process—is both more complex and more puzzling. There is a basic tension in Scotus's discussion between the desire to acknowledge the primacy of the accident's role in human cognition, and also to retain some quasi-necessary connection between an accident and its subject. His writings give the impression that he has not fully committed to the ontological independence of accidents in this epistemological context, or at least as if he has not fully realized the epistemological consequences such a position engenders.

On one side, Scotus talks about compounds of accidents and substances— what he calls "accidental beings" (*ens per accidens*). These accidental beings cannot be known scientifically, because they are composed of parts that exist in different genera.[52] Though one could know them scientifically *qua substances*, one could not know them scientifically *qua accidents*.[53] Given the problem with such compounds, perhaps Scotus could argue that accidents can be known when taken in isolation.

Unfortunately, Scotus doesn't want to allow this either, and he's quite clear about it: "an accident when understood completely cannot be understood without its subject."[54] This is a puzzling response, especially given his general movements toward granting accidents more ontological independence. One possibility is that Scotus means only that one must grasp an accident's "aptitudinal" connection to (or directedness toward) its subject to understand it completely. But if so, this also lends some support to the view one can know a substance by means of an accident that is directed toward it. Unfortunately, again, he explicitly denies this possibility. He accepts the following two arguments. First, if one can know subjects through their accidents, "one could know naturally [that] the substance is or is not in the Eucharist."[55] Second, again appealing to the relative perfection of accidents and substances, he says that a mediated knowledge of substances, through the accidents connected to them, is impossible. For him, "the species can never represent anything distinctly that is more perfect than that of which the species is."[56]

In short, accidents seem both to require, and to be forbidden from, being known in combination with their subjects. Even more puzzlingly, however, he also says that accidents are known first in generation (that is, in time), and that substances aren't known *at all* in this life.[57] Thus we have a picture in which the knowledge of subalternate sciences requires knowledge of accidents, knowledge of accidents requires knowledge of their substances, and yet substances cannot be known at all. If ever there were a recipe for skepticism, this is it.

So how can Scotus reconcile these apparent problems? One simple way is to save full, scientific knowledge for the next life. There we can know substances, and hence their accidents, and hence subalternate sciences. But this obviously puts us in a rather precarious position here, something he generally doesn't incline to do.

Conclusion

Scotus's complete *QM* account of accidents thus includes the following characteristics. First, there is the metaphysical and physical side: accidents have a large degree of ontological independence; their actual inherence in their subjects is a contingent fact about them; they are metaphysically simple; and many individuals of the same species can simultaneously inhere in the same subject. At the same time, accidents are somewhat weakened: they are less perfect than their subjects; and they have an internal "aptitude" or directedness toward their subjects.

This directedness is especially mysterious. First, what happens to the directedness of the bread and wine's accidents during the Eucharist? If the directedness ceases to exist when the conversion takes place, then the accidents appear to have undergone an internal change, which threatens their simplicity. Given this, it appears that directedness is an essential aspect of the metaphysical makeup of accidents. Perhaps it can be understood on analogy to qualities such as a stone's propensity to move down: the propensity always exists, but an impediment can prevent that propensity from being actualized.

The second worry concerning an accident's directedness is the following: is it tied to a particular, individual subject—that is, a subject token—or is it rather tied to a subject type? At first blush, token-directedness appears preferable for epistemological reasons, since a cognized accident of a subject could potentially contain within it some grounds for inferring the existence of its particular subject (despite Scotus's suggestions to the contrary).

A type-directedness, on the other hand, would at best point to the existence of some subject or other, but not to any particular subject.

Further epistemological aspects of accidents are even more problematic. The positive claims Scotus makes about accidents here are that they must be known in order to ground knowledge of subalternate sciences, and that they are temporally the first things to be known. But he also says that they cannot be known fully without knowledge of their subjects, and that knowing their subjects—that is, substances—is impossible in this life. The consequences are obvious: on this account, not only is knowledge of subalternate sciences impossible in this life, but knowledge of any science whatsoever, insofar as every science concerns itself with substances, is similarly impossible.

A straightforward way to handle this problem involves dropping the requirement that one tie knowledge of the accident to the knowledge of its substance, and thus allowing that one can know an accident fully in itself, without reference to any other existent thing. But this leads to its own cognition problems: in this case, even if we have a token-directedness in the accident, and even if the accident's token-directedness is grasped, the contingency of the accident's connection to its subject makes it impossible for us to tell whether a cognitive accident—a sensible species—is connected *in reality* to its proper subject. In short, we have divorced the sensory item from its substantial subject, thus strengthening the case for skepticism.

The more one examines Scotus's position here, the more he gives the impression of someone grappling toward an atomic theory of accidents, in the mode of Democritus or Epicurus: for these earlier thinkers, the physical world is composed of independent, eternal, internally simple atoms that play both physical and epistemological roles. Though Scotus never explicitly makes the claim, he appears to treat accidents—at least nonrelational ones—as similarly spatially located (this appears in his discussion of the accidents of sound, light, and the Eucharistic bread and wine). Now, the ancient atomists don't talk in terms of directedness or aptitude for subjects, but they do sometimes admit different types of atoms, which might be taken as equivalent to a type-directedness. Epicurus, for example, held that atoms that play a role in the cognitive process are particularly fine in nature, and are thus suited to be taken in by the senses and the soul. And we might build on this analogy even if we assume that Scotus holds token-directedness to be the proper account. In this case, the subjects of an accident's inherence would be understood to have special, individualized potentiality-receptors that fit only one individual accident, and the accident would have a mated aspect that fits only that particular potentiality-receptor.

But if this is really what Scotus is reaching toward, he doesn't fully carry it over into his epistemology. He still wants to retain a subordinate role for accidents there (due to the requirement that the substance be known for the accident to be known, and due to the accidents' lesser degree of perfection), and he doesn't fully realize the epistemological consequences that result when one separates the object of direct cognition (the accident, in this case) from the extramental object it is meant to represent or point to (the substance, in this case).

Scotus gives us a novel account of accidents in the *QM*. It has explanatory gaps, to be sure, but his attempt to give a philosophically comprehensive account of the way accidents function both metaphysically and epistemologically more than makes up for his theory's shortcomings.[58]

III UNIVERSALS

5

Avicenna Latinus on the Ontology of Types and Tokens

MARTIN TWEEDALE

Let me begin this essay with a little sophism, familiar to anyone who has tried to explain what types and tokens are:

This flag (i.e., this particular piece of cloth) is a token of a type.
This flag is the Union Jack.
The Union Jack is a type.
Therefore, this flag is a type.
Tokens of types are not themselves types.
Therefore, this flag is not a token of a type.

At the end of this essay I shall explain how, on my view, Avicenna would have resolved that sophism, but to arrive at that objective a rather arduous journey through the thickets of Avicennian ontology is required. The statement of the sophism and its resolution, then, will frame what I hope is an illuminating discussion of texts most scholars of Avicenna will be familiar with, but still, perhaps, puzzled by.[1]

Tokens as Enmattered Types

To begin with it is useful to glance back at a likely source for Avicenna's views, Alexander of Aphrodisias, whose works from around 200C.E. were known in the Islamic world from at least the ninth century. In Alexander we already find the view that when the mind considers an intelligible universal corresponding to some species or genus of material things, it is considering a form which exists in the concrete material singulars with all the accidents attendant on material existence, but nevertheless a form which in an act of abstraction the mind has removed both from matter and from the conditions attendant on matter.[2] The intelligibility of the form as well as its capacity to serve as a universal depend upon this abstraction. This is an idea that Avicenna completely accepts. In his *De anima*[3] he remarks:

Text 1

But the contemplative faculty is the faculty which is generally informed by a universal form bare of matter. If this is bare in itself, it will be easier for it to apprehend in itself its form. But if it is not bare, it will still become bare because *it will strip it so that none of what it is affected with in its association with matter remain in it.*

Sed virtus contemplativa est virtus quae solet informari a forma universali nuda a materia. Si autem fuerit nuda in se, apprehendere suam formam in se facilius erit; si autem non fuerit nuda, fiet tamen nuda quia ipsa denudabit eam, ita ut de omnibus affectionibus eius cum materia nihil remaneat in ea. [*DA* I5, p. 94, 15–p. 95, 19]

And later:

Text 2

Of the distinctive features of human beings what is particularly distinctive is the forming of universal contents completely abstracted from matter ...

Quae autem est magis propria ex proprietatibus hominis, haec est scilicet formare intentiones univer-sales intelligibiles omnino abstractas a materia ... [*DA* V1, p. 76, 4–6]

That universality is dependent on the form's being abstracted in this way is evident from many passages of which the following is perhaps one of the clearest:[4]

Text 3

Thus, just as animal in existing has many modes, so also in the intellect. In the intellect it is the abstracted form of animal in virtue of the abstraction we have talked of

Unde, sicut animal in esse habet plures modos, sic etiam est in intellectu. In intellectu etenim est forma animalis abstracta secundum abstractionem quam praediximus,

earlier, and in this mode it is said to be an intelligible form. And in the intellect the form of animal exists in such a way that in the intellect by one and the same definition it agrees with many particulars. On account of this, *one form in the intellect will be related to a multiplicity, and in this respect it is a universal. [It is a universal] because it is a single content in the intellect whose comparison does not change no matter which animal you take,* that is, when you first represent the form of any of these in your imagination, if later the intellect strips away the accidents from its content, you will acquire in the intellect this very form. Therefore this form is what you acquire by stripping away from animality any individual imagination taken from external existence, even though it does not have external existence, rather the imagination abstracts it.

et dicitur ipsum hoc modo forma intelligibilis. In intellectu autem forma animalis taliter est quod in intellectu convenit ex una et eadem definitione multis particularibus. Quapropter una forma apud intellectum erit relata ad multitudinem,

et secundum hunc respectum est universale,

quia ipsum est una intentio in intellectu,

cuius comparatio non variatur ad quodcumque acceperis animalium, videlicet quoniam, cuiusque eorum primum repraesentaveris formam in imaginatione, si postea exspoliaverit intellectus intentionem eius ab accidentibus, acquiretur in intellectu haec ipsa forma. Ergo haec forma est quae acquiritur de exspoliatione animalitatis a qualibet imaginatione individuali accepta de esse extrinseco, quamvis ipsa non habeat esse extrinsecus, sed imaginatio abstrahit eam. [*PP* V1, p. 237, 28–p. 238, 42; *MH* p. 156, 16–31.]

A corollary of this view is that the individual is formed by the enmatterment of what is common to all individuals of the same species. This is explicitly stated by Alexander and Avicenna adopts this position too, as the following passages attest:[5]

Text 4

An individual does not become an individual until extraneous distinctive features, either shared

Individuum autem non fit individuum nisi cum adiunguntur naturae speciei proprietates extraneae

or unshared, are joined to the nature of the species and this or that particular matter is designated for it.	communicantes aut non communicantes, et designatur ei aliqua materia haec vel illa. [L 12va 50–52]
But those of these natures which require matter have existence only when matter has been prepared. Thus their existence receives accidents and circumstances from outside by which they are individuated.	Quae vero ex istis naturis eget materia, non habet esse nisi cum materia fuerit praeparata; unde ad eius esse adveniunt accidentia et dispositiones extrinsecus per quae individuatur. [PP V2, p. 240, 83–85; MH, p. 158, 22–25]

I hold the view, which is frequently accepted, that it is fair enough to treat Avicenna as talking about the distinction we often designate as that between "type" and "token". The tokens are the individuals, and their forms, once abstracted by the intellect, are the types of which they are the tokens.[6] Tokens of the letter 'A', for example, are particular trails of ink or chalk or graphite or whatever at particular locations in the physical world. You get tokens by "enmattering", if you will, the type, and then those tokens differ from one another only by the accidents which accrue to them by their enmatterment at a particular time and place. Since this idea is familiar and even its use in explaining Avicenna's ontology is widely accepted, I shall not belabor the point but proceed to what is distinctive in Avicenna's handling of the whole topic.

Since Avicenna thinks that the accidents which distinguish tokens of the same type are separable, that is, of the sort that the individual can lose while remaining in existence, there can be for him no definition of an individual in the strict sense. In the following passage (which immediately follows the passage from L given in text 4) Avicenna says that the accidents serve merely to distinguish the individual, that is, token, by ostension:

Text 5

It is impossible for the distinguishing features we have thought of to be added to the species, however many they are, because in the end they will not succeed in showing the individuating content on account of	Impossibile est autem adiungi speciei proprietates intellectas quotquot fuerint, quia ad ultimum non erit earum demonstrare intentionem individuantem propter quam individuum constituatur in

which an individual is established in the intellect. For if you say that Plato is tall, a beautiful writer, and so on, no matter how many distinguishing features you add still they will not describe in the intellect the individuality of Plato. *For it is possible that the content which is composed from all of them is possessed by more than one item and shows you only that he exists, [as does] also an ostension of the individual content.* For example, if we said that he is the son of this person and at a given time is a tall philosopher, [and] it happened at that time that no one else was like him in having those distinguishing features, and you happened to know this appearance, then you would know his individuality just as you would know that which is sensible if it were pointed out to you with a finger. For example, if Plato were pointed to at the third hour. For then his individuality would be determined for you, and this would be a case of pointing out his individuality to you.

intellectu. Si enim diceres quod Plato est longus, scriptor pulcher, talis et talis, quotquot proprietates apposueris, non tamen describetur per illas in intellectu individualitas Platonis. Possibile est enim ut intentio quae componitur ex his omnibus habeatur a pluribus quam ab uno; non autem demon-strat tibi eum nisi esse, et ostensio intentionis individualis. Velut si diceretur quod est filius illius et est in tali hora longus philosophus, contingeret illa hora nullum alium convenire cum eo in illis propretatibus, et contingeret te scire hunc visum, tunc scires eius individualitatem, quemadmodum scires id quod est sensibile si digito ostenderetur tibi. Veluti si osten-deretur Plato hora tertia,tunc enim certificaretur tibi individualitas illius, et hoc esset tibi ostendens individualitatem eius. [L 12va 53-vb 3]

Avicenna sums up this theory of the distinctness of tokens very nicely in this short passage from his *De anima*:

Text 6

Otherness occurs among individual things only on account of diversity

Alteritas etenim non cadit inter singulares rerum nisi aut ex

either of materials or of accidents
and circumstances, that is, on
account of the diversity which
exists between universal and
particular, that is, between what is
abstracted from matter and what is
taken with matter.

diversitate materiarum aut
accidentium et dispositionum
aut ex diversitate
quae est inter universale et
particulare aut abstractum a
materia
et acceptum in materia. [DA V2,
p. 94, 77–p. 95, 81]

I have gone into some detail on this point in order to show how Avicenna's view runs a real danger of falling into monism, at least at the level
of species. What inseparably belongs to any given token is exactly the same
as what inseparably belongs to any other token of the same species-type.
An individual human has nothing inseparable from himself that any other
individual human does not or could not have. But what stays the same
about me despite whatever changes afflict me without destroying me is
surely just that which is me! Likewise for you and every human being.
Consequently, that which is me is just the same as that which is you and
so on for all our fellow humans. Like reasoning applies to any set of tokens
of the same species-type.

Another danger threatening Avicenna's view arises because universality
belongs to form only once the form is thought by the mind in abstraction
from material circumstances; consequently, it seems that the form will belong
to many singulars only after it is thought, for, when all is said and done,
what is it to be a universal other than to belong to many? But since, as we
have just seen, this form is the very essence of those singulars, the singulars
themselves will not exist independently of abstract thought. To put it in
modern terms, if a token has to be of a certain type to be anything at all, and
if we do not have any types until the mind goes to work abstracting something
from the conditions of physical existence, then, it seems, the tokens depend
on the mind for being whatever they are. This is basically an idealist position, and we can be sure that Avicenna did not intend to advocate that.

Universality is Accidental: Alexander's Way

I read Avicenna's further elaborations on our topic as largely an effort to avoid
both of the above pitfalls, that is, of monism on the one hand, and idealism on

the other. One way of approaching this is first to look at Alexander's position, note its failings, and then see how Avicenna modifies Alexander. Let me review, then, what I proposed quite some time ago as the Aphrodisian position on universals.[7]

Alexander claimed that universality is only an accident of the form, that is, if indeed the form is common to many, its being common to many is something the form could exist without. Further he says that when the form ceases to be thought in abstraction it ceases to be universal, but that does not mean that it ceases to be full stop. Presumably, then, it may continue in existence as the form of various concrete particulars. However, Alexander's view gets into difficulty at this point because he says that to be a universal is just to belong to many, and in fact he shows that universality is an accident of the forms it belongs to by noting that whether there is just one or more than one particular possessing that form is in no way determined by the form itself. The existence of the form itself does not entail that there is more than one particular possessing it, and thus that form can exist even though only one particular possesses it, that is, even though it is not a universal in the sense he defined. But now how can being a universal depend on being thought abstractly, unless the form's belonging to several things can occur only after it is thought? Since the form makes the individual be something, idealism seems to be the conclusion we would have to reach.

Alexander does not, so far as I know, confront this problem squarely, but certain passages suggest that he thought that only by mental abstraction could there be *one and the same* entity existing in many particulars.[8] My guess here is that Alexander would say that the form as something peculiar to one individual does exist in that particular prior to any thought, and it can be grasped as peculiar to that individual by the senses. But there is no *one and the same* thing in several particulars until the mind has abstracted such an item in thought.

So elaborated, Alexander would seem to be saved from both species monism and idealism, for on the one hand in extramental reality we do not find some one thing being the essence of all the particulars within a given species but rather a multiplicity of particularized forms, and on the other hand each particular has its essence quite independently of abstract thought. The only problem is that this whole line seems contrary to Alexander's own claim that what he calls the "common item" is ontologically prior to the particulars; it is their essential constituent. The elaboration we have just suggested in effect turns the common items or universals, insofar as they exist prior to the particulars, into thoughts or concepts, and hence they cannot be used to ground the existence of those particulars unless we want to allow that that existence is mind-dependent. But Alexander certainly wants particulars to exist independently of thought. Can this basic realism possibly be reconciled with the claims that (1) the common item is ontologically prior to the particulars it is common to, and (2) that the only sort of existence a common item or universal has prior to its existence in particulars is a mind-dependent one?

The whole problem can be translated nicely into talk of types and tokens. If we think about tokens of the letter 'A', their all falling into that class, that is, the class of tokens of the letter 'A' is dependent on there being the letter 'A' in the first place. We invent this type, the letter 'A', thereby giving it a sort of mental existence, and then by instancing that type all these material particulars get classed as tokens of that letter. The existence of the particulars as particular 'A's is mind-imposed. But if we are going to try type-token ontology on the natural world, as both Alexander and Avicenna, along with the mainstream of ancient and medieval thinkers generally, intended to do, and we do not want natural tokens of types to turn out to be artifacts of our own thinking, we are going to have to grant that types have some sort of existence prior both to the existence of the tokens *and to our thinking of those types,* and that is just what is incompatible with thinking nothing is a type prior to being thought abstractly. We seem then to be forced out of our Aristotelian refuge into the clutches of robust Platonism.

Universality is Accidental: Avicenna's Way

We shall see that Avicenna's views are designed to retain the core of Alexander's position while avoiding this problem. The existence of naturally unified classes of tokens of a certain type prior to thought is defended, while monism and idealism are rejected and Platonism avoided. Showing how Avicenna thinks he accomplished this feat is the task of the remainder of this essay. We can begin by noting that although Avicenna explicitly accepts Alexander's idea that universality is an accident of what it belongs to, he defined universality quite differently. In one place he cites three progressively wider definitions, opting in the end for the last:

Text 7

I say, then, that 'universal' has three senses: (1) Something is called universal because it is actually predicated of many items, for example, human. (2) A content is called a universal when it is possible for it to be predicated of many, even if none of these items actually exist; for example, the content of a seven-sided house. This is universal because its nature can be predicated of many; it is not necessary that those many items exist nor even any one of them. (3) A content is called a universal when nothing prevents its being *thought* to be predicated of many, because if something nevertheless did prevent [its being predicated of many] it would prevent this by a cause by which this is proven. Sun and earth are examples, for, so far as the idea of them is concerned, the fact that sun and earth are thought does not prevent its being possible for their content to be found in many. This is only prevented if we bring in an argument by which it may be known that this is impossible. And then this will be impossible because of an extrinsic cause, not because of the imagination of them. All of these senses can agree in this much: what is a universal is

Dico igitur quod universale dicitur tribus modis; dicitur enim universale secundum hoc quod praedicatur in actu de multis, sicut homo; et dicitur universale intentio quam possible est praedicari de multis, etsi nullum eorum habeat esse in effectu, sicut intentio domus heptangulae, quae universalis est eo quod natura eius est posse praedicari de multis, sed non est necesse esse illa multa, immo nec etiam aliquod illorum; dicitur etiam universale intentio quam nihil prohibit opinari quin praedicari de multis, quod tamen si aliquid prohibit, prohibebit causa qua hoc probatur, sicut sol et terra; hoc enim, ex hoc quod intelliguntur sol et terra, non est prohibitum quantum ad intellectum

posse intentionem inveniri in multis, nisi inducatur ratio qua sciatur hoc esse impossibile; et hoc erit impossibile ex causa extrinseca, non ex ipsorum imaginatione. Possunt autem haec omnia convenire in hoc quod universale est id quod in intellectu non est impossibile praedicari

something which in thought it is not impossible to predicate of many. The logical universal and whatever is similar to it must have this feature.

de multis, et oportet ut universale logicum et quidquid est simile illi sit hoc.

[*PP* V1, p. 227, 7–p. 228, 21; *MH*, p. 148, 8–p. 149, 7]

The first sense of 'universal' mentioned above is exactly the sense we found Alexander giving the term. It is interesting to note that this is not the meaning Aristotle himself expressly assigns it in the oft-cited passage at the beginning of *De Int.* 7 and which he mentions again at *Metaph.* Z13, 1038b11. There Aristotle says that a universal is what "is of such a nature as to be predicated of many subjects." Clearly Aristotle wants to make sure something can still be a universal even though in fact there are not many things for it to be predicated of.

Avicenna's second and third definitions move closer to Aristotle's. The second, in effect, says that something is universal as long as it is possible for it to be predicated of many. But since the impossibility of such predication may arise simply because immutable features of the universe dictate that there is no more than one item of a certain nature (e.g., no more than one sun or one earth) and not at all because that nature just is what it is, Avicenna adds his third, broadest definition, that doubtless is meant to do full justice to the passage from *De interpretatione*. Here anything which can be thought without logical incoherence to be predicated of many is to be called a universal. In other words, all that is now required is that the nature itself not block its being predicated of many, and this is probably close to what Aristotle intended.

But now what sense can we make of universality's being an accident of the natures it belongs to, that is, something they could exist without? This openness to being predicated of many seems to follow just from the nature itself. One presumably can tell whether a nature is universal or not just by examining that item by itself with no consideration of its circumstances in reality. Yet there can be no doubt that Avicenna does hold onto the Alexandrian thesis of the accidentality of universality; it is just that he defends it in an entirely different way. Some of the texts on this point are among the best known in Avicennian metaphysics. His general idea is that being a universal does not figure in the definition of that which is universal:

Text 8

Thus a universal just from being a universal is something, and from being something to which universality happens to belong it is something else. Thus one of the aforementioned definitions applies to the universal just because it has been made to be universal, for, since it is human or horse, here the content, which is humanity or horseness, will be something else outside the content of universality. *For the definition of horseness is outside the definition of universality, and universality is not contained in the definition of horseness. Horseness has a definition which does not require universality; rather universality happens to belong to it.* Consequently horseness itself is just mere horseness. It in itself is neither many nor one, existent neither in sensibles nor in the soul, nor any of these either potentially or actually in such a way that this is contained within the essence of horseness; rather [it is what it is in itself] from the fact that it is mere horseness.

Ergo universale ex hoc quod est universale est quiddam, et ex hoc quod est quiddam cui accidit universalitatis est quiddam alius; ergo de universali, ex hoc quod est universale constitutum, significatur unus praedictorum terminorum, quia, cum ipsum fuerit homo vel equus, erit hic intentio alia praeter intentionem universalitatis, quae est humanitas vel equinitas. Definitio enim equinitatis est praeter definitionem universalitatis, nec universalitas continetur in definitione equinitatis. Equinitas etenim habet definitionem quae non eget universalitate, sed est cui accidit universalitas. Unde ipsa equinitas non est aliquid nisi equinitas tantum; ipsa enim in se nec est multa nec unum, nec existens in his sensibilibus nec in anima, nec est aliquid horum potentia vel effectu, ita ut hoc contineatur intra essentiam equinitatis, sed ex hoc quod est equinitas tantum. [*PP* V1, p. 228, 24–36; *MH*, p. 149, 12–25]

Unity, singularity, as well as commonness, prove to be accidental as well:

Text 9

Unity is a distinguishing feature such that, when it is added to horseness, horseness becomes one

Unitas autem est proprietas quae, cum adiungitur equinitati, fit equinitas propter ipsam proprieta

item on account of the feature.
In similar fashion horseness has
many other distinguishing features
besides this one that happens to
belong to it. Thus from the fact
that many agree in its definition
horseness is common, but from the
fact that it is found with distinguishing features and designated
accidents it is singular. Thus in
itself horseness is just horseness.

tem unum.
Similiter etiam equinitas habet
praeter hanc multas alias
proprietates
accidentes sibi. Equinitas, ergo, ex
hoc
quod in definitione eius conveniunt
multa, est communis, sed
ex hoc quod accipitur cum proprietatibus et accidentibus signatis, est
singularis. Equinitas ergo in se est
equinitas tantum.
[*PP* VI, p. 228, 36–p. 229, 42; *MH*,
p. 149, 26–32]

The nature which may happen to be a genus or a species, Avicenna argues
in the next passage, cannot of itself be either universal or particular:

Text 10

Let us take an example of a genus:
animal is in itself something. And
it is the same whether it is sensible
or is thought in the soul. But in
itself it is neither universal nor
singular. For if it were universal in
itself in such a way that animality
from the fact that it is animality is
universal, no animal could possibly
be singular; rather every animal
would be universal. But if animal
from the fact that it is animal were
singular, it would be impossible for
there to be more than one singular,
viz. the very singular to which
animality is bound, and it would be
impossible for another singular to
be an animal.

Ponamus autem in hoc exemplum
generis dicentes quod animal est
in se quoddam; et idem est utrum
sit sensibile aut sit intellectus in
anima. In se autem huius nec est
universale nec est singulare. Si
enim in se esset universale, ita
quod animalitas ex hoc quod est
animalitas est universalis, oporteret
nullum animal singulare; sed omne
animal esset universale. Si autem
animal ex hoc quod est animal
esset singulare, impossibile esset
esse plusquam unum singulare,
scilicet ipsum singulare cui debetur
animalitas, et esset impossibile
aliud singulare esse animal. [*L* 12ra
53–61]

If animal were in itself universal, then 'universal' would appear in its definition and consequently be predicated of every animal. We then reach the absurd conclusion that every animal is a universal. Here Avicenna's reasoning is clear and unchallengeable. But when we try to apply the same line of argument to being a singular, we find, contrary to what Avicenna says, that no absurd conclusion need be drawn. Suppose 'singular' does appear in the definition of animal. All that follows is that every animal is a singular or particular, which is hardly paradoxical. Clearly what Avicenna intends is that if animal is of itself particular it is some particular and thus in being animal each animal will be some *one and the same* particular, and thus the particular that animal is will be the sole particular animal there is. But this doesn't seem to follow from just including 'singular' in the definition of animal.

There are a couple passages which shed some light on this problem. In these places Avicenna draws a distinction between the predicates 'rational animal' and 'individual rational animal', claiming that the former has a somewhat larger range of application. Here is a passage from his *Logica*:

Text 11

Further the difference which there is between human which is a species and individual human, which latter is common not just in name but also by being predicated of many, is this: we say that the idea of human, which is a species, is that it is rational animal. And what we say of the individual human is that that nature taken together with an accident which happens to belong to it is joined to some designated matter. It is just as though we said "a certain human" that is, "some rational animal". Thus rational animal is more common that that, for sometimes it

Differentia autem quae est inter hominem qui est species et individuum hominis, quod est commune non tantum nomine sed etiam praedicatione de multis, hoc est: Dicimus enim quod intellectus de homine, qui est species, est quod sit animal rationale. Quod autem dicimus de homine individuo est quod haec natura accepta cum accidente quod accidit ei coniuncta est alicui materiae designatae. Et hoc est sicut cum dicimus homo quidam scilicet aliquod rationale animal. Ergo animal rationale est communius quam hoc, aliquando

is the species, sometimes the individual, that is, this one named item. *For the species is rational animal just as the individual rational animal is rational animal.*

enim est species aliquando individuum scilicet hoc unum nominatum. Species enim est animal rationale sicut animal rationale individuum est animal rationale. [*L* 12vb 14–23

In the *Philosophia Prima* he assures us that animal is animal prior to being any particular animal:

Text 12

For the fact that animal itself in an individual is some animal does not prevent its being animal from the fact that it is animal. But this is not the case with the reservation that it be animal from the fact that it is in that [individual]. For when this individual is some animal, then some animal has being. Thus animal which is part of some animal has a being like whiteness has, which, although it is inseparable from matter, still in itself this has being-whiteness, just as in matter it is, considered in itself, something else and has a reality of being on its own, although its own being in reality happens to be joined to something else in existing.

Hoc enim quod ipsum animal in individuo est aliquod animal non prohibit ipsum esse animal ex hoc quod est animal, sed non hac condicione ut sit animal ex hoc quod est in illo: cum enim hoc individuum fuerit aliquod animal, tunc aliquod animal habet esse. Ergo animal quod est pars alicuius animalis habet esse, sicut albedo, quae, quamvis sit inseparabilis a materia, in se tamen haec habet esse albedo, sic in materia alius est considerata in se et habet veritatem essendi per se, quamvis veritati sui esse accidat adiungi alii in esse.
[*PP* V1, p. 234, 50–57; *MH*, p. 153, 29–p. 154, 3]

Once we view, as is suggested here, the *definiendum* of a definition as something which is a member of the extension of the *definiens*, it is not difficult to see how that *definiendum* would end up being a particular were 'particular' in the *definiens*. In virtue of such a definition 'particular' would apply not just to the items that fall under the *definiendum*, but to the *definiendum* itself. If we define human as particular rational animal, it is not just the concrete individual humans that will be asserted to be particularized rational animals but the species human itself as well. In other words, that species will be *a* rational animal; then all the absurdities of Aristotle's "third man" argument ensue. Hence Avicenna draws the conclusion that 'particular' cannot be part of the *definiens* of a species or genus.

To sum up, Avicenna allows that the species or genus being defined is an item in the extension of its own definition in addition to the individuals that fall under that species or genus, but he thinks that this leads to paradox of the "third man" sort only if we mistakenly think of 'particular' as also included in the *definiens*.

Avicenna's view here sounds very odd to us, but if we take types seriously I think sense can be made of it. What Avicenna calls a species is a type which has all the characteristics definitive of itself. If we take the type of flag called the Union Jack, we can say that it has three crosses superimposed on a blue field, but it is not a token of itself. It has all the properties required to produce a Union Jack in some matter (cloth, paint, paper, or whatever) but it is not a token of the Union Jack since it is not enmattered. We are led to say this if we treat types as items which have many of the properties also exhibited by their tokens, namely just those properties which are definitive of the type. (On the other hand, if you choose to take talk of types as just a shorthand way of talking generally about tokens, then, or course, you will not have to adopt Avicenna's approach, for then you will not treat the type as really an entity at all.)

I suggest, then, that we allow Avicenna this move and see where it leads. On his approach the species human will have all the characteristics which have to be enmattered to give us a particular human. It is thus human, just not *a* human. English grammar makes this very difficult to even say; Greek and Latin grammar in not requiring indefinite articles as frequently as English makes it easier. But in any language it is a conception that requires some getting used to.

The Three "Relationships" of Essence

We have seen that Avicenna adheres to Alexander's thesis that universality is accidental to whatever it belongs to, and earlier we noted that Avicenna also agrees with Alexander that universality follows on the universal's being an object of abstract thought. This leads to a conceptualist view of logic. The essences of things, Avicenna says, have three relationships in which they can be viewed:

Text 13

The essences of things either are in the things themselves or are in the intellect. Thus they have three relationships: One relationship of an essence exists inasmuch as the essence is not related to some third existence nor to what follows on it in virtue of its being such.[9] Another is in virtue of its being in these singulars. And another is in virtue of its being in the intellect. And then there follow on it accidents which are distinctive of this sort of being. For example, supposition, predication, universality and particularity in predicating, essentiality and accidentality in predicating, and others which you will come to know later. But in the items which are outside there is no essentiality or accidentality at all; neither is there some complex or non-complex item, neither proposition nor argument, nor anything else like these.

Essentiae vero rerum aut sunt in ipsis rebus aut sunt in intellectu. Unde habent tres respectus: unus respectus essentiae est secundum quod ipsa est non relata ad aliquod tertium esse, nec ad id quod sequitur eam secundum quod ipsa est sic. Alius respectus est secundum quod est in his singularibus. Et alius secundum quod est in intellectu. Et tunc sequitur eam accidentia quae sunt propria ipsius sui esse, sicut est supposition et praedicatio et universalitas et particularitas in praedicando, et essentialitas et accidentalitas in praedicando et cetera eorum quae postea scies. In eis autem quae sunt extra non est essentialitas nec accidentalitas omnino; nec est aliquod complexum nec incomplexum, nec propositio nec argumentatio nec cetera huiusmodi. [*L* 2rb 29–42]

It is in virtue of its relationship as an object of the intellect that the essence can become a subject for these accidents which give rise to the study of logic. But although the logical realm is thus ontologically dependent on the intellect, logic is not itself the study of the intellect. This comes out clearly when Avicenna says that the logician deals with non-complex contents which he recognizes are universal, but how this universality arises is not really part of his subject:

Text 14

Inasmuch as you are a logician you do not care how this relation exists, whether the idea from the fact that it is one (in which many agree) has existence in the very things which agree in it, or on its own a separate, external existence, over and above the existence it has in one intellect, or how it exists in your intellect. The consideration of these matters belongs to another doctrine or another two doctrines.

Non cures autem secundum hoc quod es logicus qualiter sit haec comparatio, et an intellectus ex hoc quod est unus (in quo multa convenient) habeat esse in ipsis rebus quae ipso convenient vel esse separatum extra per se praeter esse quod habet in uno intellectu, an qualiter habet in tuo intellectu. Consideratio autem horum alterius doctrinae est, aut doctrinarum duarum.
[L 3vb 10–17]

Further on in his *Logica* Avicenna goes so far as to draw a distinction between what he calls the "logical genus" and the "natural genus":

Text 15

Generality is called a logical genus, which means what is predicated of many items of different species in answer to the question 'What?' It does not express or designate something because it is animal or something else. Just as a white [thing] is in itself something thought, but that it is a human or a stone is outside its idea but is

Et generalitas vocatur genus logicum, de qua intelligitur quod praedicetur de multis differentibus specie ad interrogationem factam per quid; et non exprimit vel designat aliquid quod sit animal vel aliud aliquid. Sicut album quod in se est aliquid intellectum. Sed quod sit homo aut lapis esset praeter id

consequent on that, and is thought to be a single item, so also the logical genus.

But animal is a natural genus in virtue of its being animal, which is suited to having the relation of generality added to what is meant by it. For when the object of thought is in the soul, it becomes suited to having generality understood of it. Neither what is meant by Socrates nor what is meant by human are suited for this.

quod intelligitur de illo, sed consequitur ad illud, et putatur esse unum, et genus logicum est hoc.

Naturale genus est animal secundum quod est animal, quod est aptum ad hoc: ut ei quod intelligitur de illo ponatur comparatio generalitas. Cum enim iam intellectum est in anima fit apturm ut intelligatur ei generalitas; cui non est aptum id quod intelligitur de Socrate nec quod intelligitur de homine. [L 12rb 15–26]

Avicenna's point here, I believe, is that what makes something a "logical genus" is just its having "generality", that is, the property of being predicable of many differing in genus and answering the question 'What?'. The essence of animal is not a logical genus because it is animal (in the way mentioned earlier) or indeed because it has any of the features mentioned in its definition. But it is a "natural genus" in virtue of that. The natural genus has logical generality *accidentally*, that is, that character is not built into its definition but only accrues to it when it is thought of in the mind. Nevertheless, the definition is such that it is open to this generality, that is, being predicated of many things differing in species, and that is all that is needed to make animal, or whatever, a "natural genus". The distinction is elaborated further in the following text which follows not far after the preceding one:

Text 16

But if some one of the species is a genus, it has this not from its generality which is above it, but from those items which are under it. *But the natural genus attributes to that which is under it its name and definition from its own naturalness, that is, from the fact, for example, that animal is animal,*

Si autem aliquae specierum sit genus, hoc non habet ex parte suae generalitatis quae est supra eam, sed ex parte eorum quae sunt sub ea. Genus autem naturale attribuit ei quod est sub se nomen suum et diffinitionem ex parte suae naturalitatis, scilicet ex hoc verbi gratia quod animal est animal, non

and not from the fact that it is a
natural genus, that is, something
which once it has been understood
tends to become a genus from the
fact that it is the way it is. For it is
impossible that the latter [i.e., the
genus] not have what is beneath
the former [i.e., the species].
And generally when it is said that
the natural genus gives to that
which is under it its name and
definition, this is not really true
except by accident. For it does not
give this from the fact that it is a
natural genus, just as also it did not
give this to it because it is a logical
genus, since it gave it only a nature
which is suited to being a natural
genus. This nature by itself is not a
natural genus just as it is not a
logical genus.
But if natural genus means only
the primary nature on its own
which is suited to generality, and
natural genus is not understood as
we understand it, then it is correct
to say that a natural genus attributes its name and definition to
that which is under it. And then
animal is really a natural genus
only because it is mere animal.

ex hoc quod est genus naturale,
scilicet aliquod quod cum intellectum fuerit appetent
fieri genus ex hoc quod est ita;
impossibile enim est ut hoc
non habeat id quod est infra illud.
Et omnino cum dicitur quod genus
naturale dat ei quod est sub se
nomen suum et
diffinitionem, hoc non est satis
verum, nisi accidentaliter. Non
enim dat ex hoc quod est
genus naturale, sicut etiam non
dedit ei hoc quod est genus
logicum, quia non dedit nisi
naturam quae est apta esse genus
naturale; haec autem natura per
seipsam non est genus naturale
sicut[10] non est genus logicum.

Si autem non vult intelligi genus
naturale nisi natura prima per se
quae est apta generalitati, et non
intelligitur genus naturale quod
nos intelligimus, tunc congruum
est dicere quod genus naturale ei
quod est sub se attribuit suum
nomen et diffinitionem; et tunc
animal non est genus naturale
vere nisi quia est animal tantum.
[L 12rb 54-va 5]

From the above we can see that Avicenna really distinguishes three items
here. There is the nature (aka essence) itself of animal, and this is responsible
for the various species and individuals under it being animals, and it does
this by just what it itself is on its own, namely animal. There is then the
natural genus, which the nature is just by its suitability for being thought

and then used by thought as a predicate. This suitability is not part of the definition of the nature, however, even though it is consequent upon it. Finally, there is the logical genus which is the nature when it is thought and ready to be used as a predicate. Avicenna concludes by noting that the term 'natural genus' may just mean the nature itself, although that is not the way he uses it. In the *Prima Philosophia*, he opens up this possibility again, as the following passage shows:

Text 17

Therefore, from the fact that it is a nature it is something; and from the fact that it is apt to be understood as a universal form it is something; and from the fact that it is actually understood this way it is something; and also from the fact that it is true of it that if it were joined not to this matter and these accidents but to that matter and those accidents it would be this other individual, it is something. But this nature has existence in these sensibles in virtue of the first relationship, and besides this it does not have universal being either in virtue of the second relationship or even of the fourth in designated things. But if we mean by the content of universality this [last] relationship, then this nature with universality will exist in designated things. But here we are dealing with the universality which exists only in the soul.

Ergo ex hoc quod est natura est quiddam;
Et ex hoc quod ipsa est apta intelligi forma universalis et quiddam; et
ex hoc etiam quod intelligitur sic in actu est quiddam; et etiam ex hoc quod verum est de illa quod, si coniungeretur non huic materiae nec istis accidentibus, sed illi materiae et illis accidentibus, esset illud aliud individuum, est quiddam. Sed haec natura habet esse in his sensibilibus secundum primum respectum, et praeter hoc non habet esse universale
nec ex respectu secundo
nec etiam ex quarto in signatis.
Si autem accipitur hic respectus ex intentione universalitatis, tunc haec natura
cum universalitate erit in signatis;
universalitas autem de qua hic agimus
non est nisi in anima. [*PP* V2, p. 244, 69–78; *MH*, p. 161, 14–26]

What Avicenna refers to here as the "second relationship" is, as I read him, what makes a nature a "natural genus"; the "third relationship" makes it a logical genus. The "fourth relationship" is just what is meant by calling it a nature, and of course, if this is what one wants to mean by 'universal', then one can speak of a universal in "designated things", that is, the things one can point to in the world.

It is clear from the above that Avicenna does not want to be encumbered with idealist consequences of his usual claim that universality is an accident of natures contingent on their being abstractly thought. Particulars, "designated things", will have the natures they have just because the nature instantiated in them is what it is, not because that nature is thought. It is in virtue of its "first relationship", that is, its just being what it is, having the definition it has, that the nature makes a particular in which it is enmattered have the features given in that definition and thus be a token of some type. Here is Avicenna's answer to the problem we noted afflicted Alexander's analysis. The nature is ontologically prior to the particulars through this "first relationship", and it has this "relationship" *whether it exists or not*. (Horseness is horseness whether it exists in matter or not, and whether it exists in the mind or not, and that is all that is needed for it to ground the being of token horses once it does exist in matter. Existence in the mind is irrelevant to that, so something being a token horse is not in any way mind dependent.) In other words, an essence or nature need not exist either in external reality or in a mind in order to have that which enables it to give a definitive character to whatever bit of the material world it might come to inhabit. This is Avicenna's crucial contribution to the philosophical task of preserving the Platonic idea that the world should be understood as furnished with tokens of types without either giving into idealism or accepting the independent existence of types as Platonic Forms. The point is abundantly clear in the following text from the *Prima Philosophia*:

Text 18

Animal can be considered on its own even though it exists with something other than itself, for its essence is with something other than itself. Therefore its essence	Poterit autem animal per se considerari, quamvis sit cum alio a se; essentia enim eius est cum alio a se;

belongs to it on its own. Its existing with something other than itself is something which happens to it or something which goes along with its nature, for example this animality and humanity. *Therefore, this consideration precedes in being both the animal which is individual on account of its accidents and the universal which is in these sensible items and is intelligible, just as the simple precedes the composite and as the part the whole.* For from this being it is neither a genus nor a species nor an individual, nor one nor many; rather from this being it is merely animal, and merely human. But doubtless being one or many goes along with this, since it is impossible for something to exist but not be one or the other of these, even though they go along with it extrinsically.

ergo essentia est ipsi per se; ipsum vero esse cum alio a se est quiddam quod accidit ei vel aliquod quod comitatur naturam suam, sicut haec animalitas et humanitas; igitur haec consideratio praecedit in esse et animal quod est individuum propter accidentia sua et universale quod est in his sensibilibus et intelligibile, sicut simplex praecedit compositum et sicut pars totum: ex hoc enim esse nec est genus nec species nec individuum nec unum nec multa, sed ex hoc esse est tantum animal et tantum homo. Sed comitatur illud sine dubio esse unum vel multa, cum impossibile sit aliquid esse et non esse alterum istorum, quamvis sit comitans ipsum extrinsecus; ... [*PP* V1, p. 233, 36–p. 234, 46; *MH*, p. 153, 11–24]

In other words, the essence or nature as just being what it is, that is, defined the way it is, is ontologically prior ("precedes in being") to both the existence of the tokens (individuals having the nature in question) and the existence of the type (the universal), even though there is no third sort of existence (*pace* Plato) which that nature could have.

Monism Again a Threat

The question now arises whether Avicenna with all these admissions about how the nature is in particulars has not accepted the very sort of realism which will lead to species monism, that is, that all tokens of the same type are the same thing, and whether all his claims about universality being mind dependent are not just so many red herrings meant to divert our attention from this embarrassing consequence. I do think he does escape this objection, but sorting the matter out requires patient examination of still more texts. We can begin with Avicenna's own denial that there is any *one* thing which *many* things are:

Text 19

Thus common things in a way have existence outside and in a way not. But that a thing one and the same in number is predicated of many, that is, predicated of this individual in such a way that this individual is it and likewise with this [other] individual, obviously is impossible.	Ergo res communes aliquo modo habent esse extrinsecus et aliquo modo non; quod autem una et eadem res numero sit praedicta de multis, scilicet praedicata de hoc individuo ita ut hoc individuum sit ipsa et de hoc individuo similiter, impossibile esse manifestum est. [*PP* V1, p. 238, 51–54; *MH*, p. 157, 11–16]

The emphasis here, I think, should fall on the phrase 'one and the same in number', for the paradox that Avicenna wants to avoid is species monism, that is, that there is some *one* thing that all the members of a species are. There is no paradox if the thing they all are is not one and the same in number but is a multiple being.[11] Avicenna's willingness to speak of an essence as multiple can be well documented:[12]

Text 20

'Common' here is understood in two ways: In one way the common efficient cause is he who makes the first work, to which the other works are ordered. For example, he who attributes to prime matter the first corporeal form. . . .	Commune autem hic intelligitur duobus modis: uno enim modo efficiens communis est ille qui facit primum opus, ex quo cetera opera habent ordinem. Sicut ille qui attribuit primae materiae primam formam corporalem, ...

Another sense of 'common' shares in the meaning of 'universal' for example a common efficient cause is that which is predicated of all particular makers of particular things, and the universal end is that which is predicated of all particular ends of particular things. The difference between these two senses lies in this: that what is common in the first sense is in its existence as an essence one in number, the intellect indicates that it exists, and it is not compatible with it to be said of many. But what is common in the second sense does not have one essence in existence; rather it is an understood thing embracing many essences that agree in idea in respect of being efficient or final causes. Thus what is common in this sense will be said of many.

Alius autem modus est communis qui participatur ad modum universalis,
sicut efficiens commune est id quod praedicatur de omnibus factoribus particularibus
rerum particularium, et finis universalis est ille qui praedicatur de omnibus particularibus finibus rerum particularium.
Et differentia quae est inter duos modos haec est, scilicet quod commune secundum primum intellectum est in esse essentiale una numero, et innuit intellectus quod ipsa est, et non competit ei ut dicatur de pluribus. Commune autem secundo modo non habet in esse essentiam unam;
immo est res intellecta complectens essentias multas convenientes in intellectu secundum quod sunt efficientes aut finales; ergo hoc commune dicetur de multis. [S 14va 9–30]

We find in the above that Avicenna claims that in the sense of 'common' where it just means universal, what it denotes is not a single essence in extramental reality, but a single thing in the mind which "embraces many essences". In another passage, speaking of forms Avicenna says:

Text 21

... when they are in multiplicity they are not one in any way. For in sensible things on the outside there is nothing common except merely separateness and dispersion.

... et cum sunt in multiplicitate non sunt unum ullo modo. In sensibilibus enim forinsecus non est aliquid commune nisi tantum discretio et dispersio. [L 12va 30–32]

Finally, in talking about the consideration of animal *per se*, that is, by itself, Avicenna notes that considered in this way animal is neither one nor many, although it must be one or many if it is to exist at all. This is evident from text 18 where he says: "For from this being [i.e., the nature considered in itself] it is neither a genus nor a species nor an individual, nor one nor many . . ."

It is clear from these passages and others that the form or essence once it happens to be in concrete individuals ("these sensible items"), that is, inasmuch as many individuals are it apart from any consideration of the essence by the mind, is a multiple being rather than a single thing. It has in this case no more unity than does the referent of 'humans' in "Humans are rational."

On the other hand, once the essence becomes an abstract object of thought, then there is a single unitary item that can be called universal in the logical sense. This comes out quite clearly in the passage from *Prima Philosophia* quoted as text 3. But is this abstract intellectual content a universal in the sense that many are it, that is, the sense which forced us to treat the essence outside the mind as something multiple? Avicenna wavers on this crucial point. Consider the following passage from *L*:

Text 22

Next, a content of a non-complex term either will be such as does not from the fact that the object of thought is thought keep many from agreeing with it equally, so that *each of them is said to be it equally*. For example, this which we call human has a content in the soul which with a single sense goes along with Socrates, Plato, and the others, each of which is human . . .	Deinde intentio incomplexi aut talis erit quod non prohibetur intellectum ex hoc quod intelligitur multa convenire in eo equaliter, ut unumquodque eorum dicatur ipsum esse equaliter; sicut hoc quod dicimus homo habet intentionem in anima quae comitatur Socratem et Platonem et reliquos uno modo, quorum unusquisque est homo . . . [*L* 3va 42–49]

But this passage is followed a few lines later by the following:

Text 23

... [the universal] is the content in which that which is thought in the soul is not kept from having *a relation of similarity to many.* [my emphasis]

... est intention de qua id quod intelligitur in anima non prohi-betur habere comparationem similitudinis ad multa. [*L* 3vb 8–10]

Most often Avicenna just speaks of many agreeing (*convenire*) with the content, a rather vague and ambiguous phrase. (See, for example, text 3.)

In all this there seems to be a wavering between saying the abstract idea is what many equally are and saying it is what many are equally like. That Avicenna is committed to taking the former sort of talk seriously is evidenced by his criticism of Platonism, that is, the view which considers that the es-sence has an existence on its own, neither in singulars nor in the mind. This view, Avicenna says, simply undercuts the purpose we had for talking about essences in the first place:

Text 24

But if animal were separate of itself, as those[13] thought, then it would not be the animal which we investigate and of which we speak. For we investigate the animal which is predicated of many, *each of which is it.* But something separate is not predicated of them since none of them is it. Thus it does not do the job we intended it to do.

Si autem esset hic animal separa-tum per se, quemadmodum putaverunt illi, tunc non esset hoc animal quod inquirimus et de quo loquimur. Nos enim inquirimus animal quod praedicetur de multis quorum unumquodque sit ipsum. Separatum vero non praedicatur de his, quoniam nullum eorum est ipsum: unde non est opus ad id ad quod intendimus. [*PP* V1, p. 237, 16–21; *MH*, p. 156, 3–8]

At the very beginning we treated an essence as something which each of the sensible, "designated"[14] things tokening that essence *is.* But if we say the essences are separate, we implicitly deny that many sensibles could be them. However, would not this same line of objection undercut Avicenna's own positing of universals in the mind, if he were to claim that many could be them? After all, if mere similarity suffices to save Avicenna's position, it ought to suffice to save the Platonist line too. It appears, then, that Avicenna must affirm after all that there is a single thing that many are. How can this be consonant with the denial of monism?

Avicenna's Solution

The answer, if it is to be found at all, lies, I think, in the feature of essences which Avicenna most emphasizes in his discussion in *Prima Philosophia*, their *per se* indeterminateness. The essence on its own is neither proper (i.e., particularized) nor common; both of these attributes lie outside what the essence is of itself. I want to look carefully at an extended discussion where Avicenna puts this thesis to work to save his whole view from absurdity. The passage begins with an objection which attempts to show that animal cannot exist in individuals; its existence must be separate from them:

Text 25

Someone could say that animal from the fact that it is animal does not have existence in individuals, because what is in individuals is some animal, not animal from the fact that it is animal. But animal from the fact that it is animal has existence; therefore it has existence outside individuals. For if animal from the fact that it is animal has being in this individual, then necessarily either it is peculiar to it or not peculiar to it. And if it is peculiar, then animal from the fact that it is animal is not existent in it nor is it that very thing; rather some animal is. And if it is not peculiar to it, then something one and the same in number has being in a multiplicity, which is impossible.

Potest autem aliquis dicere quod animal ex hoc quod est animal non habet
esse in individuis, quia quod est in individuis est aliquod animal, non animal ex hoc quod est animal; sed animal
ex hoc quod est animal habet esse; ergo habet esse extra individua. Nam si
animal ex hoc quod est animal habet esse in hoc individuo, tunc necesse est ut aut sit proprium eius, aut non proprium. Si autem est proprium, tunc animal ex hoc quod est animal non est existens in eo nec est ipsum, sed
est aliquod animal. Si vero non est proprium, tunc aliquid unum et idem numero habet esse in

multitudine; quod est impossibile.
[*PP* V1, p. 234, 58–p. 235, 66; *MH*,
p. 154, 4–13]

The line of argument here is this: if animal *per se*, that is, "animal from the fact that it is animal", existed in an individual, either it would be peculiar to that individual, and then we should say not that animal exists in particulars but "some animal", viz. the one it is peculiar to does, or it is not peculiar, and then we have the absurdity that one thing exists in many, that is, monism.

This discussion hinges on the distinction we noted earlier between the predicates 'rational animal' and 'some rational animal' or 'a rational animal'. Avicenna insists that it is not enough to have only the latter predicate, but that is all we would have if the essence of each particular human were *of itself* peculiar to that particular human. Likewise for 'animal' and 'some animal'. And the reason I feel he would give for demanding that we have 'animal' as well as 'some animal' is that for a thing to be some animal requires as a prior condition that the animal it is *is animal*, that is, has animality. Otherwise it could not be *some animal*.

In the next text Avicenna warns against thinking that because any particular animal is *some* animal there is no place in particulars for animal *per se*.

Text 26

We have introduced this question, although it is trifling, because it has led into error many who seemed to be wise. We say, then, that in this question error arose in several ways. One was the opinion that since that which is animal is some animal, the nature of animality, considered in itself and not in respect of something else, does not have existence along with that. The exposition of this error is already obvious from what we said before.

Hanc autem quaestionem, quamvis sit
frivola, tamen induximus idem quod multos qui videbantur sapientes duxit in errorem.
Dicemus ergo quod in hac quaestione venit error multis modis.
Unus fuit opinio quod id quod est animal, cum fuerit aliquod animal, tunc natura animalitatis, considerata in se non secundum aliud, non habet esse cum illo; declaratio autem erroris iam patuit ex praedictis. [*PP* V1, p. 235, 67–72; *MH*, p. 154, 14–21]

The error he claims to have discussed earlier is simply that of thinking that because animal is not *per se* any singular (being some singular is not part of its definition) animal cannot be a singular at all. Avicenna has emphasized that all the negation implies is that being some singular will be an accident of the nature animal, if it belongs to it at all. The next text makes clear that neither being some singular nor being common to many singulars is something that belongs to a nature *per se*.

Text 27

Another was the opinion that animal from the fact that it is animal ought to be peculiar or not-peculiar in virtue of denial.[15] But this is not the case. For animal considered from the fact that it is animal and according to its animality is neither peculiar nor not-peculiar, that is, common. For both are denied of it, since from its animality it is merely animal. The content of animal from the fact that it is animal is outside the content of peculiar and common, and they do not enter into its quiddity. Therefore, since this is so, animal from the fact that it is animal is neither peculiar nor common in virtue of its animality; rather it is animal, not something other than itself on account of its circumstances, but being peculiar or common are consequent on it.

Alius fuit opinio de hoc quod animal ex hoc quod est animal debet esse proprium vel improprium secundum remotionem. Sed non est ita. Animal enim consideratum ex hoc quod est animal et secundum eius animalitatem nec est proprium nec improprium quod est commune; utrumque enim removetur ab eo, nam ipsum, ex animalitate sua, tantum est animal. Intentio vero animalis, ex hoc quod est animal, est praeter intentionem proprii et communis nec sunt intrantia in suam quidditatem. Cum igitur hoc ita sit, tunc animal ex hoc quod est animal nec est proprium nec commune ex sua animalitate, sed est animal, non aliud aliquid a se de dispositionibus, sed consequitur ipsum esse proprium vel commune. [*PP* V1, p. 235, 72–82; *MH*, p. 154, 21–32]

This is, of course, the key to solving the original objection. It had the form of a dilemma: either the nature *per se* was peculiar or it was common. In either case the result was unpalatable. Avicenna passes between the horns, claiming that the nature *per se* is neither peculiar nor common, that is, neither singular nor universal. But are not 'peculiar' and 'common' contradictory opposites, so that anything must be one or the other? Avicenna nicely replies to this objection:

Text 28

When it is said that it is impossible that it not be either peculiar or common, if this means that from its own animality it necessarily must be some one of these two, it is false, for neither of these holds in virtue of its animality. But if it means that it is impossible that it not be one or the other of these in the things which exist, because it is not possible that neither of those follow on it, it is true, since necessarily it follows that animal is either peculiar or common. Whichever of these happens to it animality will not be destroyed, since it is neither peculiar nor common; rather it later becomes peculiar or common on account of what happens to it in virtue of its circumstances.

Hoc autem quod dicit impossibile esse quin sit aut proprium aut commune, si intelligit ipsum ex sua animalitate necessario debere esse aliquid illorum duorum, falsum: nam nihil eorum est ex sua animalitate. Si vero intelligit impossibile esse quin sit aliquod eorum in eis quae sunt, quia non potest esse quin sequatur ipsum esse aliquid eorum, verax est, eo quod necessario sequitur animal esse proprium vel commune. Quodcumque autem horum acciderit, non destruetur animalitas, quae est ex hoc quod nec est proprium nec commune, sed fit postea proprium vel commune per id quod accidit ei de dispositionibus. [*PP* V1, p. 235, 82–p. 236, 91; *MH*, p. 155, 1–10]

In other words, the thing in question, for example, animal, must indeed be either peculiar or common if it exists at all, but it need not be either of these from the mere fact that it is animal. Just as although a person must be either young or mature, we can still say that they are neither young nor mature simply by being themselves, so also with the nature and its being peculiar and being common. But when we specify what it is that is predicated of many we specify only the nature *per se*, not the nature with any of its accidents; and consequently the many subjects are not made to be anything other than animal by having animal predicated of them.

At this point Avicenna tries to head off a possible misunderstanding. When he says that animal is not *per se* either peculiar or common, he is not to be understood as meaning that animal *per se* is neither peculiar nor common, that is, that part of what it is to be animal is to be neither peculiar nor common:

Text 29

But here there is something which must be understood: Although it is true to say that of animal, from the fact that it is animal, it is not the case that either peculiarity or commonness must be predicated, it is not true to say that of animal, from the fact that it is animal, peculiarity or commonness must not be predicated. For if animality made it be the case that peculiarity or commonness must not be predicated of it, then animal would be neither peculiar nor common.

Hic est autem quiddam quod debet intelligi, scilicet quia verum est dicere quod de animali, ex hoc quod est animal, non debet praedicari proprietas nec communitas,
nec est verum dicere quod de animali, ex hoc quod est animal, debet non praedicari proprietas vel communitas; scilicet nam si animalitas faceret debere non praedicari de eo proprietatem vel communitatem, tunc nec esset animal proprium nec esset animal commune.
[*PP* V1, p. 236, 92–98; *MH*, p. 155, 11–18]

We saw earlier that being animal implies neither being some particular animal nor being common to all animals, and now we see that it does not imply not being some particular animal or not being common to all animals. If it implied not being some particular animal there could be no particular animals, since whatever was animal could not be *an* animal. If it implied not being common, then everything that is animal would be *an* animal, a consequence we today find acceptable but Avicenna did not, as was noted earlier in this essay.

In the next and final text from this extended passage Avicenna expands these remarks and makes at the end a revealing distinction between animal as it exists in sensible things and animal as it exists in the intellect.

Text 30

On account of this you should realize that there is a great difference between these, and because of this it also makes a difference whether we say: "Animal, from the fact that it is animal on its own, [is] without the condition of [being] one or the other," or whether we say "Animal, from the fact that it is animal on its own, [is] with the condition of not [being] one or the other."[16] For if we allowed that animal, from the fact that it is animal on its own, were with the condition of not having being in those sensibles, then what we would not be allowing is that the Platonic Idea is in those sensibles. For the being of animal with the condition of not [being] one or the other thing is only in the intellect, while animal on its own, without the condition of [being] one or the other thing, has being in sensibles. It in itself in its own reality is without the condition of [being] one or the other thing, although it is with a thousand conditions which are added to it from outside.

Et secundum hoc debes intelligere magnam esse distantiam inter illa, et ob hoc etiam interest an dicatur quod animal, ex hoc quod est animal per se, sine condicione alterius, et an dicatur quod animal, ex hoc quod est animal per se, cum condicione non rei alterius.
Si enim concederetur quod animal, ex hoc quod est animal per se, esset cum condicione quod non haberet esse in sensibilibus istis, non tunc[17] concederetur quod platonitas[18] esset in sensibilibus istis; esse enim animalis cum condicione non rei alterius in intellectu tantum est; animal vero per se non cum condicione rei alterius habet esse in sensibilibus. Ipsum vero in se in veritate sua est sine condicione alterius rei, quamvis sit cum mille condicionibus quae adiungitur ei extrinsecus.
[*PP* V1, p. 236, 98–p. 237, 8; *MH*, p. 155, 19–30]

The distinction Avicenna makes here between being without a certain condition and being with the condition of not having some feature, is just a generalization on what he said about not being peculiar and not being common in the preceding text. 'Animal *per se* is without a certain condition' means the same as 'Animal is not *per se* with a certain condition' that is, being animal does not involve having that condition. 'Animal *per se* is with the condition of not having a given feature' means 'Animal *per se* lacks a given feature', that is, being animal does involve not having that feature. Now when it comes to the feature of having being in sensibles animal does not *per se* have that feature, but it is also not true that it *per se* lacks that feature. Consequently it can be found in sensibles. But animal as an object of the intellect by being such an abstract object positively resists being identified with any sensible. It of itself lacks the feature of being in sensibles. In this it is like a Platonic Idea, but, of course, Avicenna diverges from Plato in allowing such "Ideas" only an existence in the mind.

But how can this be compatible with the claim that the universal is in the intellect and is what many are said to *be*? The answer is not too difficult to see. That which the intellect abstracts and grasps, the nature of animality, for example, is indeed something that many can be; but in abstracting it the intellect creates an object which is that nature but with the feature of being a single, unitary entity that many could not possibly be. Avicenna's wavering between treating the universal as something many are and something many are like should, I am suggesting, be treated as his wavering between thinking of the universal as the nature the intellect abstractly grasps and the representation of that nature the intellect creates and by which it does grasp the nature. The two are intimately related, of course; the latter is the former but with certain features the mind imposes, although these features are not opposed to the nature *per se*.

Solving the Union Jack Sophism

It is time to return to the sophism with which we began;

> This flag (i.e., this particular piece of cloth) is a token of a type.
> This flag is the Union Jack.
> The Union Jack is a type.
> Therefore, this flag is a type.
> Tokens of types are not themselves types.
> Therefore, this flag is not a token of a type.

Avicenna's solution, I think, is really quite simple. He would deny the first inference, the one made at the fourth step. What this flag is is the Union

Jack nature, but that is something which is not *of itself* numerically one thing. It follows that it can have opposing accidents simultaneously and what is it need not have all the accidents it in fact has. The brightly colored rag in front of me is that nature and has some of the accidents that nature happens to have, namely those that distinguish this rag from other rags that are also the Union Jack. The reason the Union Jack nature is a type is that the mind conceives it as a single thing which is indeterminate in the sense that it lacks any features which would distinguish one particular token Union Jack from another. This indeterminacy is accidental to that nature, not opposed to it, and thus the Union Jack nature can have that indeterminacy. But no token can have that. Hence it is incorrect to say that the rag which is the Union Jack is that type, or any other type for that matter.

We do often say things like: "This is a type of flag" while pointing to a particular rag. We should read this in the same way as we read: "This wall is a certain color". What we mean is, roughly speaking, that there is a certain color and if we substituted its name in this sentence for the words 'a certain color' we would end up with a true sentence, for example, 'This wall is blue', but not one which would imply that the wall was a color, that is, a quality rather than a substance. Substitute in for 'a type of flag' the words 'the Union Jack' and you end up with a true sentence, but not one which implies that the rag is a type rather than a token. The scholastics would say that we have to understand 'a type of flag' in the sentence 'This rag is a type of flag' as being predicated *in quale* rather than *in quid*. It doesn't indicate what the rag is, only how it is characterized.

Returning to our sophism, note how the following argument is acceptable both in its inference and in its conclusion:

> This flag is the Union Jack.
> The Union Jack is *something which is* a type.
> Therefore, this flag is *something which is* a type.

But from that conclusion it does not follow that this flag is itself a type. It need not have all the accidents possessed by what it is since what it is is not *of itself* numerically one thing. Being a type is one of those accidents that no token of a type has. But once we allow a token to be a certain nature, where the nature is not *of itself* one single thing, then the token can lack accidents the nature has, even though it still *is* that nature.

6

Universal Thinking as Process: The Metaphysics of Change and Identity in John Buridan's *Intellectio* Theory

JACK ZUPKO

In his magisterial *Stanford Encyclopedia of Philosophy* article on William of Ockham, Paul Vincent Spade writes that:

> Over the course of his career, Ockham changed his view of what universal concepts are. To begin with, he adopted what is known as the *fictum*-theory, a theory according to which universals have no "real" existence at all in the Aristotelian categories, but instead are purely "intentional objects" more or less in the sense of modern phenomenology; they have only a kind of "thought"-reality. Such "fictive" objects were metaphysically universal; they just weren't real. Eventually, however, Ockham came to think this intentional realm of "fictive" entities was not needed, and by the time of his *Summa of Logic* and the *Quodlibets* adopted instead a so called *intellectio*-theory, according to which a universal concept is just the act of thinking about several objects at once; metaphysically it is quite singular, and is "universal" only in the sense of being predicable of many.[1]

Ockham's theory-change was a matter of parsimony,[2] helped along, no doubt, by the criticisms of realist opponents such as Walter Chatton. But Ockham says virtually nothing about how the new theory is supposed to cover psychological phenomena explained by the old theory, apparently leaving its application an exercise for the reader. But this is far from a straightforward question. How does the *intellectio* theory work in practice, when we get down to the business of actually explaining what is happening when we think, judge, will, and remember?

Ockham's younger Parisian contemporary, John Buridan, is someone who thought a lot about this question. In this essay, I will examine two versions of Buridan's *intellectio* theory, one presented in his mature works and the other dating from the beginning of his career as an arts master.[3] I have not been able to connect the two accounts by showing that the first is an earlier stage of the second, or by finding criticism of the first that might explain why Buridan abandoned it in favor of the second. But it should suffice to show that, even though there is no evidence indicating Buridan got the idea from Ockham, Buridan thought the *intellectio* theory was substantially correct, and that it merited further development as a tool for interpreting Aristotle's psychology. In this sense, Buridan's contribution was that of a nominalist fellow-traveler, advancing the *intellectio* theory beyond Ockham by working out its implications for the science of the soul.

I begin with the second account.

Buridan's Mature Intellectio *Theory*

Buridan composed many treatises and commentaries over his thirty-year career in the arts faculty at Paris, but the writings familiar to most scholars date from the very last decade of his career. These texts represent the final versions of his lectures on the works of Aristotle's systematic philosophy required as part of the undergraduate curriculum at Paris, most notably *Physics, De Anima, Metaphysics,* and *Nicomachean Ethics.* These texts, along with Buridan's logical masterwork, the *Summulae de Dialectica,* were influential enough to have been re-edited and printed as incunabular editions at the end of the fifteenth and beginning of the sixteenth centuries. These *incunabulae* were in turn reprinted as facsimile editions by the German publisher Minerva in the 1960s, which is how most of us are acquainted with them today.

In these works, Buridan speaks about the act by which we cognize universals as if there is no philosophical problem here at all, or as if the problem does not arise if one approaches the psychology of human cognition in the right way. He is always careful about his terminology, however, perhaps to avoid conveying the impression that universal cognition is directed toward some particular object, which is what had led Ockham to the *fictum* theory. Buridan's strategy is to use adverbial descriptions. Thus, when he lists four ways in which concepts are sometimes generated from other concepts without any kind of formal inference (something even brute animals can do in the case of "unsensed" intentions, the standard example being Avicenna's sheep "eliciting" the intention of hostility from the sight of the wolf), he says that humans are also able to do this "abstractively":

> such as when I first have a concept confusedly representing substance and accident together, e.g., when I perceive white, for I do not see the whiteness alone, but a white thing. But later, I perceive it to be moved and changed from white to black, <and> judge [the white thing] to be other than whiteness. And in that case [f. 5rb-va] the intellect naturally has the power of dividing the confusion and understanding substance abstractively from accident and accident abstractively from substance. And it can form a simple concept of both, and so as well by abstracting produce a universal concept from a singular concept, as must be seen in *De Anima* III and *Metaphysics* VII.[4]

We will follow these leads into Buridan's *De Anima* and *Metaphysics* commentaries in a moment, but for now four features should be noted about the process of abstraction presented in this passage: (1) it is a mode of understanding (hence the adverbial formulation: we cognize "abstractively"), rather than its product or object; (2) the act in question is one of "dividing" what is "confused" or separating out what is "simple" from what is complex; (3) it is based on (at least) two temporally discrete singular cognitions (e.g., perceiving the white thing and then perceiving the white thing changing color); and (4) it is noninferential, meaning that the universal concept is not something I must deduce from singular concepts; rather, it is formed, as Buridan says, "without the consequence of one proposition to another [*sine consequentia alicuius propositionis ad aliam propositionem*]" (QP I.4: 5rb).[5] It is also noteworthy that the process is referred to using three adverbs (we understand "abstractively [*abstractive*]") and an oblique-case participle (we produce a universal concept "by abstracting [*abstrahendo*]"). Buridan almost never uses the substantive noun "*abstractio*."

Buridan returns to the topic a little further on, in Question 7 of Book I of his *Physics* commentary, which asks whether universals are better known (*notiora*) to us than singulars. This is one of a trio of questions addressing what we would now call the cognitive and epistemic status of universals. The others are in the places he directed us to above: Book I, Question 5 of his *De Anima* commentary, which asks whether universals are prior or posterior to singulars,[6] and Book VII, Question 15, of his *Metaphysics* commentary, which asks whether universals exist separately (*separata*) from singulars. All three questions use similar arguments and examples to present what is basically the same theory of universal cognition. We do not know which discussion is the earliest, although if a reference elsewhere in the *De Anima* commentary to a question in the *Physics* commentary is not a later interpolation,[7] the latter must have come first. All three date from what Bernd Michael has proposed as Buridan's third and final period of philosophical activity, dating from just after the 1347 condemnation of the views of John of Mirecourt until Buridan's death in 1360 or 1361.[8] There are passages that occur practically verbatim in all three discussions, suggesting that Buridan was not above cutting and pasting materials from one series of lectures into another if he felt an earlier set of remarks was germane to what he happened to be teaching at the moment.

Buridan begins these questions with a distinction between three senses of the term "universal": universal in causation; universal in predication; and universal in being. The first sense refers to the scope of a subject's causal powers, which we order from omnipotent creator at the top to celestial bodies and down through the entire range of sublunary beings graded in terms of their power as movers. In this sense, the cause is a "universal" existing separately from its effects, which are generable and corruptible "singulars." Nevertheless, this is set aside as irrelevant to the question at hand, which concerns how universals feature in *human* cognition.[9]

The second sense is relevant to the question at hand, and becomes Buridan's standard approach to the problem of universal cognition:

> In another way, 'universal' is said according to predication or signification because it is predicable of many, indifferently signifies many, and supposits for many. In this sense its significate is opposed to the singular or discrete term, which, by a single imposition, is the significate or representative of one thing alone, e.g., Socrates or Plato. And in this way, the universal and the singular are mental, spoken, or written terms, and it is possible for the universal to exist separately from all singulars, e.g., suppose you form some common concept in your mind without forming one singular concept, even though other <minds> form many singular terms. Then that universal concept would exist in separation from all the singular concepts because it exists in you and all the singulars exist in others.[10]

In the parallel discussions in his *Physics* and *De Anima* commentaries, Buridan adds that this sort of universality is a matter of degree:

> We say that the term 'animal' is more universal than the term 'man' because it is predicated of more things and signifies more things, because every man is an animal and not vice versa. In this way, a singular significant term supposits for one thing alone and a universal term supposits for many, the specific details of which must be <seen> in logic. And the more universal a term is, the more it supposits for many.[11]

Underlying this doctrine is Aristotle's three-tiered hierarchy of spoken, written, and mental terms: "in written discourse there are universal and singular terms corresponding to spoken terms, as is held in *Perihermeneias* 1 [16a3], but the ordering of spoken and written terms is fixed by mental terms, because they are not formed except by reverting to mental terms."[12] Buridan sees that this raises the further question of whether universal terms come before singular terms in the mind (*apud mentem*), which is for him the same as the question of "whether we *conceive* things universally before we conceive them singularly [*utrum primo concipimus res universaliter quam singulariter vel econverso*]."[13] He tells us that he will not discuss this question here because it is treated elsewhere, that is, in Book III, Question 8 of his *De Anima* commentary and in Book I, Question 7 of his *Physics* commentary. But he has already made the key identification: it is not just that universals are universal terms, which moves them into the orbit of semantics, but that *concepts* are universal terms (or singular terms, depending on their semantic function). Buridan is thereby able to link the Aristotelian science of psychology to the broader research program of his *Summulae de Dialectica*, wherein dialectic is the "art of arts [*ars artium*]" and our primary means of unraveling conundrums and finding truth in the speculative sciences.[14] Indeed, the very first sentence of Book III, Question 8 of his *De Anima* commentary shows that the concept/term identification is foremost in his mind when he thinks about universal cognition: "the proposed question must be properly worded: whether the intellect understands the same thing or things universally, that is, according to a common concept, before it understands singularly, that is, according to a singular concept," to which he immediately adds: "and if in the course of the question we also sometimes use the words as first set down [e.g., where the concept of a horse or stone refers to some universal horse or stone existing outside

our minds], we nevertheless intend to use them in the sense just stipulated."[15] This is a conspicuous proviso from someone who is very careful
about his use of terms.

The third sense of the term "universal" is, like the first, set aside, but not
before Buridan remarks on it briefly because it provides an object lesson in
how *not* to understand universals. This is Plato's view (or what Buridan identifies as Plato's view) that "universal" picks out something outside the mind:

> But again, according to Plato universals are in some way said to exist
> outside the soul: that is to say, what is immediately signified by a singular
> term is a singular thing such as Socrates or Plato, this man or that; and
> what is immediately signified by a universal term is a universal thing
> outside the soul distinct from what is singular and from singular things.
> In this way, he assumed that apart from the concept in our souls, there is
> a universal man existing *per se*, which he called the 'idea' of singular
> men and their 'quiddity.' And he said that a term suppositing for that
> idea is truly and affirmatively predicable of each and every term sup-
> positing for any singular man.[16]

Plato, of course, did not write a treatise on supposition. What Buridan
has done here is translate, for the benefit of his student audience, Plato's
doctrine of universals into the language of the *logica moderna*, where it
appears as the claim that universal terms pick out or stand for universal
entities outside the soul. And Buridan is quick to tell his students what is
wrong with it: no universal term would be truly predicable of any singular
term because they would stand for different things! This, he asserts, is what
Aristotle meant when he criticized Plato for treating separate universals as
the object of scientific knowledge: "in knowing a thing separate and distinct
from Socrates, Socrates would not be known [*in sciendo rem separatam et
distinctam a Sorte non sciretur Sortes*]."[17] The correct view does not admit
universal beings because:

> Everything exists singularly and \<is\> so diverse from every other thing
> that it is never possible for a term suppositing precisely for one thing to
> be affirmed of a term suppositing precisely for another; on the contrary,
> if Socrates is a man, then absolutely the same thing is Socrates and a
> man. Therefore, we must not posit universals distinct from singulars
> outside the soul.[18]

Platonic universals make no sense if predication expresses the identity of supposits rather than inherence of properties, although admittedly, this does not so much refute Plato's theory as gainsay it. As an approach to the question of how we cognize universals, its justification must emerge at a higher level.

What happens at that higher level is the topic of Book III, Question 8, of his *De Anima* commentary. Here the semantic interest in what is universal in predication is prophylactic in the sense that Buridan wants to guard against misconstruing the words we use to ask the question. Even so, the nonsemantic part of his account is not exactly clear. He states his conclusions in a tentative way, and sometimes so indirectly that we must infer what his own view is from the way he handles opposing arguments. Whether this is because he found the question especially difficult, or because he was negotiating a heated controversy in treating it (or both), is hard to say.

Buridan begins by stressing the naturalness of the process of forming universal concepts. This seems like an odd thing to say: Natural as opposed to what? Natural as opposed to transcendent or supernatural. On the one hand, intellectual cognition is a causal process akin to sensation, as Aristotle suggests,[19] whose proper subject is the soul, which inheres in the body. We should not make the mistake of assuming that our ability to cognize universally somehow follows from our conception of the intellect as immaterial and unextended. This is what led Averroes to the erroneous conclusion that the subject of universal cognition itself "exists in a kind of universal way [*existit quasi modo universalis*]," such that it is "indivisible in relation to all men [*indivisibilis in omnibus hominibus*]."[20] Against this, Buridan points out that God is an immaterial and unextended being, and yet God "does not understand in a universal way, since this way of understanding is confused and imperfect"; rather, God understands "everything distinctly and most determinately."[21] In contrast to the more Neoplatonically influenced Islamic thinkers, Buridan sees universal cognition as an adaptation to the limits of our created minds, and specifically to our absolute reliance on phantasms or particular images generated by sensation.[22] God, who is omniscient, understands absolutely everything there is to understand in a single indivisible act, without mediation and without having to rely on imperfect procedures like inference and abstraction. Furthermore, we should not assume that universality is a feature found only in human cognition. Material and extended powers are also brought to their objects "in a universal way [*in modo universali*]," which is why the hunger or thirst of a horse is not directed to this particular hay or that particular water, but indifferently to any hay or water, as is shown by the fact that it would take whichever it finds first. We notice this even with inanimate powers like fire, which is disposed indifferently to heat whatever is placed next to it.[23]

What emerges from this line of argument is a picture of universal cognition as a natural activity in which a power is connected with a manifold of possible objects. The analogies mentioned are all natural: intellects cognize just as eyes see, horses desire, and fires burn. Now, the property that the multiple objects of an act of universal cognition share is not visibility or drinkability or inflammability but *similarity*, which Buridan ascribes to the resemblance that exists between things belonging to the same natural kind. "This sort of more essential agreement," he says, "stems from the fact that things belonging to the same species or genus come from the same causes, or from more similar causes, than other things, because in the order of being, they belong to the same grade, or to grades closer to one another than to other things."[24] But this explanation also invokes the notion of similarity, which tells us that similarity must function as a primitive in Buridan's account. Thus, he says that the claim that Socrates and Plato "agree more in the nature of the thing ... and in their essences [*conveniunt ex natura rei ... etiam quantum ad suas essentias*]" than Socrates and Brunellus, and that Socrates and Brunellus likewise agree more than Socrates and this stone, is something "we accept [*accipimus*]" based on their evident similarities, not something we prove by argument.[25]

The intellect is designed track these similarities, and its finding and isolating them just is what it means to cognize universally:

> Therefore, it follows from the fact that representation occurs by means of likeness that what was representative of one thing will be indifferently representative of others, unless something else occurs that obstructs it, as will be discussed later. From this it is finally inferred that once the species and likeness of Socrates has been in the intellect and abstracted from the species of what is extraneous to it, it will no more be a representation of Socrates than of Plato or of other men, nor would the intellect understand Socrates by it more than other men. On the contrary, the intellect would understand all men by it indifferently in a single concept, viz., that from which the name 'man' is taken. And this is to understand universally.[26]

On this model, universal cognition is a process through which undifferentiated representations of things outside the mind are progressively refined on the basis of the similarities and dissimilarities of those things.

But how, exactly, does the process work? As I mentioned above, Buridan does not say much about this, at least not in his mature writings. The closest we get to a proper account is the following paragraph from the final version of his *Questions* on Aristotle's *De Anima*, which locates universal cognition on a continuum of psychological activity that begins with singular cognition:

> I say that when the intellect receives the species or intellection of Socrates from the phantasm mixed together with size and place in this way, making the thing appear in the manner of something existing in the prospect of the person cognizing it, the intellect understands him in a singular manner. If the intellect is able to resolve this confusion and abstract a concept of substance or whiteness from the concept of place, so that the thing is no longer perceived in the manner of something existing in the prospect of the person cognizing it, then there will be a common concept. Thus, when the concept of Socrates has been abstractly elicited from the concepts of whiteness, place, and other accidents or things extraneous to it, it will not then represent Socrates any more than Plato, and there will be a common concept from which the name 'man' is taken. And whatever power can carry out an abstraction of this sort, whether it belongs to sense or to intellect, can cognize universally.[27]

Buridan's naturalism can be seen in his assumption that the common concept of man is somehow already "in" the confused concept of Socrates, which, we may assume from this example, has already been differentiated from other singulars in the sensory field of the person cognizing it. What the intellect does is actively "pull" it from its surroundings,[28] like the sheep seeing the wolf, the horse drinking the water, or the fire burning the kindling. The difference in the case of intellectual cognition is that the intellect does not need anything else to *be* in a certain way in order to perform its proper act, unlike the other examples, all of which require a properly disposed subject, object, and medium: the fire must be hot enough to burn, the kindling dry enough to be burned and sufficiently proximate to the fire; the horse must be thirsty and the water in a drinkable state (not frozen, for example) as well as proximate to the horse; the humors in the sheep's eye must be able to register changes in light and color, the wolf out in the open and not five miles away or behind a tree or in the dark. By contrast, Buridan holds that once the intellect has been supplied with a phantasm, it can cognize whatever is contained in that phantasm at will, without needing anything else to be in a certain way, that is, without requiring any mediating qualitative disposition external to the act itself.[29] That is why motion can only be a metaphor for thought, as Aristotle argued in Book I of *De Anima*.[30]

Still, it seems a mistake to suggest that dispositions are not involved in intellectual cognition, for how are we to account for intellectual memory? Aristotle, of course, distinguishes between different senses in which things are said to be potential or actual in order to explain the difference between knowers and learners—how the knower is able to recollect a complex geometrical proof at will while the learner struggles to reproduce it with the help of books and diagrams.[31] How does this phenomenon translate into Buridan's theory? Buridan devotes an entire question to this, arguing that we must posit intellectual dispositions that are "left behind and caused by the act of intellection [*derelinquitur vel causatur ab intellectione*]" (QDA_3 III.15; 164, l. 114) because there is no other way to explain how knowers differ from learners. He says that these dispositions have a different nature than either the intelligible species (which he interprets materially, as a sensory image "in the corporeal organ of imagination or the cogitative power [*in organo phantasiae vel cogitativae*]" (QDA_3 III.15; 166, l. 163) or the act of intellection itself. They cannot have the same nature as the species because then they would simply *be* species, and, with everything necessary for the formation of an act of intellection still in place, the original act would not cease—which is contrary to our experience of thinking as a transient phenomenon.[32] Nor can the disposition have the same nature as the intellection. Here Buridan dismantles the argument of an unnamed opponent that the difference between an intellection and its remaining disposition is a matter of degree, so that on a scale of ten, for example, the same form would be intensified to its maximum as an intellection (10/10), diminished by half as a disposition (5/10), and further diminished to nothing if forgotten completely (0/10). Buridan rejects this because it fails to explain the relative fluidity of intellections on the one hand and the stubborn persistence of dispositions on the other. Why is it that the top five degrees are intensified and diminished so quickly, as our thoughts move from one thing to another, whereas the bottom five are removable only with difficulty (QDA_3 III.15;

163–64, ll. 90–103)? Buridan concludes that the disposition left behind by the act of thinking cannot be a less intense version of itself.

But then what kind of thing is the disposition? The arguments Buridan gives in his *De Anima* commentary establish only that in the process of human intellectual cognition, the intelligible species, the act of intellection, and the disposition are all distinct. He chooses not to speculate about the nature of the disposition, hazarding only the observation that "the intellect together with the phantasms is immediately and naturally suited to understand any aspect of a thing previously understood, and to which it has been habituated."[33] For proof, he appeals to our own experience: "for since it perceives itself to understand A on a given day and can also understand how much time has passed since that day, it can infer that two years have passed since it first understood A."[34] The intellect must have stored its first understanding of A in dispositional form in order to make such an inference. Now admittedly, this has the look of a dormitive virtue argument: the reason the intellect can recollect its own activity is that it possesses just such a recollective capacity. But actually, I think all Buridan is doing here is signaling that the evident arguments have run out. We are acquainted with the phenomenon and can distinguish its elements, but we cannot go further and say anything about their real natures. Instead, the science of psychology must make do with nominal definitions. Thus, when asked what sort of thing the intelligible species is, Buridan says that "one must first cognize the nominal definition," which is "an act or disposition coming from a sensible thing by the mediation of sense, required in the mind and necessary for the formation of a first intellection, viz., an intellection someone can form without the assistance of any other intellection."[35] If we ask further which aspect(s) of human intellectual cognition might satisfy this definition, Buridan suggest two possibilities:

> It is apparent to me that <the intelligible species> [1] is the act of cognizing by the imagination or cogitative power (or whatever else you want to call it), which Aristotle calls the phantasm (the act, of course, would be extended and derived from the potentiality of a corporeal organ); or else [2] it is the actual intellection actually caused by the intellect and drawn out from its potentiality without extension. Everyone has to grant this disjunction, since it is necessary for every intellect to reflect on phantasms. But which disjunct is true? It seems to me better to exercise caution based

on the smallest number of entities sufficient for the phantasm, i.e., the actual cognition.[36]

Although he does not say so, the alternatives Buridan sketches here correspond roughly to Ockham's *fictum* and *intellectio* theories of universal cognition, respectively. Like Ockham, Buridan opts for the second disjunct, the *intellectio* theory, on grounds of parsimony, having already conceded that no evident truths can settle the question. This is about how many entities are contributed by the soul to its primary or initial act of intellectual cognition. The answer is that we need to posit only one.

But there is a problem with Buridan's argument from parsimony. Has he not just said that the intelligible species, the act of intellection, and the disposition are all distinct? If so, then how can he then identify the intelligible species with the phantasm, and the phantasm with the actual cognition? This would, by transitivity of identity, make the intelligible species the same as the actual cognition, which would contradict his earlier claim that they are distinct. Buridan tries to clarify his view as follows:

> It seems to me that the intellect is made sufficiently actual by the actual cognition or apprehension, so that with it, it can form an actual intellection in itself that is not already received in the body as something drawn out from its potentiality, but in the intellect alone. For this reason, it is apparent that the phantasm—i.e., the actual apprehension—is related to the intellection in the same way as the species caused by the object in the organ of sense was said to be related to the sensation. That is how I understand Aristotle's remark that "to the intellective soul, phantasms are like sensibles," because without phantasms, the soul in no way understands. For just as exterior sense cannot form a sensation without sensible species caused by an object in the organ of sense, so the intellect cannot form an intellection without the aforementioned phantasm.[37]

What Buridan is suggesting here is that the intelligible species and the act of intellection are two distinct modes of the same thing, and that the latter can be actualized at will. The distinction is quasi-physical because the human soul is an incorporeal subject whose most characteristic act resembles physical processes insofar as it unfolds in time. We might say that it involves temporally discrete quasi-movements, viz., that of apprehending a phantasm and then perceiving or understanding it as signifying something beyond itself. Ontologically, the apprehending-to-understanding phase is just the transformation of the same thing, the phantasm, from one degree of actuality to another—and it is not a necessary transformation either, since the process can be interrupted should our attention be diverted elsewhere. Borrowing an analogy from Buridan's *Physics* commentary, it is like a block of wax that we roll out with our hands into a sphere: we do not say that we have two distinct things, a cube and a sphere, but rather, one thing with two different shapes in succession, or one thing that is successively cubical and spherical.[38]

Extending this to the case of human intellectual cognition, we can talk about changes in the soul's internal states or qualities. In an earlier question from his *De Anima* commentary, Buridan says that the way in which the intellect is "differently disposed [*aliter et aliter se habere*]" (note the adverbial formulation) at different times:

> can only be explained by the generation or corruption of some disposition inhering in it and distinct from it. For it is like this with water if it is first hot and later cold; and with matter, if it is first in the form of water and then later in the form of fire; and with the intellect, if it was first believing one thing and then the contrary. For even when a man is asleep, lacking any of his sensible representations, he would still be disposed later differently than he was earlier, which can only be explained by the difference of those opinions from each other and from the intellect.[39]

This question has an identifiable historical context. In it, Buridan is replying to dispositionalists such as John of Mirecourt, whose condemnation marks the beginning of the final phase of Buridan's academic career. Mirecourt apparently held that we can explain change by means of the alteration of enduring subjects, which appear differently to us at different times because of the waxing and waning of their inherent dispositions—as if every individual were a shape-changer like Proteus. But the details of Mirecourt's theory need not detain us here.[40] What is important is Buridan's defense of the opposing view that there must be some *real* difference between the intellect and its dispositions, as well as between the dispositions themselves. This real difference does not constitute a real distinction, however, if by that we mean that the process of thinking creates new or special objects for that thinking to be about. Instead, the signification of a concept or term is altered so that it brings different things to mind.

We can now see why Buridan makes it so explicit that "our concepts exist in our intellect as singularly and distinctly from one another and from other things as do colors and flavors in bodies" even though "they do not in themselves have extension or corporeal location."[41] "A universal term," he says, "exists just as simply and distinctly from other things in your intellect or in my intellect as whiteness in a wall."[42] The universality of concepts or acts of thinking is secured not by their mode of being but by their signification, which Buridan conceives in terms of bringing to mind the particulars of which it is truly predicated. Accordingly, the transformation of concepts from singular to universal involves its further specification, when the intellect distinguishes the various elements fused together (confusa) in it by, for example, "understanding substance abstractively from accident and accident abstractively from substance."[43] It is this latter move which unlocks the potential of a singular concept to be a signifier of other things.

But Buridan's "mature" account did not come from nowhere. Although we do not know the precise influences shaping his influential and much-copied question commentaries on Aristotle, we do have an early treatise which suggests that Buridan's views were subject to criticism by various opponents. At least on the topic of universals, such opponents do not seem to have been in short supply at Paris.

Buridan's First Intellectio Theory

Although Buridan's mature works, like Ockham's, tend to be focused on the semantic dimensions of the problem of universals, he did address its metaphysical and psychological aspects in one of his earliest works, the Tractatus de differentia universalis ad individuum [Treatise on the Difference between the Universal and the Individual]. This treatise, which has been published in a modern edition by Sławomir Szyller, is one of five polemical works composed 1332–35; of its four known manuscripts, one (Uppsala C.615) indicates in the explicit that the question was determined in 1334. The text contains two questions: "Do universals actually exist outside the soul?" and "Do universals exist outside the soul with a unity that differs from numerical unity?" It is directed against two realist opponents: possibly Walter Burley, who is named ("Gualterus") as the source of one of the affirmative arguments,[44] and an anonymous member of the Picard nation (possibly Aegidius of Feno, a Flemish contemporary of Buridan's, who moved on to the faculty of theology, obtaining his doctorate there in the late 1340s).[45] Its authenticity is not in doubt.

The *Treatise* reflects what must have been an active and fairly high-level debate on the nature of universals. The first question alone gives twenty-five affirmative arguments and twelve negative arguments, with authoritative sources cited early and often. The treatise genre does not appear to be one Buridan returned to later in his career, and so this work affords us a rare look at Buridan directing his philosophical energies toward solving a problem rather than explicating a text.

The title of the work, which may also be translated, "Treatise on How What Is Universal Differs from What Is Individual," suggests that individuality is relatively unproblematic for Buridan, which is hardly surprising for someone who thinks that "everything exists singularly" and that "we must not posit universals distinct from singulars outside the soul."[46] It turns out that he also has something to say about the metaphysical status of individuality, although the dialectic of the question treats individuality as the *explanans* of universality, so that problems connected with our cognition of singulars are addressed only in the elaboration of his main reply to the question.

Do universals exist outside the soul? Buridan gives a very direct answer:

> I advance three main conclusions. The first is that the universal as a form does not exist outside the soul. The second is that the universal as a subject as distinct from the individual as a subject—e.g., man as distinct from Socrates and Plato—does not exist outside the soul. The third is that the universal as a subject does exist outside the soul with respect to its relation. And we will see later the sense in which the relation is outside the soul and the extent to which and how it is from the soul.[47]

The distinction between existing "as a form" and existing "as a subject," which is how Buridan understands the terms of the question, corresponds to "the common distinction by which 'universal' is usually said to be capable of meaning the intention or the thing."[48] The first two conclusions deny that universals exist outside the mind either as formal beings or as entities unto themselves, respectively. But the idea brought into play in the third conclusion, "the universal as a subject with respect to its relation," is not a common or customary distinction. It does most of the work in what follows.

Buridan offers five arguments for the first conclusion, all of which turn on his understanding of formal being as conceptual or intentional being, which would make the formal universal a second intention, or concept of concepts. This is what happens, he says, when the mind uses its reflexive power to form further concepts based on concepts it has already formed:

> But things in the soul can be founded not only on things outside the soul but also on things in the soul due to the soul's capacity to reflect on itself and its operation. The minor is known, for just as we call man or animal or stone 'universals' because each of them is predicable of many, so too we call the intelligible species, act of understanding, intention, proposition, syllogism, and other entities in the soul 'universals,' because each of them is predicated of many.[49]

On this view, universals are just terms or concepts that are predicable of (many) other terms or concepts, which means that only certain terms or their corresponding concepts are eligible to be called "universal," since extramental beings are not predicable of anything.

Buridan then gives eight arguments for the second conclusion that the subjective universal as distinct from individuals such as Socrates and Plato does not exist outside the mind. The most interesting for our purposes are the first two:[50]

> The first [argument] is as follows: the formal universal is a second intention. This is conceded, but it would not be true for the subject it denominates because the subject supposits for the first intention and not precisely for the thing. Therefore, etc.
>
> Second, we argue as follows: assume that only two men exist, Socrates and Plato. Then man is affirmed of Socrates and Plato for all, its reality preceding the operation of the soul. This seems evident *per se*. But man is not affirmed of Socrates and Plato as distinct from them, but rather denied, for negation is on the basis of the distinction of terms and affirmation on the basis of their indistinction. Therefore, man as distinct from Socrates and Plato does not exist without some operation of the mind.[51]

The first argument involves a dangerous ambiguity: if formal universals such as species are second intentions, then they denominate subjects such as man, which are first-intentional names or concepts, whereas first-intentional names or concepts should denominate subjects such as Socrates and Plato, which are extramental things. But Buridan does not say that.

Instead, he appeals to what the first-intentional name supposits or stands for—the singular things of which it is truly predicated—refusing to unpack its signification (or denomination). The reason he puts it this way is that he sees first-intentional names as somehow already tied to their corresponding particulars, such that their content—what it is that makes them universal—doesn't just fall out of them without effort. It requires an act of mind to get man out of Socrates and Plato. What is denominated by man is therefore not a simple but a complex concept: it is *Socrates signified as a man* or *Plato signified as a man*, neither of which has a simple or straightforward referent outside the mind, as Plato's view suggests.

So the second conclusion is that the subjective universal—first-intentional terms or concepts, such as man, which are denominated by "universal"—do not exist outside the mind as distinct from individuals such as Socrates or Plato. But this threatens to leave universal concepts ungrounded. Hence the third conclusion: subjective universals conceived relationally do exist outside the mind.

Buridan signals that this is where he will make his stand on the ontological question of universals: "the subjective universal with respect to its relation is that upon which the intention of universality is founded," he says. Furthermore, it is the subjective universal, for example, man, "that is verified essentially and *in quid* of real individuals such as Socrates and Plato—which would not be the case if it had no import outside the soul."[52] Buridan is anxious to demonstrate that import because otherwise, the distinction between what is individual and what is universal "would be a fiction fabricated by the mind, to which nothing corresponds in reality."[53]

But what could it mean to conceive of a universal relationally? If it has terms, which *relatum* is in the mind and which outside the mind? Buridan prepares the way for his answer by offering several *notabilia* on the epistemic aspects of the question. First, he reminds his readers of his ontological commitments:

Whatever exists outside the soul exists individually in the thing itself, i.e., distinct from everything else, from its own species as well as from the species of other things, so that there is absolutely nothing except things that exist individually, nor is there anything else distinct from them. For Socrates and his humanity or animality or being exist distinctly in a thing from Plato and his humanity and animality.[54]

No matter how hard it looks, the intellect will never find any one thing outside the mind that possesses a universal mode of being. But it is not as if the intellect is in touch with individuality either. Buridan is adamant that neither the intellect nor the senses nor any other power of cognition can distinguish between two things belonging to the same species except through extraneous considerations—differences in size, shape, color, and so on. This is obvious by experience. He gives a nautical example: suppose you were living at sea and could only see water; if you fell asleep while your ship was at rest and it slowly drifted and came to rest in another place, you would not be able to tell that the ship had moved when you woke up, as obviously you would if you were acquainted as such with the particular bits of water that surrounded your ship.[55]

So we are possessed of an intellect that is directly acquainted with neither universals nor singulars. Things are looking pretty grim for us human knowers. But Buridan uses our indirect acquaintance with singulars as represented by our imagination to bootstrap his way to an account of how we cognize universally:

> If the species man were in the imagination and all other species extraneous to it were removed or stripped off, the resulting species will not represent either Socrates or Plato determinately, but both of them, or any other man, indifferently. And so the intellect would not understand this man determinately through that species, but this one or that one or some other one indifferently, and this is what it means to understand man by a universal act of understanding.[56]

Buridan says the same thing, using almost the same words, some twenty years later in his account of universal cognition in Book III, Question 8 of his *De Anima* commentary.[57] Now one might wonder how the intellect can remove extraneous considerations from the species. How does it know which ones are extraneous, so that what remains is a projectable predicate, the true likeness of a natural kind? Buridan says that the answer to this does not really pertain to the present question (but rather to Book III of *De Anima*), but he does mention two possibilities: the "*opinio famosa*" that it is due to the operation of the agent intellect, and another opinion that universality is conferred upon things as soon as they are taken in by an immaterial and indivisible intellect. Either, he says, suffices to show that "the intellect can understand a thing universally even though there is nothing distinct from singulars outside the soul, and that an intellection of this sort is not a fiction."[58]

Notice, however, that in both cases the intellect has done something to bring about its understanding universally. This leads Buridan to the insight that perhaps it is not any kind of object that is universal, but the way something singular is conceived: "sometimes concepts are distinct not because of diversity in the things conceived, but because the modes of conceiving them are different, just as the concepts of a rational animal and a man are different, though it is the same thing [that is both]."[59] He surmises that what we call universal must in reality be a kind of aggregate:

> I say that the subjective universal is an aggregate of the thing and the concept, or of the thing and the mode of conceiving. It is therefore outside the mind in relation to the thing and dependent on the mind in relation to the concept and mode of conceiving. And because in an aggregate of this sort the thing is like the subject of the concept and the second intention is more properly and formally attributed to the aggregate because of the concept than because of the thing, we call the concept the 'proximate subject' of the second intention, the thing the 'remote subject,' and the aggregate the 'total subject.'[60]

The "subjective universal [*universale pro subiecto*]" is that of which second-intentional concepts/terms like "species," "genus," or "universal" can be truly predicated. Buridan says that this is an aggregate of the first intentional concept/term (e.g., "man") and the thing (Socrates or Plato)—the former being the proximate subject, the latter the remote subject, and the two together the total subject. He proceeds to argue that the subjective universal is "partly from the soul and partly outside the soul [*partim ab anima et partim praeter animam*]," and that *qua* remote subject it is not outside the soul in a way that is distinct from individuals such as Socrates and Plato—unless we say that it is distinct *in potentia*. But each component in this complex object is metaphysically particular: the thing, the concept, and the mode of conceiving the thing. What Buridan is saying is that universals are structured aggregates with a mental component and an extramental component standing in a certain relation. The glue that holds them together is the intellection, in this case the act of cognizing universally: "man as distinct from Socrates and Plato requires some mental operation."[61]

Although we cannot tell whether he was influenced by it directly,[62] Buridan's distinction between subjective and formal universals looks very close to a distinction Thomas Aquinas draws between first- and second-intentional concepts. A first-intentional concept is "a likeness of the thing existing outside the soul [*similitudo rei existentis extra animam*]," whereas a second-intentional concept only "follows upon the mode of understanding the thing existing outside the soul [*consequitur ex modo intelligendi rem quae est extra animam*]."[63] The thing existing outside the soul is thus conceived in two ways: as the proximate object of the first intention—proximate because "it has an immediate foundation in the thing [*talis conceptio intellectus habet fundamentum in re immediate*]"—and the remote object of the second intention, which must operate through the first intention.

Buridan then takes his account of universal cognition a step further. In his reply to one of the initial arguments, he says that the division of things using *differentiae* such as rational and irrational is not some real act outside the mind; instead, we are to imagine three things at work here: "a starting point [*terminus a quo*], a finishing point [*terminus ad quem*], and a subject that remains the same throughout."[64] This is of course the language of the analysis of motion, and the example he offers is the action of dividing a line: before it is divided, a line has a unity of parts, but afterwards not; the starting point in the division of a line is therefore its unity and the finishing point is its multiplicity; but the subject of the change, the essence of the line, remains the same throughout, for no part of the essence of a line is corrupted through division. Applying this to the case at hand, Buridan tells us that:

> In the division of animal into rational and irrational, a single general concept, indifferent to Socrates and Brunellus, is just like the starting point; the special concepts, viz., of man and ass, by which we differently conceive Socrates and Brunellus, are the finishing points; and the thing existing singularly outside the mind—Socrates or Brunellus, or other things of this kind—are like the subject that remains the same under both concepts.[65]

This sounds like some kind of metaphysical dissection has been performed, but we are not to think that anything has been really divided here; rather, we say that:

> Several things existing outside the soul are divided in this way like the subject of a division—things whose single general concept is the *terminus*

a quo and whose different specific concepts are the *terminus ad quem*. And that division is a *per se* and essential division, first because the same essence is subject to both concepts, and then because the concepts of those diverse things themselves are essential concepts.[66]

Buridan's idea here is that universals are dynamic aggregates of extramental particulars, concepts, and the thinking or "mental motion" required to connect the two. In dividing the concept "animal," we begin with a singular general concept indifferent to both *relata*, the underlying subjects of Socrates and Brunellus, and then differentiate it into man and donkey, without producing any real change in either *relatum*. When Buridan says that universals are aggregates, he is referring to the entire movement, from indifferent general concept to differentiated specific concepts. The movement in the other direction, from singular concepts to common concept, begins from multiple singular concepts and then converges on a point of similarity.

Buridan does not further elaborate on this account, although the concept of aggregation is sometimes used in his later writings when he wants to harmonize apparently disparate views, such as whether true human happiness consists in the exercise of prudence or moral virtue (answer: both).[67] What is most enticing about it is that it seems to take Ockham's final word on the matter, that universal concepts are a kind of mental act or "*intellectio*," almost literally, appropriating terminology used to analyze motion to model what happens in the mind when we think. And if universal cognition is something that unfolds in time, like physical motion, then we can see not only why God does not cognize universally but also why Buridan is so keen to treat it as a natural phenomenon rather than as some sort of quasi-divine insight, in the way the Islamic commentators wanted to treat it.

Conclusion

Although it would be useful to find some substantive link between Buridan's two accounts, the aggregative and relational conception of universality outlined in his *Treatise on the Difference between Universals and Individuals* appears to play no role in his mature discussions of the problem of universals and, as far as I know, is never mentioned by him again. Whether he was forced to abandon it because of insurmountable difficulties or whether he simply didn't have occasion to model universal thinking again is difficult to say. He is usually very good about referencing previous discussions of a question in his Aristotle commentaries, although he refers to his early treatises hardly at all. Perhaps the genre gap between his *tractates* and *quaestiones* was too great for him to introduce the former comfortably into the latter. Perhaps he thought the students in his Aristotle lectures would not be able to find copies of his early treatises very easily, which would obviate the point of referring to them.

Ontologically, Buridan's appeal to motion looks promising as a solution to the problem of universals. For a nominalist, actions complicate ontology not by adding new things but by rearranging old things, or by placing these old things in special relations to one another by virtue of their inherent qualities; thus, by using the term "white" of one supposit and then considering it indifferently, I am connecting this term to everything else of which it is truly predicated: past, present, future, and possible. Now, if this is a causal relation, it must be a very special type because I don't have to be physically proximate to the other supposits which bear this quality in order to signify them. We might imagine universal cognition in Buridan's sense as a signifying gesture, like the outward sweep of a hand over many things, whereas singular cognition would correspond to a different gesture, like pointing to one thing in particular.[68] In the end, it is not clear that a nominalist can get much beyond metaphor here, since gestures are conventional. What does seem clear is that no static model of human cognition is going to work for Buridan, because if we were to take snapshot of creation at any moment and count up the things, we would "see" only particular substances and certain particular accidents. We would not see their similarities, let alone what makes them similar, without a "second look" that relates those particulars to each other. That is where the dynamic element comes in.[69]

IV LANGUAGE, LOGIC, AND METAPHYSICS

7

Can God Know More?
A Case Study in Later Medieval
Discussions of Propositions

SUSAN BROWER-TOLAND

In this essay, I trace the development of a peculiar debate between William of Ockham (d. 1347) and some of his immediate successors at Oxford over the question of whether "God can know more than he knows." Discussion of this question (which begins well before the fourteenth century) has its origin in specific theological concerns about the compatibility of divine omniscience and immutability. At the hands of Ockham and his colleagues, however, it comes to take on much broader philosophical significance. This is because, as they see it, whether or not God can know more depends entirely on the nature of the entities which serve as objects of his knowledge. And this, in turn, raises a further question about the nature of objects of propositional attitudes generally—divine or otherwise. Thus, for Ockham and his successors, this traditional question about God's knowledge serves as an occasion for debating issues surrounding the nature of what we, nowadays, might refer to as "propositions."[1] Yet, even if it is clear that these thinkers are addressing issues closely connected to contemporary debates about propositions, the theories that emerge from their discussion will, no doubt, strike most contemporary philosophers as rather peculiar (to say the least). The types of entity Ockham and his colleagues introduce to serve as objects for propositional attitudes are a far cry from propositions as they are conceived now.[2] The aim of this essay is to clarify both the nature of the debate itself and the theories that emerge from it.

My discussion falls into three sections. In the first section, I provide an overview of the debate itself. I begin by sketching Ockham's answer to the question about whether God can know more; I then trace the reception of his views among two of his immediate successors, namely, Walter Chatton (d. 1343) and Robert Holcot (d. 1349). As will be clear, the sorts of positions these thinkers defend—both on the issue of divine knowledge and on the issue of propositions generally—are deeply puzzling. Indeed, part of my aim in the first section is simply to call attention to the difficulties (both interpretative and philosophical) their discussions raise. In the second section, I go on to advance a hypothesis about what's needed in order to make sense of their discussions. The key, I argue, lies in getting clear about how each of the participants in the debate conceives of propositional attitudes and, more specifically, how they conceive of the role played by the "object" of propositional attitude relations. In a third, and final, section, I briefly discuss how my interpretation of this debate can be seen as opening up some new ways of thinking about (and classifying) later medieval theories of propositions.

Can God Know More? A Debate about the Objects of Propositional Attitudes

As I indicated above, the debate about whether God can know more begins well before the fourteenth century. In fact, the origin of this particular debate traces to the twelfth century and, more specifically, to Book 1, d. 39 of the *Sentences* of Peter Lombard (d. 1160), where he considers "whether God's knowledge can increase, diminish, or be changed in some way."[3] What prompts discussion of this issue, both in Lombard and in later figures, is a general concern about the compatibility of divine omniscience and immutability. If God is omniscient, he must know everything. But since what is true can change from one time (or world) to the next, it is difficult to see how divine omniscience is to be squared with immutability. If what God knows is changeable, does it not follow that God himself is changeable? Now, in Lombard's case, the concern seems to be primarily one about whether God's immutability is consistent with changes in his knowledge across worlds. In subsequent authors, however, the concern gets focused more on whether divine immutability is compatible with changes in God's knowledge *across times*. This is, in any case, the focus of concern for Ockham and his colleagues. For them, the issue at stake is whether God can know something more (or less, or simply other) than what he knows *right now*.

As we shall see, Ockham, Chatton, and Holcot all think that answering this question requires first getting clear about the nature (and mutability) of the "truths" to which God's knowledge relates. And this, in turn, requires taking a stand on the nature of the entities which serve as objects for propositional attitudes generally. Thus, for these thinkers, this traditional theological question about divine knowledge serves as an occasion for theorizing about the nature of propositions. As we shall see, their discussion not only highlights their views about the nature of propositions, but also a host of difficulties associated with their proper interpretation.

Ockham on Whether God Can Know More

Ockham begins his discussion by drawing two preliminary distinctions.[4] The first is a distinction between different ways of understanding the question itself. In asking whether God can know more one might, Ockham thinks, be asking either of the following two questions:

(I) Is it possible for God to come to know a greater quantity of things than he knows now?

(II) Is it possible for God to come to know something other than what he knows now?[5]

Understood the first way, the question is about the *measure* or *quantity* of what God knows: Can it increase? Understood in the second way, however, the question is merely about the *mutability* of what God knows: Can it change? As we'll see, Ockham thinks it makes a difference which of the two questions we are asking. Indeed, he gives different answers to each.

The second distinction Ockham draws is between two different types of knowledge corresponding to two difference senses of the term "to know."

> 'Know' is taken in two ways—in a broad sense and in a strict sense. In the first way it is the same as 'cognize' insofar as cognizing [is a relation that] extends to all things. And, in this way, God knows—that is, cognizes—all things: propositional and non-propositional, necessary and contingent, true, false, and impossible. In the [second,] strict sense, 'know' is the same as 'cognize what is true'; and in that sense nothing is known but what is true.[6]

Here, Ockham distinguishes two different cognitive relations that the term "know" might be taken to designate. In the broadest possible sense, to know (or have knowledge of) something is just to cognize it. Understood in this way, knowledge is just a relation that holds between a cognizer and whatever she cognizes. Thus, objects of knowledge in this sense can be either propositional or nonpropositional (necessary or contingent, true or false) in nature. In the strict sense, however, knowledge is a distinctively *propositional* attitude. For, taken strictly, "knowledge" is not mere cognition, but cognition of and assent to what is *true*.[7] Taken in this sense, therefore, "knowledge" designates a relation which obtains between a cognizer and whatever she (correctly) cognizes *as true*.

If we take this latter distinction between two senses of "to know" in conjunction with the foregoing division of the question, it should be clear that each of the questions at I and II above admit of a further twofold division. Thus, in asking whether God can know more one might be asking any of the following:

(Ia)   Is it possible for God to come to cognize a greater quantity of things than he does now?

(IIa) Is it possible for God to come to cognize something other than what he does now?

(Ib)   Is it possible for God to come to know a greater quantity of truths than he knows now?

(IIb) Is it possible for God to come to know some truth other than what he knows now?

Over the course of his discussion Ockham addresses all four of these questions. As we shall see, however, he is primarily interested questions Ib and IIb—that is, in the questions having to do with the quantity and the mutability of *truths* known by God. For this reason, these same questions become the focus debate among subsequent thinkers.

Once Ockham dispatches with these preliminary distinctions, he turns to address the question itself. Beginning with the first of the two senses of "know," namely, cognition, he says that regardless of how we interpret the question—whether as a question about the quantity (viz., Ia) or mutability (viz., IIa) of what God cognizes—it must be answered in the negative. For, insofar as God's knowledge in this broad sense is just his cognition of all things, there can be no question of its increase or change at all, since it already extends to everything (whether actual, merely possible, impossible, propositional, or nonpropositional).

When Ockham turns to knowledge in the strict sense, matters are a bit more complicated. If the question is interpreted along quantitative lines (viz., IIa), that is, as having to do with the quantity of truths God can know, Ockham thinks we must, again, give a negative reply. God cannot know any more (or, for that matter, any fewer) truths than he knows now. Even so, Ockham insists, God can come to know *other* truths than those he knows now. Hence, if the question is interpreted along the lines of mutability (viz., IIb), that is, as a question about whether he can come to know *different* truths, then here we must answer in the affirmative.

On the face of it, these latter two answers seem inconsistent. If God cannot know a greater number of truths than he knows now, how is it possible for him to know any truth other than those he knows now? Ockham's idea is that while the quantity of truths always remains fixed, nevertheless, the members of the set of truths can vary over time.

> It is not possible that there are more truths at one time than at another. This is because at each time one or the other part of a contradiction is true, and nothing is true but what is one or the other part of a contradiction. And since it is not possible for both parts of a contradiction to be true [simultaneously] it is always the case that there are as many truths at one time as at another. Thus, while there are neither more nor fewer truths [from one time to another], some things may be true at one time that are not true at another time.[8]

Although Ockham never explicitly specifies the precise nature of these "truths" to which God's knowledge relates, it is clear, nonetheless, that as he conceives of them they are entities capable of changing their truth-value over time. What is more, as Ockham argues in this passage, the mere fact that what is true changes over time does not by itself entail that the overall quantity of truths changes. For "if one thing becomes false that was true earlier, another thing will become true that was false earlier."[9] Thus, even if the quantity of truths known by God never varies, it still remains an open question precisely *which* truths are known by God at any given time. "For everything true, when it is true, is known by God; and when it is not true it is not known by God."[10]

In light of the foregoing, we may summarize Ockham's argument this way:

1. God is omniscient.
2. Therefore, God knows every truth.
3. The quantity of truths never varies.
4. Therefore, God cannot know more—that is, a larger quantity of truths—than he knows now.
5. But what is true at one time may be false at another (and vice versa).
6. Therefore, God can come to know different truths than those he knows now.

The conclusions at steps 4 and 6 correspond to Ockham's views about the quantity and mutability of what God knows in the strict sense (i.e., his answers to questions Ib and IIb, respectively). As he sees it, while God cannot know *more* truths than he knows now, he can know *other* ones.

Ockham's treatment of God's knowledge in d. 39 raises a number of questions—both interpretive and philosophical. Foremost among these is a question about the implications of d. 39 for his theory of propositions generally. While Ockham says nothing in d. 39 about the nature of the truths that function as objects for divine knowledge, in a number of other contexts he makes quite clear that the primary bearers of truth and falsity are linguistic entities—namely, true and false sentences (*complexa*). Consider, for example, his remarks in the following passages:

Everything that is true or false is a sentence (*complexum*).[11]

Truth and falsity are in composition and division. Thus, an expression (*oratio*) composed affirmatively from a noun and a verb—or such an expression composed negatively—is true or false. [12]

Nothing is believed except what is true [or false], and nothing is true [or false] except a sentence. [13]

What these passages show is that Ockham takes sentences (and apparently only sentences) to be the primary bearers of truth (and falsity) and, hence, holds that sentences function as objects for propositional attitudes. What is more, insofar as his remarks in these passages are about expressions as they occur (or, are "composed") in natural language, it would appear that when Ockham speaks of sentences as the bearers of truth-value he has sentence *tokens* in mind. And, since sentential expressions occur not only in spoken and written language, but also in mental language, for Ockham (as for most medieval thinkers), truth-bearers will include not only spoken and written tokens, but also tokens in the language of thought.

The foregoing passages seem to represent Ockham's considered view regarding the nature of truth-bearers. Even so, they seem to be in tension with his account of divine knowledge in d. 39. Indeed, it would seem that a token-sententialist account of truth-bearers is simply inconsistent with the conclusions Ockham draws regarding the quantity of what God knows. Holcot calls attention to precisely this point when he responds to Ockham's discussion. He argues that, given Ockham's *own* views about the nature of truths, Ockham is simply not entitled to claim, as he does, that God cannot know a greater number of them.[14] After all, Holcot reasons, if Ockham holds that sentence tokens (spoken, written, and mental) are the bearers of truth and falsity, then to say that God knows every truth is just to say that he knows every true sentence token. But, of course, if the objects of God's knowledge are sentence tokens—namely, contingently existing, transient entities—the quantity of things known by God would be changing constantly. Thus, Holcot claims that "according to him [namely, Ockham], it ought to be entirely granted that God can know more than he knows."[15] Accordingly, Holcot concludes that "in this article he [namely, Ockham] seems to contradict his own views in many places."[16]

Of course, if Holcot's criticism is right, then Ockham is guilty of a serious philosophical blunder, namely, that of failing to see the consequence of his own views about the nature of truth-bearers and objects of propositional attitudes in their application to God's knowledge. Rather than lay such a charge at Ockham's feet, more recent commentators have instead preferred to challenge the accuracy of Holcot's interpretation. Norman Kretzmann, for example, has argued that "much of Holcot's criticism of Ockham is founded on the assumption that Ockham was attempting to use the [sentence] token as the object of knowledge. That is an unfounded assumption about Ockham's position generally."[17] Thus, rather than draw the uncharitable conclusion that Ockham's solution to d. 39 is evidence of inconsistency, Kretzmann recommends that we take d. 39 as evidence that Ockham did not, in fact, mean to be defending a token-sententialist account of propositions. E.A. Moody and Marilyn Adams argue in much the same vein. Indeed, all three of these commentators take d. 39 as evidence for an alternative interpretation of Ockham's account of propositions—one according to which sentence *types* function as the ultimate bearers of truth and, likewise, as the objects for knowledge, belief, and so on. Thus, as Moody argues:

> All of Holkot's arguments turn on his extremely nominalistic refusal to construe the word "proposition" (and hence the word "true") as designating anything other than particular complexes of terms or concepts actually formed by particular men at particular times. . . . In modern parlance, Holkot uses the word "proposition" for *token-sentence* and not for *type-sentence*. The fact that Ockham does not do this has perhaps not received the notice that it deserves.[18]

Adams concurs with this assessment: "Ockham . . . in assuming that the number of truths and falsehoods is constant and equal seems to treat propositions as [sentence] types."[19]

But it is not at all clear that this alternative reading of Ockham's account saves Ockham from inconsistency. In saddling Ockham with sentence *types*, these commentators also saddle Ockham with a commitment that runs directly counter to his own strict nominalism. After all, on the most natural construal of them, sentence types look to be a kind of universal.[20] But as is well known, Ockham is resolute in his rejection of universals. And even if, contrary to fact, Ockham were willing to admit such entities, it is by no means clear that he would thereby be entitled to claim that the quantity of truths does not change over time. For sentence types are not obviously eternally existing entities; one might, for example, suppose that they come into and go out of existence when a new language is born and an old one dies. What is more (and worse), it is not obvious that sentence types are themselves truth-bearing entities. Indeed, to the extent that truth belongs to sentences at all it looks to be a feature of token sentences, not types, since only the former (i.e., only sentences in a context) can make specific truth-evaluable claims. It is not clear, therefore, that this alternative reading does anything to resolve the original difficulties raised by Ockham's discussion in d. 39. Indeed, if anything, it simply relocates the inconsistency and leaves Ockham with a less plausible theory of propositions.

What's needed, therefore, is a way of understanding Ockham's discussion in d. 39 that not only yields a consistent theory of propositions, but also accommodates his broader nominalist proclivities while also preserving God's omniscience and immutability. On the face of it, the prospects for such an account look dim.

Chatton on Whether God Can Know More

Chatton's discussion of the question regarding whether God can know more comes at Book I, d. 39 (article 2) of his own commentary on the *Sentences*.[21] His account is essentially a critical reaction to Ockham's earlier treatment of the same issue. Accordingly, Chatton begins by summarizing Ockham's account, calling attention both to his division of the question and his distinction between the two senses of "knowledge." Unlike Holcot, who criticizes Ockham for not allowing more change in what God knows, Chatton is critical of Ockham's allowing any change at all in what God knows. Chatton claims that it is impossible not only for God to know something more (or less) than he knows now, but likewise for him to come to know something *other* than what he knows now. Ultimately, therefore, Chatton wants to resist Ockham's second conclusion (that is, his answer to IIb); instead, he argues that God's knowledge relates to the same objects—the same "truths"—at all times.

As becomes clear from Chatton's discussion, his disagreement with Ockham about divine knowledge is a direct consequence of a broader disagreement over the nature of objects of propositional attitudes. Chatton himself hints at this broader disagreement at the very outset of his discussion. Thus, after reviewing Ockham's distinction between two notions of knowledge, Chatton proceeds to introduce his own, preferred analysis. "For me," he says, " 'to know' is to cognize the thing (*res*) that is signified by a true sentence."[22] And, again, a bit later, he repeats the same point: "strictly speaking, to know is to assent to something that is signified by a true sentence."[23] According to Chatton, therefore, the objects of God's knowledge (and indeed, of propositional attitudes generally) are not, as Ockham holds, sentences or linguistic signs ("*signa*") of any sort; they are, rather, the entities *signified* by them. "After all," he explains, "it is certain that there are no sentences in God's mind, and God does not assent to our [spoken, written, or mental] sentences."[24]

Although Chatton says very little in d. 39 about the precise nature of the "things" which are signified by sentences, his discussion in other contexts makes fairly clear that he takes these items to be concrete, worldly entities. This view emerges most clearly in his discussion of objects of belief in the prologue to his *Sentences* commentary.[25] In this context, he argues that the object for a given propositional attitude is the individual entity (typically, a substance) signified by the (categorematic) terms which occur in sentences expressing that attitude. For example, he claims at one point that the object of the belief that God is three and one is just that entity which is signified by the terms that occur in the sentence "God is three and one." And, as he goes on to make clear, this is nothing other than God himself. For, as he explains, "each part of that sentence is a way of thinking about God."[26] Indeed, in general, Chatton seems to think that the subject and predicate expressions occurring in affirmative atomic predications (i.e., sentences whose logical structure is of the form "a is F") refer to one and the same object.[27]

Although Chatton's view about the nature of objects of propositional attitudes is treated explicitly only in the prologue of his *Sentences* commentary, he makes clear in subsequent discussions that this general account applies equally in the case divine knowledge:

> I am supposing what was made clear in the *Prologue*, namely, that it is not necessary that one assents to a sentence (*complexo*), but rather one can [assent] directly to the thing signified by a sentence. And, therefore, in this case, when God assents to the thing signified by 'A exists,' it is not the case that he assents to a sentence, but rather [he assents] to some *thing*.[28]

Clearly, therefore, on Chatton's view, God's knowledge is a relation not to true sentences, but to the objects that are "signified" by them.

Despite Chatton's insistence that knowledge is primarily a relation to *things* and not to representational or linguistic entities, he is willing, none-theless, to follow Ockham in speaking of God's knowledge as a relation to "truths."[29] For, as Chatton sees it, sentences are not the only items to which the notion of truth applies; on the contrary, he thinks that the concrete worldly things (*res*) to which they correspond, and which they signify, can also be said to be true. What is more, he thinks that truths of this latter sort are such that they do not alter their truth-value over time. Thus, says Chatton, "as far as truth applies to the thing that is known (*res cognitae*), it is impossible that something be true [in this sense] at any time without its also being true now."[30] In light of all this, of course, Chatton rejects Ockham's claim that God can know something different than what he knows now. If God knows all true *things*, and if what is true now is true at all times, it follows, as Chatton says, that it is "impossible for God to know something that he does not know now."

Interestingly, toward the end of his discussion in d. 39, Chatton acknowledges that his disagreement with Ockham regarding God's knowledge owes to broader differences in their accounts of the nature of the "truths" to which God's knowledge relates.

> As to the argument he [viz. Ockham] offers (that God can know something that he does not know, because something can be true which is not now true), I respond that if he means to be talking about ["truth" as] the denomination of a *thing* by a sign, then his [conclusion] is impossible. But if [he intends to be talking about truth as something] on the side of the sign—[i.e., of the "truth"] by which a sign is now true—then, in that case, something that is not [now] true *can* be true. But this question asks about the truth of the *thing* cognized, not about the truth of the sign.[31]

Chatton here concedes that if the truths in question were sentences, then what is true could change over time; indeed he is even willing to "concede that [in such a case] God can know or cognize something that is not true now."[32] But he insists that what God knows principally is things, not sentences, and thus, that when it comes to questions about the quantity and mutability of the objects of God's knowledge the question is "about the truth of the thing . . . not about the truth of a sign."[33]

Given what Chatton wants to say about the objects of knowledge generally, his response to this question is perfectly in keeping with his broader views about propositional attitudes. But his discussion of divine knowledge does bring into relief the oddity of these broader views. As the foregoing makes clear, Chatton wants to treat ordinary concrete things not only as objects for propositional attitudes but even as things that can be said to be true. The problem with this view, of course, is that such entities seem utterly unsuited for the job; to the extent that Chatton is appealing to these sorts of entity to fill roles traditionally associated with propositions (namely, that of truth-bearer and object of belief) his account seems confused.

As a way of illustrating the point we may, once again, take a page from Holcot, whose discussion of God's knowledge includes not only a critique of Ockham's account, but also a critique of Chatton's.[34] Regarding Chatton's view, Holcot has the following to say:

> Against this view, I argue as follows: Only what is true is known, but an external thing (*res*) signified by a [sentence] is not true. Therefore, etc. Again, only what is known as true (*tantum . . . quod vere est scitum*) in an act of knowing is the object of that act of knowing. But an external thing is not known as true by an act of knowing. Therefore, an external thing is not an object of an act of knowing.[35]
>
> Indeed, ordinarily, it is not proper for philosophers [to use] the expression 'I know stone,' or 'I know wood,' rather this is proper: 'I know *that* stone is hard,' 'I know *that* wood is soft' and so forth. Likewise, ordinarily, for Catholic theologians this is not a proper expression 'I believe God,' but rather 'I believe *that* God exists,' or 'I believe that God is three and one.'[36]

Holcot's aim in these passages is precisely to call attention to the oddity of Chatton's position. Not only are things like individual substances not susceptible of truth (or falsity), but it is for just this reason that they are the wrong sort of entity to serve as objects for knowledge (or any other propositional attitude). After all, to believe or to know something is to assent to its truth—that is, to take it *as true* (as Holcot says "only what is true can be known"). But we do not assent to individual entities, nor do we take them to be true (or false). That this is the case is clear, Holcot thinks, just from the structure of ordinary knowledge and belief ascriptions. After all, if Chatton's account were right, we would expect such ascriptions to take an altogether different form than they in fact do. We would say "S knows x" (where x is an expression that stands for an individual object—a stone, in Holcot's example), rather than "S knows that p" (where p is a sentential expression). The very fact that we do not ascribe knowledge and belief in this way appears, as Holcot rightly points out, to tell against Chatton's view.

Unlike the case of Ockham, therefore, the central difficulty for Chatton's discussion in d. 39, is not that of identifying a theory of propositions consistent with his various conclusions about divine knowledge. On this score, his account is fairly straightforward. Rather the difficulty is in understanding why Chatton would hold such a theory in the first place.

Holcot on Whether God Can Know More

Holcot is the third of our three authors to take up the question about whether God can know more. As we have seen, his discussion is informed by his disagreement with both Ockham and Chatton. Unlike the latter two, however, Holcot addresses the issue not in his *Sentences* commentary, but in the course of a quodlibetal disputation (Quodlibet I, question 6). What is more, Holcot explicitly connects this question about God's knowledge to the broader issue about the nature of propositions and propositional attitudes generally. Thus, his discussion in q.6 is divided into two separate articles: in the first, he inquires about the nature the objects of propositional attitudes and only after that, in the second article, does he take up the issue of whether God can know more.

In the first article, Holcot addresses his disagreement with Chatton. For reasons we have already canvassed, Holcot rejects as implausible Chatton's account of "things" as truth-bearers and objects for propositional attitudes. Accordingly, he concludes his discussion in the first article by defending (what he takes to be) Ockham's position, namely, the view that sentence tokens are the primary bearers of truth and the immediate objects of belief and knowledge.[37] In the second article, when Holcot turns to the question about whether God can know more, Ockham becomes his target of criticism. As we have already seen, Holcot holds that Ockham's account of God's knowledge is inconsistent with his broader, token-sententialist account of truth-bearers. As Holcot sees it, Ockham has simply misapplied his own theory of propositions to this question about God's knowledge. Holcot's central aim in article 2, therefore, is to demonstrate the inconsistency in Ockham's account and to correct it. In this regard, he takes himself to be defending the true "Ockhamist" position—that is, the position to which he believes Ockham himself is committed.

The problem Holcot identifies for Ockham's account has to do with the first of Ockham's two conclusions (i.e., step 4 in his argument), namely, the claim that God cannot know a greater *quantity* of truths. As we have seen Ockham's defense of this conclusion turns on his contention that the quantity of truths is constant at all times since one or the other of a pair of contra-dictories is always true. As Holcot sees it, however, this line of reasoning violates Ockham's own principles. As he explains:

Each of these claims, namely, that "one part of a contradiction is always false" and "there are always equally many true things, so that there are not sometimes less and sometimes more" are false. This is the case given two other claims that belong to this doctor, namely, [his claim that] "everything true is an existing thing (*esse*)" and that "only a sentence is true, whether it is a concept, something written, or a spoken utterance."[38]

Given Ockham's own views about the nature of truth-bearers, Holcot insists, there is no reason to suppose that the number of truths will be fixed at all times. For, if what Ockham is calling "truths" are token sentences (spoken, written, or mental), the quantity of truths must be changing constantly, namely, with every sentence spoken, every thought entertained (or dismissed), with every line penned (or erased). And, as Holcot goes on to point out, there is simply no reason to think that each existing truth comes paired with its contradictory. As he explains, "it is possible that some sentence is true but has no [existing] contradictory"[39]; or again "it is possible that there could be a thousand true sentences to contradict one false sentence."[40] Given these sorts of considerations, Ockham's claim that the number of truths always remains the same over time appears utterly unfounded.

In article 2, therefore, Holcot goes on to offer the answer he thinks Ockham himself should have given:

In this article, I argue otherwise [than Ockham himself did]: [First, I claim] that God can know something that he does not know, and can know both more than he knows and less than he knows. . . . Second, it must be said that, whenever I wish, I can make God not know many things that he [now] knows, and make him know many things that he does not [now] know. For if I say or think many true things, or set out in a book many true things, then it is certain that God knows all those things. Now suppose that I burn my book and fall asleep. All these truths will perish, and if they cease to exist, they cease to be true, and as a consequence they cease to be known by God.[41]

Obviously, if God's knowledge extends to all truths, and truths are nothing other than true sentences tokens, God's knowledge involves a relation to entities that are constantly coming into and out of existence. Indeed, as Holcot says here, the number of things God knows increases whenever we write something down, and decreases whenever we go to sleep (since this reduces the number of mental sentence tokens). Thus, God can know not only more than he knows, but also less than he knows. In fact, as Holcot goes on to point out, "even this is possible: *God knows nothing.*"[42] After all, "it is possible for nothing to be true."[43] What all this shows, Holcot concludes, is that "on Ockham's own view it ought to be granted that God can know more than he knows."[44]

Unlike Ockham, Holcot provides an account of divine knowledge that is perfectly consistent with a broader, token-sententialist theory of propositions. Even so, Holcot's discussion of God's knowledge calls attention to a number of difficulties with that broader theory.[45] Not only does Holcot's token sentialism about propositions seem incompatible with divine immutability (since the view entails that God could know more than he knows now, less than he knows now, or even nothing at all), but it also seems incompatible with commonsense views about propositional attitudes. How, for example, can entities as ephemeral and transient as utterance tokens or thought tokens serve as objects for attitudes which seem to persist over long periods of time? If, as Holcot supposes, belief, knowledge and every other propositional attitude involves a relation to some token utterance (or inscription, or mental sentence), it follows that what we know (believe, etc.) is constantly changing as such tokens go into and out of existence. Yet, knowledge and beliefs are states that persist over extended durations—not only in God's case, but in humans' too.

Again, even supposing it could be shown that token sentences are suitable objects for belief and knowledge, there are further problems. To see why, note first of all that we need some explanation of precisely which of all the relevant existing tokens are supposed to serve as the object of a given act of belief or knowledge. In God's case, the answer is easy enough: insofar as God is omniscient his knowledge relates him to all true sentence tokens. But what about the case of human knowers? It appears that, on Holcot's view, any sort of token—that is, any written, spoken, or mental sentence—may serve as the object for an act of believing or knowing. Indeed, as Holcot's remarks about the objects of God's knowledge make clear, the token believed by a subject need not be one uttered, written, or thought by the believing subject herself. But if this is right, then, we need some explanation of precisely which of the relevant existing tokens functions as the object for a given act of believing. Suppose, for example, I form the belief that a triangle is a three-sided figure.

Which among the class of suitable sentence tokens will serve as the object for this belief? Surely, not all of them. But, if not all of them, what will be the criterion for including some rather than others in a class of equally suitable candidates? How can the answer be anything other than arbitrary?[46]

In light of these sorts of considerations, Holcot's discussion of God's knowledge, and the theory of propositions on which it rests, turns out to be every bit as puzzling as those developed by Chatton and Ockham.

Making Sense of the Debate

By now it should be clear that this theological dispute over God's knowledge serves for Ockham and his colleagues as a context for addressing purely philosophical issues about the nature of the entities which function as objects of propositional attitudes generally. At the same time, it should also be clear just how puzzling the general theories that emerge from this discussion are. One might be forgiven for wondering whether they are even coherent. In what follows, I propose a way of reading these accounts that not only renders them coherent, but also defensible—at least against the sorts of difficulties discussed in the previous section.

Ockham on Objects of Knowledge Revisited

As we have seen, Ockham's account of divine knowledge in d. 39 is difficult to reconcile with the account of truth-bearers he develops in other contexts. In particular, his contention that the quantity of truths known by God never varies looks to be incompatible with a token-sententialist theory of truth-bearers. Nor are matters improved, as I have argued, by reading Ockham's claim about the fixed quantity of truths as evidence of a commitment to sentence types. But then what is the alternative?

As it turns out, there is a fairly straightforward way to resolve the apparent conflict in Ockham's account. To see what it is, we may begin by noting that Ockham's claim about the quantity of truths being fixed conflicts with his broader token sententialism *only* if he intends that claim to range over *all* true sentence tokens. But why should we suppose that he intends this? When Ockham argues in the context of d. 39 that "the number of truths never varies," it is natural to assume that the "truths" he has in mind are just those that serve as objects for God's knowledge. Of course, if God's knowledge relates him to every true sentence token (written, spoken, or mental), this qualification will do nothing to restrict the scope of the claim. But, again, why should we suppose that Ockham thinks divine knowledge is a relation to all true tokens? Admittedly, Ockham does claim that (1) sentence tokens are the primary bearers of truth (and falsity), and, likewise, that (2) God, insofar as he is omniscient, knows every truth. But these two claims do not by themselves entail a commitment to the further claim that (3) God's omniscience consists in relation to every true sentence token. Indeed, given that this further claim conflicts with Ockham's claim about the fixed quantity of truths, there is good reason for thinking he is not committed to it. As I understand Ockham, therefore, God's omniscience does not consist in a relation to *every* existing true sentence token, but rather just to a proper subset of them—namely, those that are tokened in his own mental language.

This way of reading Ockham provides a means for reconciling his sententialism about truth-bearers with his claims in d. 39 about the quantity of truths known by God. For, on this interpretation, Ockham's claim (in premise 2 of my reconstruction of the argument) that God knows every truth asserts nothing more than that God stands in the relation of knowing to every true sentence in his own language of thought. Accordingly, when Ockham goes on to assert (in premise 3) that the number of truths never varies, the "truths" in question are those which serve as objects of divine knowledge. Unlike other sentence tokens, however, sentences in the mind of God, insofar as they depend for their existence on God's eternal act of thinking, do not come into nor go out of existence—they exist at all times. On this interpretation, therefore, Ockham can conclude quite plausibly that the quantity of truths known by God does not change.

Clearly, then, we have a way of making sense of Ockham's discussion in d. 39 without appealing to sentence types. Not only that, but this way of reading him also squares with what I take to be his overarching views about propositional attitudes and, in particular, his conception of the role played by the "object" of propositional attitude relations. I have argued in great detail elsewhere that Ockham conceives of knowledge, belief, and other propositional attitudes as the holding of a relation between a mental act or state (i.e., the subject's act of knowing, believing, etc.), on the one hand, and its representational content, on the other. Thus, for Ockham, the items which function as objects for propositional attitudes are what we might think of as "*content* objects"—that is, as items which function both as the object (or *relatum*) of propositional attitude relations and as representational content of the acts or attitudes relating to them.[47] Given this way of thinking about propositional attitudes and their objects, it should be clear why Ockham would suppose that only a subset of existing sentence tokens function as objects for divine knowledge (or belief etc.). After all, linguistic tokens (whether written, spoken, or mental) produced by creatures surely do not supply the representational contents of God's knowledge. The *only* token entities which could plausibly be thought to function as content objects for divine knowledge are token thoughts in the mind of God himself. Indeed, in general, it would seem that the only sentence tokens that *could* serve as representational contents for attitudes such as knowledge, belief, etc. are just those that occur in the subject's own language of thought. It is no doubt for this same reason that Ockham, in contexts outside of d. 39, often argues explicitly for the view that the objects of knowledge and belief are mental entities—namely, *mental* sentences.[48]

In light of all of this, we can now see that Ockham's discussion of God's knowledge in d. 39 is not only perfectly coherent, but is also perfectly consistent with his broader nominalist (and token-sentientialist) proclivities. For, given Ockham's broader analysis of propositional attitudes, it should by now be clear that, for him, God's knowing every truth does not entail that God stands in the relation of knowing to every existing true sentence token; rather, all it entails is that God's mental language include a representation of all possible states of affair (paired as contradictories) and that, at any given moment, God stands in the relation of knowing to just those representations (i.e., those tokens of his mental language) that are, at that moment, true.

Chatton on Objects of Knowledge Revisited

Returning now to Chatton's discussion, recall that the central difficulty with his account was not that of identifying the theory propositions it presupposes, rather the difficulty is in understanding why Chatton would want to hold such a theory in the first place. Once again, however, the solution lies in getting clear about Chatton's conception of propositional attitudes and the role he assigns to the objects of such attitudes.

Just as Ockham's discussion of God's knowledge comes into focus once we recognize that he is supposing that objects of knowledge are *content* objects, so too, I now want to suggest, much of Chatton's discussion falls into place once we read it as an account of what we might call the *referential* objects of God's knowledge. Though distinct from the notion of a content object, the notion of a referential object is closely connected to it. To see how, simply note that there is a connection between the way a belief represents the world as being (i.e., its content) and what it is that is thusly represented. We might think of the latter as the belief's "referent." Understood in this way, the object of a given propositional attitude is not to be identified with its representational content, but rather with that object to which the attitude relates *in virtue of* its content. In order to distinguish this notion of object from that operative in Ockham's discussion, let us call it the "referential object" of the attitude.

When read as an account of the *referential* objects of propositional attitudes, much of what initially seems puzzling in Chatton's discussion begins to make sense. For example, his central contention that nonlinguistic, nonmental *things* function as objects for propositional attitudes now appears much more plausible. For, read in this way, Chatton merely means to be offering an account of what propositional attitudes are *about* or directed at in virtue of their content. Thus, for him, the object or *relatum* of a given propositional act or attitude is just the entity that is represented by it; it is that which is believed, known—or otherwise judged—*about*. Thus, for example, on Chatton's view, the belief that *Socrates is pale* has Socrates for its object.[49] Understood this way, Chatton's claim that individual, concrete *things* function as objects for propositional attitudes looks far less controversial.[50]

But what about Chatton's willingness to refer to the *things* to which God's knowledge relates as "truths"? What sense is there in saying that nonlinguistic, nonmental, things are truths? Indeed, what notion of truth could even apply to them? I think we can begin to make sense of Chatton's way of speaking if we note that Chatton is thinking of individual things not only as the *referents* for acts of belief and or knowledge (and for the sentences which express them), but also as what corresponds to them and, hence, as what makes them true. Thus, Chatton is supposing that the entity which serves as the object and referent of a given attitude is also that in virtue of which it is true (when it is true). Although this claim, namely, that beliefs (or the sentences which express them) are made true by the individual things to which they refer may be contentious, it nevertheless does provide a basis for explaining why Chatton should think there is a sense in which such things are appropriately called "truths." Chatton is very likely adopting the

Aristotelian notion that certain expressions can have "focal meaning"—that is, can apply to different things in different, but related senses.[51] Thus, just as food or exercise can be called "healthy" in virtue of causing or being generally productive of health so too, nonlinguistic, nonmental *things* can called "true" or "truths" insofar as such things are truth-makers.

So far so good. But as yet, it may still seem unclear why Chatton holds that the truths to which God's knowledge relates are such that they are true at all times. After all, even if there is a sense in which "truth" can be applied to things one might still wonder why Chatton holds the predicate applies to it at all times. Yet this is precisely what he does say. Consider, for example, his remarks in the following passage:

> It is impossible that something ever (*unquam*) be signified by a true sentence without now (*modo*) being signified by a true sentence. For the same thing that is signified by an affirmative sentence is also signified by its negative contradictory. And, from the fact that it is impossible to prevent one or the other of [a pair of] contradictories from being true, it follows, therefore, that whatever *can be* signified by a true sentence is now signified by a true sentence. And since this is [a thing's] being true (*Et cum hoc sic esse verum*), it is therefore impossible for God know something [that is, some *true thing*] that he does not now know.[52]

As we have already seen, Chatton claims that the things to which true sentences refer can themselves be said to be true insofar these things ground the truth of that sentences. Interestingly, Chatton also seems to think that everything that exists is at all times the referent of some true sentence. His argument for this claim takes its start from the following assumptions: (1) contradictory sentences refer to one and the same thing and (2) that for every existing entity, there exists a pair (at least) of contradictory sentences which refer to it.[53] But since at all times one or the other of a pair of contradictories is true, it follows that "whatever can be signified by a true sentence is now signified by a true sentence." Hence, if truth applies at any time to some thing, it applies to it all times and, so, the number of true *things* will not vary over time.

Admittedly, this argument calls attention to a number of further questions about Chatton's account that I cannot pursue further here—in particular, questions about the precise ontological status of sentences and of the objects signified by them. Even so, what I have said so far is, I think, sufficient to resolve the *prima facie* difficulties associated with his theory about the objects of knowledge. For we can now see that his account as a whole is motivated by the assumption that the "objects" of propositional attitudes are just those items to which such attitudes refer or which they are about.

Holcot on Objects of Knowledge Revisited

Recall that Holcot's attempt to treat sentence tokens as objects of knowledge faces at least two difficulties. First, it seems implausible to suppose that persisting states such as knowing, believing, etc. involve relations to objects as ephemeral and transient as spoken, written, and mental sentence tokens; second, there seems to be no nonarbitrary means of specifying precisely which of any class of relevant tokens is the object for a given act or attitude. Once again, however, the key to resolving these difficulties lies in getting clear about the role "objects" play in Holcot's account of propositional attitudes.

The first difficulty can be handled simply by recognizing that for Holcot, as for Chatton, objects of propositional attitudes do not function as content objects. Clearly, it *would* be absurd to suppose that a mental state's having a given representational content is to be explained in terms of a relation to entities which are constantly coming and going out of existences (as are utterances and thought-tokens). Such a view would seem to entail that the content of my knowledge and belief is changing constantly—which is obviously false. But, so long as Holcot does not take sentence tokens to function as the content objects of propositional attitudes his account entails no such thing.

That Holcot does not take sentence tokens to function as content objects is evident from a variety of claims he makes about the nature of God's knowledge. Holcot, as we have already noted, maintains that the quantity of truths (i.e., quantity of existing, true, written, spoken, and mental sentence tokens) changes over time and, hence, that the number of truths known by God also changes over time. But, as Holcot is well aware, this raises questions about divine immutability. Does not his view violate the traditional doctrine? Holcot explicitly addresses this worry, and his reply is significant:

> When it is said that God's knowledge cannot be increased or diminished, I grant this, since his knowledge is his essence. Nevertheless, that knowledge sometimes knows more and sometimes less given that there are

sometimes more true things (and, as a result, more knowable things) and sometimes there are fewer.[54]

As Holcot sees it, to say that God can know more or less than he does is just to say that God can be related by his single, everlasting act of knowing to more or fewer objects. But, as he seems to be saying here, this entails nothing about the content of what he knows.[55] In fact, Holcot allows that even if no one had ever formed a sentence at all, the content of God's knowledge would be just what it is now.

> God by knowing his own essence knows every truth. Thus, supposing that no sentence existed [about, say, triangles], God would in that case know no less about triangles than he knows now, although he would not have known as *many truths* about triangles.[56]

Thus, which objects God's knowledge relates him to makes no difference to the content of his knowledge.[57]

But if sentence tokens do not function as content objects, then how are they functioning? Are we to take them as "referential objects"? Understood this way, Holcot's view would be that sentence tokens function merely as those objects *about which* a subject believes or knows (e.g., when she believes or knows that that token is true). Although some of Holcot's remarks do suggest this interpretation, in the end, I think we must resist it. After all, if Holcot conceives of objects of propositional attitudes as *referential objects*, his objections to Chatton's lose much of their force. If the objects of belief are just those objects *about* which we form beliefs and judgment, then Chatton's contention that individuals can function as objects of the attitudes would hardly be objectionable. In fact, Holcot's own position (on this reading) would seem far less plausible than Chatton's since it entails that our beliefs (etc.) are always directed at sentences. Yet, there's no reason to think that all or even the majority of our thoughts or beliefs are about or directed at sentence tokens.

But if Holcot's objects of belief are neither content objects nor referential objects, what else could they be? In order to answer this question, as well as to see what Holcot has in mind when he speaks of objects of propositional attitudes, consider again the sorts of claims Holcot makes about the objects of God's knowledge. As we have noted already, Holcot holds that since God's act of knowing relates him to every true proposition, the question of which objects God knows is a completely contingent matter—having to do only with what true sentence tokens happen to exist at a given time. One of his favorite ways of calling attention to this fact is by pointing out that he himself can, if he so desires, alter what God knows. We have already seen him make this point in a passage cited earlier, but compare also the following remarks:

> Suppose that I order the sentence "Socrates runs" to be written in a thousand places (and that it is the case [that Socrates runs] in the truth of reality). . . . Say I likewise order the sentence "Socrates does not run" (which is false) in one place alone. . . . Suppose then that Socrates sits down. Assuming the truth of all other sentences remains fixed, it follows necessarily that God knows less than he knew—by 999 sentences. For of those 1000 sentences that he once knew, he now knows, *de novo*, only one.[58]

While Holcot's radical way of stating the view does not contribute much to its *prima facie* plausibility, it does give us some clues about the alternative notion of object that he has in mind. Clearly, Holcot wants to say that because God is omniscient, he stands in the knowledge relation to every presently existing true proposition. And if we ask what it is about God's act of knowledge, on the one hand, and (true) sentence tokens, on the other, that explains the obtaining of this relation, Holcot seems to have a perfectly natural explanation to hand. A propositional attitude relation is one that obtains between a given mental state and an object just in case that object expresses—or, we might say, *encodes*—the representational content of the state in question.

Thus, to say that God stands in the knowledge relation to every true sentence is just to say that every existing true sentence token is such that it specifies or encodes (some portion of) the representational content of God's (single) act of knowing. Holcot puts it this way: "God is [in virtue of his act of knowing] equivalent to every sentence that would be true if it existed."[59] This claim makes perfect sense if we suppose (as Holcot does) that every existing true sentence token is such that it encodes (some part of) the representational content of God's knowledge—every such token is "equivalent in signification" to one of God's acts of knowing (or, more accurately, to some aspect of his one, eternally existing knowledge state). Thus, what is "known" by God are certain linguistic objects—namely, those sentences that are equivalent in signification to God's act of knowing.[60] And, according to Holcot, every existing true sentence token is of this sort.[61] Of course, inasmuch as the sentences that do the encoding are entities that come into and go out of existence and change their truth-value over time, Holcot is forced to allow that God's eternal act of knowing does not always relate him to the same objects. Hence, as we have seen, Holcot thinks that divine "knowledge sometimes knows more and sometimes less given that there are sometimes more things (and, as a result, more knowable things) and sometimes there are less."[62]

Recognizing that sentence tokens function on Holcot's account as what we might call "encoding objects" also provides the resources for resolving the second of the two difficulties for his account, namely, the problem of specifying, in a nonarbitrary way, which among the class of relevant tokens is the object for a given act or attitude. In fact, by now, the answer should be clear: a given state of belief or knowledge (or other attitude) will relate to *every* token that encodes its content. Thus suppose, for example, that at time t1, S believes that triangles have three sides. And suppose further that at t1, S utters assertively the sentence "triangles have three sides." This token utterance will, on Holcot's view, be an object of S's belief since it encodes the content of that belief. But, S's utterance at t1 need not be the only object of her belief.

> When I know this token sentence (formed by me): *A Triangle has three [sides]*, then I know (or am truly said to know) another equivalent sentence formed by you, since that one [viz. yours] is equivalent in its signification to this one [of mine].[63]

Even in the case of human (or non-divine) subjects, therefore, the relation of believing or knowing is conceived by Holcot to obtain between a token and a subject just in case that token encodes the content of the subject's belief state. And, as he makes clear in this passage, it is perfectly possible that there may be more than one object of her belief. Indeed, any tokens that are "equivalent in signifying," as Holcot describes them here, will be counted among the objects of the belief. For such tokens are, according to Holcot, equally said to be the objects believed by her. Even with human beings, therefore, it will often be the case that a subject is related by a single act of knowing or believing to a plurality of objects. Hence, if tokens are in fact functioning on Holcot's account as encoding objects, there is an obvious and nonarbitrary way of specifying which, among the relevant class of suitable tokens, will be the objects for a given propositional attitude: all of them. Clearly, therefore, if we read Holcot along these lines, we are in a position not only to resolve the main difficulties for his account, but also to see why the claims which initially seemed so radical are, in fact, not so very radical at all.

Broader Implications

Obviously, there's much more that could be said about Ockham, Chatton, and Holcot's (respective) theories as well as about the debate as a whole. The purpose of my discussion, however, has not been to provide an exhaustive treatment of the debate, or even to resolve all the difficulties associated with the theories that emerge from it. Rather, my purpose has been merely to find a way of rendering their discussions intelligible. If the argument of the preceding section is correct, however, it should be clear that doing so requires that we be clear about the precise role played by "objects" in these thinkers' analyses of propositional attitudes. What is more, if my argument is correct, it turns out that there are no less than three different notions of object at issue in the context of this single debate about God's knowledge. Although this is perhaps a surprising result, the explanatory power of the interpretation itself counts strongly in its favor. After all, this way of reading the debate goes a long way toward resolving the puzzles and difficulties it presents. I can, moreover, think of no other way of making sense of the various claims Ockham and his colleagues make either about God's knowledge or about propositional attitudes in general.

If my interpretation is correct, however, it also has significant implications about our understanding of the later medieval debate about propositions as a whole. Until now, scholarship on medieval discussions of propositions has typically proceeded on the assumption that when medieval philosophers debate questions about the objects of belief, knowledge, and other propositional attitudes, they employ the notion of "object" in a single, univocal sense. As a consequence, commentators have generally assumed that medieval theories of propositions can be classified simply in terms of the ontological *type* or *category* of entity introduced to serve as the object for propositional attitudes.[64] Indeed, according to the scheme now standard in the secondary literature, medieval theories of propositions are divided into three main categories: "*complexum* theories," namely, theories that take objects of propositional attitudes to be complex linguistic expressions (i.e., sentences); "*res* theories," namely, theories which hold that "things" (i.e., ordinary substances) are objects for the attitudes; and "*complexe-significabile* theories," which argue for the introduction of some *sui generis* entity.[65]

Given what we have now seen, however, it should be clear that this standard tripartite taxonomy is far too coarse-grained to capture what's really going on. Not only does it fail to capture the nature of the various theories on offer, but it also misrepresents the structure of the debate itself. Because these thinkers are often operating with a different conception of what it is for is for something to be an object of a propositional attitude they are also often operating with very different conceptions of the nature of propositional attitude relations. It follows, therefore, that any taxonomy that classifies positions in the debate solely in terms of the ontological type to which the objects of such relations belong will be inadequate. In order to properly understand the nature of the various positions within the debate, we must first get clear about what each thinker means to be offering a theory of. And this requires developing a classificatory scheme capable not only of sorting theories according to the ontological type of object introduced by each, but also—and, perhaps, more importantly—of sorting them according to the theoretical role such objects play in an account of propositional attitudes. Only then will we be in a position to understand the differences among the various theories or to assess their respective merits. Indeed, as we have just seen in the debate between Ockham and his colleagues, it is only by getting clear about the precise role played by objects of propositional attitudes that we are able to arrive at a coherent interpretation of their accounts respectively.

Not only will a more refined taxonomy yield a better understanding of the nature of various theories on offer in this debate, it will also yield a rather different picture of relationship between various positions within the debate. Indeed, what we will find, I suspect, is that philosophers previously supposed to be on opposite sides of the debate—and even those typically thought be on the same side—turn out not to be disagreeing (or, for that matter, agreeing) at all, but merely (and perhaps unbeknownst to themselves) talking past one another.[66] To see this, consider what we have just seen in the debate between Ockham, Chatton, and Holcot over whether God can know more. A moment's reflection makes clear that Ockham and his colleagues may not actually disagree either about the nature of the objects of God's knowledge or about the nature of propositions generally. Indeed, to the extent that each thinker approaches this particular debate with his own, distinct conception of the nature of propositional attitude relations as well as a distinct conception of the role played by the objects of such relations, the theories they develop are not necessarily competing theories at all. In principle, one could hold all three views in conjunction without any inconsistency. In such a case, one would simply be holding one view about the nature of the entities which function as the representational content of propositional attitudes, a second view about the items which encode that content, and a third about the nature of the entities to which such attitudes refer in virtue of their content. Clearly, therefore, the mere fact that Ockham, Chatton, and Holcot introduce entities of different ontological type to serve as objects for propositional attitudes does not entail any disagreement between them. Of course, none of this is to say that there are not genuine disputes among later medieval philosophers on questions about objects of propositional attitudes (indeed, Ockham and his colleagues clearly disagree about is *what it is for something to be the object* of propositional attitudes), but it does make clear that understanding where these disagreements occur and precisely what the disagreements are will require more caution in how we identify them.[67]

8

The Power of Medieval Logic

TERENCE PARSONS

Aristotelian logic has been very well studied. By "Aristotelian logic" I mean the system of logic that appeared in logic texts in the nineteenth and twentieth centuries under that name. It consists primarily of conversion principles and principles for judging the validity of syllogisms. The theorems of this system are theorems of the monadic first-order predicate calculus. It is known to be inadequate for many very important logical applications since relational statements cannot be formulated in the system. So "Aristotelian logic" is an unflawed but importantly incomplete system.

What about medieval logic? Is it also unflawed? Is it also incomplete? How incomplete? This seems like a natural question to ask, and it is the topic of this paper. It turns out to be a somewhat complicated issue.

What Is Medieval Logic?

The first task is to decide what to count as medieval logic. Medieval logic consists of centuries of work by some very smart people working in a difficult area. I will be libertine about what is included in medieval logic. If any medieval logician ever said it, and if it is worthwhile, it is part of medieval logic.

Conversions and Syllogisms

The first thing to look at, of course, is the logic passed down to the medievals by Aristotle (Aristotle's logic,[1] not nineteenth-century "Aristotelian logic"). The best-known parts of this are the principles of conversion and of the syllogism:

> Example of conversion: *Some A is B ≈ Some B is A.*
> Example of a syllogism:[2] *Every P is M*

Some S is not M
∴ *Some S is not P*

These parts of Aristotle's logic are extremely important, but highly limited. This is because the logic that Aristotle formulates is limited to exactly four very specific forms of propositions:

Every S is P
No S is P
Some S is P
Some S is not P

Conversions and syllogisms involve propositions of these forms, and no others. There is no hope of considering additional inferences within it, inferences such as:

Some donkey sees every cleric
∴ *Every cleric is seen by some donkey (or other)*

However, Aristotle contributed much more than this. I have in mind the principles of reasoning that Aristotle himself actually used, most of which he used self-consciously, and that he identified and discussed. These principles are *much more* important to the potential of medieval logic than the conversions and syllogisms. The prominent examples of such principles are what Aristotle called *reductio* and what he called exposition (Greek *ecthesis*).

Reductio

The principle of *reductio* is this: if you want to prove a given proposition, it suffices to assume its contradictory and then derive an absurdity. To apply this principle you need to know a contradictory of the proposition you are trying to prove, because that is what you will assume, and you also need to know what an absurdity is. As for contradictories, Aristotle himself (*On Interpretation* 7) specified that:

Every X is Y contradicts *Some X is not Y*
Some X is Y contradicts *No X is Y*

An absurdity is the contrary or contradictory of a premise, or an assumption, or of something you have previously proved. The contradictories have just been given. The contraries are:

Every X is Y and *No X is Y*

Here is a *reductio* argument. It is Aristotle's proof of conversion of particular affirmatives from the already established conversion of universal negatives:[3] the task is to show that from *Some A is B* one may infer *Some B is A*. The job is to fill in the lines in a proof of this form:

1 | *Some A is B*
   |————

   |

   |

4 | *Some B is A*

(I use here the modern lines-and-bars notation to keep track of premises and conclusion. For Aristotle, this is all implicit. He just states things, and leaves it up to the reader to keep track of their status. The lines-and-bars notation is one way among many to explicitly keep track.)

The proof is by *reductio;* you assume the contradictory of what you are trying to prove, and then you show that that contradictory is false by deriving something absurd from it.

1 | *Some A is B*
   |————

2 || *No B is A*   ← assume the contradictory of line 4
   ||————
   ||

3 || ← get something absurd here
4 | *Some B is A*

We are considering a point in Aristotle's reasoning where he has already proved the principle of conversion for universal negatives, so he can use this in the proof. So from the assumption of the subproof—line 2—we can infer line 3:

1 | *Some A is B*
   |————

2 || *No B is A*
   ||————

3 || *No A is B* ← from line 2 by conversion of universal negative

4 | *Some B is A* ← line 3 contradicts line 1, so *reductio* is complete

And the proof is done. For line 3 is the contradictory of line 1. Line 3 is "absurd" *because* it contradicts line 1.

We see here that the key both to setting up the *reductio* and to knowing when you have reached something absurd is knowing when two propositions contradict one another. And here is one place where Aristotle's logic is so limited; we are told what contradicts what, one propositional form at a time, and we are only given this information about the four forms of proposition that occur in the square of opposition. Two pairs of contradictory forms are given, and that is all.

Fortunately, medieval authors had ways to expand the stock of contradictory propositions, so as to give the *reductio* technique much broader application.

Contradictories and Equipollences

Medieval logicians vastly expanded the stock of contradictories. One fundamental useful principle was this general doctrine that applies to a proposition *P* of any form:[4]

Not P contradicts *P*   (for any proposition *P*)

This looks fundamental to us, but it needed recognition by medieval logicians to make the technique of *reductio* be widely available. This, however, is too limited, because it only applies to pairs of propositions in which one of the propositions is the other one preceded by *Not*. We need additional forms of contradictories. This was done using the medieval analogue of what we call quantifier exchange principles. We have these exchange principles in modern logic:

$$\forall x \approx \sim\exists x \sim$$
$$\exists x \approx \sim\forall x \sim$$

Assuming that the available quantifier signs are *every*, *some*, and *no*, William Sherwood gives a verse whose lines consist of triples of equipollent signs. According to this verse, each of these combinations of symbols may be substituted for any other on the same line, for any denoting phrase in the proposition (so long as the result is grammatical).[5]

every X	≈	*no X not*	≈	*not some X not*
no X	≈	*every X not*	≈	*not some X*
some X	≈	*not no X*	≈	*not every X not*
some X not	≈	*not no X not*	≈	*not every X*

It is inevitable that some such principles be posited, since otherwise the three quantifier words *every*, *some*, and *no* are just unrelated signs. You either posit these "definitions" or else you posit some logical rules that let you prove them. The following use of equipollents was clearly presupposed: if A contradicts B, and if B differs from C only by an interchange of equipollent expressions, then A contradicts C. We now have available many cases of contradictories. Examples are:

Every A is B contradicts	*Some A is not B*
Not every A is not B contradicts	*No A is B*
No A is not B contradicts	*Some A is not B*

The first pair of contradictories was stipulated by Aristotle; here it is derived from the stipulations about equipollent signs and the principle that *Not P* contradicts *P*. The other pairs go beyond Aristotle's limited notation in ways that medieval logicians were comfortable with, so they were in a position to make wider application of the *reductio* technique.

Exposition and Expository Syllogisms

Suppose that we want to prove the principle of conversion for particular affirmatives and we have not yet proved any of the conversion principles. Here is a way to do it. We want to show:

1 | *Some A is B*

4 | *Some B is A*

We can fill this in if we—using Aristotle's way of talking—"take one of the
As that is B, call it C":

1 | *Some A is B*
  |————————
2 | *C is A*   From 1: "take one of the As that is B; call it C"
3 | *C is B*
4 | *Some B is A*   From 2, 3

The "setting-out" on lines 2 and 3 Aristotle called exposition. Step 4 is
a kind of existential generalization; medieval philosophers called it "expository syllogism." The technique of proof used here is familiar to twenty-
first-century logicians. Given an existentially quantified proposition (that
is, a proposition beginning with *Some A*), produce an instance of it, using
a name that does not occur elsewhere in the proof. Then reason with
the instance in ordinary ways. After that, generalize away the inserted
name. Aristotle applies exposition to particular propositions, but medieval
writers could apply the principle to propositions that Aristotle did not use,
such as:

Some donkey not every animal is not
∴ *n is a donkey*
∴ *n not every animal is not*

Likewise, the accompanying expository syllogism could apply generally to
more complex propositions, such as:

n is a donkey
n some running animal is
∴ *Some donkey some running animal is*

With the techniques of *reductio*, exposition, and expository syllogism, supple-
mented by the quantifier sign equipollences, we are well on our way to
having a general logic.

Transitivity of Consequence

Aristotle also uses an assumption that he did not comment on, but which
was recognized and articulated in medieval times. This is that you can get a

good proof by stringing together good inferences. This is a major way in which you get complex proofs. Aristotle did it, and medieval authors formulated it: the principle of the transitivity of consequence:[6]

If A ∴ B is a good consequence, and B ∴ C is a good consequence, then A ∴ C is a good consequence.

Truth-Functional Logic

Aristotle had no truth-functional logic; in fact he seemed to be of the opinion that it did not exist.[7] But the Stoics had developed it, and it became part of the liberal arts curriculum, and was inherited by medieval logicians. I will take for granted that medieval logicians had all of propositional logic at their disposal.[8]

With all this in hand, we can use lots of modern proof techniques. For example, given principles of existential instantiation and generalization along with *reductio*, we can derive principles of universal instantiation and generalization, and these, along with truth-functional logic, are most of the principles that are needed for modern first-order predicate logic. But that is not the direction in which things proceeded.

Ascent and Descent

Brand new in late medieval times is the theory of ascent and descent, in which one can define what are now called "modes of supposition" as understood by Burley, Ockham, Buridan, and others.[9] There are three modes: Determinate, Distributive, and Merely Confused. Determinate has something to do with being existentially quantified with wide scope, and Distributive with being universally quantified (with either wide or narrow scope). These are the criteria that are usually given for them:

DETERMINATE

A term has Determinate supposition if you can descend under it to a disjunction of instances, and you can ascend from that disjunction back to the original. Equivalently, you can ascend from any instance. Illustration:

The term *donkey* has determinate supposition in *Some donkey is grey*, because you may "descend to"—that is, you may infer:

This donkey is grey <u>or</u> that donkey is grey <u>or</u> that donkey is grey <u>or</u> . . .

and you may ascend from any instance; for example, from:

that donkey is grey

you may infer:

Some donkey is grey

DISTRIBUTIVE

A term has Distributive supposition when you can descend under it to a conjunction of instances, but you may not ascend from any one instance. Illustration:

The term *donkey* has distributive supposition in *Every donkey is grey*, because you may "descend to"—that is, you may infer:

This donkey is grey <u>and</u> that donkey is grey <u>and</u> that donkey is grey <u>and</u> . . .

but you may not ascend from any instance; for example, from:

that donkey is grey

you may not infer:

Every donkey is grey

MERELY CONFUSED

A term has merely confused supposition when you may not descend in either of the above ways, but you may ascend.[10] Illustration:

The term *donkey* has merely confused supposition in *Every animal is a donkey*, because no descent is possible, but you may ascend from any instance; for example, from:

every animal is that donkey

you may infer:

Every animal is a donkey

Causes of the Modes of Supposition

These principles are not useful all by themselves, since they are usually taken to be definitions of the modes. For example, whether a term has determinate supposition is defined in terms of whether the ascents and descents behave as above. However, there is an independent theory about how quantifier signs and negations *cause* terms to have the various modes,[11] and this theory allows one to mechanically assess by inspection of the syntactic form what mode of supposition a term has (at least in many cases). For example, one common rule is that a negation distributes all main terms within its scope (unless they are already distributed, in which case it removes that distribution). With this and other principles you can often figure out the mode of supposition merely by inspection of the syntax, and then do the related inferences. This is very useful, since it licenses use of the corresponding ascents and descents.

With these principles come some more powerful ones. For example, if a term is distributed then you can descend to any *inferior* term under it, and if it is determinate or merely confused you can ascend to a *superior* term over it. Since *animal* is distributed in *Every animal is running* you can infer *Every donkey is running*, given that *donkey* is inferior to *animal* (given that the donkeys are included in the animals). And since *donkey* is determinate in *Some donkey is running* you can infer *Some animal is running* given that *animal* is superior to *donkey* (given that the animals include all the donkeys).[12]

Reflection on Conversion and Syllogisms

Earlier I suggested that Aristotle's conversion principles and syllogisms are too special to be of interest. That can now be rationalized. They can all be proved, and so they cease to have the fundamental position that they had for Aristotle. This was already the case for the conversion principles, since Aristotle himself proved them, and we can just repeat his proofs. As for the syllogisms, well, Aristotle assumed the argument forms Barbara and Celarent, and with these assumptions he proved the rest. Fortunately, medieval logicians had the resources to prove Barbara and Celarent, using the principle I just mentioned of descent to subterms under distributed terms:

Barbara is:

Every X is Y	*X* is distributed (by the sign *Every*)
Every Z is X	*Z* is inferior to *X*
∴ *Every Z is Y*	

Celarent is:

No X is Y	*X* is distributed (by the sign *No*)
Every Z is X	*Z* is inferior to *X*
∴ *No Z is Y*	

In addition to these principles are some others that allow you to infer a proposition with a term having determinate supposition from one having that same term with distributive supposition, and a proposition with merely confused supposition from one with the same term having determinate supposition.[13]

Generalizing: in late medieval times there were some prevailing logical principles used, articulated, discussed, and endorsed, from which all of the inherited logic could be derived as special cases. This logic included all modern principles of monadic propositional logic with identity[14] as well as analogues of rules for existential instantiation and generalization.

Reasoning with Relations

All of the terms we have discussed so far are monadic. What about relational terminology? Well, it is easy to introduce relational terminology; just write:

Socrates sees Brownie

This departs from standard propositional form by having a transitive verb rather than a copula, but it can be changed into:[15]

Socrates of-Brownie a seeing-thing is <In Latin the -*thing* is not present>

The *of* is there on the front of *Brownie* to indicate that it has accusative case; there is nothing logically complicated about *Brownie*. It is the *seeing-thing* that is complicated; this term must have a variable extension; in this sentence it consists of things that see Brownie, whereas in another sentence it will have to consist of things that see something else. This is a complication that I have not found discussed in the medieval literature, and this is a serious gap in their theorizing. However, it does not usually affect the inferences that are sanctioned.

So perhaps we can include relational terminology, but can we use it to make interesting inferences? Here is a famous test case; it is Demorgan's challenge, issued in 1860:[16]

> Given that *all horses are animals*, prove that *all heads of horses are heads of animals*.

Demorgan was sure that this was a solid inference, and he insisted rightly that it was not an Aristotelian syllogism, and could not be validated within purely syllogistic logic. Could it be handled within medieval logic?

The answer is "sort of." Here is a way to do it. The conclusion to be derived is:

Every head of-a horse is a head of-an animal

We must, of course, make an additional assumption. The conclusion we are trying to reach is a universal affirmative, and universal affirmatives have existential import. But the fact that every horse is an animal does not entail that there are any heads of horses. We need to make this an additional assumption. So our premises are:

1 *Every horse is an animal*
2 *Some head of-a horse is*

The argument goes as follows. A number of writers noted that if *A* is nonempty then a proposition of the form *every A is A* is automatically true. So from 2 we will have:

3 *Every head of-a horse is a head of-a horse*

Now if we merely apply the rule "from an inferior to a superior" and ascend from *horse* in the consequent to its superior *animal*, we have what we are after:

13 *Every head of-a horse is a head of-an animal*

May we ascend in this way? If we do, the proof is done. And we can ascend if we know that the term *head* is merely confused in the consequent of 3. And indeed *head is* merely confused there. But in a proof, you need a *principle* that will *tell* you that it is merely confused there. And we do not have such a principle. That is because this *horse* is a part of the complex term *head of a horse*, and the rules that I mentioned above about signs causing modes of supposition apply only to main terms, not to terms that are parts of other terms. So we are not in a position to get to the conclusion in this extremely simple way.

Still, there *is* a way to do the proof. The logic is more perspicuous if we put the verb last (as some authors tended to do); I will do this. So we have:

1 | *Every horse is an animal*
2 | *Some head of-a horse is*
| —————————————
3 | *Every head of-a horse a head of-a horse is*   from line 2
|
|
13 | *Every head of-a horse a head of-an animal is*

We can get the desired conclusion by a *reductio* argument. The proof takes the form:

1 | *Every horse is an animal*
2 | *Some head of-a horse is*
| —————————————
3 | *Every head of-a horse a head of-a horse is*   2
|
4 || *Not every head of a horse a head of an animal is* <assumption>
| |—————————————
| |
| |
| | ← GET A CONTRADICTION HERE
|
13 | *Every head of-a horse a head of-an animal is.*

Rules of equipollence applied to 4 give 5:

1 | *Every horse is an animal*
2 | *Some head of-a horse is*
| —————————————

3 | *Every head of-a horse a head of-a horse is*
  |

4 || *Not every head of-a horse a head of-an animal is*
  ||——————————————

5 || *Some head of-a horse every head*
     of-an animal is not   4 equipollences
  ||
  |

13 | *Every head of-a horse a head of-an animal is*

We now use exposition to get lines 6 and 7:

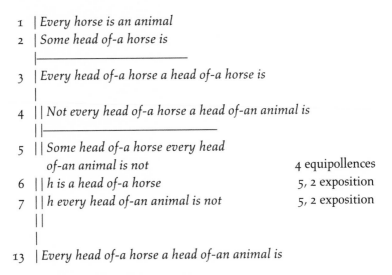

1 | *Every horse is an animal*
2 | *Some head of-a horse is*
  |——————————————

3 | *Every head of-a horse a head of-a horse is*
  |

4 || *Not every head of-a horse a head of-an animal is*
  ||——————————————

5 || *Some head of-a horse every head*
     of-an animal is not   4 equipollences
6 || *h is a head of-a horse*   5, 2 exposition
7 || *h every head of-an animal is not*   5, 2 exposition
  ||
  |

13 | *Every head of-a horse a head of-an animal is*

We now need one of those trivial moves that I have not seen discussed, but that would surely be appealed to in practice. It is the equivalence [*] of the phrase *h is a head of an F* with the phrase *h is of an F a head*.[17] We will use this twice. The first use is to get line 8:

1 | *Every horse is an animal*
2 | *Some head of-a horse is*
  |——————————————

3 | *Every head of-a horse a head of-a horse is*
  |

4	|| *Not every head of-a horse a head of-an animal is*	
	||———————————	
5	|| *Some head of-a horse every head*	
	of-an animal is not	4 equipollences
6	|| *h is a head of-a horse*	5, 2 exposition
7	|| *h every head of-an animal is not*	5, 2 exposition
8	|| *h is of a horse a head*	6 [*]
	||	
	|	
13	| *Every head of-a horse a head of-an animal is*	

Finally:[18]

1	| *Every horse is an animal*	
2	| *Some head of-a horse is*	
	|———————————	
3	| *Every head of-a horse a head of-a horse is*	
	|	
4	|| *Not every head of-a horse a head of-an animal is*	
	||———————————	
5	|| *Some head of-a horse every head*	
	of-an animal is not	4 equipollences
6	|| *h is a head of-a horse*	5, 2 exposition
7	|| *h every head of-an animal is not*	5, 2 exposition
8	|| *h is of a horse a head*	6 [*]
9	|| *h is of-an animal a head*	1,8 Infer. to super.
10	|| *h is a head of-an animal*	10 [*]
11	|| *every head of-an animal is not h*	7 equipollences
12	|| *h is not h*[19]	10,11 Universal App.
	|	12 is *absurd*
13	| *Every head of-a horse a head of-an animal*	

This proof was carried out without appeal to any special principles for relational predicates. Perhaps this should not be a surprise. After all, in the first-order predicate calculus there are no special principles for relations.

Instantiate—Reason—Generalize

Do we now have a system as adequate as the modern one? Here is where the "sort of" comes in. In symbolic logic courses students are given complex proofs to do, in which they make heavy use of the technique of "instantiate away the quantifiers, then use tautological logic a bit, and then generalize the quantifiers back on." This is done all the time. It is customarily taught. And so far as I can see, except for Aristotle's simple use of exposition, this technique was not widely used in the Middle Ages. I have argued that it could indeed be done, using accepted medieval principles, but it was rarely done in proofs more complicated than Aristotle's. So even if the resources were at hand, there is a kind of practice that was mostly unknown. Since the technique was theoretically there, one could say that it was there, and that this is not a way in which medieval logic fell short. But since it was an unpracticed kind of application, this is a way in which the logic, in practice, falls short.

What Can Be Formulated?

Here is another worry. We have seen that certain inferences concerning relations can be validated by means of principles that medieval logicians, in principle at least, had at their disposal. But this depended on the statements in question being formulable in the canonical notation. And here there remains a problem. One can formulate analogues of natural language claims, and perhaps account for logical relations among them. But predicate calculus logic allows, and uses, formulas that do not correspond to anything in natural language.

It would be nice to show that anything formulable in the predicate calculus can be duplicated within medieval logic. I do not know how to show that. But even if the medieval logic notation does not allow any old thing that can be formulated in predicate logic, it still might be adequate for some important applications. For example, suppose that medieval logic provides a framework within which mathematical claims can be formulated and theorems proved. This is something that predicate logic is valued for. Might medieval logic do this as well?

I will address this question in a preliminary way by asking whether some important mathematical notions are formulable within the logic. I propose two tests. One is whether Peano's Postulates can be formulated, and the other is whether the notion of transitivity can be formulated. The results follow below. In each case I give the proposition worded in the way it is usually stated. Then I give it a stilted reading that still captures what it is saying. Then there is a little change of word order (to a Latin form that is close to a form that medieval logicians might have used). Finally I give a formula in logical notation that I see as revealing a useful logical form that clarifies the logical relations meant by the proposition.

Peano's Postulates

ZERO IS A NUMBER

Zero is a number
Zero a number is
(Zero x)(a number y) x = y

ZERO IS NOT A SUCCESSOR OF A NUMBER

Zero isn't of-a number a successor
Zero not of-a number a successor is
(Zero x) not (a number y)(a successor-of-y z) x = z

EVERY SUCCESSOR OF A NUMBER IS A NUMBER

Of-every number every successor is a number
Of-every number every successor a number is
(every number x)(every successor-of-x y)(a number z) y = z

IF TWO NUMBERS HAVE THE SAME SUCCESSOR, THEY ARE IDENTICAL

Of-every number no successor of-some number other than it is a successor
Of-every number no successor of-some number other than it a successor is
(every number x)(no successor-of-x y)(of-some other-than-it number z) (a successor-of-z u) y = u

IF ZERO IS ϕ AND IF FOR EVERY NUMBER THAT IS ϕ ITS SUCCESSOR IS ϕ THEN EVERY NUMBER IS ϕ

IF	*(Zero x)ϕ[x]*
AND	*(every number-which$_x$-ϕ[x] y)(every successor-of y z)ϕ[z]*
THEN	*(Every number x)ϕ[x]*

Transitivity Stated

Every number exceeds every number which a number which it {the first number} exceeds exceeds.

> *Every number exceeds every number which a number which it exceeds exceeds*
>
> *Every number, every number which a number which it exceeds exceeds, exceeds*
>
> *(Every number x)(every {number which$_z$ (a {number which$_z$ (it u) u exceeds z} v) [z exceeds v]} y) x exceeds y*

I think that everything is fine with these symbolizations, with one exception. This is the need to use pronouns having antecedents, such as the *it* in the fourth Peano Postulate and in the statement of the transitivity of exceeding. I have not been able to find a way to avoid all such uses of pronouns. In predicate logic this would be no problem; we would just turn the *it* into a bound variable. But that is not possible within the medieval logic framework. The word *it* is a singular term on its own, and there are no variables to turn it into. When I use variables in the logical forms above, they are nonmedieval terminology that I insert for my own purposes, to represent invisible grammatical structure. A pronoun is not an invisible element.

What is lacking is clear; we need a theory of the logic of pronouns with antecedents. At least, we need a theory of pronouns that behave like bound variables in modern logic. There is a medieval theory of such terms, and it is not very helpful. All theorists agree that the kind of term corresponding to *it* in English is a term like any other, and it has a mode of supposition, just like other terms. The basic view seems to be that an anaphoric pronoun has the same mode of supposition as its antecedent,[20] though according to some theorists that mode is modified in some way. For example, Burley holds that a reflexive pronoun has a mode which adds "singulation" onto the mode of supposition of its antecedent, so that if its antecedent supposits confusedly and distributively, the pronoun has confused and distributive "singled" supposition.[21] This is said to affect how descent is carried out under the term. But the details are unclear. However, none of this matters from the point of view of the theory of inference, because there are two principles which seem to provide an adequate theory of inference for the type of pronouns we are concerned with here (for the "bound variable" type). The first principle, which is widely endorsed, is that if a pronoun has a singular term as its antecedent, the proposition containing the pronoun is equivalent to one in which the pronoun is replaced by a repetition of its antecedent.[22] The second principle is not explicitly endorsed by anyone that I have found, but it is uniformly employed. This is the principle that if the antecedent of a pronoun is instantiated, or generalized, then the pronoun remains unchanged, though its new antecedent is now whatever term replaces the term being instantiated or generalized.[23] Example: from the statement of transitivity for *exceeds*, together with the assumption that 3 is a number, one can universally instantiate under the first *number* to:

3 exceeds every number which a number which it exceeds exceeds

The *it* now has 3 as its antecedent instead of *every number*. By the principle governing pronouns with singular antecedents, this inferred proposition in turn entails:

3 exceeds every number which a number which 3 exceeds exceeds

This is correct, and the theory, developed in this way, seems to work well.

In conclusion, the logic that was practiced by medieval logicians is, from a contemporary perspective, rich and powerful. Unfortunately, its power was not exploited in detail by writers at the time, which must have been a factor in its gradually fading influence.

9

Iteration and Infinite Regress in Walter Chatton's Metaphysics

RONDO KEELE

Under the pressure of a foreign military campaign, soldiers will sometimes improvise weapons and armor for themselves with an alacrity unmatched by military engineers back home whose motivational level is affected by their more peaceful surroundings. So too for the soldier in medieval theological battles; sometimes in the heat of discussion there is innovation in argumentation that logicians outside the conflict never have time to catch up to.

For the most part, medieval logicians stayed up with the theologians. Many logical and semantic theories are well discussed by logicians in the Middle Ages and are in turn well used by philosophers, theologians, etc. To take an obvious example, categorical syllogistic was constantly discussed and developed as an explicit object of theory, and was also constantly used to display the validity of reasoning on every imaginable subject. Similarly, the idea of consequences in the late medieval period was systematized into rules and cases, and one often sees such rules actually referred to and applied in theological debates. To take two narrower examples, William of Ockham gives us a theory of truth conditions in his account of personal supposition, but also uses this theory as part of his rejection of universals existing outside the mind, and again, his treatment of connotation theory and his application of it against realist metaphysicians is legend.

By contrast, some logical theories are extremely well developed but are, strange to say, seldom applied, as far as we know. An obvious example would be *obligationes*. These elaborate rule systems for detecting and maintaining logical consistency were worked out, sometimes in remarkable detail, by diverse thinkers from the thirteenth to the fifteenth centuries; yet we still do not have a clear idea what the theory was for, that is, how it really applied to actual reasoning, if indeed it did.

I want to draw attention to a third category, as presaged in my military example above: namely, those argument strategies and patterns of reasoning which, although relied upon in difficult situations by philosophers and theologians, are nevertheless not explicitly discussed in logical theory; that is, patterns on whose logic medieval philosophers rely, but whose logic is, so to speak, unknown, or at least is relatively unknown. One argument strategy often used even today, but seldom explicitly analyzed, involves appeals to infinite regress. Philosophers have made arguments about the eternity of the world, about the existence of God, and the nature of language which have an appeal to infinite regress at their core, and yet apart from some attempts to distinguish vicious and nonvicious regresses, philosophers have seldom taken time to evaluate the epistemic weight of such appeals.

Walter Chatton used a complex and interesting argument strategy involving infinite regress, together with a kind of operational iteration. He uses this strategy in a couple of tight spots in doing his metaphysics, but the strategy receives no explicit development by him outside these contexts, nor, as far as I know, was it developed by anyone else. But he is clearly quite proud of this method; he relies on this iteration technique in two very different philosophical contexts, concerning issues very dear to his heart. I will examine these two applications of his iteration rule in reverse-chronological order, because the later one, in his c.1324–28 *Lectura*[1] discussion of the anti-razor, is in fact the clearer and more elaborate of the two. I will then apply what we learn there to an earlier instance of the same reasoning, exhibited in very condensed fashion in his c.1322 *Reportatio*[2] discussion of future contingents. Overall I will show that Chatton fairly successfully uses this strategy against an Ockhamist semantic analysis, but that he rather defends himself from this very same strategy, again successfully, in his discussion of future contingents. I intend to keep the philosophical background of the larger theological issues pared down the minimum needed for illuminating his iteration strategy. I wish to focus on the general, abstract, and common features in the reasoning itself, not the issues in which the reasoning is embedded.

The Anti-Razor

Our first case study comes from Chatton's defense of his anti-razor against certain Ockham-style objections.[3] Chatton's anti-razor is a principle for determining ontological commitment. Say we have a true proposition p, whose truth we want to use to help establish an ontology. Briefly, Chatton's anti-razor procedure is to ask how many instances of what kinds of things (*res*) would be required for the truth of p. We determine the answer to this basic question by thought experiment. If proposition p is about Plato and Socrates, say, then we know they must exist to make it true, but to go deeper we must also imagine that *only* Plato and Socrates exist, and then ask "Is this bare situation is consistent with the falsehood of p?" If it is, then Plato and Socrates alone are not enough to make p true, and we know more things are required in our ontology. Consequently, we must then posit whatever metaphysical items sensibly fill this ontological gap we have detected, and in general, if n entities aren't enough to make a sentence p true, we must posit an $n + 1$th entity, etc., until we have enough things such that they are inconsistent with the falsehood of p. (I find it useful to think of Chatton's anti-razor as a kind of *a priori* version of Mill's joint method; by controlled experiment we discover what things are necessary and sufficient to cause a proposition's truth.)

An informal example of how Chatton applied his anti-razor will help to clarify all this. Chatton believed that we had to posit the existence of certain kinds of real relations, in particular relations of causality, as distinct Aristotelian accidents inhering in individual substances.[4] Thus, if this light ray is caused by the sun, then we must certainly posit the ray and the sun, but Chatton believed the situation could only be fully explained by the existence of two other entities: (1) an active relational entity we could call *production* (=Latin *actio*), which inheres in the sun and "points to" the ray as its product; and (2) and passive relational entity *being produced* (=*passio*), which inheres in the light ray and "points to" the sun as its producer. Now the anti-razor is used to support this kind of realist ontology as follows. Imagine that nothing exists except the sun and a light ray, and that we have before us the proposition "This light ray is from the sun."[5] There is nothing which guarantees that these two distinct so-called absolute entities, ray and sun, have the right relationship so that the proposition "This light ray is from the sun" is true; that is, with only the ray and the sun existing, no part of reality speaks to the "producer/produced-relation" that the proposition asserts for these two absolute entities, ray and sun. Since the two-element ontology {ray, sun} is consistent with the falsehood of the proposition "This light ray is from the sun," this ontology is in general insufficient to guarantee its truth.

However, if we add to this ontology two respective accidents, one of *production* and one of *being produced,* as described above, then the ray and the sun would be related in such a way that the proposition would be true. Having completed this thought experiment, we deduce that, in the real world, where the proposition "This light ray is from the sun" is sometimes in fact true of certain light rays, there must in fact be such respective accidents (partially) causing the truth of the proposition. The intuitive center of Chatton's anti-razor is that whatever makes a difference to truth must be real, and since in our experiment respective accidents make a difference to truth, they must be real.

An interesting Ockham-style objection to this application of Chatton's ontological principle would say that propositions sometimes require more than just *things* (*res*) to make them true; sometimes, for example, they require instead that certain *conditions* be met. To put it briefly, Ockham certainly agreed with Chatton that while there must *be* in actuality all that is necessary to account for the truth of actually true propositions, he objected that, nevertheless, not everything that propositions require for their truth is therefore some *thing* in one of Aristotle's ten categories (i.e., a *res*). For example, Ockham objected that we do not need to posit an Aristotelian accident *motion* in order to explain the truth of "Object *a* moved," rather, we only need to posit the object *a* and the following three conditions:[6]

(i)   *a* was in a place and now is in another;
(ii) this change happened continuously and successively;
(iii) this change happened without any intervening rest on the part of *a*.

Ockham insists it is not the positing of more *things* (*res*) that clarifies the meaning of "motion" here, but rather the positing of more conditions on moving object *a,* and as conditions are not to be reified as *things,* we have clarified the truth conditions of the proposition without expanding our ontology. An ontology of one thing, together with these three conditions, does the same thing as a Chattonian ontology of two things.

Chatton must have had just such an Ockhamist objection in mind when he defended his anti-razor principle in the *Lectura,* for in that place he gives the following complex argument against the Ockhamist objection:

The following method ought to be used against these objections and against all other similarly derived objections. Whenever a new, added condition is designated by an objector as required for some original proposition p to be true, we ought simply to accept the condition, whether the proposition expressing it is affirmative or negative. We then ought to ask what things are required for the proposition expressing the condition to be true. Either: (1) the proposition requires n things such that it is inconsistent with the existence of these n things, equally present without another thing, that p be false, or, (2) not n things, but only fewer than n things are required . . . If the first alternative is the case, then I have the plurality I proposed. After all, the [anti-razor] already requires n things such that it is inconsistent with the existence of these n things, consistently present without another thing, that p be false; [therefore the anti-razor holds;] therefore, it is required to posit the *thing*, not just the proposed condition, to account for the truth of the proposition. If the second option is given, then I argue in this way: since fewer than n things, howsoever they are present without another, are consistent with the falsehood of the proposition, it follows that these things so present are not sufficient to account for the truth of it, and, consequently, besides the [first] added condition, it is required to posit yet another condition.

In that case, I accept the proposition that expresses this additional condition and I ask what things are required to account for *its* being true. Either as many things, present in a certain way without a new thing, as are consistent with p's being false, or as many things as are inconsistent with p's being false. If the second answer is given, then I have the plurality I originally proposed, since in order that it be true, this latest proposition requires that the condition be true, and the condition requires that just as many things be posited [as the anti-razor originally claimed were required]. But therefore the proposition requires that just as many things be posited [as the anti-razor originally claimed were required]. If the first answer is given, I then add that other condition, form its proposition, and ask about it, as previously, and so on to infinity.

Whosoever labors . . . in adducing reasons why the anti-razor is false, let it be objected against him through the method sketched above, . . . since if the interlocutor should not want to object against his own position through this method, then he proceeds insufficiently, even by his own standards. [7]

The full import of this quotation is not immediately clear, but Chatton employs a very clever argument strategy using self-referential iteration and infinite regress. We will be aided in our analysis if we use as scaffolding a more formal and precise step-by-step presentation of the anti-razor method. As we construct this general and abstract description of the anti-razor below, it will be useful to keep in mind the concrete example of the ray and the sun previously discussed.

Given a true proposition p and an original stock of n entities, $a_1, a_2, \ldots a_n$, the anti-razor sets out a two-stage meditation, forcing us to posit the existence of suitable $n + 1$th thing, call it a_{n+1}, to explain the truth of p:[8]

(i) It must be that the original n entities, $a_1, a_2, \ldots a_n$, are required for the truth of p, and yet it must be that the existence of these n entities, $a_1, a_2, \ldots a_n$ is consistent with the falsehood of p. That is, $a_1, a_2, \ldots a_n$ alone are necessary but not sufficient for the truth of p. Then . . .

(ii) . . . we must ask whether with the presence of a suitable a_{n+1} thing it is still consistent to say that p is false. If it is, then we have not yet filled the truth gap, so to speak, since we have not yet explained p's truth, and so, obviously we would have to come up with another entity a_{n+2}, add it to the mix, and start again. If, however, it is inconsistent that the a_{n+1} thing exist and yet p is false, fithen p obviously requires this a_{n+1} thing for its truth, and this a_{n+1} thing is enough. Hence, since p is in fact true, this a_{n+1} thing must exist.

Chatton's Rule of Iterated Analysis

Let this be the general method of the anti-razor. Now we can ask: What is Chatton's general response in the previous paragraph to the Ockhamist objection—namely, the objection that the insufficiency the anti-razor detects is not always to be remedied by positing even more *things*, but rather, by sometimes instead by positing more *conditions* which need to be met by the things we already recognize?

In the long quotation, Chatton seems to be asking us to apply the anti-razor method to the propositional content of the very condition the objector insists on adding. Let us try to do this in detail using our previous example of the ray and the sun.[9] Let the machinery of the anti-razor be assumed as above. Now, take the proposition "This light ray comes from the sun," and suppose that it is in fact true. As we have already seen, Chatton would say the truth of this proposition requires that a light ray exist, that the sun exist, and that besides these two absolute entities, one relative accident of *production* and one of *being produced* exist in the sun and the ray, respectively.

Now an Ockhamist objector can challenge the whole basis of this analysis in a manner similar to Ockham's challenge to realist theories of motion, by saying that the consistency of the existence of the light ray and the sun with the falsehood of "This light ray is from the sun" shows, not that other *things* must exist, but that there are in reality more *conditions* on the truth of "This light ray is from the sun," which conditions have not yet been met. What kind of conditions? To take one example, we might say that God could make a ray, the sun, and the two respective accidents, and yet could make "This light ray is from the sun" still be false because he refuses to co-act with the causal power of the sun for producing this ray. Continuing with this counter-example, we might say that what would be needed to bring about the truth of "This light ray is from the sun," is not that there are other things, but instead a further condition is met, namely, that God cooperate, and co-act with the causality in the sun to let this ray be from it. The point of the objection is that sometimes not only *things* but also *conditions* must be posited for the truth of propositions.

Now, in his *Lectura* text, Chatton attacks such an objection this way. Take the new condition the objector claims is necessary, in this case the condition *that God co-acts so that this ray is from the sun*, and make the condition into a proposition, thus: "God co-acts so that this ray is from the sun." Since "God co-acts so that this ray is from the sun" is just a proposition, we can simply apply the anti-razor to it and see what happens. That is, we ask, what kind and how many *things* must exist in order for the truth of the new proposition "God co-acts so that this ray is from the sun"?

Now, there are two possible answers to this last question. Option 1: "God co-acts so that this ray is from the sun" requires us to posit the same number of things as the anti-razor would say the original proposition "This ray is from the sun" itself requires. That is, one possibility is that "God co-acts so that this ray is from the sun" requires that four things exist {sun, ray, two respective accidents}, which is just as many as the anti-razor said were required. Option 2: The truth of "God co-acts so that this ray is from the sun" requires that fewer than four things exist, presumably just the two things outside of the dispute, that is, the ray and the sun. (We do not consider that "God co-acts so that this ray is from the sun" could require *more* than four things, since the objector is obviously a nominalist, and would not introduce a condition that *expanded* our ontology beyond even Chatton's requirements!)

But under either option the objector has a problem. If the first option holds, then four things exist, and Chatton and his anti-razor were right all along anyway, since application of his anti-razor showed that, indeed, we had to posit four things. If the second option holds, then even with the new condition added, the ray and the sun are still insufficient for the truth of "God co-acts so that this ray is from the sun." That this is so is shown this way. Everyone agrees that two things, the ray and the sun, are insufficient for the truth of "This ray is from the sun'"; they only disagree on how to fill the gap. But since "This ray is from the sun" is an embedded dictum in "God co-acts so that this ray is from the sun," clearly "God co-acts so that this ray is from the sun" requires at least as many things for its truth as the dictum "This ray is from the sun" does. Hence, if two things were insufficient for the truth of "This ray is from the sun," obviously two things are also insufficient for the truth of the new proposition, "God co-acts so that this ray is from the sun."

So, *on his own principles*, even the objector would have to agree that, on Option 2, the insufficiency we detected at the first level is pushed up to this new, higher-level proposition. Now, the objector holds that insufficiency for propositional truth in this case requires posting, not more things, but rather more conditions, so by his own lights, the insufficiency of these two things for the truth of "God co-acts so that this ray is from the sun" requires us to posit the existence of still *another* condition, this time a condition on the proposition "God co-acts so that this ray is from the sun." It is difficult to say what this new condition would be, but let us try, for example, the condition *that God wills that God co-act so that this ray is from the sun.* Some such new condition is clearly necessary to fill the insufficiency that still exists, and, so to speak, make up the ontological gap.

Now we can again propositionalize this new condition *that God wills that God co-act so that this ray is from the sun,* just as we did previously with *that God co-act so that this ray is from the sun,* to yield the new, even more complex proposition "God wills that God co-act so that this ray is from the sun." We then proceed exactly as before, and ask: What is required for the truth of "God wills that God co-act so that this ray is from the sun"? Either as many things as the anti-razor says, or fewer. If as many as, Chatton was right all along; if fewer, then the objector's own strategy forces us to posit still *another* condition, which new condition we can propositionalize as before, etc.

Now either this process proceeds to infinity, with each new condition in its turn requiring we posit yet another condition to explain the previous proposition's truth—and in that case we have an explanatory regress, since the truth of "This ray is from the sun" never finally gets explained—or else at some level we jump off this infinity train. But the only station through which we can exit is Option 1 or its equivalent, that is, the only way to break the regress is to admit that Chatton was right to begin with: more than two *things* are needed for the truth of "This ray is from the sun." But then of course, the entire nominalist line of objection was for naught.

To recapitulate briefly and more formally, the general structure of this objection and Chatton's reply is as follows:

(1) Assume the machinery of the anti-razor for the sake of objection.

(2) Objection: the consistency of the existence of $a_1, a_2, \ldots a_n$, with the falsehood of p shows, not that we must posit a new thing a_{n+1}, but rather a new condition on the truth of p, call it Cp.

(3) Form the proposition expressing the new proposed necessary condition Cp, written $\pi(Cp)$. Ask: What must exist in order for $\pi(Cp)$ itself to be true?

(4) Now, there are two possible answers. Option 1: $\pi(Cp)$ requires more than n things exist, just as Chatton's anti-razor says p did. Option 2: The truth of $\pi(Cp)$ requires that than n or fewer things exist.

(5) If Option 1, then the anti-razor was correct after all.

(6) If Option 2, then even with $C(p)$ added, entities $a_1, a_2, \ldots a_n$ without a_{n+1} are still insufficient for the truth of $\pi(Cp)$. *Proof:* By hypothesis, n or fewer things are ontologically insufficient for the truth of p, but since p is an embedded dictum in $\pi(Cp)$, clearly $\pi(Cp)$ requires at least as many things for its truth as p does. Hence, if n or fewer things are insufficient for the truth of p, obviously n or fewer things are insufficient for the truth of $\pi(Cp)$ as well. QED.

(7) The objector's general method would therefore require us to posit still *another* condition to explain the truth of proposition $\pi(Cp)$; call the new condition $C^*\pi(Cp)$. This $C^*\pi(Cp)$ is necessary to fill the insufficiency which, by (6) above, still exists for $\pi(Cp)$.

(8) But we can propositionalize $C^*\pi(Cp)$ just as we did Cp, to yield $\pi C^*\pi(Cp)$, and then proceed again as in (4)–(7) above, for the positing of $C^{**}\pi C^*\pi(Cp)$, which we can make into $\pi C^{**}\pi C^*\pi(Cp)$, etc.

(9) Now either this process proceeds to infinity, with the nth requirement of a new condition producing a true proposition of the form $\pi C^{*\,n+1} \ldots \pi(Cp)$—and in that case, p's truth conditions never having been finally stated, we have an explanatory regress—or else admit (4) Option 1 above, and the entire objection was for naught.

Assume for the moment that this argument strategy works. What has Chatton accomplished thereby? He has shown that one cannot fill ontological gaps with nonentities; positing conditions only generates more propositions whose truth conditions must be similarly explained by the nominalist, which explanation requires yet more conditions, and so on. Only real things are ontologically sturdy enough to fill the chinks in this sinking semantic ship. The Ockhamist analysis in which conditions make propositions true, even if it is correct, still depends upon the more basic fact that propositions about things are made true by things, which basic fact is given more proper due by the realist analysis. Hence the Ockhamist objection sheds no light upon the correctness or incorrectness of Chatton's own realist ontological analysis with his anti-razor. Put simply, Chatton has shown that the Ockhamist analysis is dependent upon a more basic realist analysis, and so is not capable of adjudicating on questions raised about that more basic level of analysis.

How though can we briefly summarize Chatton's argument strategy in plain English? I think the following statement captures what is important:

Chatton's rule of iterated analysis: Given two competing analyses A and B, where we want to show that A is more fundamental, and B as less so, we can ask what happens if we self-referentially iterate B, that is, what happens when B is used to analyze its own outputs (assuming this is legitimate). If the legitimate iteration of B leads to an explanatory regress unless analysis A is used to terminate it, then clearly B at bottom depends upon A.[10]

I wish to stress that this rule of iterated analysis we have discovered is not identical with the anti-razor, nor is it a part of it. The anti-razor is a semantic theory which Chatton here defends with the rule of iterated analysis, but, as the next section will reveal, the rule can be easily applied to very different philosophical contexts just as easily. In short, A and B can be any two analyses at all.[11]

Is Chatton's strategy a good one? I think that it is, if we add some provisos on its application and results:

(i) Clearly B may depend upon things other than A; that is, with his rule we show at most that the success or truth of analysis A is necessary for the success or truth of B, but there may of course be other factors upon which B depends, or upon which A depends. Chatton's *Lectura* discussion does not show any awareness of this issue.

(ii) Although other things may be necessary, in addition to analysis A, in order to terminate B's iteration, it really must be the case that A is strictly *necessary* to terminate B's iteration. If there is another way of doing so that is independently acceptable and that does not involve A, then all bets are off.

(iii) The application of analysis B to itself must be otherwise logically and philosophically legitimate, for example, it must not make a category mistake. Chatton's discussion in *Lectura* does show awareness of this issue.

The best way to argue against a particular application of Chatton's rule of iterated analysis is, obviously, to show that it fails on one of the provisos above, or, still more directly, to show that the regress that drives the argument is not really a problem: for example, that it is not vicious, or that the regress is not infinite, but instead collapses to the finite. Perhaps such a response could be made above on behalf of the Ockhamist above.

Chatton Defends against His Own Rule

In his highly original treatment of future contingents in *Reportatio* I, d. 38, Chatton again faces this complex iteration strategy. Only on this occasion it seems that, instead of applying the strategy, he is rather defending against it, since in that text he is at pains to show that a certain seemingly infinite regress stemming from an iterated analysis in fact collapses to the finite level. Hence, in this second example, Chatton is trying to show that there is not (despite initial appearances) a case of infinite regress of the sort to which his rule would apply, quite the opposite of what he was doing in the first example.

For complex reasons that we need not go into, Chatton's solution to the problem of future contingents requires that there be two distinct, independent analyses of what it means to be committed to the proposition "Socrates will be sitting," and in general to any future-tensed proposition of the form "*a* will be P," where *a* names a contingent thing. Our commitment to "*a* will be P" can have two particular, distinct analyses, according to Chatton. Thus "*a* will be P" can mean either:[12]

(i) "*a* will be P" is true [A future-tense proposition *is true*.]
     or
(ii) "*a* is P" will be true [A present-tense proposition *will be true*.]

Although Chatton thinks true propositions of the first form lead to fatalism, he thinks those of the second form do not, and hence the distinction between these two forms can be the basis of a stable solution to the problem of future contingents.[13] That is, to avoid fatalism but still safeguard veridical prophecy and divine foreknowledge, we have to say that Analysis (i) yields a proposition which is really indeterminate in truth value, while Analysis (ii) yields a proposition which can be regarded as true. Consequently, it is absolutely critical to Chatton's solution that these two analyses are distinct and independent, and in particular, it cannot be that Analysis (ii) depends at all on Analysis (i). At the point where he should naturally make an argument for this important point, he instead offers this extremely compressed and obscure remark:

> If 'The Antichrist will come' is true according to the second mode of assertion, then if it were again asserted to be true, it would again be true in that very same mode in which it was originally asserted. The reason is that from the opposite of something the opposite conclusion follows (this dictum being understood here in a general sense).[14]

What could he mean here?

I believe what we have learned above from his rule of iterated analysis can shed light on this remark. Imagine someone opposed Chatton's claim that Analyses (i) and (ii) above are distinct and independent. She could attack his whole strategy by applying the iterated analysis rule against him, in particular, she might try to show that Analysis (ii) in fact depends upon (i). This would of course finish off Chatton's solution to future contingents.

How could we go about using Chatton's rule against him in this way? Chatton's rule of iterated analysis suggests we iterate Analysis (ii) on its own outputs in such a way that a regress is generated which only Analysis (i) can break. Now, Analysis (ii) says that the truth of "*a* will be P" commits you to the truth of "'*a* is P' will be true." Notice that the original sentence is future-tensed, and that, after we apply Analysis (ii), the result is another future-tensed proposition. Consequently we can legitimately iterate Analysis (ii), applying it to its own original output, to get a proposition of a higher "level," so to speak: from "'*a* is P' will be true" we get "'*a* is P is true' will be true." This could continue, and, using parentheses instead of quotation marks, we would then have, schematically:

Level 0   *a* will be P *commits you to:*
Level 1   (*a* is P) will be true *commits you to:*
Level 2   ((*a* is P) is true) will be true *commits you to:*
Level 3   (((*a* is P) is true) is true) will be true *etc.*

At each new level we have used Analysis (ii) to obtain a new future contingent sentence, the truth of which is entailed by the previous level.

Chatton claims that Level 0 and Level 1 are equivalent. But this analysis could obviously be repeated to infinity, so that Level 1 automatically generates Level 2, and it seems the truth conditions of the sentence on Level 1 might seem to await determination by what happens at Level 2, but 2 generates 3, so 2 awaits determination by 3, which generates 4, etc. Hence we seem to have an explanatory regress. How could the regress be broken? The only way would be to determine *independently* the truth conditions for any arbitrary Level $n > 0$ of the schema above. So consider, under what conditions are any of these higher sentences in the above schema true? Since at any Level $n > 0$ of this analysis we are dealing with a future-tensed proposition, to answer this question we must ask: Under what conditions is a future-tensed sentence generally true? And this is just to ask, how do we know that, for example, the sentence "(((*a* is P) is true) is true) will be true" is true? But—and here is Chatton's worry—*to ask this is really just to ask what makes a sentence of the form in Analysis (i) true.* To see this clearly it is best to approach the matter formally. Note that no matter what level we are at in the schema above we have a long proposition on the left, and the main logical operator—the phrase "will be true"—on the right. Now regard "true" in this phrase as a predicate, P; we then have at every level a proposition function "will be P." Since a proposition is a contingent thing, the long proposition on the left can be represented by a, which symbol you recall can stand for any contingent thing. We see immediately that each level of the schema actually has the logical form "a will be P," thus:

Level n of Analysis (ii): $(\ldots \underline{(a \text{ is P}) \text{ is true}}_1) \text{ is true}_2) \ldots)$ will be $\underline{\text{true}}_n$

Analysis (i): a will be P

Hence, to ask of any Level n in the schema for Analysis (ii) whether it is true is just to ask whether a sentence of the form "a will be P" is true, which sentence is as the form in Analysis (i); hence, to terminate the regress in the schema of Analysis (ii) we are forced to resort to Analysis (i), which Chatton said leads ultimately to fatalism.

Chatton seems to face here the same stark choice we just saw him put before the Ockhamist. For in order to give the truth-conditions of any arbitrary future-tensed proposition of any Level $n > 0$ in his schema, by his own lights Chatton has only two choices: use Analysis (i) or use Analysis (ii). If he uses Analysis (i) the fatalist was right all along. If he uses Analysis (ii) he simply obtains the $n + 1$th level of the schema, and the regress continues unless Analysis (i) finally be admitted. In sum, by Chatton's own rule of iterated analysis, since Analysis (i) is needed to break the regress on the iteration of Analysis (ii), we have shown that (ii) depends upon (i). So it seems that Chatton has been sunk with his own rule here.

It is just such an objection that Chatton is trying to head off, I think, when he asserts the compressed remark with which we began this section of the essay:

> If 'The Antichrist will come' is true according to the second mode of assertion, then if it were again asserted to be true, it would again be true in that very same mode in which it was originally asserted.

The reply suggested in this quotation amounts to this. Analysis (ii) does not really create a new irreducible sentence whose determinate truth cannot be explained otherwise—rather, the product of Analysis (ii) is a new, contingent, future-tense sentence that can be understood *in just the same way as the original*, and so is reducible to the original, because the iteration outputs of Analysis (ii) are all equivalent to the original sentence, that is, each Level n > 1 really reduces by equivalence to Level 1. And it is just here where Chatton's remark about the *ex opposito* dictum comes in—it turns out we can in fact reason *ex opposito* to collapse the infinite schema down to the finite. Without an infinite regress, the rule of iterated analysis does not apply, Chatton can have his distinction, and we can all avoid the iron hand of fate. The gist of the strategy becomes clearer if we look a bit deeper at the details.

How though can we collapse these levels to the finite by reasoning *ex opposito*? In general, reasoning *ex opposito* is just reasoning by what we call contraposition, viz., p → q therefore ~ q → ~ p, or vice versa. Now, we already have that Level 0 ↔ Level 1, and also the ascending set of implications that Level 1 → Level 2 → Level 2 → Level 3 → . . . from Analysis (ii) itself. Hence, if we could establish set of a corresponding descending implications, showing that for any n > 1 that (Level n → Level n − 1), then we would have proven the equivalences Level 0 ↔ Level 1 ↔ Level 2 ↔ Level 2 ↔ Level 3 ↔ . . . This would collapse the infinite regress.

The argument from contraposition that collapses these levels is easy to establish in full generality by mathematical induction, but tediously long to state in that form; instead I will illustrate the method by using contraposition to reduce Level 3 to Level 2:

Take a sentence of Level 3; it has the form (((a is P) is true) is true) will be true. We want to show this entails the Level 2 sentence ((a is P) is true) will be true. The proof is by contraposition. We assume *(((a is P) is true) will be true) is false* and show *((((a is P) is true) is true) will be true) is false*.

1. (((a is P) is true) will be true) is *false*   *given; this implies that*
2. ((a is P) is true) will *not* be true   *which implies that*
3. ((a is P) is *not* true) will be true   *which implies that*
4. ((a is *not* P) is true) will be true
5. (a is *not* P) = (a is P) is *not* true   *law of negation; substitution in 4 yields*
6. (((a is P) is *not* true) is true) will be true   *which implies that*
7. (((a is P) is true) is *not* true) will be true   *which implies that*
8. (((a is P) is true) is true) will *not* be true   *which implies that*
9. ((((a is P) is true) is true) will be true) is *false*   QED

Hence, Level 3 → Level 2.

Although my hypothesis explains a great deal about what Chatton has in mind, I may be wrong, of course, and this might not be the way to exposit the *ex opposito* portion of this compressed remark. After all, the reduction from Level 3 to Level 2 can be done directly and more simply by using the logical equivalence "*a* is P" is true if and only if *a* is P, and substitution into sentence at level *n*, for example, merely from

(((a is P) is true) is true) will be true

and

"*a* is P" is true if and only if *a* is P

alone it follows immediately by simple substitution that

((a is P) is true) will be true

Hence, Level 3 → Level 2. But if Chatton did not intend this reasoning as I have reconstructed it here, it is difficult to imagine how else to sort out his very obscure remark.

Conclusion

It seems Chatton's defense against his own strategy is sound here. But it is possible that an Ockhamist might adopt a somewhat similar form of reply, by trying to find added conditions which explain relational sentences but which nevertheless do not add another entity to ontology when they are propositionalized to embed the original sentence.[15] What such a condition might be I leave to the reader to consider.

Despite what I said in the Introduction about the behavior of regress arguments not being well studied, it should be noted in closing that the other aspect of Chatton's strategy, iteration of sentential operators, has definitely received great scrutiny in modern logic. Indeed, Chatton's intense interest in the logical behavior of certain sentential analyses under iteration puts one in mind of modern modal logicians and their worries about the axiom sets under which iterated modalities collapse. For example, it can be shown that under the powerful and seemingly useful assumptions of the modal system S5, one ends up with a logic that cannot sustain iterated modalities, in the sense that any string of unary operators $\sim$, $\square$, $\lozenge$, in front of a formula p is S5 equivalent to one of only four basic (nonempty) modalities, $\sim\square p$, $\square p$, $\sim\lozenge p$, or $\lozenge p$. Thus S5 is axiom rich but theorem poor.

And again, modern philosophers have found that they must grapple with infinite regress in order to sort out their own debates. One thinks of Russell and the paradoxes of self-reference plaguing set theory early last century. It is interesting that we have now found Chatton six centuries ago combining these two powerful tools, self-referential iteration and infinite regress, into one interesting argument strategy, although this strategy itself is apparently never named or discussed explicitly by logicians.

10

Analogy and Metaphor from Thomas Aquinas to Duns Scotus and Walter Burley

E. JENNIFER ASHWORTH

In the history of Aristotelianism and Thomism people often speak about *analogia entis*, the analogy of being,[1] or what, following Giorgio Pini and Silvia Donati, I shall call metaphysical analogy.[2] In fact, this notion was foreign to Aristotle, and for Thomas Aquinas analogy, under that name, was semantic analogy.[3] It belonged to the theory of language, since it was regarded as a type of equivocation, the medieval name for homonymy. Metaphor too was closely related to equivocation, although, unlike analogy, it was an improper use of language, and produced by usage rather than imposition. In the second half of the thirteenth century logicians began to worry about how semantic analogy could be produced by imposition, and how analogical terms could be related to concepts. If a single term is used in different but related senses, does this come about through one original act of imposition, or through two related acts? If there are two acts, can we speak of a single term? If there is just one act, what of the concept or concepts to which that term is subordinated? Can there be a single concept which conveys related senses, and if not, how can the relationship between two concepts be captured by a single act of imposition? As a result of such worries some thinkers, especially John Duns Scotus, abandoned semantic analogy. What was called analogy was now metaphysical analogy, and, at the linguistic level, metaphor replaced semantic analogy. It is the history of these developments that I shall discuss in this essay, and in so doing, I shall show something of the interplay between logic, metaphysics, and philosophy of mind.

Semantic Analogy and Metaphor

I shall start by sketching the metaphysical and theological doctrines which provided the motivation for semantic analogy. Aristotle had transmitted a metaphysics of real natures, genera, and species, which exist in some way in the external world, and which are organized in accordance with the ten categories. This Aristotelian ontology was considerably enriched by the Neoplatonists, who emphasized a hierarchy of being. Things are ranked in accordance with the varying degrees of perfection, including existence, that they possess. For a Christian Neoplatonist that meant that God is the one who has the highest degree of existence, truth, unity, goodness, and justice, while every creature has less existence, truth, unity, goodness, and justice. What makes the hierarchy of being possible is participation. God, who is entirely simple, is all that he is by virtue of his essence, and all creatures are what they are through their varying degrees of participation in the divine perfections. In Christian theology, Neoplatonism was modified both by the doctrine of creation and by belief in a God who reveals himself in Jesus Christ. It remained true that God is infinitely removed from creatures, transcending all created reality and all possible knowledge. Nonetheless, as created substances we reflect the perfections of God, and as Christians, we have at least some knowledge of God. Both these facts give us reason to suppose that meaningful discourse about God is possible.

But for meaningful discourse about God to be possible we need an adequate theory of language, and the main elements of the theory of language prevalent in the mid-thirteenth century posed a problem. The first thing to note is that in their discussion of signification, logicians focused on single categorematic terms, those which can serve as subjects or predicates in propositions. Complex terms, phrases, and propositions are posterior to simple terms, and by virtue of the principle of compositionality, the sense of a phrase is a function of the sense of its parts. This approach downplayed the importance of context and speaker meaning. Secondly, logicians saw human language as conventional (*ad placitum*), and believed that spoken terms receive their signification through an original institution, usually called imposition. Modist logicians in particular were reluctant to accept that the original imposition could be modified by context, or linked to some subsequent imposition. Moreover, for the *modistae*, the speculative grammarians of the second half of the thirteenth century, a word drew from its imposition not only its signification but its consignification, its grammatical properties, the set of its *modi significandi*.[4] For Roger Bacon, the imposition of a term was constantly renewed, but for most logicians, terms received their signification and their consignification just once. In the second half of the thirteenth century, a number of logicians claimed that the context of a word, including the purely linguistic context, changed neither the signification, nor, in most cases, its consignification. This rigid view of imposition seems to be tied to the modistic desire to treat grammar as a science, whose objects cannot be contingent and variable. Thirdly, logicians held that spoken terms signify things through their relation to concepts, which are naturally significative and which, from the second half of the century, were themselves regarded as representative signs. This theory of signification went hand in hand with the ontology of natures and categories. For Lambert of Auxerre (or Lagny) the primary significate of a categorematic term was an intelligible species and its secondary significate was a common nature.[5] For others the primary significate was not an intelligible species but a concept, Aquinas's inner word, and for yet others, the primary significate was the common nature itself, whether this was identified with the content of a universal concept, or was ontologically separate from the concept and its external referents, the individuals.[6] Finally, everything that was univocally predicated of individuals in a strict sense of univocation was taken to belong to a category, and to be either a genus, a species, a difference, an accident, or a property (in the technical sense).[7] It was the abandonment of this doctrine that allowed Scotus to view the word *ens* (being) as strictly univocal in his later works.

I will leave aside the problems this theory of language caused for fictional terms, negative and privative terms, and for concrete accidental terms or adjectives, and I will consider just the problems posed to theology and metaphysics. Human language is constructed in order to speak about created natures, to put them in their genera and species, and to predicate their accidents, properties, and differences, but God is not part of the created world, and he transcends all the categories. How then should we construe the divine names such as "good" and "just"? And how should we construe the word "being" in its two forms *esse* and *ens*? Is God a being in the same sense as created beings? Is substance a being in the same sense as accidents? More generally, there is the problem of the transcendental terms, including *ens* but also *verum, bonum,* and *unum*. We use these terms of everything that exists, and so they are terms that transcend the categories. How can they signify univocally if univocal signification is linked to the categories?

If the theory of language posed problems, it was in the linguistic sciences— grammar, rhetoric, and logic—that the philosophers and theologians found the tools to resolve these problems. I will begin with grammar and rhetoric, which provided the theory of tropes, especially metaphor. Here we must make certain distinctions in relation to the vocabulary. Sometimes the word *metaphora* was used in medieval Latin, but the more common words are *translatio* and *transumptio*, which were often treated as synonymous, but which were used in a variety of ways.[8] Sometimes they refer to metaphor in particular, sometimes to any figure of speech, and sometimes, especially in twelfth- and early-thirteenth-century theology, they refer to any kind of semantic transfer.[9]

In origin, the notion of *translatio* was part of the theory of tropes, itself of Stoic origin.[10] According to Quintilian, "A trope is the change (*mutatio*) of a word or phrase from its proper signification to another signification, with some <added> force (*cum uirtute*)"[11] and metaphor is "the transfer of a noun or verb from the place in which it is proper to another place where the proper word is lacking or where the word which has been transferred is better."[12] In his definition of tropes, the grammarian Donatus, whose work was read in all the medieval schools, added a reference to similitude and wrote: "A trope is an expression transferred (*translata*) from its proper signification to an improper similitude (*ad non propriam similitudinem*), either for ornament or out of necessity."[13] Metaphor was then defined as the *translatio* of things and words. There are three points to emphasize. First, the use of words is said to be proper when the word is used in accordance with the sense received by imposition, and all other uses are by definition improper, even if they are both useful and legitimate. This by itself prevented *translatio* from providing a solution to the problem of divine names if we want, as Aquinas did, to insist that the divine names are used properly of God.[14] Secondly, some logicians such as William of Ockham insisted that a second act of imposition, related to the first, was required to produce a metaphor,[15] but the most usual view insisted on just one initial act of imposition which had nothing to do with the later transfer of sense. The Oxonians Thomas de Wyk and Walter Burley argued that two senses could not be linked by two acts of imposition.[16] Each such act had to be totally arbitrary (*ad placitum totaliter*), but when one transfers a word, there is always a reason, which is the presence of a similarity of relations. We call the bottom of a bridge the foot because the bottom of a bridge supports the bridge just as the foot of a man supports the man. Only usage, and not imposition, explains the transfer of sense. This brings me to the third point to be noted, namely that metaphor was closely linked to analogy in the Greek sense of an equality or likeness between two proportions. Thus in his *Summa theologiae* I.13.6, Aquinas referred to the standard example *prata rident* ("the meadows are laughing") and he wrote that "laughing" said of meadows signifies that flowering is to meadows as laughing is to human beings, and in the same way "lion" said of God signifies that God acts vigorously in relation to his works just as the lion acts vigorously in relation to its own works.

So far as the attitude of Aquinas toward metaphor is concerned, we should begin by noting that unlike his modist successors, he had a relaxed attitude. When he speaks of language in general, he leaves room for the exigencies of usage, without appealing to equivocation or analogy or metaphor. He was very conscious of the fact that language changes and evolves,[17] that a word can enjoy several senses without being strictly equivocal, and without having several senses linked by priority and posteriority. From sources such as Aristotle and Boethius he drew histories of such words as "natura," "persona" and "spiritus," and he presented each history as the history of a series of transformations, without insisting on a new imposition.[18] In his *Summa theologiae* he explained that it is possible to employ a word in several senses without its becoming improper. For instance, the word "verbum" has four senses, of which only one is improper.[19] His discussion of the word "light" in the *Summa theologiae* is of equal importance.[20] He said that there are two ways of employing this word, either in accordance with its first imposition, or in accordance with usage (*usus nominis*). The name "vision" signifies eyesight through its imposition, but by extension it signifies cognition by the other senses. In the same way, by its imposition the word "light" signifies what produces a manifestation to the sense of vision, but by extension it signifies all manifestation by any mode of cognition. If one takes the word in the sense of its first imposition, and uses it of spiritual things, one is speaking metaphorically. But if one takes the word in accordance with ordinary usage (*usus loquentium*), one can assert it properly of spiritual things. In commentaries on the *Sophistical Refutations*, ordinary usage was identified with metaphor, but here Aquinas separates them. What is more, he offers us a choice between two interpretations of the word.

However, where the divine names are concerned, there is no choice. If a word, "lion" for instance, implies reference to a corporeal reality or a deficiency (*imperfectio*) of some sort, it can only be said of God metaphor-ically.[21] For Aquinas, metaphor was part of the literal sense of a text, but if one speaks of the right arm of God, the literal sense is not the figure of speech but what is figured, that is, the power of God.[22] In one of his biblical commentaries, he said that there are two ways to signify according to the literal sense: properly, as when one says that a human being laughs, and according to a similitude or metaphor.[23] When we say that the meadows are laughing, we signify their flowering.[24] Nonetheless, even if metaphor is part of the literal sense, it is not part of a rational discourse. One cannot use metaphorical locutions in an argument, because there is no fixed meaning. The Bible predicates the word "lion" of the devil as well as of God.[25] More-over, even if metaphor gives us a way of talking about the properties of God, its use requires antecedent knowledge of these properties. The explanation of a metaphor takes us back to the proper sense of words. For all these rea-sons, metaphor offers no solution to the problems of theological language, or, for that matter, of metaphysical language.

For many twelfth- and early-thirteenth-century theologians, *translatio*, taken in the very wide sense of any semantic transfer, offered the best solu-tion to the problem of the divine names,[26] but such theologians as Aquinas viewed *translatio* more narrowly, and preferred to turn to logic and the notions of equivocation and of analogy in a new, non-Greek sense, for their solution. Their starting point was provided by Aristotle's *Categories* 1a1–3, which opens with a definition of equivocal terms. Aristotle writes: "When things have only a name in common and the definition or nature (*substantiae ratio*) which corresponds to the name is different, they are called equivo-cals."[27] For Aristotle, equivocals were things in the world, but obviously a thing is equivocal if and only if it is named by an equivocal term. As a result, logicians focused on terms in relation to things, and not on terms in relation to other terms in a linguistic context. Note that this remark ties in with what I identified as the first element of the theory of language, its focus on single categorematic terms.

In his commentary on the *Categories*, Boethius proposed a classification of equivocals.[28] In conformity with the material he had taken from Greek commentators, he divided them into two groups. Some are chance equivocals (*a casu*) and others are deliberate equivocals (*a consilio*). There is no rela-tionship between the multiple senses of chance equivocals, and although Boethius himself gave the example of a proper name, the standard example was the common name "dog," said of a barking animal, a marine animal, and a constellation. As later logicians would emphasize, three acts of imposition were required, and three separate concepts. Deliberate equivocals had four subdivisions. The first is *similitudo*, resemblance, and the standard example was the human being and his pictured likeness, *homo pictus*.[29] The second subdivision is *proportio* (*analogia* in Greek). The example given is *principium*, principle, which denotes unity with respect to number or a point in relation to a line. It is important to note that analogy in the Greek sense of an equality between two proportions was largely absent from medieval discussions of analogy.[30] The third subdivision is *ab uno*, of one origin, and the example used was the word "medical." The last is *ad unum*, in relation to one end, and the standard example was "healthy" (*sanum*). Medieval thinkers, following Averroes, added a fifth subspecies, in relation to one subject, and the standard example was *ens*.[31] These last three can be easily assimilated to Aristotle's *pros hen* equivocation, and they appear as a package in Aquinas's early *Principles of Nature*, as well as in his late commentary on Aristotle's *Metaphysics*.[32] Equivocation *ab uno* and the example "medical" were often omitted, and it is the possible distinction between treatments of *sanum* and *ens* that will be crucial for logicians and theologians.

After his initial analysis, Boethius goes on to say that there seems to be another mode of equivocation that Aristotle is silent about, namely *translatio*.[33] He states that *translatio* has no property of its own (*translatio nullius proprietatis est*), by which he means that it is not a particular class of word.[34] It may or may not fall under equivocation. If, for reasons of ornament, one calls a steersman a charioteer, the word "charioteer" is not equivocal, for the man is already properly named steersman. However, if the object has no name of its own, as in the case of the picture of a man, one can transfer the word *homo* from the living man to his picture, and so the word *homo* is equivocal. Note that we are encountering *homo pictus* for the second time, for he was also the standard example of *similitudo*, the first subdivision of deliberate equivocation.

Another classical source that brought metaphor, under that name, together with equivocation is Simplicius' commentary on the *Categories*, translated by William of Moerbeke in 1266. Simplicius remarked that there was a possible link between one of the subdivisions of deliberate equivocation, analogy in the Greek sense, and metaphor, when he wrote "Others, among whom is Atticus, bring together the mode according to metaphor (*secundam metaphoram*) and the mode according to analogy (*secundum analogiam*) and affirm that their reunion constitutes one single mode of equivocation."[35] He went on to quote and elaborate on Porphyry's point that when a word is transferred to something that has a name, there is metaphor and no equivocation, but when it is transferred to something that has no name, it is not a case of metaphor at all, but is straightforward equivocation. The example cited is that of "foot," said on the one hand of the lower part of a mountain in place of the Greek word *hyporia* and on the other hand of a table or bed, because of the similitude to the foot of an animal. Here there are two *rationes* and one common name. Simplicius added that the first case will count as equivocation if similitude is involved.

In effect, *translatio* reappears in the *Sophistical Refutations* 165b–166a6. In this work, Aristotle distinguished three modes common to equivocation and amphiboly, though only the first two are relevant to our discussion. Aristotle (according to the Latin translation) wrote that the first mode occurs "when either a phrase or a name such as *piscis* or *canis* principally signifies more than one thing," and the second mode occurs when it is in virtue of custom that the word or phrase is so used.[36] Burley argued that only the first mode related to equivocation,[37] but in order to harmonize the common modes with the two groups of equivocals given by Boethius, logicians usually said that chance equivocals belong to the first mode and deliberate equivocals to the second.[38] The reference to custom in the second mode, linked with the discussion of *translatio* in Boethius's commentary on the *Categories*, invited logicians to include metaphor under deliberate equivocation. Thus a number of logicians put metaphor alongside analogy in the new medieval sense in the second mode of equivocation. Moreover, some argued that metaphor should be reduced to analogy,[39] while others, including the author of the *De fallaciis* sometimes attributed to Aquinas, argued that analogy should be reduced to metaphor.[40] The latter position prevailed at Oxford. Of the logicians I have read, only Peter of Spain notes that metaphors can become fixed in the language, and thereby turn into straightforward equivocal terms.[41]

In order to understand what was at issue here, we need to consider the new medieval sense of analogy. This had its roots in Aristotle's *Metaphysics* and in Arabic sources. In the *Metaphysics* 4.2 (1003a33–35) Aristotle wrote: "The word 'being' is said in many ways, but in relation to one (*ad unum*) and to one nature, and not by equivocation but rather as 'salubrious' in relation to health."[42] Among the logicians of the Arab world, there was a long tradition of ambiguous words which were intermediary between univocals and equivocals and which were said in a prior and a posterior sense (*per prius et posterius*).[43] This tradition was transmitted to the Latin world by the *Logic* of Al-Ghazâlî (Algazel)[44] and by the *Metaphysics* of Avicenna, where he said that *ens* was neither a genus nor a predicate predicated equally of all its subordinates, but an intention in which they agreed according to a prior and a posterior sense.[45] To this idea of being said in a prior and a posterior sense, logicians added Averroes's notion of the attribution of one thing to another,[46] which served as a metaphysical foundation for signifying in a prior and a posterior sense. It seems that it was in the 1220s that people began to call ambiguous words analogical in the new sense, and a little later, logicians and theologians began to use the word *analogia* for deliberate equivocation.[47] This new theory of analogy posed various problems for the theory of language. If an analogical term corresponds to two concepts, were there two linked acts of imposition, or one act of imposition and an extension by virtue of usage? If an analogical term corresponds to one concept by one act of imposition, is this concept simple or complex? Can a simple concept include priority and posteriority?[48] Can a complex concept include conditions for use, such as the condition that the word will need to be distinguished in one context but not in another?[49] Echoes of all these debates are found in the logical writings of Scotus.

From Aquinas to Scotus and Burley: Tripartite Divisions of Analogy

Now that I have laid out the background, I will turn to a sequence of tripartite divisions of analogy in order to investigate the developments that took place after Aquinas. In his commentary on the *Sentences* I, d. 19, q. 5, a. 2, ad 1, Aquinas had presented a threefold division of analogy which seems to be original, and which was particularly influential in late-thirteenth-century Oxford (as well as in the fifteenth century).[50] Aquinas focuses on semantic analogy, opening with the words: "Something can be said according to analogy in three ways."[51] I shall go directly to the second case, in which a word is said "according to *esse* and not according to intention, and this happens when many things are made equal [*parificantur*] in the intention of some common <nature>, but this common <nature> does not have the *esse* of one characteristic [*ratio*] in all. Thus all bodies are made equal in the intention of corporeity, whence the logician, who considers intentions alone, says that this name 'body' is predicated univocally of all bodies; but the *esse* of this nature does not have the same *ratio* in corruptible and incorruptible bodies, whence for the metaphysician and natural <philosopher> who consider things according to their *esse*, neither this name 'body' nor any other is said univocally of corruptibles and incorruptibles." This type of analogy was usually discussed in response to Aristotle's *Physics*, where, according to the current Latin translation, he claimed that many equivocations are hidden in the reference to a genus.[52] Aquinas's presentation is important for the distinction he draws between the logician, who treats the word "body" as univocal, and the metaphysician, who treats it as equivocal. We might think of the distinction as still broadly semantic, insofar as the metaphysician is said to speak differently. However, in the hands of subsequent logicians, especially at Oxford, the emphasis will be rather different. First, the distinction will be extended to those who use the word *ens*. Second, even if the way the metaphysician speaks is still alluded to, there will be a sharper division between semantic analogy, which involves signification and modes of predication, and metaphysical analogy, which does not.[53] Third, the issue of the concept correlated with the term will become central. The concept of a genus is not analogical, and so the word will remain univocal. Whether the concept of *ens* can be analogical remains to be seen.

I now return to Aquinas's first case, in which a word is said "according to intention alone and not according to *esse*. This is when one intention is referred to several things *per prius et posterius*, which however does not have *esse* except in one. Thus the intention of health is referred to <an> animal, urine and diet in diverse ways, according to prior and posterior; not however according to diverse *esse* because there is no *esse* of health except in an animal." In other places, Aquinas uses a different vocabulary and speaks of the *ratio substantiae*, the phrase found in Boethius's translation of the *Categories*. Moreover, sometimes he speaks of a single *ratio* which is partly the same and partly different, and sometimes he speaks of many *rationes*.[54] Despite his various ways of putting the matter, we can legitimately attribute to Aquinas the notion that when we call an animal healthy, we employ the central concept of health, and when we call a diet healthy, we employ a secondary concept, that of producing the health of an animal. Later authors were concerned to be more precise about the number of concepts, and in the case of the word "healthy" most agreed that there were at least two related concepts. For those who accepted related acts of imposition, the analogical term is clearly a deliberate equivocal. However, if it is impossible for two acts of imposition to be related, as various Oxonians including Burley thought, we will either have to resort to the unconvincing claim that the word is after all univocal, as does Scotus in his questions on the *Sophistical Refutations*,[55] or appeal to *translatio*, with Burley and other Oxonians. Indeed, Burley construes all of Boethius's subdivisions of deliberate equivocation as cases of *translatio*.[56] This poses a problem. There are real relations between the healthy animal and its healthy food, but not between a man who runs or laughs and the running river or the laughing meadow. So far as most deliberate equivocals are concerned, it seems that there is an established order between the things signified and the acts of signifying, but metaphor is founded on an accidental ordering.

Aquinas's third division introduces the crucial example of the word *ens*. This occurs when a word is said analogically "according to intention and according to *esse*; and this is when they are neither made equal in a common intention nor in *esse*. In this way *ens* is said of substance and accident; and in these cases, it is necessary that the common nature should have some *esse* in each one of those of which it is said, but differing according to the *ratio* of greater or lesser perfection." According to Aquinas in this passage, the word *ens* seems to correspond to one concept at the semantic level and to one nature (or quasi-nature) at the ontological level, but both involve an inequality.

If we try to summarize Aquinas's divisions in the form of a table, we get a relatively simple result:

	According to esse	*Not according to* esse
According to intention	*ens*	*sanitas*
Not according to intention	*corpus*	

For subsequent authors, matters were considerably less simple, as they were concerned to harmonize the divisions of analogy with their differing doctrines of equivocation and imposition. Four solutions were possible, two of which were adopted by Scotus. For the early Scotus as for the late Scotus, true analogy is metaphysical analogy, and no semantic analogy is involved. However, for the early Scotus, as for a number of earlier Oxonians, the word *ens* is a chance equivocal, with two unrelated senses,[57] while for the late Scotus, *ens* is a strictly univocal term. The third view sees *ens* as a deliberate equivocal which corresponds either to more than one related concept or to a single complex concept such as a disjunction. Semantic and metaphysical analogy are parallel. Finally, there is the view that *ens* is intermediary between univocals and deliberate equivocals, in such a way that it is not equivocal in any of the normal senses, since there is just one *ratio* involved, but it is not truly univocal, since the *ratio* allows a prior and a posterior sense. In this case too, semantic analogy and metaphysical analogy are parallel.

This fourth thesis was apparently first presented in the 1270s in the framework of a threefold division of analogy proposed by the Parisian authors of *Questions on the Sophistical Refutations*.[58] These authors, however, trade on the ambiguity of the word *ratio* which can mean either concept or nature, and their thesis seems to be presented in ontological terms, without attention to the intervening concepts. Some Oxonian presentations of the same thesis are more precise. Let us consider another anonymous set of questions on the *Sophistical Refutations* which could date anywhere from the last decade of the thirteenth century to the first decade of the fourteenth century.[59] The author asked whether a word equivocal according to the second mode was analogical, and in his reply, wrote that there are three types of analogy. The first is the analogy of a cause to what is caused. Substance is the cause of an accident, and so the word "being" (*ens*) is given by imposition to a thing (*res*) common to the substance and accident, but more perfect in substance than in accident. This analogy is primarily in things and as a result it is found in both concepts and words. The second type of analogy is the analogy of genus, the analogy of more and less perfect, and the anonymous author speaks neither of an analogy of concepts nor of an analogy of words. The two types of analogy do not prevent univocation, since the terms signify one nature, and so the terms *ens* and "animal" do not belong to the second mode of equivocation. That is to say, they are not deliberate equivocals, even if they are not univocal in the strictest sense, which includes only the lowest species of a genus.[60] The third type of analogy is the transfer of sense (*transsumptio*) because of a similitude, and the two examples are "healthy" and "running" said of a man and of water. This type belongs to the second mode of equivocation in the *Sophistical Refutations*, because there are at least two significates (*significata*), the first produced by imposition and the second because of usage (*ex consuetudine loquendi*), and it is a type of analogy found principally in words.

A very similar classification is found in an early work by Burley.[61] In his commentary on a *Treatise on Fallacies*, he wrote:

> Analogy is threefold, that is, on account of (*a parte*) the concept, on account of the thing, and on account of transference. In the first way *ens* is analogical to substance and accident, since *ens* signifies (*importat*) one concept which is found in substance before accident. In the second way animal is analogical to man and donkey, and any genus is analogical in this way to the species which is more perfect and the species which is less perfect. But this analogy pertains not to the logician but to the natural philosopher—it is not the logician who posits analogy in genus but the natural philosopher. In the third way 'foot' is analogical, and any utterance that signifies one thing by imposition and another by transference.

Burley does not explicitly discuss the notion of an intermediate type of analogy between strict univocals and deliberate equivocals. However, his analysis of different types of univocation and equivocation allows us to assume that the notion is there. In his last commentary on the *Categories*, as in his last commentary on the *Physics*, Burley distinguishes three levels of univocation.[62] In the broadest sense, a univocal term has a single concept which corresponds to a number of things either equally or according to a difference between priority and posteriority. In the stricter sense, the single concept corresponds to a number of things equally. In the strictest sense, the concept cannot be divided in accordance with essential differences, such as rationality. There is a corresponding hierarchy of equivocal terms. In the broadest sense, an equivocal term signifies either several concepts or a single concept that can be divided by appeal to essential differences, or a single concept that applies to more than one thing according to a difference between priority and posteriority.

The views of Burley and some earlier thinkers can be summarized in the following table:

	Analogical Word	Analogical Concept	Analogical Reality
Strict univocal, i.e., species term	No	No	No
Broader univocal, i.e., genus term [also broadest equivocal]	No	No	Yes
Broadest univocal, e.g., *ens* [also broader and broadest equivocal]	Yes	Yes	Yes
Deliberate equivocal = case of *translatio*	Yes	No	No
Strict equivocal, e.g., *canis*	No	No	No

Scotus: The Treatment of Analogy in His Logical Works

Let us now turn to Scotus and his logical works, which probably date from the last decade of the thirteenth century, and which are heavily influenced by the doctrines of other English logicians. Here I should add a note about chronology. Donati has found in her reading of *Physics* commentaries that the Oxonian account of a single analogical concept of *ens* was subsequent to and influenced by Scotus's discussion of *ens* as univocal, and Burley's discussions in his logical works were also subsequent to Scotus.[63] However, I read Scotus's early logical works as making most sense in a context in which the notion of a single concept of *ens* which involves prior and posterior senses while being in some way univocal was already the subject of discussion.

In his commentary on the *Categories* (see Appendix I), Scotus asked whether the word *ens* was purely equivocal or analogical, and he began by saying that some authors attribute analogy to terms in three ways.[64] The first is when a word principally signifies a *ratio* which, when it exists in things, applies to its analogues differently. We should note here that Scotus distinguishes three elements: the concept; the *ratio* as significate and object of the intellect; and the *ratio* as a real nature in the things that exist.[65] For the logician, these terms are simply univocal. At the other extreme, there is the case of *translatio*, which is equivalent to deliberate equivocation. Neither the first nor the third case apply to the word *ens*.[66] The second case is the one that interests us. According to those who accept it, a word is analogical when it signifies one thing as prior and a second thing as posterior. It is against this case that Scotus directs his arguments, both here and in Question 15 of his commentary on the *Sophistical Refutations* (see Appendix II), where he asked whether a name could signify one thing as prior and another as posterior.[67] He claimed that this kind of analogy seems to be impossible.[68]

First of all, he was strongly opposed to the doctrine of a single analogical concept which represents its objects according to priority and posteriority. In his commentary on the *Sophistical Refutations*, he argues that to signify is to represent something to the intellect, and that what is signified must be conceived. However, everything that is conceived by the intellect should be conceived by a distinct determinate *ratio* which cannot be both absolute and comparative.[69] Either one has a concept which represents all its objects equally and as separate from other things, or one has a concept which represents a relation between two things. If one has a concept of substance, the concept is absolute, but if one has a concept which represents accidents as attributed to a substance, one has a comparative concept. It follows that it is impossible to find a single analogical concept of *ens* that applies to both substance and accidents, and, in general, that it is impossible to find a concept which represents one thing according to priority and another thing according to posteriority, by virtue of attribution to the first thing.

So far as words are concerned, Scotus was strongly opposed to the doctrine that words can signify according to priority and posteriority.[70] Although things are in fact ordered according to priority and posteriority, the original impositor is under no necessity to pay attention to this order. One can name the posterior thing without knowing the prior thing, or one can understand the prior thing as prior without giving it a name. In these two cases, the name given by the impositor signifies principally (*primo*) the posterior thing, and it is impossible to change this first imposition.[71] The claim that it signifies according to priority and posteriority results from a confusion between the order of signifying, the order of understanding, and the order of things.[72] In his commentary on the *Sophistical Refutations*, he considered the number of acts of imposition in relation to the number of *rationes*.[73] If a word receives its signification from a single act of imposition, the word should correspond to a single *ratio*, and as a result, it will be univocal, since a single *ratio* cannot produce signification according to priority and posteriority. There is no intermediary between pure equivocation and univocation where *rationes* are concerned. If a word receives its signification from two acts of imposition, it must correspond to two *rationes,* and this on an equal footing, since it is impossible to order two acts of imposition according to priority and posteriority. As a result the word will be a chance equivocal. No word can signify according to priority and posteriority, and so there is no analogical predication.

Scotus concluded that all the words which are supposed to signify a real relation between things ordered in accordance with priority and posteriority should be reduced to chance equivocals. Hence no genuine deliberate equivocal can exist, and it is our knowledge of the world, not our knowledge of semantics, which helps us to understand how such words as *ens* are to be used. There is indeed an analogy of being, and the metaphysician considers it, but the analogy of words and concepts does not exist.[74] Only such words as "laughing" said of a man and a meadow belong to the second mode common to equivocation and amphiboly, which is the mode of *translatio* and *transumptio.*[75] Hence it is metaphor, which cannot be explained without reference to a term that has already received its imposition,[76] that replaces semantic analogy. For Scotus, there are three distinct phenomena: analogy, which is an ontological phenomenon; equivocation, a linguistic phenomenon produced by imposition; and metaphor, a linguistic phenomenon produced by usage. Semantics and ontology are now independent, and the analogy of being is recognized as such.

Appendix I: John Duns Scotus on the Categories

[From *Question 4:* "Whether *ens* is <said> univocally of the ten categories." I have often altered the punctuation of the edition in this and in the subsequent translations.]

[280] Hence one should say that *ens* is not <said> univocally of the ten categories. However, one must ask in what way it is <said>, whether purely equivocally or analogically.

Analogy is posited with respect to utterances in three ways.

(1) Either because [281] they primarily signify one *ratio* which at the level of existence applies in different ways (*in exsistendo diversimode convenit*) to two or more things, called analogates. In this way the names "cause" and "principle," along with many others which are distinguished in *Meta-*

physics V, signify one *ratio* primarily, yet it is in diverse things according to an order.

(2) Analogy in utterances is posited in another way, when the utterance signifies one thing primarily (*per prius*) and the other secondarily (*per posterius*). The reason given for this is that signifying follows understanding. Thus what is understood prior (*per prius*) to another, if it is signified by the same utterance by which that other is signified, will be signified primarily (*per prius*).

(3) The third way: when an utterance is imposed properly on one thing, and, because of some similitude to that on which it is first imposed, is transferred to signify another thing, as happens in the second mode of equivocation, where there is indeed some order of signifying, since an utterance is never transferred to signify something <else> unless it is supposed that it has been imposed to signify something properly, and <the utterance> signifies the second thing only because that thing has some similitude to the thing on which <the utterance> was first imposed. [282]

Analogical utterances of the first sort seem to be simply univocal to the logician. For a genus, according to the logician, is simply univocal, even though the *ratio*, which it primarily signifies, applies to diverse species according to an order. As Aristotle said in *Metaphysics* X, "In every genus there is one <that comes> first, that is the measure of all those that come after."

However, perhaps the case of utterances analogical in this way is not entirely similar to the case of genus in relation to species, for although the species of a genus have an order among themselves of more and less perfect in being (*in essendo*), they do not have an order with respect to their participation in the *ratio* of that genus, for they participate in it equally primarily, for a genus is equally immediately predicated of the primary species which divide it. Thus there is no difference in primacy between these predications, "whiteness is a color," "blackness is a color," even though, when one compares whiteness and blackness to each other, whiteness is the more perfect. But in utterances, which are said to be analogical in the first way, there is an order among the participants in participating that <which they participate>, so that end and matter are not equally primarily a cause, nor perhaps are contrariety <and> {added from apparatus} contradiction equally primarily an opposition.

The second type of analogy given above seems to be impossible, for it can happen that one is unaware of the <thing that is> simply first when the name is imposed on the posterior thing, for the simply posterior can be first for us, and thus will be understood first, and signified first. If therefore this utterance is secondly (*secundo*) imposed on what is simply first, it is clear that it will <not> {added from apparatus} signify secondarily (*per posterius*) [283] the thing on which it was first imposed, because once that was signified primarily, it will always <be signified primarily>. After an utterance has been imposed, it will not change with respect to signifying the thing on which it was imposed, and so the order of things does not entail any order in the signification of utterances.

The reason given for the position seems to be invalid, for signifying does not follow understanding by a necessary consequence, as an effect follows a necessary cause. <This is> because something can be understood to be prior to another in both time and nature, and yet not be signified then. For it is not necessary that the one who understands should impose an utterance on that which he understands, but it is up to him (*ad placitum*) whether he imposes <an utterance> or not. But this proposition "signifying follows understanding" should be understood <in terms of> "that without which," for nothing can be signified unless it is understood; but one does not follow the other necessarily, nor according to a similar order in understanding and signifying.

But in what way should a logician posit an analogical utterance? The third way seems most probable, because otherwise there will be no difference between the first mode of equivocation and the second. Either [if *deleted*] an utterance will signify several things primarily in both <modes>; or, if in the second mode, the utterance does not signify that to which it applies improperly, then that mode will not seem to be a mode of equivocation, because that utterance will be simply univocal, in that it signifies only one thing.

But whatever <the solution is> with respect to the mode of positing analogy, none of these modes seem to be appropriate to *ens* in relation to the ten categories. [284]

That the first mode does not apply, is proved by the reasons given for the opposite view. [pp. 277–80: reply to view that *ens* is univocal, and involves one *ratio*.] Similarly, <the categories> do not seem to have an order in participating *ens*, for of each of them <*ens*> is predicated *in quid, per se* in the first way, and immediately.

The second mode is not possible for the logician.

The third mode is not relevant to the present case, since this name *ens* does not seem to be transferred from substance to accident because of some similitude of accident to substance, since it is predicated *in quid* of both, as Aristotle says in *Metaphysics* IV, and thus it <is predicated> improperly of neither.

Similarly, accidents are in the senses prior to substance, and so the same applies to the intellect. Thus it is possible to impose a name on them that signifies them without any relation to substance being involved. Even if accident was signified by this name *ens* as an attribute of substance, it would thereby be signified by a proper *ratio*, as the *ratio* of attribute is the proper *ratio* of accident. And so *ens* would be simply equivocal to substance and accident, because it would signify each according to its proper *ratio*. [285]

Because of this we should say that this name *ens* is simply equivocal to the ten categories by the first mode of equivocation, and especially because of the last <argument>, for it is certain that substance is signified by a proper *ratio*, and accident <is signified> in another way. For if accident is signified by this name *ens* in accordance with a proper *ratio*, this will be proper to it in accordance with the *ratio* by which it is attributed to substance or to something similar, <and> this is proper to an accident; hence it follows that both <substance and accident> are signified by a proper *ratio*.

We should understand, however, that the utterance which is simply equivocal for the logician, because it signifies (*importat*) several things equally primarily, is analogical for the metaphysician or the natural philosopher, who do not consider the signifying utterance but rather those things that are signified insofar as they exist, for the things that are signified have an order among themselves insofar as they exist, although not insofar as they are signified. Thus the metaphysician in *Metaphysics* IV and VII holds that *ens* is analogical to substance and accident, because those things that are signified have an order in being; but to the logician, it is simply equivocal, because insofar as <the things> are signified by the utterance, they are signified equally primarily.

Appendix II: John Duns Scotus on the Sophistical Refutations

[Such sequences as I.1R2OR should be read from right to left as "reply to objection to second reply to argument I.1."]

Question XV: Is it possible for a name to signify one thing primarily and another thing secondarily?

I. <IT IS NOT POSSIBLE> [331]

I.1 It seems that it is not, for if it were possible, this would be on account of the utterance (*ex parte vocis*), or on account of the impositor, or on account of the thing itself. Not on account of the utterance, for the utterance, insofar as it is an utterance, determines no thing <in relation> to itself; nor on account of the impositor, for since the impositor imposes as he pleases (*ad placitum*), he can first impose a name on that which is posterior in reality; nor on account of the thing itself, for although things have an order among themselves, it does not follow from this that they have an order to each other insofar as they are signifiable, for that which is posterior, as was said, can be signified first.

I.1R1 To this reasoning one can say that there are some things that do not have an order among themselves, and some that do. If those things that do not have a relation to each other are signified by an utterance, they are signified purely equivocally. But those things that do have a relation to each other will be signified in the mode of priority and posteriority. For understanding follows being (*esse*), just as signifying <follows> understanding. From the fact that there is an order [332] of priority and posteriority in reality, it follows that there will be an order of priority and posteriority in signifying.

I.1R1O But one can argue against this solution in two ways.

(i) Signifying is a certain act of the intellect, <insofar as it> {added from apparatus} is attributed to the things themselves, but that which is posterior in reality, can be better <known> and <first> {added from apparatus} known by the intellect than that which is simply first in reality. And as the intellect understands, so it imposes a name to signify; therefore, it can first impose a name on that which is posterior in reality; hence priority and posteriority in the intellect do not entail priority and posteriority in things insofar as they are signifiable; hence <the argument does not hold>.

(ii) If some name is imposed on diverse things, either it is imposed on them by one imposition, or by several impositions. If by one imposition, then since one imposition is accepted through one *ratio significandi*, both <things> are made univocal by one *ratio*. If it is imposed on them by diverse impositions, then since the first imposition no more imprints representation on the utterance than does the second, the two <things> are represented equally.

I.1R2 Because of these <remarks> another reply is given, namely that the analogical name signifies one common *ratio* primarily, but this *ratio* is found in diverse things according to prior and posterior (*per prius et posterius*). And in the same way that this *ratio* is found in diverse things, the name is said of them according to prior and posterior. For instance, *ens* primarily signifies entity, and "one" primarily signifies lack of division, but the *ratio* of being (*essendi*) primarily belongs to substance, and then to quantity and the other categories. And so this name *ens* is first (*per prius*) said of substance, and secondarily (*per posterius*) [333] is said of quantity and the other <categories>. And similarly for "one."

I.1R2O But against this:

(i) There is no medium between same and diverse, therefore everything that is conceived is either conceived under the same *ratio* or a diverse <*ratio*>. But those things that are conceived under the same *ratio* are made univocal under that *ratio*. Those that are conceived under a diverse *ratio* are made equivocal by the diverse *rationes*. Since therefore there is no medium between same and diverse, every name will be either simply equivocal or univocal.

(ii) The term puts what it primarily signifies as subject to the predicate. If therefore the analogical name signifies one common <thing>, it will put that as subject to the predicate, and as a result, one will not have to respond to <the use of> that name by making a distinction, since there is a unity there, and not a duplication, and as a result such an analogy will not cause equivocation.

(iii) What is added about *ens* is not true, since it does not primarily signify some *ratio* common to those of which it is said. This is so for three reasons:

(iii.1) According to Aristotle in *Metaphysics* VIII and *Metaphysics* II there are two kinds of matter, sensible and intelligible. The things that have intelligible or sensible matter are not immediately that which they are, for in them matter awaits the coming of form. But in those things that have no matter, whether sensible or intelligible, they are immediately that which they are, for there is nothing there that awaits the coming of form. And he gives the example of *ens* and *unum*, for *ens* and *unum* are immediately what kind, or how, or how much, [334] and so they do not have to be put in definitions. But if *ens* were to signify some common *ratio*, that *ratio* would await some addition by which it would be determined to substance or accident. Since therefore it is the ten categories immediately, it will not signify any common *ratio*.

(iii.2) If *ens* and *unum* were to signify some common *ratio*, the diverse categories would differ less than two species of the same genus, for two species of the same genus agree in the common *ratio* of the genus, and they differ by essential differences. But if *ens* were to signify a *ratio* common to the diverse categories, they would agree in this common *ratio*, and they would not differ by essential differences, for *ens* is not a genus, because difference falls outside the understanding of genus, and vice versa. And a genus is not predicated *per se* of a difference, but *ens* is predicated *per se* of a difference. Thus *ens* is not divided into ten categories by essential differences, but by diverse modes of being (*essendi*), to which diverse modes of predication (*praedicandi*) correspond, and that is why they are called categories (*praedicamenta*), therefore <the argument fails>.

(iii.3) Every concept is either comparative or absolute, therefore the common concept of being (*conceptus entis*) is either absolute or comparative. But an absolute concept is the concept of <a> substance, and a comparative concept is the concept of <an> accident, therefore the concept of <a> being is either the concept of <a> substance or of <an> accident.

(iii.3O) Perhaps someone will say that this argument commits the fallacy of figure of speech, as if one were to argue "every animal is either rational or irrational, therefore [every *deleted*] animal signifies rational or irrational." This is the fallacy of figure of speech, from personal to simple supposition. Even though an actual animal has to be either rational or irrational, [335] "animal" can signify in such a way that it is indifferent with respect to rational or irrational. Similarly, although any concept must be either absolute or comparative, *ens* can signify what is indifferent to this or that.

(iii.3OR) But this reply does not impede the argument, for absolute and comparative are differences of the concept itself as it is conceived, just as rational and irrational are the differences of animal, as it exists in reality. But it is impossible to find any animal in reality which is indifferent to rational and irrational; therefore it is impossible to find any concept which is indifferent to absolute and comparative.

<{Interpolated Conclusion}: Thus it remains true that *ens* does not primarily signify a *ratio* common to those of which it is said. Similarly, <it remains true> that an analogical name does not primarily signify a common *ratio* which is found in diverse things according to prior and posterior. As a

result, the reply that was given was not adequate or well founded; therefore <the argument fails>.>

II. <It is possible>

II.1 There is a difference between univocal, equivocal, and analogical. The univocal signifies one thing principally, the equivocal signifies several things, but equally. Therefore the analogical signifies one thing primarily (*per prius*) and the other secondarily (*per posterius*).

II.2 According to Aristotle in *Metaphysics* IV, "*ens* is said in many ways," and by this he suggests that it is not <said> entirely univocally, nor equivocally, but in relation to one <thing> and one nature, just like "healthy."

II.3 Understanding follows being (*esse*), and signifying <follows> understanding, therefore the mode of understanding follows the mode of being, and the mode of signifying follows [336] the mode of understanding. But there is a relation in reality; therefore there is <a relation> in signifying.

II.4 In *Metaphysics* V, Aristotle distinguishes the names which are said primarily and secondarily (*per prius et posterius*), therefore <this is possible>.

III. <Answer to the question>

In reply to the question, one should say that so far as the signifying utterance is concerned, it is not possible for an utterance to signify one thing primarily (*per prius*) and another secondarily (*per posterius*), for to signify is to represent something to the intellect. Thus what is signified is first conceived by the intellect. But everything that is conceived by the intellect is conceived under a distinct and determinate *ratio*, because understanding (*intellectus*) is a certain act, and thus what it understands, it distinguishes from another <thing>. Therefore everything that is signified is signified under a distinct and determinate *ratio*. This is obvious, because prime matter which in itself is *ens* in potentiality, if it is understood, must be understood under a distinct *ratio*. And so if this applies to <prime> {added from apparatus} matter, much more obviously (*fortius*) will it be true of everything else.

If, therefore, an analogical word (*dictio*) or utterance is imposed on diverse <things>, it is necessary for it to be imposed on them under a distinct and determinate *ratio*. If therefore an analogical word is imposed on diverse things under diverse *rationes*, it is necessary that it represent them equally so far as the signifying utterance is considered. Hence there can be analogy in reality, but in a signifying utterance no priority or posteriority can occur. For there is some property which belongs more properly to one thing than to another, but there is no property which belongs more properly than another to the substance of an utterance. This is also obvious from the fact (*signum*) that in the *Categories*, where Aristotle determines <what> significant utterances <are>, he makes no mention of the things that are analogicals in reality, but only discusses univocals and equivocals. Hence [337] Boethius says in <his commentary on> the same passage, that when Aristotle says "equivocals are those whose name is common but the *ratio substantiae* is diverse," he includes things that are analogical in reality, and every kind of equivocation, under this one definition. Hence he takes *ratio substantiae* there for a determinate *ratio* which the intellect attributes to things, and not for the *ratio* as it is composed out of genus and difference. Because of this I say that so far as the role of the signifying utterance is concerned, there is no priority or posteriority, even though the things signified have a relation to each other.

IV. <Reply to II>

II.1R So far as the signifying utterance is concerned, there is no medium between univocal and equivocal.

II.2R The natural philosopher and also the metaphysician consider the things themselves. The logician however considers beings of reason. Hence there are many <things> that are univocal for the logician but are called equivocal by the natural philosopher. The natural philosopher will say that "body" is said equivocally of higher and lower body, but the logician will say that it is said univocally of both. Hence whatever things a logician can abstract one common *ratio* from are said to be united or made univocal in that common *ratio*. Hence because one can find one common *ratio* in higher and lower body, since these and those bodies agree in having three dimensions, the logician will say that both these <bodies> and those are univocated in the common *ratio*. But because the natural philosopher applies his consideration to the things themselves, and corruptible body has a different nature from incorruptible body, hence the natural philosopher says [338] that "body" is said equivocally of this body and that. The logician also says that all species of the same genus are made univocal in their genus, but the natural philosopher says that many equivocations are hidden in a genus. Hence the logician considers the things themselves as they fall under a *ratio*. And because there is no medium between same and diverse, the logician posits no medium between equivocal and univocal. Hence because of this one should say to the form of the argument that it is because the metaphysician (*primus philosophus*) considers things according to their quiddities, and in reality some things do have a relationship to each other, that the metaphysician {*primus* added from apparatus} says that *ens* is said of substance and accident analogically. But because the logician considers things as they fall under a *ratio*, he says that *ens* is said equivocally of substance and accidents. Hence Porphyry says in his chapter on species that "if anyone calls all things *entia*, he is speaking equivocally, not univocally."

II.2RO But against this it is argued: If then the utterance which is called analogical, so far as the signifying utterance is concerned, does not signify one thing primarily and the other secondarily, it will follow that the first and second mode of equivocation do not differ, for the first mode is when some word signifies several things equally.

II.2ROR Thus one must say that analogy does not cause the second mode of equivocation, because properly speaking, analogy is reduced to the first mode of equivocation. So at the moment it should be said that transference (*translatio et transumptio*) from proper signification to improper <signification> on account of some similitude [339] is what causes the second mode of equivocation. This is obvious from what Aristotle says in the text. For he says that the second mode of equivocation and amphiboly results from what we are accustomed to say, just as "laugh" properly signifies the act of a man, and through some *translatio* is transferred to the flowering of meadows. Hence I will say that we find the second mode of equivocation here: "whatever laughs has a mouth; the meadow laughs; therefore <the meadow has a mouth>." Hence in this second mode no relation is involved, and if those things that in reality do have a relation to each other are signified under distinct *rationes*, then they are signified equivocally so far as the utterance is concerned. This sort of analogy should be reduced to the first mode of equivocation.

[omit p. 339:12–13.]

II.3R One should say that if accident is understood as it has a relation to substance, and if the name is imposed on <accident> in that sense then <the name> is imposed on <accident> under a distinct and determinate *ratio*. As a result, if the same name is imposed on both <accident and substance>, it will represent them equivocally. Hence although the cause of posterior being (*esse*) is prior, it is not necessary that the cause why the posterior is signified should be prior, for the posterior in reality can be more <known> and first known by the intellect, and as a result a name can be first imposed on it; hence a relation in reality does not necessarily imply priority and posteriority in a meaningful word (*sermo*).

II.4R <The reply is obvious.> {added from apparatus}

NOTES

Introduction CHARLES BOLYARD AND RONDO KEELE

1. This is a close paraphrase of the views of Spade, especially as expressed in his *A Survey of Mediaeval Philosophy, Version 2.0* (online at http://pvspade.com /Logic/docs/Survey%202%20Interim.pdf), ch. 4.

1. Duns Scotus on Metaphysics as the Science of First Entity
REGA WOOD

1. Paul Vincent Spade, "The Unity of a Science according to Peter Aureol," *Franciscan Studies* 32 (1972), pp. 203–17, esp. pp. 206–7.
2. Aristotle, *Posterior Analytics* 1.2.71b10–12.
3. Dominique Demange and I arrived independently at similar positions for many of the same reasons. Dominique Demange, "Pourquoi Duns Scot a critique Avicenna," in *Medioevo* 15 (2008). *Giovanni Duns Scoto: Studi e ricerche nel VII Centenario della sua morte in onore di P. César Saco Alarcón,* ed. M. Núñez (Rome, 2008), pp. 195–232. Rega Wood, "The Subject of the Science of Metaphysics," in *The Cambridge History of Medieval Philosophy,* ed. R. Pasnau and C. Van Dyke (Cambridge, 2009), pp. 609–26. As the reader will note, Demange published first and his account is more detailed than mine.
4. John Duns Scotus, *Quaestiones super libros Metaphysicorum Aristotelis* 1.1, ed. G. Etzkorn et al. (St. Bonaventure, NY, 1997), OPh III: 15–72.
5. For a nice summary of M1, see D. Demange, "Pourquoi Duns Scot," pp. 208–12, esp. 212.
6. Both M1 and M2 refer to the St. Bonaventure edition cited in Note 4 above. Citations list the paragraph number and the page number in that edition and take the following form: M1/M2 paragraph number, page number.
7. Citations of the Paris prologue will include page numbers from both works. "RP" refers to K. Rodler, *Der Prolog der Reportata Parisiensia des Johannes Duns Scotus,* Mediaevalia Oenipontana 2 (Innsbruck, 2005); "AM" refers to *Reportata Parisiensia,* Opera omnia 11, Lyons 1639, repr. (Hildesheim, 1969). References take the following form: RP 1A Question.Article, paragraph number, page number; AM Question.Article, paragraph number, page number. The abbreviation "Qlae." stands for Quaestiunculae.
8. Demange, "Pourquoi Duns Scot," pp. 230–32.

9. John Duns Scotus, *In Praedic.*, 4.26, 48, ed. G. Etzkorn et al. (St. Bonaventure, NY, 1999), OPh 1: 280, 288; M1 91, pp. 46–47.

10. Aristotle, *Ethica Nicomachea* 10.8.1177a12–b13; M2 123, p. 58.

11. Aristotle, *Metaphysics* 4.2.1003b7–8; M1 18, p. 21; M2 115, p. 55.

12. M2 142, 143, p. 65.

13. Demange excludes all the additions (*additiones*) from M1, but whether he assigns them to M2 is not clear. See Demange, "Pourquoi Duns Scot," pp. 205, 208.

14. Paragraphs 32–33 are about whether God's attributes are sufficiently distinct from him to permit predication, and the problem is not completely resolved.

15. M2 52, p. 34; see also M2 57, p. 35.

16. Namely, that God does not act necessarily (M2 41, p. 31).

17. The fourth addition in paragraphs 79–83 (pp. 41–43) cannot pertain to M1, but also need not pertain to M2; it assumes that entity is the subject of a *propter quid* science of metaphysics and deals with the question whether *ens qua ens* should be understood specificatively or reduplicatively.

18. For 6.1 see Demange, "Pourquoi Duns Scot," pp. 217–20, citing M2 131, p. 60; for 8.1 see M2 46–48, pp. 32–33.

19. But cf. Demange, "Pourquoi Duns Scotus," p. 231.

20. Ludger Honnefelder, *Ens inquantum Ens*, Beiträge zu Geschichte der Philosophie und Theologie des Mittelalters, Neue Folge 16 (Münster in. W., 1979), p. 307.

21. Demange, "Pourquoi Duns Scot," pp. 204, n. 20; pp. 220–23, 230. Pages 220–23 cite M2 125–26, pp. 58–59; 134, pp. 61–62; and 153, p. 68—the last two as decisive. And I agree that M2 153 makes it clear that Scotus regards univocity as compatible with first entity as the subject of metaphysics. But 134 seems to suggest that only created entity is univocal, so I would not suggest that M2 "reconnaît formellement l'univocité de l'étant."

22. Demange, "Pourquoi Duns Scot," pp. 224–26.

23. RP 1A 3.1, 191, p. 60; AM 3.1, p. 20b.

24. M2 163, pp. 71–72.

25. For useful reflections on this topic see Demange, "Pourquoi Duns Scot," pp. 227–30.

26. RP 1A 3.1, 191–92, pp. 60–61; AM 3.1, pp. 20b–21a. Cf. Aquinas, *Summa contra Gentiles* III.25.

27. RP 1A 1.4, 105–6, pp. 32–33; AM 1.4, 42, pp. 12a–b.

28. RP 1A 3.2, 197, p. 63; AM 3.2, p. 21a. Cf. RP 1A 1.4, 103, p. 32; AM 1.4, 40, p. 12a. Cf. etiam *Ordinatio* 1.3.1.3 n. 151; Opera omnia 3: 93.

29. RP 1A 1.2, 20–27, pp. 8–11; AM 1.2.7, pp. 3b–4b.

30. Cf. Aquinas, *Summa theologica* 1a 17.

31. M2 153, p. 68: ". . . nunquam principale subiectum ponetur genus, quando de ipso et aliis speciebus traditur scientia principaliter propter cognitionem unius speciei, sed tantum tunc quando aeque primo de omnibus propter cognitionem

de genere habendam . . ." This quotation shows that metaphysics is not generically unified. See also M2 115, p. 55 and the arguments it references (M1 18, p. 21 and M1 64–65, p. 37). Note, however, that Demange makes an interesting case that according to M2 metaphysics is generically unified, basing himself on the discussion in M2 103, pp. 50–51, a discussion that is echoed at M2 131, p. 60. For a further discussion see below and cf. Demange, "Pourquoi Duns Scot," pp. 213–20.

32. RP 1A 3.1, 191, p. 60; AM 3.1, p. 20b.

33. For the Paris prologue statement of the objection that first entity can be known only accidentally, see RP 1A 1.4, 106, p. 33; AM 1.4, p. 12b.

34. RP 1A 1.2, 24, p. 9, RP 1A Q3 Qlae. 210, p. 67; AM 1.4, p. 11b. Note, too, that even M1 assumes that there is an adequate response to this objection; see M1 25, p. 25. But this is an issue about which Scotus hesitates; see M2 33, p. 29.

35. Or alternatively that the common concept of first entity is not knowable, as codices E and H indicate.

36. RP 1A 3.1, 191, p. 60; AM 3.1, p. 20b.

37. See M2 145, p. 65, l. 20.

38. Aristotle, *Ethica Nicomachea* 10.8.1177a12–b13; M2 123, p. 58.

39. RP 1A 3, 182, p. 58; AM 3, p. 20a; RP 1A 3, 200; AM 3, p. 22a.

40. Of course, for Aristotelians no *quia* science is as certain as a *propter quid* science. See Aristotle, *Posterior Analytics* 1.27.87a31–33.

41. RP 1A 1.1, 8–11, pp. 4–5; AM 1.1, p. 2.

42. RP 1A 1.2, 23, p. 9; AM1, p. 2. Cf.1 *Ord.* prol., 4.1–2.208, Vat. 1: 141; Lect. 107, Vat. 16: 39.

43. RP 1A 3.3, 200, pp. 63–64; AM 3.3, p. 21b.

44. RP 1A 3.3, 201, p. 64; AM 3.3, 7, p. 22a.

45. RP 1A 2, 132, p. 42; AM 2, 4, p. 15a; RP 1A 3.1, 191, p. 60; AM 3.1, p. 20b.

46. RP 1A 3.3, 200, pp. 63–64; AM 3.3, p. 21b.

47. RP 1A 3 Qlae., 209, p. 67; AM 3 Qlae., p. 22b. Still, this very disagreement suggests that as a metaphysician, Scotus has reason to prefer M2. For as the Paris prologue states, the nobility of a science depends as much on the nobility of its subject as on its certainty. And on those grounds the metaphysics M2 describes is more noble than the Paris prologue's metaphysics. See RP 1A 3 Qlae., 218; AM 3.3, Qlae., 15, p. 23b.

48. See also Demange, "Pourquoi Duns Scot," pp. 231–32.

49. RP 1A 3.2, 196, p. 62; AM 3.2, p. 21a.

50. Spade, "The Unity," p. 214.

51. Demange, "Pourquoi Duns Scot," pp. 213–20.

52. The manuscript witnesses for the changes I propose in M2 32 and 131 are as follows: Balliol College 234 (B), Padua Bibl. Antoniana (D), Berlin Staatsbibl. lat. fol. 420 (E), Erfurt, UB Ampon. Quarto 291 (F), and Paris Bibl. Nat. lat. 16110 (M).

53. Duns Scotus, *Quaestiones super libros Metaphysicorum* 6.1, OPh IV: 5–6.

54. Ibid., 703–6, appendix.
55. Ibid., 15–17.
56. RP 1A 3.2, 196–97, pp. 62–63; AM 3.2, p. 21.

2. Aquinas vs. Buridan on Essence and Existence GYULA KLIMA

1. Thomas Aquinas, "On Being and Essence," c. 5, in Gyula Klima (ed.), *Medieval Philosophy: Essential Readings with Commentary* (Oxford: Blackwell Publishers, 2007), p. 240.
2. Anthony Kenny, *Aquinas on Being* (Oxford: Oxford University Press, 2002).
3. Gyula Klima, "On Kenny on Aquinas on Being: A Critical Review of *Aquinas on Being* by Anthony Kenny," *International Philosophical Quarterly*, 44 (2004), pp. 567–80.
4. A nominal essence is what is described by a nominal definition, which merely provides the meaning of a name, regardless of whether there is or even just can be anything that fits that description, while a real essence is what is signified by a real or quidditative definition, which identifies the essential features of the thing that is referred to by name according to the meaning specified by the corresponding nominal definition. Therefore, we can have nominal essences expressed/described by nominal definitions even of nonentities or mere *impossibilia*, whereas real essences can only be had by really existing genuine entities. For a good description of the contrast between nominal and quidditative definitions in the Thomistic tradition see "Thomas de Vio Cardinalis Cajetanus Super Librum De Ente et Essentia Sancti Thomae," in *Opuscula Omnia* (Bergomi, Typis Comini Venturae, 1590), p. 290.
5. Johannis Buridani, *Quaestiones in Aristotelis Metaphysicam: Kommentar zur Aristotelischen Metaphysik* (Paris, 1518; reprint, Frankfurt am Main: Minerva, 1964) selections from lb. 8, q. 4, emended *ad sensum* and translated by Gyula Klima in Klima (ed.), *Medieval Philosophy*, p. 250.
6. Buridan uses these sentential nominalizations equivalently with the abstract nouns formed from their verbs. This issue need not detain us here.
7. Buridani, *Quaestiones in Aristotelis Metaphysicam*, p. 250.
8. Ibid.
9. See the end of c. 1 of *De Ente et Essentia*. The quidditative definition of the thing Aquinas has there in mind is the definition of its most specific species consisting of its proximate genus and its specific difference.
10. For this point see for instance the entire discussion of c. 4 of his *De Ente et Essentia*.
11. For a painstaking and extremely illuminating discussion of distinct versus confused concepts or acts of cognition, see q. 1 of Cajetan's question commentary on Aquinas's *De Ente et Essentia*.
12. Thomas Aquinas, *Summa theologiae* 1, q. 2, a. 2.
13. I owe the original objection and the retort to my initial response to it to my student Timothy Kieras, S.J.

3. The Form of Corporeity and Potential and Aptitudinal Being in Dietrich von Freiberg's Defense of the Doctrine of the Unity of Substantial Form BRIAN FRANCIS CONOLLY

I am very grateful to Charles Bolyard and Rondo Keele for their very helpful comments on an earlier version of this essay. Translations from the Latin texts of medieval authors quoted throughout are mine, except as otherwise noted.

1. For a brief overview of the life and works of Dietrich von Freiberg (hereafter referred to as "Dietrich"), see Markus Führer, "Dietrich of Freiberg," *Stanford Encyclopedia of Philosophy* (Summer 2010 Edition). Edited by Edward N. Zalta, URL = http://plato.stanford.edu/archives/sum2010/entries/dietrich -freiberg/.

2. See Dietrich, *De iride et radialibus impressionibus*, edited by Loris Sturlese and Maria Rita Pagnoni-Sturlese in *Opera Omnia*, IV (Hamburg: Felix Meiner Verlag, 1985).

3. See William A. Wallace, O.P., *The Scientific Methodology of Dietrich von Freiberg* (Fribourg in Switzerland: University Press, 1959).

4. See especially Kurt Flasch, "Kennt die mittelalterliche Philosophie die konstitutiven Funktion des menschlichen Denkens? Eine Untersuchung zu Dietrich von Freiberg." *Kant-Studien* 63 (1972), pp. 182–206; and Burkhard Mojsisch, *Die Theorie Des Intellekts bei Dietrich von Freiberg* (Hamburg: Felix Meiner Verlag, 1977).

5. See especially Armand Maurer, "The *De Quidditatibus Entium* of Dietrich of Freiberg and its Criticism of Thomastic Metaphysics" in Armand Maurer, *Being and Knowing. Studies in Thomas Aquinas and Later Mediaeval Philosophers* (Toronto: Pontifical Institute of Mediaeval Studies, 1990), pp. 177–99; and Ruedi Imbach, "Pourquoi Thierry de Freiberg a-t-il critiqué Thomas d'Aquin? Remarques sur le *De accidentibus*," *Freiburger Zeitschrift für Philosophie und Theologie* 45 (1998), pp. 116–29.

6. Aquinas has a much different theory of generation, known as the "succession of forms," in which the previous stages of generation are not preserved in the latter stages. This will be discussed in some detail below.

7. See Dietrich, *De accidentibus*, edited by M.R. Pagnoni-Sturlese in *Opera Omnia* III (Hamburg: Felix Meiner, 1983). See also Imbach, "Pourquoi Thierry de Freiberg."

8. In addition to the problem of accounting for the numerical identity of the living and dead body of Christ, to be discussed below, the opponents of the theory maintain that it runs into problems in regard to the Eucharist, the Incarnation, the doctrine of Creation, and the remission of sins! See Giles of Lessines, *De unitate formae*, edited by Maurice de Wulf (Louvain: Institute supérieur de philosophie de l'Universite, 1901), tertium capitulum primae partis, pp. 12–17.

9. Giles of Lessines, *De unitate formae*, p. 14.

10. Cf. Thomas Aquinas, *On Spiritual Creatures* (English translation of *De spiritualibus creaturis* by Mary Fitzpatrick and J. Wellmuth [Milwaukee: Marquette University Press 1949]), art. III, ad 12: "As to the twelfth, it must be said that the body, before it receives a soul, has some form; however, that form does not remain when the soul comes. For the coming of the soul takes place through a kind of generation, and the generation of one thing does not occur without the corruption of the other; thus, for instance, when the form of fire is received in the matter of air, the form of air ceases to be in it actually and remains in potency only. Nor must it be said that the form comes into being or is corrupted, because coming into being and being corrupted are characteristics of that which has actual being, and actual being does not belong to a form as to something that exists, but as to that whereby something is. And hence, too, nothing but the composite is said to come into being, insofar as it is brought from potency into act."

11. See, for instance, Aristotle, *Metaphysics* VII, 1035b 23–25.

12. I say "at least" specifically distinct, since in late medieval philosophical and theological contexts, *equivocation* usually entails a difference between the things thus compared which precludes a generic and even an analogous community.

13. Matthew of Aquasparta, for instance, quite consciously steers away from any notion of aggregation. See Roberto Zavalloni, O.F.M., *Richard de Mediavilla et la controverse sur la pluralité des formes* (Louvain: L'institut supérieur de philosophie, 1951), pp. 324–25 and 328–30.

14. See Thomas Aquinas, *Summa theologiae* (hereafter cited as "*ST*") I, q. 76, art. 6.

15. Thomas Aquinas, *Quodlibet* IV, q. 5. See also *ST,* III, q. 50, art. 5, where Aquinas tries to resolve the *numerical identity* of the living and dead body of Christ with the *equivocity* of the living and dead body of Christ and of any other man. On this see also Zavalloni, *Richard de Mediavilla*, pp. 267–72.

16. See Zavalloni, *Richard de Mediavilla*, pp. 259–60. Zavalloni provides a detailed and comprehensive discussion of the Dominican and non-Dominican defenders (or sympathizers) of the doctrine of the unity of form on pp. 247–302.

17. Cf. Aquinas, *ST* III, q. 50, art 2, ad 1: "The Word of God is said to be united with the flesh through the medium of the soul, *inasmuch* as it is through the soul that the flesh belongs to *human nature*, which the Son of God intended to assume; but not as though the soul were the medium linking them together. Rather it is due to the soul that the flesh is human even after the soul has been separated from it—namely, inasmuch as by God's ordinance there remains in the dead flesh a certain relation to the resurrection. And therefore the union of the Godhead with the flesh is not taken away" (Blackfriars translation).

18. Cf. Aquinas, *ST* III, q. 50, art. 5, ad 1: "The dead body of everyone else does not continue united to an abiding hypostasis, as Christ's dead body did; consequently the dead body of everyone else is not the same 'simply,' but only in some respect: because it is the same as to its matter, but not the same as to its

form. But Christ's body remains the same simply, on account of the identity of the suppositum, as stated above" (Blackfriars translation).

19. Edited by Zavalloni in *Richard de Mediavilla*, p. 108.

20. See ibid., pp. 303–42.

21. Aquinas, *ST* III, q. 50 art. 5.

22. Earlier in the body of the question Aquinas explains that in the first sense of *simpliciter* the living and the dead body of Christ are absolutely and simply the same: "The expression 'simply' can be taken in two senses. In the first instance by taking 'simply' to be the same as 'absolutely'; thus 'that is said simply which is said without addition,' as the Philosopher put it (*Topic*. ii): and in this way the dead and living body of Christ was simply identically the same: since a thing is said to be 'simply' identically the same from the identity of the subject. But Christ's body living and dead was identical in its suppositum because alive and dead it had none other besides the Word of God, as was stated above (Article 2). And it is in this sense that Athanasius is speaking in the passage quoted" (*ST* III, q. 50 art. 5; Blackfriars translation).

23. Dietrich, *De origine rerum praedicamentalium*, edited by Loris Sturlese in *Opera Omnia* III (Hamburg: Felix Meiner Verlag, 1983), pp. 119–201.

24. Dietrich, *De corpore Christi in mortuo*, edited by Maria-Rita Pagnoni-Sturlese in *Opera Omnia* II (Hamburg: Felix Meiner Verlag, 1980).

25. See Maria-Rita Pagnoni-Sturlese, "Per una datazione del De Origine di Teodorico di Freiburg," *Annali della Scuola Normale Superiore di Pisa* 33, no. 11 (1981), pp. 431–45.

26. Dietrich's arguments against the pluralist position actually proceed along two fronts. In chapter 4 of *De origine rerum praedicamentalium* we find one set of arguments that concerns the *physics of generation* and focuses upon the *form of corporeity* (which is our main concern in the present discussion). We also find another set of arguments that approach the pluralist position with regard to *metaphysics*, that is, apart from all consideration of motion and change: "For the evidence of this it is to be considered that there are two ways in which a being tends to the completion that is befitting to it according to act and form. In one way, insofar as it is considered in relation to its causes, and this with respect to the first mode named above in the beginning. In another way, insofar as a thing is considered with respect to the *ratio* of its quiddity and absolute essence, namely, insofar as it is a being, and this with respect to the mode named above" (*De origine rerum praedicamentalium*, ch. 4, pp. 169–70). These latter arguments conform closely to what can be found in Aquinas's own discussions of the problem. Dietrich's arguments against the pluralist position are much more distinctive (and therefore more interesting) when he considers the problem from the point of view of the physics of generation and corruption. Indeed it is here that Dietrich demonstrates the independence, originality, and cogency of his thinking with respect to this problem.

27. See Aquinas, *On Spiritual Creatures*, p. 41, for further references.

28. Except for a brief mention of the notion of the organized body in *Quaestiones de anima*, q. 9, Aquinas does not appear to discuss such organization or harmony as an accidental disposition that mediates the union of body and soul. Inasmuch as this notion of harmony also appears not to be discussed by Giles of Lessines in *De unitate formae*, Dietrich's discussion provides an excellent witness to how far the debate advanced within the decade following Giles's treatise.

29. Dietrich, *De origine rerum praedicamentalium*, ch. 4, pp. 171–72.

30. Dietrich, *De corpore Christi in mortuo*, ch. 4, p. 150.

31. See Aquinas, *On Spiritual Creatures*, art. III.

32. Dietrich, *De origine rerum praedicamentalium*, ch. 4, p. 110.

33. In other words, the accidental dispositions must reside in either the form itself or the proper subject itself, or the relation between them.

34. It is clear that Dietrich is here considering harmony as a disposition that is *accidental* to the substantial form of flesh or body; for if it were *essential* then obviously he could just argue that the presence or absence of such harmony is tantamount to a numerical if not also specific distinction of the forms of corporeity in question. The point is that *harmony* cannot in any case be an accidental disposition the presence and absence of which distinguishes the living body and the dead body without at the same time compromising their numerical identity, simply because *harmony* cannot be an accidental disposition to this or any other substantial form, since substantial forms are simple and harmony requires a diversity of things.

35. Cf. Dietrich, *De origine rerum praedicamentalium*, ch. 4, p. 172: "Furthermore, it happens that the harmony that they refer to, is not found in the substantial form of flesh, which is *simple*, whereas a harmony seems to be the proportion that several things owe to each other. Also, the harmony that is between the form of flesh and its proper matter, according to them, is not transformed after death. For otherwise the same form of flesh would not now exist in the matter as was before, since there could not be the same proportion between form and matter as was before. Therefore, it is necessary that such transformation of a harmony, according to them, be made in things that are in the *subject* of the form of flesh."

36. Cf. ibid., pp. 172–73: "Hence, whether they mean that such a harmony is found in such things completely accidentally or completely substantially, provided that there is not so much transformation that such things would still remain in that proportion whereby they can be the subject of the form of flesh, it still follows that, since flesh, according to the *ratio* of its substantial form, is *per se* in potency and in an ordered relation to the form of the soul, if the same form remained, flesh would be in an ordered relation to the form of the soul. <This is> because that which befits a thing *per se* according to the reason of its quiddity, cannot *not* exist while the thing itself remains, and because in every essential order of causes the second is not found without the first, as is clear by

running through any number of things. For in the genus of material causes, an element is not found without prime matter; in efficient causes, sperm does not move without a celestial power; in formal causes, 'life' is not found without 'being,' and so on, concerning the others. Hence, in the thing proposed, the form of flesh by which flesh is *per se* in an ordered relation to the form of the soul, is not found without soul or without the ordered relation to it. For although the soul is the final form in the path of generation, it is nevertheless the first in nature and in defintion. Therefore, the transformation of the harmony, in the manner that was said, does nothing to change the relation of the form of flesh to the soul, yet the same form of flesh remains what it was before. Therefore, it would be possible for an animal to resurrect, as was concluded above."

37. Dietrich seems to think that it is in any case impossible to account for the living body's potency to the soul in terms of an *accidental* disposition of harmony or temperment, as indeed his argument seems to suggest. For the pluralist has maintained all along that it is only by virtue of this harmony alone that there can be a union of body and soul, which is to say, a living body. Hence, this harmony must be considered to be something *essential* to the composite substance that is the union of body and soul. Cf. *De origine rerum praedicamentalium*, ch. 4, p. 172: "For this harmony, whereby a thing receives being or falls away from substantial being, is not an accident, nor is it something that exists in the manner of an accident. Rather, it is a certain moderation of the thing that is considered completely essential. <For> otherwise, an accident would be an intrinsic principle of a substance and within its essence, which is absurd. Therefore, if the harmony of a thing, according to which it is considered to be or not to be according to substance, is transformed, it is necessary for the thing to be transformed in its essentials. Now, if the essentials of the thing are transformed, then the essence is transformed; but if the essence does not remain the same as it was before, it is impossible for the thing to exist under the act of the same substantial form. Therefore, if the harmony of the flesh is transformed through death, it is necessary that the same substantial form of flesh does *not* remain after death."

38. That the pluralists consider and discuss each form in the course of generation as something *positive* should be clear from the discussion of their position throughout. For Aquinas's account of generation in terms of a succession of forms, each of which being understood positively, see, for instance, *On Spiritual Creatures*, art. III, ad. 13.

39. To some extent this move can be seen as simply the strict application of those principles of change that are to be found in Aristotle's analysis of change, namely, *form* and *privation*. See, for instance, Aristotle, *Physics* I.7–9 and *De generatione et corruptione* I.3. Aquinas is aware of form and privation as the fundamental principles of change in nature, as is evident from his discussion in *De Principiis Naturae*, yet he does not seem ever to have applied these principles in the manner proposed here by Dietrich.

40. See Dietrich, *De corpore Christi in mortuo*, ch. 3, pp. 148–49.

41. Cf. ibid., p. 148: "as in the process of generation a thing proceeds from potency to act, so with respect to the fall or withdrawal from entity or from the act by which it is a being, it falls into a certain aptitude, so that when from seeing it becomes blind or from living it becomes dead. For something blind is by nature apt to see, but not seeing, and something dead is apt by nature to live, but not living."

42. Aristotle, *Metaphysics* V, 1022b25–28. (Translation by Hippocrates G. Apostle [Bloomington, Indiana: Indiana University Press, 1966], p. 95.) See also *Metaphysics* IX, 1046a32–35. The term "aptitudinal being," by contrast, might be innovative on Dietrich's part; or at least I don't know where the term in this sense originates.

43. As will be seen below, Dietrich maintains that despite these differences in the various stages of the process of generation, there persists an essential unity throughout. It should be noted that there is perhaps some equivocation on the use of "form" here as well. On the one hand, there is the substantial form, for example, man, which informs prime matter and makes the substance to be and to be what it is; on the other hand, there is the shape, as it were, that something takes in the process of generation (or corruption), for example, embryo, infant, child, adolescent, adult, senile, and, upon death, corpse. In other contexts Dietrich of course shows a clear understanding of the former sense; but in the present context he means the latter. It is, however, "form" understood in the former sense that provides the underlying essential unity throughout the course of generation for Dietrich. This essential unity, or numerical identity between the being in the various stages of generation, will be discussed in detail below.

44. Dietrich, *De origine rerum praedicamentalium*, ch. 3, pp. 158–59.

45. Ibid., pp. 159–60.

46. Ibid., pp. 160–61.

47. Ibid., p. 161.

48. Ibid., p. 162.

49. Ibid. While the ontological or essential properties of a substance (as opposed to its substantial properties) may be said to dispose a substance formally, they do not do so by the *ratio* of any natural operation.

50. Ibid., p. 168.

51. Ibid.

52. The intrinsic principles of beings, for example, matter and form, taken on their own, run into problems with this second condition, as do privated beings, for example, beings in the process of corruption. For the former, see ibid., p. 162; for the latter, see ibid., pp. 166–68. This aspect of Dietrich's thought will be discussed below in some detail.

53. Ibid., pp. 159–60.

54. Ibid., p. 163. Cf. also ibid., ch. 4, p. 169: "But it is to be known, according to the Philosopher in IX *Metaphysics*, that a being in potency neither is nor has a

definition unless by reason of the act to which it is <in potency>. Hence, by virtue of the act that something *already* participates, and according to its proper reason, such a being in potency has both a *ratio* of being and that by which it differs from non-being absolutely; and so the complete act is primarily and principally both the *ratio* of its being and of its difference from nothing." And ibid., ch. 4, p. 170: "Therefore, because a thing is a *being in potency* according to each of those things that precede the ultimate act, it follows that according to none of them is it a being absolutely; and consequently, such a thing is not determined to any genus of being, that is, so that it would be in a genus absolutely and in act. Rather, <it is a being absolutely> only according to the ultimate act of the form by which a thing has its complete and specific being, since according to this alone is a thing a being in act."

55. Ibid., ch. 3, p. 164.

56. Dietrich, *De corpore Christi in mortuo*, ch. 2, p. 147. Cf. also *De origine rerum praedicamentalium*, ch. 3, p. 166: "Now similarly, as was said concerning beings in potency, privated beings, (such as a dead animal and similar things), also pertain to the same genus as the beings that the privations imply: *originally*, indeed because of the nature and *ratio* of the subject; *formally*, however, and *completively*, by reason of privation. For privation has a *ratio* from the form and habit of which it is the privation; and thus it is necessary for them to belong to one ordered arrangement. For privation succeeds the substantial form in the subject. Hence, in such beings, that is, privated beings, in order that they be in an ordered arrangement with other things under a genus, the privation is in place of the substantial form. For they are not reduced to the genus by the substantial form, which once existed in <the thing>. For they are privated beings, as dead animal <is reduced> by the form of body and flesh, which once existed in <the thing>. For such a form is found and intended by nature accidentally, since it is the principle of no operation <that is> intended through itself by nature, but <is found> only as a being is in the process of dissolution, so that it should arrive at the principles of its nature, <that is>, at the terminus in which the corruption of one thing can be the generation of another. Therefore, such beings are reducible to the ordered arrangement under a genus in which previously they were related to the form which through itself and absolutely is a being in a genus. Now such is the privation by which privated beings are related to form through something prior, just as a being in potency through something prior is related to the act of the form through that which is in potency, and so, is reducible to the same genus. Now when I say 'a form intended by nature accidentally,' I call nature not only the first principle of all beings, but also properly the determinate and proper period of each beings, within which the being of each generable things is enclosed. For, just as in the generation of a being absolutely intended by nature, <nature> intends the being and the completion of the thing according

to the act of the form, so in corrupting by something prior, <nature> intends the corruption or privation of form, not to introduce a form, but as a privated being exists, to which it is not fitting that it have through itself a period in nature, just as it is not a being through itself in nature, as was said. The Philosopher suggests this in VIII *Metaphysics*, where he says that life is not the matter of death nor wine <the matter> of vinegar, nor does matter through itself receive the form of death or of vinegar, but accidentally, according to the process of the corruption of animal and of wine."

57. Dietrich, *De corpore Christi in mortuo*, ch. 2, p. 146. Dietrich's theory of the reciprocal transformation of the elements is somewhat more complicated in his treatise *De miscibilibus in mixto*, edited by William A. Wallace in *Opera Omnia* IV (Hamburg: Felix Meiner Verlag, 1985), pp. 27–47. Therein he introduces a notion of *proper matter* even for each of the elements, and a corresponding corequisite notion that *prime matter* is intrinsically complex. For only thereby could one account for such a notion as *proper* matter for each of the elements. Closely related to this concern is the desire to preserve a clear distinction between *alteration*, on the one hand, and *generation and corruption*, on the other.

58. Dietrich, *De corpore Christi in mortuo*, ch. 2, p. 146.

59. Ibid., ch. 2, pp. 146–47. Cf. also *De origine rerum praedicamentalium*, ch. 4, p. 173: "Furthermore, that the form of flesh in the dead animal, which had been in the living animal, is not the same as it was before, the Philosopher manifestly shows in VIII *Metaphysics*, and the Commentator in the same place, where he says that matter is related in two modes to diverse forms in receiving them. In one way, it is related to the diverse forms 'according to privation.' This is when matter is related to either form in the same order, and these forms can succeed each other reciprocally in the same matter, as when fire is generated from air and conversely. Now this mode of reception and of the relation of matter to these forms is here said to be according to privation. For in matter there is required only the privation of the form to be received; it is not necessary that one of them exists in it in order that it receive the other. In another way, matter is related to diverse forms in receiving them 'according to possession.' This happens when matter receives form according to a certain order that is *per se* found among forms, so that it does not receive any of them unless there is first found in matter another according to the path and order of generation of corruption. For example, it is clear that matter does not receive the form of flesh unless the form of blood precedes it in the matter, and so on concerning the others."

60. Dietrich is justified in doing so because substantial change in nature is distinguished into generation and corruption; and *form* is the terminus of *generation*, whereas the *privation of form* is the terminus of *corruption*. If, on the contrary, the terminus of corruption were *form* and not the *privation of form*, then either corruption would not be corruption, but generation, or

"generation" and "corruption" would be reduced to being merely relative terms. Thus, the adult human being could be seen not only as the product of generation, but also as the product of corruption, with respect to that generation which has the embryo as its terminus. Conversely, if the terminus of corruption were *form*, then the corpse could be seen, in such relative terms, not only as the product of corruption, with respect to the generation that has the living human being as its terminus, but also as the terminus of a generation, in which the living human being would be but a being in potency in relation to the corpse, which, relative to this being in potency, is the complete being in act.

61. See Dietrich, *De origine rerum praedicamentalium*, ch. 3, p. 166.

62. Ibid., ch. 4, pp. 173–74. With respect to the phrase "innuens per hoc huiusmodi ordinis accidentalitatem," ms. B used in the edition has "modum essentialem" here instead for "accidentalitatem," which seems to make more sense in the context of the argument. Cf. also *De corpore Christi in mortuo*, ch. 4, p. 150, where Dietrich argues precisely along these lines that the pluralist position is contrary to what Aristotle says: "And this position about a living and a dead man is manifestly contrary to the Philosopher in VIII *Metaphysics*, where he shows that it is impossible for matter to receive the form of 'death' unless the form of 'life,' which is to be a soul, were previously in the matter. And it is impossible for matter to receive the form of vinegar unless the form of wine precedes <it> in the matter. Precedes <it>, I say, by nature and by time, as he shows there and is clear from his discussion. Wherefore it is impossible that the form of 'death' exist in the body unless it is preceded in the matter, by nature and by time, by the form of life in man, which is the rational soul." In the same section of the text, Dietrich also argues along similar lines that the pluralist position leads to a consequence that is contrary to Christian faith, namely, that Christ was not truly dead. But the argument is not clear.

63. Aristotle, *Metaphysics* VIII, 1045a29–33.

64. Averroes, *In VIII Metaphysica*, comm. 15 (Venice: 1562), 224ra.

65. Dietrich, *De corpore Christi mortuo*, ch. 3, p. 148.

66. Ibid., p. 149.

67. See Dietrich, *De ratione potentiae*, ed. Maria-Rita Pagnoni-Sturlese et al. in *Opera Omnia* III (Hamburg: Felix Meiner Verlag, 1983), wherein Dietrich distinguishes several different meanings of this term in physics and in metaphysics.

68. Dietrich, *De corpore Christi mortuo*, ch. 3, 149.

69. As Dietrich neatly explains in *De origine rerum praedicamentalium*, ch. 3, pp. 164–65, the manner in which these are in potency to the human being is specifically quite distinct from the manner in which the embryo, the infant, etc. are in potency to the adult human being that stands at the culmination and completion of the process of generation.

70. Aristotle, *Metaphysics* VII, 1035b23–25.

71. Dietrich, *De origine rerum praedicamentalium*, ch. 3, pp. 167–68.

4. Accidents in Scotus's Metaphysics *Commentary* CHARLES BOLYARD

1. Boethius, *De Trinitate*, in *Theological Tractates and The Consolation of Philosophy* (Loeb ed.). (Harvard, 1973), p. 7: "Sed numero differentiam accidentium uarietas facit. Nam tres homines neque genere neque specie sed suis accidentibus distant; nam uel si animo cuncta ab his accidentia separemus." As translated by Paul Vincent Spade, *Survey of Mediaeval Philosophy, Version 2.0:* "Now it is the variety of accidents that makes for difference in number. For three men are distinguished not by genus or species, but by their accidents." For a discussion of William of Champeaux's view, especially as interpreted by Abelard, see Spade, *Survey*, ch. 40, pp. 1–16.

2. All references to the *QM* will be threefold. The first will be to the book, question, and paragraph numbers; the second will give the pagination from the recent Latin critical edition of the text: B. Ioannis Duns Scoti, *Quaestiones Super Libros Metaphysicorum Aristotelis, Opera Philosophica III–IV*, ed. Andrews et al. (St. Bonaventure: The Franciscan Institute, 1997); and the third will give the pagination from the recent translation: John Duns Scotus, *Questions on the Metaphysics of Aristotle*, trans. Etzkorn and Wolter. (St. Bonaventure: The Franciscan Institute, 1997). As the editors of the critical edition point out, though it had been thought that the *QM* was one of Scotus's early works, there is now ample evidence that he continued to revise it throughout his career. Thus dating it to any particular period in his life is difficult at best.

3. Giorgio Pini, "Substance, Accident, and Inherence: Scotus and the Paris Debate on the Metaphysics of the Eucharist," in *Duns Scot á Paris 1302–2002: Actes du colloque de Paris, 2–4 Septembre 2002*, ed. O. Boulnois, E. Karger, J.-L. Solère, and G. Sondag (Turnhout: Brepols, 2004), p. 287. Pini's article focuses much more on the development of Scotus's mature position, with substantial attention paid to his medieval precursors and to many of his works. He gives the *QM* some attention, but he focuses primarily on VII.1. It should also be noted that Pini is focused on the question of how an accident inheres in a subject, rather than on giving a multifaceted account of accidents.

4. For the best recent treatment of the topic, see Theodor Ebert, "Aristotelian Accidents," in *Oxford Studies in Ancient Philosophy: Vol. XVI*, ed. C.C.W. Taylor (Oxford, 1998), pp. 133–58. My brief discussion of Aristotle's view here is indebted in particular to Ebert's paper. Other scholarship of note includes Robert Heinaman, "Aristotle on Accidents," *Journal of the History of Philosophy* 23.3 (July 1985), pp. 311–24; Irving M. Copi, "Essence and Accident," *Journal of Philosophy* 51.23, pp. 706–19; W. Donald Oliver, "Essence, Accident, and Substance," *Journal of Philosophy* 51.23, pp. 719–30; Michael V. Wedin, *Aristotle's Theory of Substance: The* Categories *and* Metaphysics *Zeta* (Oxford, 2000), esp. pp. 38–66; and R.J. Hankinson, "Philosophy of Science," in *The Cambridge Companion to Aristotle*, ed. Jonathan Barnes (Cambridge, 1995), pp. 109–39.

5. All translations of Aristotle in this essay are taken from the edition of Jonathan Barnes, *The Complete Works of Aristotle* (2 vols.) (Oxford, 1984).

6. Ebert, "Aristotelian Accidents," p. 158.

7. Porphry, *Isagoge et in Aristotelis Categorias commentarium*, ed. Adolfus Busse ("Commentaria in Aristotelem Graeca," Vaol. 4.1) (Berlin: George Reimer, 1887). I follow the translation of Paul Vincent Spade, *Five Texts on the Mediaeval Problem of Universals* (Hackett, 1994), p. 11.

8. For a clear exposition of a generic medieval account of relational accidents, see Rondo Keele, "Can God Make a Picasso? William Ockham and Walter Chatton on Divine Power and Real Relations," *Journal of the History of Philosophy* 45.3 (2007), pp. 398–401. For a fuller treatment of relational accidents, including a discussion of Scotus's view, see Mark G. Henninger, *Relations: Mediaeval Theories 1250–1325* (Oxford: Clarendon Press, 1989).

9. Pini terms this Scotus's "independence thesis." See Pini, "Substance," p. 288.

10. For Augustine's discussion of the vanishing extent of the present instant of time, see the final line of his *Confessions* XI.14: ". . . ut scilicet non vere dicamus tempus esse, nisi quia tendit non esse."

11. QM VII.2, nn. 25–26; Ed. IV, pp. 111–12; Trans. II, p. 104. Richard Cross speculates that the Scotus of the *Ordinatio* might hold such a position, though he gives no textual evidence to support his assertion. See Richard Cross, *The Physics of Duns Scotus* (Oxford, 1998), p. 106. Berthold Wald also holds this view. See Berthold Wald, "*Accidens Est Formaliter Ens*: Duns Scotus on Inherence in his *Quaestiones Subtilissimae* on Aristotle's *Metaphysics*," in *Aristotle in Britain during the Middle Ages*, trans. Roger Wasserman and ed. John Marenbon (Brepols, 1996), pp. 177–93. Pages 187–88 are particularly relevant here.

12. QM VII.1, n. 19; Ed. IV, p. 96; Trans. II, p. 91. Cf. Wald, "*Accidens*," p. 185. For a thorough treatment of the way in which Scotus handles the metaphysical issues surrounding the sacrament of the Eucharist, with special attention given to his mature, *Ordinatio* view, see Pini, "Substance," pp. 273–311. On pp. 273–74, Pini gives a particularly lucid overview of the basic doctrine of the Eucharist, which bears repeating. When the host is consecrated, "[t]he substance of bread and the substance of wine are said to be converted into the body and blood of Christ, while the accidents of bread and wine (for instance, their color, smell, and taste) remain there without inhering in any subject." While Pini argues that it is only Scotus's later, Parisian view of this event that is metaphysically coherent, I intend to give more insight into the nature of his early position from the QM. For another, theologically focused treatment of Scotus on this issue, see David Burr, "Scotus and Transubstantiation," *Mediaeval Studies* 34 (1972), pp. 336–60. Burr gives little attention to the role of accidents in the doctrine. The most comprehensive account of the metaphysical issues involved in transubstantiation during this period is Marilyn McCord Adams, "Aristotle and the Sacrament of the Altar: A Crisis in

Mediaeval Aristotelianism," in *Aristotle and His Mediaeval Interpreters*, ed. R. Bosley and M. Tweedale (University of Calgary Press, 1992) [=*Canadian Journal of Philosophy* Suppl. vol. 17], pp. 195–249. Adams discusses (in turn) Aquinas, Giles of Rome, Scotus, and Ockham. For her most focused treatment of Scotus on accidents, see pp. 232–35.

13. *QM* VII.1, n. 22; Ed. IV, p. 96; Trans. II, p. 92.

14. Cross points out that for the Scotus of the *Ordinatio*, accidents can at best supernaturally, but not naturally, move from substance to substance. It is unclear whether the Scotus discussed here, the Scotus of the *QM*, would see the movement of sound across a void as a movement from substance to substance, though if the sound is eventually received by the senses, it would be difficult not to interpret it this way. Furthermore, Cross also reads the Scotus of the *Ordinatio* as allowing the supernatural possibility, but denying the natural possibility, that an accident can exist separately from a subject when he explains that for Scotus, " 'accident' and 'inherence' are synonyms." See Cross, *Physics*, pp. 101–4. Also, it should be noted that the Condemnation of 1277 demanded that one maintain the possibility of an accident's noninherence in a subject. On this, see Pini, "Substance," p. 286.

15. *QM* VII.4, nn. 17–18; Ed. IV, p. 125; Trans. II, p. 114.

16. Though he does not make the comparison himself, one might construe this as the same sort of relationship Aquinas holds to exist between an intelligible species and the phantasm from which it is abstracted—although the intelligible species itself is metaphysically divorced from the phantasm, it still "tends toward" the singular item represented there. See Thomas Aquinas, *Summa Theologiae* I, Q. 86, a. 1. (See also Adams, "Sacrament," p. 201 for a mention of a related point in Aquinas: that for him, a soul can remain individuated upon leaving a material body simply because of its prior association with a material body.) Also, it is informative to note the way Scotus himself speaks of relations in *QM* V.7, n. 99. As he says there, a relation is "not simply in [a subject]— speaking absolutely and strictly—but in it with respect to another" (Ed. II, p. 515; Trans. I, p. 463). Thus this "directedness" is common to other kinds of accidents. Aquinas too appears to admit such directedness in some cases, though interestingly it is only in his theological works that he allows this, and not in his philosophical works, such as his own commentary on the *Metaphysics*. See Pini, "Substance," pp. 276–83.

17. Save those involving what he calls "discrete and continuous quantities." See *QM* VIII.1, n. 23; Ed. IV, p. 404; Trans. II, p. 349. Also important for understanding his view is how he views an accident's "inherence" in a subject as something nonessential to the accident itself. See Pini, "Substance," pp. 295–98.

18. *QM* VIII.1, n. 22; Ed. IV, pp. 403–4; Trans. II, p. 349.

19. *QM* VIII.1, nn. 1–2; Ed. IV, p. 397; Trans. II, p. 343.

20. *QM* VIII.1, n. 24; Ed. IV, p. 405; Trans. II, p. 350.

21. Or at least he thinks Aristotle would make this claim. See *QM* VIII.1, n. 25; Ed. IV, p. 405; Trans. II, p. 350.
22. *QM* VIII.1, n. 3; Ed. IV, p. 397; Trans. II, p. 343.
23. *QM* VIII.1, n. 27, Ed. IV, p. 406; Trans. II, p. 351.
24. *QM* VIII.1, n. 4; Ed. IV, p. 398; Trans. II, pp. 343–44.
25. *QM* VIII.1, n. 28; Ed. IV, pp. 406–7; Trans. II, pp. 351–52. Scotus makes a related point about light, which will be discussed below. See *QM* V.7, n. 101.
26. *QM* VIII.1, nn. 5–6; Ed. IV, p. 398; Trans. II, p. 344.
27. *QM* VIII.1, nn. 29–30; Ed. IV, p. 407; Trans. II, p. 352.
28. Wald, "*Accidens.*"
29. VII.2–3 is the by far the longest treatment Scotus gives to a single question/set of questions in *QM*. It comprises seventy-six pages of the modern critical edition, while the next longest question, VII.13, comprises seventy-five pages (though much of the latter question's page length is attributable to the MS. variances noted in the critical apparatus). Despite their length, I discuss these questions only in passing here.
30. *QM* VIII.2–3; Ed. IV, pp. 413–88; Trans. II, pp. 357–436. For a helpful discussion of some earlier ancient and medieval treatments of this issue, focusing in particular on Godfrey of Fontaines and Scotus's interpretation of him, see John F. Wippel, "Godfrey of Fontaines on Intension and Remission of Accidental Forms," *Franciscan Studies* 39 (1979), pp. 316–55.
31. *QM* V.7; Ed. III, pp. 489–521; Trans. I, pp. 437–74. Adams briefly discusses this issue with respect to relations. See Adams, "Sacrament," p. 227.
32. *QM* V.7, n. 71; Ed. III, p. 507; Trans. I, p. 455.
33. *QM* V.7, nn. 14–15; Ed. III, p. 494; Trans. I, p. 443.
34. *QM* V. 7, n. 42; Ed. III, p. 500; Trans., I, p. 449.
35. *QM* V.7, n. 43; Ed. III, p. 500; Trans. I, p. 449.
36. *QM* V.7, n. 44; Ed. III, pp. 500–1; Trans. I, p. 449.
37. *QM* V.7, n. 45; Ed. III, p. 501; Trans. I, p. 450.
38. *QM* V.7, n. 47; Ed. III, p. 501; Trans. I, p. 450.
39. *QM* V.7, n. 18; Ed. III, pp. 494–95; Trans. I., p. 444.
40. The subjects of accidental predication might be thought of as pincushions with an infinite number of holes, each of which could admit a single particular accident, to run a variation on Spade's frequently used "pincushion" analogy of substance.
41. *QM* V.7, n. 54; Ed. III, pp. 502–3; Trans. I, p. 451.
42. For a discussion of Giles of Rome's view that such a return is impossible naturally, but possible by divine power, see Adams, "Sacrament," pp. 207–8.
43. *QM* V.7, n. 65; Ed. III, p. 505; Trans. I, p. 453. This claim is echoed in n. 98 as well.
44. *QM* V.7, n. 101; Ed. III, p. 516; Trans. I, p. 464.
45. *QM* V.7, n. 108; Ed. III, p. 518; Trans. I, pp. 466–67. A "sensible species" is a type of accident, and it can be particular—"image," "vision," or "impression" might be a more easily understood translation, but those terms come with

their own philosophical baggage. "Species" in this sense is different that the "species" of genus/species fame.

46. *QM* V.7, n. 111; Ed. III, p. 519; Trans. I, p. 467.

47. *QM* V.7, n. 94; Ed. III, p. 513; Trans. I, p. 461.

48. *QM* V.7, n. 68. Ed. III, p. 506; Trans. I, p. 454.

49. Though not directly relevant to the central topic of this essay, Scotus gives an interesting account of location in space in this question. Here, he appears to say that it is within God's power to cause one thing to exist simultaneously in many places. See *QM* V.7, n. 99. Cf. Adams, "Sacrament," p. 226.

50. *QM* I.9, n.40; Ed. III, p. 175; Trans. I, p. 151.

51. *QM* VI.2, n. 24; Ed. IV, p. 45; Trans. II, p. 48.

52. *QM* I.9, n. 18; Ed. III, pp. 169–79; Trans. I, p. 147.

53. *QM* VI.2, n. 21; Ed. IV, pp. 43–44; Trans. II, pp. 46–47.

54. *QM* VII.4, n. 28; Ed. IV, p. 127; Trans. II, p. 116. Or, as Robert Pasnau has pointed out in private conversation, it might simply be that for Scotus, an accident can't be fully known without knowing that it naturally inheres in *some-substance-or-other*, rather than in a *particular* substance. Even if this is so, the skeptical problems remain, as discussed in the remainder of the essay.

55. *QM* VII.3, n. 10; Ed. IV, pp. 116–17; Trans. II, p. 108. Note that although these are presented as objections to Scotus's view in the text, Scotus's distinction between knowledge in this life and in the next suggests that he allows this to hold here and now.

56. *QM* VII.3, n. 14; Ed. IV, pp. 117–18; Trans. II, p. 109.

57. *QM* VII.3, n. 7; Ed. IV, p. 116; Trans. II, pp. 108–109.

58. An earlier and shorter version of this essay was presented both at a colloquium at James Madison University and at the 2007 SIEPM International Congress in Palermo, Sicily. I thank my audiences for their helpful comments. I would also like to thank Rondo Keele and Robert Pasnau for their suggestions and objections. A brief version of some of these ideas may be found in "John Duns Scotus on Accidents," in Alessandro Musco (ed.) *Société Internationale pour l'Étude de la Philosophie Médiévale (SIEPM) Universalità della Ragione. Pluralità delle Filosofie nel Medioevo. 12. Congresso Internazionale di Filosofia Medievale: Palermo, 17–22 settembre 2007.* (Palermo: Officina di Studi Medievali, 2012), vol. II.2, pp. 911–922.

5. *Avicenna Latinus on the Ontology of Types and Tokens*
MARTIN TWEEDALE

On account of my ignorance of Arabic I have been forced to rely on Latin translations of Avicenna's works produced in the medieval period, and to a lesser extent on Michael E. Marmura's English translation of *The Metaphysics of* The Healing , that is, the *Prima Philosophia* (Provo, Utah: Brigham Young University Press, 2005), henceforth abbreviated as *MH*. Consequently, it may be safest to see this essay as more a treatment of how Avicenna appeared to the medieval scholastics of the thirteenth century; hence the insertion of "Latinus" in the title. Nevertheless, after reading Marmura's translation of the Arabic, I do not find any major discrepancies between his translation and a translation of the corresponding Latin text. Nor has my reading of works by other scholars who have studied the Arabic texts revealed any major divergence from what one reads in the Latin. I would be surprised, then, if what is said here turned out on account of errors by the Latin translators to mislead the reader significantly as to Avicenna's true position. I should also add that it is possible that Avicenna's views changed over time and that some of the difficulties I try to sort out result from that. But it is beyond the scope of this essay (and the abilities of the author) to determine whether this is in fact true as regards the present topic. Instead, I have simply tried to read the relevant texts in a way which produces a single coherent view.

1. Needless to say, in my translations of texts emphasis by italics is not found in the original, but has been added by myself in order to direct the reader's attention to the key phrases.

2. The textual support for this can be found in Martin M. Tweedale, "Alexander of Aphrodisias' Views on Universals," *Phronesis* 29 (1984), pp. 279–303.

3. I rely here on *Avicenna Latinus, Liber de Anima seu Sextus de Naturalibus* (henceforth abbreviated *DA*), 2 vols., ed. S. Van Riet; vol. 2 (Editions Orientalistes, Louvain, & E.J. Brill, Leiden, 1968); vol. 1 (E. Peeters, Louvain, & E.J. Brill, Leiden, 1972).

4. For this passage I rely on *Avicenna Latinus: Liber de Philosphia Prima sive Scientia Divina* (henceforth abbreviated *PP*), 2 vols., ed. S. Van Riet (E. Peeters, Louvain, & E.J. Brill, Leiden, 1977, 1980).

5. For the first passage I rely upon Avicenna's *Logica* (henceforth abbreviated as *L*) as found in *Opera Philosophica*, Venice 1508 (reimpression en facsimile, Louvain, 1961).

6. I shall take it for granted that a type is a sort of universal and that there can be a ranking of types in terms of their relative specificity or genericness, that is, determinateness or indeterminateness. I recognize that it may be wise to distinguish subtly (with the Subtle Doctor) tokens from individuals, but that degree of refinement is not required here. Certainly if we allow that there are immaterial individuals those individuals will not be "tokens" and the universals they instantiate will not be "types" in the sense that I am using those terms here.

7. See Note 2.

8. See Tweedale, "Alexander of Aphrodisias," p. 300.

9. The reference here is to the essence *per se* where only that is true of it which is included in its definition. Note that Avicenna is anxious even here to make sure the reader does not think of this as some sort of third mode of existence of the essence, an existence as a Platonic Form.

10. Reading *sicut* for *sive*.

11. The idea that a universal is many things rather than one has good Aristotelian credentials. See *Categ.* 5, 3b10–18; *Post Anal.* I, 24, 85a31. Note also 83a24,

where it is said that a substantial predicate is identical with its subject. This makes any universal in the category of substance the same as many.

12. I rely here in part on Avicenna's *Sufficientia* (henceforth abbreviated *S*) found on folios 13r to 36v of *Opera Philosophica*, Venice 1508.

13. A few lines earlier Avicenna has referred to the Platonic Ideas (see text 30). It is fair to presume, then, that it is the Platonists that Avicenna refers to, perhaps those mentioned by Aristotle at the beginning of *Metaph.* Z 14.

14. The word means something you could point to, that is, which has a position in space and time.

15. Avicenna refers here to the principle that given contradictory opposites if one is denied the other must be affirmed; in other words the principle of excluded middle.

16. The ambiguity here can be seen as between a large and a small scope for the negation: (1) It is not the case that animal *per se* has the condition of being X. (2) Animal *per se* has the condition of not being X. I take the two sentences quoted to be saying (1) that it is not the case that animal just by being animal has the condition of being some one or the other individual animal, and (2) that animal just by being animal has the condition of not being any individual animal. *MH* (p. 155, 22) takes the condition to be that of there being no other thing, but this hardly seems to fit the overall argument Avicenna is pursuing. A.-M. Goichon in *Lá Distinction de l'Essence et de l'Existence d'après Ibn Sina* (Desclèe de Brouwer, Paris 1937), p. 82, took the condition to be that of not being "soumis à aucune autre condition," but this would exclude the condition of being apprehended by thought, and it seems from the passage that this is not intended, since Avicenna immediately proceeds to say that what of itself has the condition in question can exist only as an object of thought.

17. The editors of *PP* have "tamen" here, but one manuscript has "tunc," which seems to me to provide a better reading. Goichon seems to have used this reading too.

18. The term *platonitas* seems to have resulted from a misunderstanding by the original translator. The Arabic terms mean Platonic Ideas (see Goichon, *Lá Distinction*, p. 82). Hence *MH* has "Platonic Exemplars," and I follow this reading in my translation.

6. Universal Thinking as Process: The Metaphysics of Change and Identity in John Buridan's Intellectio Theory JACK ZUPKO

1. Paul Vincent Spade, "William of Ockham," *The Stanford Encyclopedia of Philosophy (Fall 2006 Edition)*, Edward N. Zalta (ed.), URL = http://plato.stanford.edu/archives/fall2006/entries/ockham/.

2. Claude Panaccio points out that underlying Ockham's *intellectio* theory is the realization that "each cognitive act does not need exactly *one* object . . . if conceptual acts are seen as general signs, only their singular *significata* are

needed to serve as their objects" (*Ockham on Concepts* [Burlington, VT: Ashgate, 2004], 27).

3. Buridan never considers the *fictum*-theory, almost as if the criticisms Ockham raised against it were decisive.

4. John Buridan, *Subtilissimae Quaestiones super octo Physicorum libros Aristotelis* (Paris, 1509); rpr. as *Kommentar zur Aristotelischen Physik* (Frankfurt a. M.: Minerva, 1964) (*QP*, by Book, Question, and Folio): *QP* I.4: f. 5rb-va: "Tertiomodo abstractive, ut quia habeo primo conceptum confuse et simul representantem substantiam et accidens, ut cum percipio album, non enim solam albedinem video, sed album; et tamen postea percipio idem moveri et mutari de albo in nigrum, iudico hoc esse aliud ab albedine. Et tunc [f. 5rb-va] intellectus naturaliter habet virtutem dividendi illam confusionem et intelligendi substantiam abstractive ab accidente et accidens abstractive a substantia. Et potest utriusque formare simplicem conceptum et sic etiam abstrahendo fit conceptus universalis ex conceptu singulari sicut debet videri tertio De Anima et septimo Metaphysice."

5. The force of "noninferential" here is simply that the process of abstraction occurs naturally in us, without deliberation or conscious reflection on the content of our singular cognitions—although it can of course occur deliberately as well, for example, when we rationally reconstruct the process by means of "the consequence of one proposition to another."

6. As we shall see, this Question has an epistemic correlate in Book III, Question 8 of Buridan's commentary, which asks whether the intellect *understands* what is universal before (*prius*) what is singular.

7. QDA_3 III.11; 123, ll. 240–41: "Ad hanc obiectionem responderi debet per ea quae dixi supra secundo Physicorum, in tertia questione" (see *QP* II.3: 31ra-rb). I should mention here that the incunabulum containing Buridan's *De Anima* commentary does not correspond to any known manuscript of that work. Therefore, I use the working edition of the final version of Book III of that commentary contained in J.A. Zupko, "John Buridan's Philosophy of Mind: An Edition and Translation of Book III of his 'Questions on Aristotle's *De Anima*' (Third Redaction), with Commentary and Critical and Interpretative Essays," Cornell University, doctoral dissertation, 1989 (hereafter QDA_3 by Book, Question, page, and line number—except Book I, which is from Vat lat. 2164, by Question and Folio).

8. Bernd Michael, "Johannes Buridan: Studien zu seinem Leben, seinen Werken und zu Rezeption seiner Theorien im Europa des späten Mittelalters," 2 vols., doctoral dissertation, University of Berlin, 1985, 274–75.

9. Actually, Buridan does mention one epistemic consequence, citing Aristotle's remark (*Metaph.* I.2.982a23–24) that those causes which are most universal (like God and the intelligences, on this interpretation) are the hardest for us to know. See *QP* I.7: 8ra; QDA_3 I.5: 127ra; *QM* VII.15: 50va.

10. John Buridan, *In Metaphysicen Aristotelis Questiones argutissimae* (Paris, 1588 [actually 1518]); rpr. as *Kommentar zur Aristotelischen Metaphysik* (Frankfurt a. M.: Minerva, 1964) (hereafter *QM*, by Book, Question, and Folio): *QM* VII.15: 50va (cf. *QP* I.7: 8ra-rb; *QDA*₃ I.5: 127ra): "Alio modo dicitur universale secundum predicationem vel significationem quia de multis est predicabile et indifferenter significant multa et supponit pro multis. Et tunc significatum ipsi oppositum est terminus singularis seu discretus qui una impositione significatum vel representativum est unius tantum, ut Sortes <vel> Plato. Et sic universale et singulare sunt termini mentales, vocales, aut scripti, et possibile est quod sit universale separatum ab omnibus singularibus, scilicet posito quod in mente tua tu formares aliquem conceptum communem et non formares unum singularem, licet alii forment multos terminos singulares. Tunc illud universale est separatum ab omnibus singularibus quia est in te et omnia singularia sunt in aliis."

11. *QP* I.7: 8ra-rb; cf. *QDA*₃ I.5: 127ra: "istum terminum animal diceremus universaliorem isto termino homo quia predicatur de pluribus et significat plura, omnis enim homo est animal et non econverso. Et isto modo singulare dicitur terminus significativus supponens pro uno solo et universale terminus supponens pro pluribus, prout hoc debet specificari in logica. Et tanto est universalior quanto supponit pro pluribus."

12. *QDA*₃ I.5: 127rb: "in scriptura sunt termini universales et singulares corre-spondentes vocalibus, ut habetur in primo Perhermeneias <Posteriorum del. in ms.>, termini autem vocales et scripti debent ordinari secundum exigentiam mentalium, quia non formantur nisi ad revertandum mentales."

13. *QDA*₃ I.5: 127rb.

14. For the role played by dialectic in Buridan's nominalism, see Jack Zupko, *John Buridan: Portrait of a Fourteenth-Century Arts Master* (Notre Dame, IN: University of Notre Dame Press, 2003). Gregory Landini uses similar terminology to describe the project of logical atomism in a recent book, *Wittgenstein's Apprenticeship with Russell* (New York and Cambridge: Cambridge University Press, 2007): ix. Though their aims are different, there are interesting methodological similarities between fourteenth-century nominalism and twentieth-century logical empiricism, such as the emphasis on procedural rigor over formal structure.

15. *QDA*₃ III.8; 64, ll. 7–13: "ideo dicta quaestio in propriis verbis formanda est: utrum easdem res vel eandem rem intellectus prius intelligat universaliter, id est, secundum conceptum communem, quam singulariter, id est, secundum conceptum singularem. Et si in processu quaestionis etiam aliquando utamur verbis primo positis, tamen volumus uti eis ad sensum verborum immediate positorum."

16. *QP* I.7: 8rb (cf. *QDA*₃ I.5: 127va-vb; *QM* VII.15: 50va-vb): "Sed iterum secundum Platonem aliomodo dicuntur universalia in essendo extra animam, videlicet illud quod ad extra significatur immediate per terminum singularem

est res singularis ut Sortes vel Plato, hic homo vel ille, et id quod ad extra immediate significatur per terminum universalem est res universalis extra animam distincta a singulari et a rebus singularibus. Ita quod iste ponebat praeter conceptum animae nostrae hominem universalem per se existentem quem vocabat ydeam hominum singularium et quidditatem eorum. Et dicebat terminum supponentem pro illa ydea esse vere et affirmative praedicabilem de unoquoque termino supponente pro aliquo hominum singularium."

17. Cf. Aristotle, *Metaph.* I.9.991a12 (tr. Ross): "for they are not even the substance of these, else they would have been in them."

18. *QP* I.7: 8rb (cf. *QDA*₃ I.5: 127va; *QM* VII.15: 51vb): "omnis res singulariter existit ita ut sit diversa ab unaquaque aliarum rerum quod nunquam possibile est terminum supponentem precise pro una re affirmari vere pro termino supponente pro alia precise. Immo si Sortes est homo, eadem res penitus est Sortes et homo. Ideo sic non sunt ponenda universalia preter animam a singularibus distincta." On Plato's view, according to Buridan, the term "man" would supposit precisely for the separately existing form of humanity, which of course is not identical to Socrates; therefore, the predication would fail.

19. Aristotle, *De An.* III.4.429a13–18.

20. *QDA*₃ III.8; 70, ll. 173–75.

21. *QDA*₃ III.8; 72, ll. 219–23: "Deus super me immaterialis et inextensus non intelligit modo universali, quia talis modus intelligendi est confusus et imperfectus. Deus autem non intelligit res imperfecte nec confuse, sed omnia distincte et determinatissime." Thus, when Buridan says in his *Physics* commentary that God "does not understand in a universal way as we do [*non intelligit modo universali sicut nos*]," he is not saying that God understands universally in some *other* way (*QP* I.7: 8va).

22. Buridan is agnostic about our mode of cognition in beatitude. This is for two reasons. First, he thinks that because the beatific vision is a supernatural rather than a natural phenomenon, it is beyond the scope of philosophical inquiry, which he sees as concerned with propositions and arguments whose truth is evident to our senses; thus, the beatific vision is like the inherence of immaterial human souls in material bodies in that it is something we believe but cannot (in this life) know or understand. Second, as a career arts master, Buridan was forbidden by statute from determining questions that pertain to the faculty of theology; this is a boundary he generally respects, though he never refers to what the theologians do as constituting a *scientia* or body of knowledge. For discussion, see my *John Buridan*, pp. 139–45 and 180–82.

23. *QDA*₃ III.8; 73, ll. 225–28: "virtus materialis et extensa fertur bene in obiectum suum modo universali, nam appetitus equi secundum famem aut situm non est singulariter ad hanc avenam vel ad hanc aquam, sed ad quamlibet indifferenter; unde quamcumque primitus inveniret illam caperet. Et intentio naturalis vel appetitus ignis ad calefaciendum non se habet modo singulari ad hoc

calefactibile vel ad illud, sed ad quodlibet indifferenter quod ipse posset calefacere; ideo quodcumque sibi praesentetur, calefaceret ipsum."

24. QDA_3 III.8; 74, ll. 256–61: "Et huiusmodi maior essentialis convenientia provenit ex eo quod illa quae sunt eiusdem speciei vel generis proveniunt ex eisdem causis, vel similibus magis, quam alia, propter quod in ordine entium sunt eiusdem gradus, vel propinquorum graduum ad invicem, quam alia."

25. QDA_3 III.8; 74, ll. 250–56: "Tunc accipimus quod res extra animam singulariter existentes de eadem specie vel de eodem genere habent ex natura sui similitudinem seu convenientiam essentialem maiorem quam illae quae sunt diversarum specierum vel diversorum generum. Plus enim conveniunt ex natura rei Sortes et Plato quam Sortes et Brunellus (etiam quantum ad suas essentias), et plus etiam conveniunt Sortes et Brunellus quam Sortes et ille lapis, quod propter hoc patet quia in eis inveniuntur accidentia naturaliter convenientia essentiis eorum, magis similia et magis convenientia in hiis quae sunt eiusdem speciei vel generis quam in aliis."

26. QDA_3 III.8; 75, ll. 279–90: "Ideo consequitur ex quo repraesentatio fit per similitudinem quod illud quod erat repraesentativum unius erit indifferenter repraesentativum aliorum, nisi aliud concurrat quod obstet, sicut dicetur post. Ex hoc finaliter infertur quod cum species et similitudo Sortis fuerit apud intellectum et fuerit abstracta a speciebus extraneorum, illa non magis erit repraesentatio Sortis quam Platonis et aliorum hominum, nec intellectus per eam magis intelliget Sortem quam alios homines. Immo sic per eam omnes homines indifferenter intelliget uno conceptu, scilicet a quo sumitur hoc nomen 'homo'. Et hoc est intelligere universaliter." The obstruction mentioned here is possibly in reference to qq. 15–16 of Buridan's commentary, where he discusses natural limitations on the capacity of the human intellect, for example, its inability to consider fully more than one thing at once.

27. QDA_3 III.8; 79–90, ll. 391–405: ". . . dico quod cum intellectus a phantasmate recipit speciem vel intellectionem Sortis cum tali confusione magnitudinis et situs, facientem apparere rem per modum existentis in prospectu cognoscentis, intellectus intelligit illum modo singulari. Si intellectus potest illam confusionem distinguere et abstrahere conceptum substantiae vel albedinis a conceptu situs, ut non amplius res percipiatur per modum existentis in prospectu cognoscentis, tunc erit conceptus communis. Unde cum elicitus fuerit conceptus Sortis abstracte a conceptibus albedinis et situs et aliorum accidentium vel extraneorum, ille iam non magis repraesentabit Sortem quam Platonem, et erit conceptus communis a quo sumitur hoc nomen 'homo'. Et quaecumque virtus potest facere huiusmodi abstractionem, sive illa sit sensus sive intellectus, illa potest universaliter cognoscere."

28. *Extrahere* is the verb Buridan sometimes uses here. See QDA_3 I.5: 127vb: "et sic intellectus poterit a conceptu singulari extrahere conceptum universalem animalis."

29. *QDA₃* III.15; 165, ll. 142–45: "But once the intellect has been actualized by its first intellections, it is potentially actually thinking everything that has been deduced from those first intellections, or from others similar to them, and their dispositions have remained in it [*Cum autem intellectus actuatus fuerit per primas intellectiones, ipse est potens actu considerare de omnibus quae ex illis primis intellectionibus vel ex similibus aliis deductis fuerunt, et quorum habitus in eo remanserunt*]." On Buridan's view, what is distinctive in human intellectual cognition is precisely this capacity to exercise it at will, over whatever objects it is potentially thinking.

30. Hence, "it is doubtless better to avoid saying that the soul pities or learns or thinks, and rather to say that it is the man who does this with his soul. What we mean is not that the movement is in the soul, but that sometimes it terminates in the soul and sometimes it starts from it" (*De An.* I.4.408b14–17; tr. Smith).

31. See Aristotle, *De An.* II.5.417a22–30.

32. *QDA₃* III.15; 167, ll. 176–87: "it is impossible for the species to remain in the intellect without the intellection because nothing else is supposed to be required for the formation of an intellection but our intellect and the universal agent, which is God, and also the species, which is the representation of the thing either understood or to be understood and also <the representation> of other things necessary for <the object of> that species to exist. For saying that something else is required for understanding appears to be fictitious and altogether superfluous. Everything remains, however, if the species remains in the intellect, because neither the approximation nor the other condition appears to be lacking. Therefore, it is evidently impossible that the species remain in the intellect, and the intellection not remain [*impossibile sit illam speciem manere in intellectu sine intellectione, quia nihil aliud ponitur requiri ad formationem intellectionis nisi intellectus noster et universale agens, quod est deus, et illa species quae est representatio rei vel intelligendae vel intellectae et aliarum ad esse illius speciei requisitarum. Dicere enim alia requiri ad intelligendum apparet esse ficticium et omnino superfluum. Haec autem omnia manent si species illa maneret in intellectu, quia non apparet deficere approximatio nec alia circumstantia. Ideo impossibile esse videtur quod maneat in intellectu illa species, et non maneat intellectio*]." The principle behind this argument is stated a little further on: "once the causes sufficient for some effect have been posited, and posited in the way in which they are sufficient, it is necessary that the effect be posited [*necesse est, positis causis sufficientibus ad aliquem effectum, et eo modo quo sufficiunt, poni istum effectum*]" (ibid., 170, ll. 263–64).

33. *QDA₃* III.15; 172, ll. 321–23: "intellectus autem cum phantasmatibus statim innatus est quodlibet rei intelligere prius intellectum, et ad quod est habituatus."

34. QDA_3 III.15; 172–73, ll. 323–27: "Cum enim percipit se intelligere A in tali die, etiam potest intelligere quantum tempus transiret post illam diem, ipse potest inferre duos annos esse praeteritos postquam primo intellexit A."

35. QDA_3 III.15; 168, ll. 206–14: "Quantum ergo ad hoc quod primo dubitatur, quae res sit illa species intelligibilis, ego dico in respondendum illi dubitationi: oportet praecognoscere quid nominis. Et ponamus quod huiusmodi species nec est habitus intellectualis nec actualis intellectio, sed quod sit actus vel dispositio proveniens a sensibili mediante sensu, requisitus vel requisita in mente et necessaria ad formationem primae intellectionis, scilicet quam aliquis potest formare non proveniente alia intellectione."

36. QDA_3 III.15; 168, ll. 214–24: "Tunc apparet mihi quod illa [1] est actus cognoscendi per phantasiam aut per cogitativam (aut a quocumque alio nomine illa nominetur), quem Aristoteles vocat phantasma <vide Arist. *De An.* III.3.427b28ff.> (quidem actus sit extensus et eductus de potentia organi corporei); vel [2] est intellectio actualis actu causata ab intellectu et educta de potentia illius sine extensione. Hanc disiunctivam omnes habent concedere, cum necesse sit intellectum quemcumque phantasmata speculari <Arist. *De An.* III.7.431a15–16>. Sed quae pars disiunctivae sit vera? Videtur mihi quod melius ad praecavendum de minima entium multitudine quod sufficiat illud phantasma, id est, illa actualis cognitio."

37. QDA_3 III.15; 169, ll. 227–41: "videtur mihi quod per illam actualem cognitionem seu apprehensionem, intellectus sit sufficienter in actu, ut ipse cum illa posset actualem intellectionem formare in se quae iam non recipiatur in corpore (tanquam educta de eius potentia), sed in intellectu solum. Unde sic apparet quod illud phantasma, id est illa actualis apprehensio, se habet proportionaliter ad intellectionem sicut species causata ab obiecto in organo sensus dicebatur se habere ad sensationem. Sic ergo intelligo illud dictum Aristotelis quod intellectivae animae, phantasmata ut sensibilia sunt <*De An.* III.7.431a15>, propter quod sine phantasmate, nequaquam intelligit anima. Nam sicut sine specie sensibili causata ab obiecto in organo sensus non potest sensus exterior formare sensationem, sicut nec intellectus sine praedicto phantasmate intellectionem."

38. *QP* II.3: 31ra-rb. The wax analogy, which was probably a commonplace, recurs often in QDA_3 III.11, which explicitly refers to the *QP* II.3 discussion QDA_3 III.11; 123, ll. 240–41. The latter basically recaps the main points of *QP* II.3, where Buridan introduces a distinction between three ways in which "something, while remaining the same, can be differently disposed, such that contradictory predicates are true of it—that is, of the term suppositing for it—at different times [*aliqua res manens eadem tripliciter potest se habere aliter et aliter quod de ipsa, id est de termino supponente pro ipsa, verificentur praedicata contradictoria prius et posterius*]" (*QP* II.3: 31ra). The first two ways refer to relational changes of material subjects, that is, (1) between a subject and what is external to it (e.g., when a person turns around so that a

column that was on his right is now on his left and (2) between the integral (physical) parts of the same subject (e.g., a block of wax rolled into a sphere). If the first two ways do not apply, Buridan says, "then no other cause appears natural to me than the addition, generation, or corruption of something belonging to that thing. For in this way, a man is white and non-white, or first white and later black; thus the distinction of forms and accidents from their substances can be known and defended [*tunc nulla causa apparet mihi naturalis nisi quia illi rei est aliqua res addita generata vel corrupta. Sic enim est homo albus et non albus, vel albus et niger prius et posterius. et sic potest sciri et argui distinctio formarum et accidentium a substantiis suis*]" (*QP* II.3: 31rb). The third way thus covers qualitative change, including—as Buridan uses it in *QDA*₃ III.11—the dispositional changes of immaterial subjects such as the intellect. For discussion, see Calvin Normore, "Buridan's Ontology" in *How Things Are: Studies in Predication and the History and the Philosophy of Science*, edited by James Bogen and James E. McGuire (Dordrecht-Boston-Lancaster: Reidel, 1985): 189–203, and Zupko, *John Buridan*, ch. 11.

39. *QDA*₃ III.11; 124, 256–67: "non potest salvari, nisi per generationem vel corruptionem alicuius dispositionis sibi inhaerentis et distinctae ab ea. Sic enim est de aqua, si prius est calida et post frigida; et de materia, si prius est sub forma aquae et post sub forma ignis; et de intellectu, si prius fuit sic opinans et post contrarie. Nam homine dormiente et omni repraesentatione sibi per sensum circumscripta, adhuc aliter haberet se posterius quam haberet se prius, quod non potest salvari nisi per alietatem illarum opinionum ab invicem et ab intellectu."

40. The way Buridan presents it, Mirecourt's theory is easily reduced to absurdity (*QDA*₃ III.11; 122, 204–15): "For it is said that they were not such as to believe that this man is the same in number as that one, but [they did believe this] of things that appear to be generated one from another: e.g. if from earth A comes water B, and from water B comes grass C, and from grass C, horse D, and so on for all species of generable and corruptible things, then horse D is the same as what was the grass, the water, and the earth, for the same matter which they said is the entire substance of the thing was first the earth and then the water, the grass, and the horse, differently disposed. But these remarks are extremely obscure and dangerous, for in the same way, an ass was a stone, and a stone has always existed, and no horse or human being has ever been generated, although matter has been made into a human being or horse [*Non enim erant ita fatui quod crederent illum hominem esse idem in numero cum illo, sed de hiis quae apparent ex se invicem generari: ut si ex terra A fiat aqua B, et ex aqua B herba C, et ex herba C equus D, et sic de omnibus speciebus generabilium et corruptibilium, tunc equus D est idem quod fuit herba et aqua et terra, eadem enim materia quam dicebant esse totam substantiam rei fuit prius terra, et post aqua et herba et equus, aliter et aliter se habens. Haec autem dicta sunt valde obscura et periculosa, sic enim asinus fuit lapis, et lapis*

semper fuit, et nunquam equus vel homo fuit genitus, licet materia facta fuit homo vel equus]."

41. *QDA₃* III.8: 73, ll. 233–37: "conceptus nostri in intellectu nostro ita singulariter et distincte ab invicem et ab aliis existunt sicut colores et sapores in corporibus; quamvis conceptus tales in eis non habeant extensionem nec situm corporeum, immo omnia existunt singulariter."

42. *QP* I.7; 8va: "terminus universalis ita simpliciter et distincte ab aliis existit in intellectu tuo vel meo sicut albedo in parietem."

43. See *QP* I.4: f. 5rb-va, quoted at Note 4 above. A universal concept, then, is the mind's activation of the potential of a singular concept to bring to mind the other individuals that are naturally related to it in a given respect, for example, my coming to see that this wall and this piece of paper are alike in whiteness. It should not be thought of objectively, as the distilled output of the process of abstraction, although Buridan sometimes talks this way. A big problem for *intellectio* theorists is that our metaphors for thinking all seem to view it as a step-wise process involving discrete objects, as if the wall's whiteness were some additional thing to be considered, apart from the wall.

44. This is the argument that if the intention of fire is only to ignite another *particular* fire, its existence would be superfluous once it has actually done so (superfluity being a kind of pointlessness, which is incompatible with a divinely ordered world): all dressed up and nothing to burn. See Sławomir Szyller (ed.), "Jan Buridan, *Tractatus de differentia universalis ad indivi-duum*," *Przeglad Tomistyczny* 3 (1987): 138, ll. 17–22 (hereafter *TDUI*, by page and line number).

45. Unlike Buridan, Aegidius was very successful at obtaining benefices, prebends, and other academic emoluments, perhaps because he knew the future Pope Clement VI personally when he was studying at Paris. Another ms. (München SB Clm 18 789) mentions that Buridan wrote the treatise "against certain Englishmen who assume that universals are entities existing outside the soul, just like the heresiarch Wyclif and his followers [*contra quosdam Anglicos ponentes universalia esse encia extra animam, sicut posuit Vickleff heresiar-cha cum suis sequacibus*]," though of course Wyclif himself could not have been Buridan's target, as he would have only been a child when Buridan's *Treatise* was composed. See Michael, "Johannes Buridan," 434. John Wyclif (c. 1330–84) had his views condemned twice: first in 1382 by Archbishop Courtenay and finally at the Council of Constance, 1414–18.

46. *QP* I.7: 8rb, quoted at Note 18 above.

47. *TDUI*: 146, ll. 16–23: ". . . pono tres conclusiones principales. Prima est, quod universale pro forma non est praeter animam. Secunda est, quod universale pro subiecto, prout distinguitur contra individuum pro subiecto, verbi gratia: homo prout distinguitur contra Socratem et Platonem, non est praeter animam. Tertia est, quod universale pro subiecto est praeter animam quantum

ad aliquid sui. Et postea videbitur, quantum ad quid est praeter animam et quantum ad quid est ab anima et quomodo."

48. *TDUI*: 146, ll. 11–12: "Talia enim dicimus esse individua et haec est illa distinction qua communiter universale dici solet potest capi pro intentione vel pro re."

49. *TDUI*: 146, l. 37–147, l. 7: "Sed res animae non solum fundari potest super rem extra animam sed etiam super rem animae propter reflexionem animae super se et super suam operationem. Minor autem nota est, quia sicut hominem vel animal aut lapidem universalia esse dicimus ex eo, quod quodlibet illorum de pluribus praedicatur, ita etiam speciem intelligibilem, actum intelligendi, intentionem, propositionem, sillogismum et alia entia animae dicimus esse universalia, quia quodlibet illorum de pluribus praedicatur."

50. The other arguments just tease out some of the inference rules that would be violated if we were to treat subjective universals as existing outside the mind.

51. *TDUI*: 148, ll. 17–26: "Primo sic: universale pro forma est intentio secunda. Hoc conceditur, sed hoc non esset verum in subiecto quod denominat, quia supponeret intentionem primam et non rem praecise, ergo, etc.
   "Secundo arguitur sic: pono, quod non sint homines nisi Socrates et Plato, tunc homo pro omni eius realitate praeveniente operationem animae affirmatur de Socrate et Platone. Ista videtur per se nota; sed homo non affirmatur de Socrate et Platone prout distinguitur ab eis, sed magis negatur, nam negatio est propter distinctionem terminorum et affirmatio propter eorum indistinctionem, ergo homo prout distinguitur a Socrate et Platone non est sine operatione animae."

52. *TDUI*: 152, ll. 23–28: "Deinde probo tertiam conclusionem, quod universale pro subiecto est praeter animam quantum ad aliquid sui, quia universale pro subiecto est illud super quod fundatur intentio universalitatis, sed ipsa universalitatis fundatur super rem extra, aliter videtur, quod esset ficta . . . universale pro subiecto, ut homo, verificatur essentialiter et in quid de individuis realibus, scilicet de Socrate et Platone, quod non esset, si nullam rem praeter animam importaret."

53. *TDUI*: 152, ll. 36–39: "si universale non distinguitur praeter animam ab individuo, videtur quod numquam per animam distingui possit nisi illa distinctio esset ficta, cum illud fabricatum per animam fictum sit, cui nihil correspondet ex parte rei."

54. *TDUI*: 153, ll. 10–14: ". . . quidquid praeter animam existit, in re ipsum existit individualiter, scilicet distinctum ab omnibus aliis tam suae speciei quam aliarum, ita quod ibi nihil est omnino praeter res, quae individualiter existunt, nec est distinctum ab eis. Socrates namque et eius humanitas vel animalitas vel entitas distinctim existit in re a Platone et eius humanitate et animalitate."

55. *TDUI*: 153, ll. 26–29.

56. *TDUI*: 155, ll. 29–35: ". . . si species hominis fuerit in phantasia et denudetur seu prescindatur ab omnibus extraneis seu a speciebus extraneorum, quod ipsa non representabit determinate Socratem vel Platonem, sed indifferenter

quemlibet ipsorum aut aliorum omnium hominum et ita intellectus non intelligeret per illam speciem hunc hominem determinate sed indifferenter hunc vel illum vel alium, et hoc est intelligere hominem universali intellectione."

57. See Notes 25 and 26 above.

58. *TDUI*: 156, ll. 23–25: "sufficit enim ad praesens, quod intellectus potest rem universaliter intelligere, licet praeter animam nihil sit distinctum a singularibus et quod huiusmodi intellectio sit ficta."

59. *TDUI*: 156, ll. 34–37: "aliquando conceptus sunt diversi non propter diversitatem rerum conceptarum, sed propter diversitatem modi concipiendi, sicut alius est conceptus animalis rationalis et alius hominis, licet sit eadem res."

60. *TDUI*: 158, ll. 16–23: "Dico enim, quod universale pro subiecto est congregatum ex re et conceptu sive ex re et modo concipiendi. Est ergo quantum ad rem praeter animam et quantum ad conceptum et modum concipiendi est ab anima. Et quia in tali aggregato res est sicut subiecta conceptui et quod intentio secunda magis proprie et magis formaliter attribuitur illi congregato ratione conceptus quam ratione rei, ideo istum conceptum possumus vocare subiectum propinquum secundae intentionis et rem subiectum remotum et congregatum subiectum totale."

61. *TDUI*: 148, ll. 25–26: "homo prout distinguitur a Socrate et Platone non est sine operatione animae."

62. The distinction was much debated in the decades between Aquinas and Buridan (see L.M. de Rijk, *Giraldus Odonis, O.F.M.*, Opera Philosophica, *Vol. 2: De intentionibus, Critical Edition with a Study on the Medieval Intentionality Debate up to ca. 1350*, Studien und Texte zur Geistesgeschichte des Mittelalters, 86 [Leiden and Boston: Brill, 2005]), so the question of Buridan's unnamed source or sources here is impossible to determine. There is also an interesting passage in Duns Scotus where he identifies the subjective universal with the first intention ("pro subiecto, scilicet pro re primae intentionis cui applicatur intentio universalis"), the formal universal with the second intention ("pro forma, scilicet pro re secundae intentionis, causata ab intellectu et applicabili rebus primae intentionis"), and the aggregate with the subject and form together ("pro aggregato ex subiecto et forma"). But the aggregative conception is set aside by Scotus as irrelevant to philosophy because it is only a collection of diverse natures not making something one *per se*, and Aristotle says that there is no science of the accidental (*Metaph.* VI.6) (*Quaest. in Porph.* 4, *Prooemium*; OP I: 21, ll. 5–15).

63. Thomas Aquinas, *In I Sent.* d.2, q.1, a.3, c. Aquinas has a third category of concepts that are fictional entities. These "have neither a proximate nor a remote foundation in the [extra-mental] thing, like the concept of a Chimera [*non habet fundamentum in re, neque proximum neque remotum, sicut conceptio Chimerae*]." But Buridan does not mention this third category, perhaps because he has other ways of handling nonreferring concepts/terms.

64. *TDUI*: 167, ll. 11–12: "Ad nonam rationem, quando dicitur: res praeter animam dividitur per rationale et irrationale, dicendum est, quod huiusmodi divisio non est aliquis actus realis praeter animam, sed est ibi tria imaginari, scilicet terminum a quo et terminum ad quem et subiectum manens idem sub utroque termino."

65. *TDUI*: 167, ll. 17–23: "in divisione animalis per rationale et irrationale conceptus unus generalis, qui est indifferens Socrati et Brunello, est sicut terminus a quo, conceptus vero speciales, scilicet hominis et asini, quibus differenter concipiuntur Socrates et Brunellus, sunt terminus ad quem; res vero praeter animam singulariter existentes, puta Socrates et Brunellus aut alia huiusmodi, sunt sicut subiectum manens idem sub utrisque conceptibus."

66. *TDUI*: 167, ll. 31–34: "res plures praeter animam existentes est terminus a quo et diversi conceptus specifici sunt terminus ad quem; et illa divisio est divisio per se et essentialis tum quia eadem est essentia subiecta utrisque conceptibus, tum quia utrique conceptus sunt ipsarum rerum diversarum conceptus essentiales."

67. See John Buridan, *Quaestiones super decem libros Ethicorum Aristotelis ad Nicomachum* (Paris, 1513); rpr. as *Super decem libros Ethicorum* (Frankfurt a. M.: Minerva, 1968): X.4: 209vb.

68. Demonstration by pointing is in fact the model for Buridan's theory of singular cognition. See Ryszard Tatarzynski (ed.), "Jan Buridan, *Kommentarz do Isagogi Porfiriusza*," *Przeglad Tomistyczny* 2 (1986) ch. 9; 162, ll. 1437–39: "as for the terms 'Socrates' and 'Plato', I say that they are truly and properly individual terms, because the name 'Socrates' was imposed on this man by an act of pointing [*de istis terminis "Socrates" et "Plato" dico, quod vere et proprie sunt termini individuales, quia hoc nomen "Socrates" impositum fuit huic homini per demonstrationem*]."

69. Earlier versions of this essay were delivered at a session of 42nd International Congress of Medieval Studies (May 12, 2007) and a workshop on medieval nominalism at the Université de Québec à Montréal (May 17, 2008). I am grateful to both audiences, and to the editors of this volume, for many helpful comments and suggestions, especially Antoine Côté, Benjamin Hill, Peter King, Gyula Klima, Tim Noone, Calvin Normore, and Claude Panaccio.

7. Can God Know More? A Case Study in Later Medieval Discussions of Propositions SUSAN BROWER-TOLAND

1. "Proposition" is, of course, a term of art; these days, philosophers use it to designate entities that play a number of theoretical roles—including not only (1) objects of propositional attitudes, but also (2) truth-bearers, and (3) meanings of sentences. In what follows I will be using the expression "proposition" primarily for entities playing the first of these three theoretical roles. As will become clear, however, Ockham and his colleagues think of the entities that serve as objects of propositional attitudes as filling some of other roles as

well—most notably that of truth-bearer. Also, it is worth emphasizing that I am *not* using "proposition" as a translation for the Latin expression *propositio*. This is because *propositio* approximates more nearly the notion expressed by our English expression "sentence" as it applies to sentence *tokens*. While medieval philosophers do regard sentences as bearers of truth and falsity, there is no consensus among them as to whether (natural language) sentence tokens (i.e., *propositiones in voces/in scriptum*) serve as objects for the attitudes or as the *primary* bearers of truth and falsity.

2. In contemporary discussions propositions are typically taken to be some type of abstract entity. Although this broad characterization leaves open a number of important questions about the exact nature of such entities (e.g., whether they are structured or not and, if so, whether they include particulars as constituents; whether they exist necessarily or contingently, etc.), the general assumption is that they are abstract entities of some sort or other. Among medieval thinkers, however, there is considerable resistance to the idea that the entities that function as truth-bearers and objects of propositional attitudes are abstract.

3. Peter Lombard, *Sententiae in IV libris distinctae*, ed. PP. Collegium S. Bonaventurae (Grottaferrata: Collegium S. Bonaventurae ad Claras Aquas, 1971–81), I.39, 280. In the course of this discussion, Lombard specifically asks (in article 3 of D. 39) whether "God can know more than he knows." Lombard's *Sentences* is a theological treatise that was used as a textbook for training students of theology in thirteenth- and fourteenth-century universities.

4. "Utrum Deus possit scire plura quam scit?" In what follows, citations of Ockham's Latin texts are to his *Opera Philosophica et Theologica* (St. Bonaventure, New York: St. Bonaventure University Press, 1967–88). The *Ordinatio* (=*Ord.*) is part of Ockham's commentary on Peter Lombard's *Sentences*. Distinction 39 of Ockham's *Ordinatio* has been translated by Marilyn Adams and Norman Kretzmann in William Ockham, *Predestination, God's Foreknowledge, and Future Contingents*, ed. and trans. M.M. Adams and N. Kretzmann, 2nd ed. (Indianapolis: Hackett Publishing Co, 1983), 92–95. In what follows, I adopt their translation, with some modification.

5. Ockham himself puts the two questions this way: "First, we must consider how the question is to be understood. Here it must be noted that it is one thing to ask whether God can know more than He knows, but it is another to ask whether God can know something that He does not know" (*Ord.* d. 39 [*OTh* IV, 589]); cf. Ockham, *Predestination*, 92.

6. *Ord.* d. 39 (*OTh* IV, 589); cf. Ockham, *Predestination*, 93.

7. The distinction Ockham has in mind is similar to the one he marks in other contexts as a distinction between "apprehension" and "judgment." To apprehend something is just to consider or be aware of it. Thus, apprehension extends to propositional and nonpropositional objects. Judgment, on the other

hand, is always a propositional attitude inasmuch as it involves not only awareness of some object, but also some further attitude (such as assent or dissent) with respect to its truth. See for example, *Ord.* Prologue, q.1 (*OTh* I, 16).

8. *Ord.* d. 39 (*OTh* IV, 589–90); cf. Ockham, *Predestination*, 93.
9. *Ord.* d. 39 (*OTh* IV, 590); cf. Ockham, *Predestination*, 93.
10. Ibid.
11. *Expositio in Librum Praedicamentorum Aristotelis* 17, sec.13 (*OPh* II, 317). *Complexum* is a term Ockham uses (often interchangeably with *propositio*) to designate complex—i.e., sentential—linguistic expressions.
12. *Expositio in Librum Perihermenias Aristotelis, Prooemium, sec. 12.* (*OPh* II, 373).
13. *Quodlibeta Septem* III.8 (*OPh* IX, 236).
14. Holcot takes up this issue in one of his quodlibetal disputations, namely Quodlibet I, question 6 (hereafter "Q.I.6"). Although several of Holcot's quodlibetal questions have been edited individually, there is no single critical edition of all of his Quodlibeta. In what follows, I rely on William Courtenay's 1971 edition of Holcot's Q.I.6. See William Courtenay, "A Revised Text of Robert Holcot's Quodlibetal Disputation on Whether God is Able to Know More than He Knows," *Arichiv fürGeschichte der Philosophie* 53 (1971): 3–21. Translations are my own, though I have consulted Robert Pasnau's English translation of Holcot's text in *The Cambridge Translations of Philosophical Texts*, vol. 3, *Mind and Knowledge*, ed. and trans. R. Pasnau (Cambridge: Cambridge University Press, 2002), 302–17.
15. Holcot, Q.I.6, 9.
16. Ibid., 11.
17. Norman Kretzmann,"Medieval Logicians on the Meaning of the *Propositio*," *The Journal of Philosophy* 67 (1971): 781–82.
18. E.A. Moody, "A Quodlibetal Question of Robert Holcot, O.P., on the Problem of the Objects of Knowledge and Belief," *Speculum* 39 (1964): 69.
19. Marilyn M. Adams, *William Ockham* (Notre Dame, IN: Notre Dame University Press, 1987), 1088.
20. There are perhaps other ways of construing sentence types. Moody and Kretzmann offer no alternative account, but Adams does attempt to provide some notion of types that would be acceptable to Ockham. On the account she offers, sentence types turn out to be, roughly, divine ideas. Developing the details of her account is neither feasible here nor necessary since, in the end, Adams herself gives up the project. Ultimately, she is forced to admit that Ockham is not entitled to sentence types. As she points out, even if Ockham intended to construe sentence types as ideas in God's mind such entities would not be eternal. After all, even if God had in mind an instance of every possible sentence (of every possible natural language), in order for such a sentence to be true, on Ockham's view, there must be an interpretation of these conventional sentence types. But interpretations come into and out of existence with linguistic communities. See Adams, *William Ockham*, ch. 26.

21. References to Book I of Chatton's *Sentences* commentary are to his *Reportatio super Sententias: Liber I, distinctiones 1–48*, ed. J.C. Wey and G.J. Etzkorn (Toronto: Pontifical Institute of Mediaeval Studies, 2002). All translations are mine.

22. *Rep.* I d. 39, q.u, a.2 (*Reportatio dd. 10–48*, 365).

23. Ibid. Although Chatton recognizes that this notion of knowledge maps neither of Ockham's, he insists nonetheless that Ockham would have to allow that God's knowledge includes a relation of this sort. As he says: "he too would have to say this, [namely, that God cognizes the thing signified by a true sentence]—whether he does so directly or indirectly" (Ibid.).

24. Chatton makes this point, not in d. 39, but just afterward at dd. 40–41, q.2, a.1 (*Reportatio dd. 10–48*, 393).

25. Chatton's most extensive treatment of objects of propositional attitudes occurs in q.1, a.1 of the Prologue to his *Sentences* commentary in *Reportatio et Lectura Super Sententias: Collatio ad librum Primum et Prologus*, ed. J.C. Wey (Toronto: Pontifical Institute of Mediaeval Studies, 1989). For a fuller treatment of Chatton's discussion in that context see Susan Brower-Toland, "How Chatton Changed Ockham's Mind: William Ockham and Walter Chatton on Acts and Objects of Judgment," in *Intentionality, Cognition, and Mental Representation in Medieval Philosophy*, ed. G. Klima (New York: Fordham University Press, forthcoming).

26. *Sent.* Prol. q.1, a.1 (*Collatio et Prologus*, 39).

27. Thus, for example, speaking of sentences in the language of thought, Chatton says: "A mental sentence is a certain propositional cognition. Thus, it is a cognition of just that which is cognized through the subject, or the predicate or the copula [of that mental sentence]. For its being a cognition accrues to it through its parts—but its parts are cognitions of an extramental thing. An external thing (*res*) is cognized through the subject, the predicate, and the copula since those terms are cognitions of an external thing. Throughout the whole time in which the sentence signifying an external thing is formed in the mind, the external thing is cognized—sometimes by the subject of the sentence, sometimes by the copula, sometimes by the predicate" (*Sent.* Prol. q.1, a.1 [*Collatio et Prologus*, 24]).

28. *Rep.* I dd. 40–41, q.2, a.1 (*Reportatio dd. 10–48*, 393).

29. Indeed, Chatton even follows Ockham in characterizing God's omniscience as a matter of God's assenting to every truth. As he explains, "every unqualified perfection is suited to God, and to assent to every truth whatsoever is an unqualified perfection, therefore, [God assents to every truth]." *Rep.* I dd. 40–41, q.2, a.1 (*Reportatio dd. 10–48*, 395).

30. *Rep.* I d. 39, q.u, a.2 (*Reportatio dd. 10–48*, 366).

31. *Rep.* I d. 39, q.u, a.2 (*Reportatio dd. 10–48*, 367).

32. Ibid.

33. Ibid.

34. Holcot explicitly considers and rejects Chatton's account of truth-bearers and objects of knowledge in article 1 of his discussion in Q.I.6.

35. Holcot, Q.I.6, 4

36. Ibid., 7.

37. Holcot begins article 1 by summarizing both Ockham and Chatton's view: "One view, which Ockham holds, is that only a sentence [*complexum*] is known. But another view—a view held by Chatton—is that the object of knowing or believing is not a sentence, but the thing signified by a sentence. Accordingly, the act of believing that *God is three and one* has God himself as its object, and the act of knowing that a *human being is an animal* has *a human being* for its object" (Holcot , Q.I.6, 3).

38. Holcot, Q.I.6, 11. Holcot goes on immediately after this to cite further evidence from Ockham: "For in his *Summa logicae*—which is so usefully compiled—Ockham himself says (at part two, chapter two, at the end, where he speaks of necessary propositions):

> It must be known that a sentence is not said to be necessary because it always was true or always will be true, but because it is true and cannot be false. For example, the spoken sentence 'God exists' is necessary, nevertheless, it is not always true since when it does not exist, it is neither true nor false. But it is necessary because when it exists it is true and cannot be false. Here, he explicitly says that the sentence 'God exists' was not always true; but it is also certain that its opposite was never true. Therefore, there was a time at which neither part of this contradiction, 'God exists'/'God does not exist,' was true. This is the case since at some point in time neither of these sentences existed" (Holcot, Q.I.6, 11–12).

39. Holcot, Q.I.6, 15.

40. Ibid., 10. After all, Holcot goes on to explain, "suppose I order 'Socrates runs' to be written in a thousand places (and suppose it is the case in fact [that Socrates runs]) . . . and suppose I order 'Socrates does not run' to be written in just one place . . . then the thousand true sentences contradict this one."

41. Holcot, Q.I.6 , 13.

42. Ibid., 9

43. Ibid., 11.

44. Ibid., 13.

45. The two worries I discuss below are similar to ones raised for sententialist views of assertion (i.e., views according the things asserted or said are sentences) first raised by Richard Cartwright in "Propositions" in *Analytical Philosophy*, 1st ser., ed. R.J. Butler (Oxford: Basil Blackwell, 1962), 81–103, and later discussed by Howard Wettstein in his paper, "Can What is Asserted Be a Sentence?" *Philosophical Review* 85 (1976): 196–207.

46. There are actually two issues here. We are not only going to need some account of why, among a class of relevantly similar tokens, one token is the

object of a given belief rather than another; we also need some way of specifying the class itself. How Holcot specifies the relevant class as well as his account of which member of the class is the object for a given instance of belief (and why) will emerge presently.

47. This claim applies only to Ockham's early views about the objects of propositional attitudes. Ockham's views about the nature of the objects of propositional attitudes evolve over time. Since d. 39 is among Ockham's earlier writings, however, the subsequent developments in his thinking need not concern us here. For a more detailed treatment of Ockham's account and of the developments it undergoes see Susan Brower-Toland, "Ockham on Judgment, Concepts, and the Problem of Intentionality," *Canadian Journal of Philosophy* 37 (2007): 67–109.

48. As he insists: "every science (*scientia*) whatsoever—whether it is real or rational—concerns only mental sentences. For it concerns those things which are known (*scita*) and only mental sentences are known (*scitur*)" (*Ord.* d.2, q.4 [*OTh* II, 135]). Here too it is worth emphasizing that Ockham's views about mental sentences serving as objects of judgment evolve over time—my remarks in this context apply only to his earlier theories.

49. Indeed, as we have seen, Chatton holds that the object of a given attitude is just the entity (or entities) that the terms which comprise the sentence expressing that attitude "signify." See Note 28 above.

50. It is not altogether uncontroversial, however. Indeed, one of Chatton's contemporaries—Adam Wodeham—does in fact take issue with precisely this claim; Wodeham contends that what propositional attitudes refer to are not things, but rather facts, or concrete states of affair. For more on Wodeham's criticisms of Chatton's position see Susan Brower-Toland, "Facts vs. Things: Adam Wodeham and the Later Medieval Debate about Objects of Judgment," *Review of Metaphysics* 60 (2006): 597–642.

51. G.E.L. Owen coined the term for this Aristotelian notion in his "Logic and Metaphysics in some Earlier Works of Aristotle," in *Aristotle and Plato in the Mid-Fourth Century*, ed. I. Düring and G.E.L. Owen (Göteborg: Almquist and Wiksell, 1960),163–90.

52. *Rep.* I, d. 39, q.u, a.2 (*Reportatio dd. 10–48*, 365–66).

53. As he puts it at another point in d. 39: "The same thing that is now signified truly by 'you are sitting' will immediately be signified by its contradictory when you arise. For contradictories signify the same thing altogether—otherwise they would not be contradictories" (*Rep.* I, d. 39, q.u, a.2 [*Reportatio dd. 10–48*, 366]). This is a point Chatton repeats elsewhere. In the next question, for example, he says: "I am supposing that that very thing which is signified by 'Socrates is sitting' is also signified by this 'Socrates is not sitting'—otherwise they would not be contradictories" (*Rep.* I, dd. 40–41, q.2, a.1 [*Reportatio dd. 10–48*, 393]). Chatton's idea here is not, of course, that such sentences have the same content, but rather merely that such sentences *refer*

to—or are about—the same thing—namely, Socrates. After all, if such sentences were about different things they would not be contradictory.

54. Holcot 1971, 21. Notice that Holcot speaks of God's "knowledge" (rather than God himself) as knowing more or less. This is typical of Holcot's way of speaking throughout Q.I.6; he alternates between speaking of the *relations* of belief and knowledge as holding between subjects—that is, knowers—and certain objects, on the one hand, and as holding between mental acts and those same objects on the other.

55. This is because, on Holcot's view, "God himself is Truth and is a single true cognition equivalent to and preexisting every true sentence" (Holcot, Q.I.6, 7). Or, as he puts it elsewhere, "God is something equivalent to every sentence that would be true if it existed. Thus, if he had only known that [truth] which is himself, he would be as wise as he is now" (Holcot, Q.I.6, 13).

56. Ibid., 5.

57. Holcot's claim (in the foregoing passage) that God would "know" no less about triangles even if he'd not "known" as many truths about them makes clear that he is willing to use propositional attitude expressions such as "know" and "believe" in two different senses. In one sense (e.g., in the first occurrence above), he uses such expressions to talk about the content of a mental act, in another sense (e.g., in the second occurrence) to talk about a relation to the object of that act. While he does not do so in the passage just quoted, Holcot sometimes signals these different senses by actually using a different expression to talk about a belief's content. For example, in the passage cited in Note 50 above he claims that while God can "know" more or fewer truths, he is at all times "just as *wise* (*sapiens*) as he is now." At other points he uses the Latin expression *novit* in place of *scivit* when discussing what God knows in the sense of content. Also, Holcot never uses the expression *object* (*obiectum*) in contexts in which he's talking about a belief's content.

58. Holcot, Q.I.6, 10–11.

59. Ibid., 7. See also Note 50 above.

60. Actually, while Holcot thinks that it is sentence tokens that primarily function as objects of propositional attitudes, he does allow that some nonlinguistic entities can be objects for propositional attitudes as well. For some nonlinguistic objects are truth-bearers. In this connection, Holcot mentions the example of a barrel hoop which signifies equivalently to this sentence: "Wine is sold here." See Holcot, Q.I.6, 7.

61. There are, of course, certain truths for which this claim raises problems and, hence, in virtue which it might require further qualification. For while the claim that God's omniscience is a matter of God's knowing (standing in the knowing relation to) every truth is, on the face of it, an intuitive explication of omniscience, one might suspect that there are some sentences that may be true and yet are not equivalent to—and so do not encode—anything God can be said to know. Here I have in mind situations that might arise with

demonstratives. For example, is there anything in God's mental language which the true token (in my mouth) "I am Susan" encodes? What Holcot would say about this depends on how fine-grained a notion of content he has—or how strict a notion of equivalence is required for encoding. (I make clear how equivalence enters into the notion of encoding below.)

62. Holcot, Q.I.6, 21.

63. Ibid., 5.

64. Scholars have, of course, been sensitive to the fact that medieval authors, in developing a theory of propositions, are often addressing different sorts of issues. That is to say, they typically distinguish between three different questions medieval authors discuss in theorizing about propositions: (a) what sort of entity functions as the bearer of truth/falsity; (b) what sort of entity function as the meaning (*significatum*) of sentential expressions; (c) what sort of entity functions as the object of propositional attitudes. See, for example, Rondo Keele, "The So-Called *Res* Theory of Walter Chatton," *Franciscan Studies* 61 (2003): 37–53; E.J. Ashworth, "Theories of the Proposition: Some Early Sixteenth Century Discussions," *Franciscan Studies* 38 (1978): 81–121; Norman Kretzmann, "Medieval Logicians on the Meaning of the *Propositio*," *The Journal of Philosophy* 67 (1970): 767–87. What has been overlooked, however, is the fact that even in cases where the debate is focused specifically on one of these subquestions—say, on the question about objects of propositional attitudes—participants in the debate may still be addressing different sorts of questions. Thus, in the case at hand, Ockham, Chatton, and Holcot are clearly all addressing the third of these three questions. Nonetheless, insofar as they are each operating with different conceptions of what it is for something to be an object of judgment they are not addressing the same question.

65. This classificatory scheme owes to Gabriele Nuchelmans's pioneering study of ancient and medieval theories of propositions in his *Theories of the Proposition: Ancient and Medieval Conceptions of the Bearers of Truth and Falsity* (Amsterdam: North Holland, 1973). Since then, his scheme has been widely adopted by scholars. See, for example, Keele, "The So-Called *Res* Theory"; Elizabeth Karger, "William of Ockham, Walter Chatton, and Adam Wodeham on the Objects of Knowledge and Belief," *Vivarium* 33 (1995): 171–86 ; Jack Zupko, "How It Played in the rue de Fouarre: Reception of Adam Wodeham's Theory of the *Complexe Significabile* in the Arts Faculty at Paris in the Mid-fourteenth Century," *Franciscan Studies* 54 (1994): 211–25; Onorato Grassi, "The Object of Scientific Knowledge in Some Authors of the Fourteenth Century," in *Knowledge and the Sciences in Medieval Philosophy: Proceedings of the Eighth International Congress of Medieval Philosophy*, ed. S. Knuuttila, R. Tyorinoja, and S. Ebbesen (Helsinki: Luther-Agricola Society, 1990), 180–89; Adams, *William Ockham*, ch. 26; Gabriele Nuchelmans, "Adam Wodeham on the Meaning of Declarative Sentences," *Historiographia Linguistica* 8 (1980): 177–87.

66. Thus, for example, Ockham and Chatton are often characterized as holding opposed positions regarding the nature of propositions (Ockham as a *complexum*-theorist, Chatton as a *res*-theorist) whereas Holcot and Ockham are depicted as falling in the same camp (both being *complexum*-theorists). (See, for example, Nuchelmans, *Theories of the Proposition*, chs. 12–13; Keele, "The So-Called *Res* Theory"; Karger, "William of Ockham, Walter Chatton, and Adam Wodeham"; Adams, *William Ockham*, ch. 26.) But not only are their positions not clearly opposed, there is reason to suspect that there might be a fair amount of agreement between them. Indeed, Chatton and Holcot would agree with Ockham that the content of a propositional attitude is to be identified with a mental sentence; Ockham and Holcot would concede to Chatton that the referential objects for such attitudes are entities falling within the Aristotelian categories of substance or accident; and, finally, I suspect that Ockham and Chatton would have no objection to Holcot's claim that token sentences encode the content of propositional attitudes. I have discussed the extent of agreement and disagreement between Ockham and Chatton on these issues in much more detail elsewhere (see Brower-Toland, "How Chatton Changed Ockham's Mind").

67. I am grateful to Jeffrey Brower for his valuable comments and feedback on earlier drafts of this essay.

8. The Power of Medieval Logic TERENCE PARSONS

Except for Calvin Normore, I have learned more about medieval logic and philosophy from Paul Vincent Spade than from any other (secondary) source, especially about the topics of the modes of personal supposition. This essay is essentially a progress report on a longer work in progress, tentatively titled *Basics of Medieval Formal Logic*.

1. Aristotle, *Prior Analytics* I 1–2, 4–7.

2. This form of syllogism was later called Barocho. See *Prior Analytics (27a36)*, for this discussion.

3. See *Prior Analytics* I, ch. 2.

4. In his *Introductiones in logicam*, William of Sherwood states the rule: "Pre-negation produces the contradictory." See Martin Grabmann (ed.), *Die introductiones in logicam des Wilhelm von Shyreswood (nach 1267): Literarhistorische Einleitung und Textausgabe*, Sitzungsberichte der Bayerischen Akademie der Wissenschaften, Philosophisch-historische Abteilung, Jahrgang 1937, H. 10 (Munich: Verlag der Bayerischen Akademie der Wissenschaften, 1937), I.19, p. 38. English translation: *William of Sherwood's Introduction to Logic*, trans. Nicolas Kretzmann (Minneapolis: University of Minnesota Press, 1966). See also Peter of Spain, *Tractatus* (or *Summule Logicales*), ed. by L. M. De Rijk (Assen: Van Gorcum & Co, 1972), I.18. English translation by Brian Copenhaver forthcoming from Oxford University Press.

5. Grabmann, pp. 37–38. According to footnote 54 of chapter 1 in Kretzmann, *William of Sherwood*, Peter of Spain also gives a verse which contains most of these equivalences, along with some others, such as *neither* and *not either*. His source is Bochenski's edition of Peter's *Summulae Logicales* (= *Tractatus*). I cannot find this verse in De Rijk's edition of the *Tractatus*, indicating that it was a later addition.

6. Cf. John Buridan, *Tractatus de Consequentiis*. In *Iohannis Buridani tractatus de consequentiis: Édition critique*, ed. Hubert Hubien, vol. XVI of Philosophes médiévaux (Université de Louvain, 1976). Hereafter cited as "*TC*." English translation: Jean Buridan, *Jean Buridan's Logic: The Treatise on Supposition, the Treatise on Consequences*, trans. Peter King (Dordrecht: D. Reidel, 1985). See also section III.2 in Paul of Venice, *Logica Parva*. English translation: Paulus Venetus, *Logica Parva: Translation of the 1472 Edition*, trans. Alan Perreiah (München: Philosophia Verlag, 1984).

7. Aristotle characterizes propositions in *On Interpretation*; molecular propositions are not included. See *Prior Analytics* 1.44 for a discussion of what we call disjunctive syllogism, where it is characterized as the result of a kind of agreement.

8. One difference is that conditionals usually had to be necessary in order to be true (though material conditionals were sometimes discussed; cf. *TC* I.4.7–8). Peter of Spain, *Tractatus*, I.17, gives truth conditions for molecular propositions, as does Albert of Saxony at III.5 of an unpublished translation by Ernest Moody of selections from his *Summa Logicae*. Paul of Venice, *Logica Parva*, III.7, gives propositional rules of inference. General laws were well known, such as the principle that anything follows from a contradiction; see *TC* I.8.32.

9. Cf. sections 4.3.5–6 in John Buridan, *Summulae de Dialectica*, trans. G. Klima (New Haven and London: Yale University Press, 2001).: Chapter VI of Anonymous *Dialectica Monacensis*, in De Rijk, L.M. 1967 *Logica Modernum* II.2 Koninklijke Van Gorcum, Assen, The Netherlands, 605–16: Chapter VII of Anonymous *Logica "Ut Dicit"*, in De Rijk ibid., 408–11: and Marsilius of Inghen, *Treatises on the Properties of Terms*, translated in Egbert Bos, *Marsilius of Inghen: Treatises on the Properties of Terms*, Reidel, 1983, pp. 57–61.

10. I omit here a discussion of Ockham's idea that in merely confused supposition one can descend to a disjoint term. For an argument that this kind of descent rests on grammatical rather than logical considerations see Terence Parsons, "Supposition Theory in the later 12th through 14th Centuries," in *Handbook of the History of Logic: Medieval and Renaissance Logic*, ed. D. Gabbay and J. Woods, vol. 2 (Amsterdam: Elsevier, 2008), 157–280.

11. The study of how signs cause changes in mode of supposition was widespread. Cf. pp. 613–16 in Anonymous *Dialectica Monacensis* in de Rijk op. cit., pp. 408–11 in Anonymous *Logica "Ut Dicit" in de Rijk* Op. cit., and pp. 713–21 in Anonymous, Tractatus de Proprietatibus Sermonum in De Rijk op. cit.

12. Cf. Walter Burley, *Consequences* in *The Cambridge Translations of Medieval Philosophical Texts*, ed. Norman Kretzmann and Eleonore Stump, vol. 1 (Cambridge: Cambridge University Press, 1988), p. 300. See also section 3.7.8 of *The Treatise on Supposition* in Jean Buridan, *Jean Buridan's Logic*.

13. See Kretzmann, *William of Sherwood*, section 5.13.

14. Once multiple quantification is introduced, as in *No animal is every donkey*, it is no longer possible to use only the monadic calculus *without* identity to formalize propositions.

15. Cf. John Buridan, *Summulae de Dialectica*, sections 1.3.3.

16. Augustus De Morgan, *Formal Logic: The Calculus of Inference, Necessary and Probable* (Honolulu: University Press of the Pacific, 2003; reprint of the 1847 edition), p. 114. I have changed *head of a man* to *head of a horse* to match discussion in the secondary literature.

17. The first of these phrases contains a single complex term, and the second has two terms. This equivalence may seem ad hoc, but the complex term is a special construction, so something special is needed to deal with it. This issue would be avoided in modern logic by symbolizing both phrases in the same way, thus smuggling a logical equivalence into the symbolization technique. For example, *h is a head of an F* might be symbolized as $\exists x(Fx$ & h is-a-head-of x$)$, and *h is of an F a head* would then be symbolized in exactly the same way. Since the Latin forms are different, I have retained the differences and invoked their equivalence as an explicit logical assumption.

18. The notation "Universal App" is short for "Universal Application," a principle that Aristotle used without mention. It sanctions going from *Every A is B* and *n is an A* to *n is a B*.

19. Actually this justification is not fully stated. For *h is not h* will be true if the term *h* is empty. We need an appeal to line 6 to validate *h is not empty*.

20. Cf. Marsilius of Inghen, p. 75 in Bos 1983 op. cit.; Peter of Spain, *Tractatus*, VIII.15.

21. Walter Burley, *On the Purity of the Art of Logic*, trans. Paul Vincent Spade (New Haven: Yale University Press, 2000), paras. 125–26. Albert of Saxony espouses a similar view in his 18th Question in Michael J. Fitzgerald, *Albert of Saxony's Twenty-five Disputed Questions on Logic*. (Leiden/Boston/Köln: Brill, 2002). Likewise Ockham in section I.76 of Michael J. Loux, *Ockham's Theory of Terms: Part I of the Summa Logicae* (Notre Dame, IN: University of Notre Dame Press, 1974).

22. See for example Burley, *On the Purity of the Art of Logic*, para. 117.

23. Terence Parsons, "Anaphoric Pronouns in Very Late Medieval Supposition Theory," *Linguistics and Philosophy* 17 (1994): 429–45.

9. Iteration and Infinite Regress in Walter Chatton's Metaphysics
RONDO KEELE

A version of this essay was first presented at the American Catholic Philosophical Association meeting, in a session organized by the Society for Mediaeval

Logic and Metaphysics, October 2006, and first published in the *Proceedings
for the Society for Mediaeval Logic and Metaphysics*, 2006. Thanks to Gyula
Klima for suggesting I present the paper at this venue, and for permission
to use the work here. Thanks also to Jack Zupko, whose comments at the
conference helped me revise the text.

1. The *Lectura* has been edited by Jerry Etzkorn, and is being published by the
   Pontifical Institute of Mediaeval Studies as part of their Studies and Texts
   series, the first volume of which appeared in 2007. All references to the *Lectura*
   in this essay are to the paragraph numbers in Etzkorn's edition, which he has
   graciously allowed me to see in advance of publication.

2. The *Reportatio* has been fully edited in four volumes. The relevant volume
   here is *Reportatio super Sententias: Liber I, distincitones 10–48*, ed. Joseph C.
   Wey and Girard J. Etzkorn [Studies and Texts 142] (Toronto: Pontifical
   Institute of Mediaeval Studies, 2002). Hereafter cited as "*Reportatio I.*"

3. Throughout the essay I leave to one side the question of whether Ockham
   ever made *exactly* the objections Chatton attributes to him; the objections
   are certainly Ockhamist in spirit. Nevertheless, Ockham's *Quodlibet* I.5 gives
   an example of an objection very like the one I here characterize as
   "Ockhamist."

4. Chatton defends this in many places, for example, *Reporatio* I, d. 30, q. 1, a. 4,
   38, pp. 233–34: "Quartus articulus est respondere ad formam quaestionis,
   an aliqua accidentia respectiva sint in orbe. Sunt, ut dixi, quattuor vel tres
   opiniones . . . quod non . . . Sed teneo conclusionem oppositum . . ." He goes on
   to give six examples of cases where one needs to posit causal respectives, viz., a
   case of generation, one of production, one of motion, one of condensation, one
   of seeing, and one of understanding.

5. This example comes from *Lectura* I, d. 3, q. 1, a. 1, paras. 43–46.

6. See for example *Quod.* I.5.

7. *Lectura*, dist. 3, q. 1, a. 1, paras. 40–42.

8. This theory is most fully developed in *Lectura* I, d. 3, q. 1, a. 1, paras. 4–22.

9. This discussion comes from *Lectura* I, d. 3, q. 1, a. 1, paras. 43–46, and is a
   response to an objection first mentioned in objection in ibid., para. 25.

10. Chatton does not give a name to this strategy, but simply refers to it as a
    "method."

11. Thanks to Jack Zupko for pointing out the need for this clarification.

12. *Reportatio* I, d. 38, q. unica, a. 1, para. 22, p. 351.

13. *Reportatio* I, d. 38, q. unica, a. 1, paras 24–29, pp. 351–52. Paragraph 28
    contains the heart of his solution. For a full explanation, see Rondo Keele,
    "Walter Chatton," *The Stanford Encyclopedia of Philosophy (Fall 2006
    Edition)*, ed. Edward N. Zalta, URL = http://plato.stanford.edu/archives
    /fall2006/entries/walter-chatton/, section 5.

14. *Reportatio* I, d. 38, q. unica, a. 1, para. 23, p. 351. He says "Si est vera in
    secundo intellectu, igitur si asserat se esse veram, illo modo vera est ut asserit

se veram, quia ex opposito sequitur oppositum, si intelligatur illud dictum generaliter."

15. Thanks to Charles Bolyard for pointing out this possibility to me.

10. Analogy and Metaphor from Thomas Aquinas to Duns Scotus and Walter Burley E. JENNIFER ASHWORTH

1. For the analogy of being see Pierre Aubenque, "Sur la naissance de la doctrine pseudo-aristotélicienne de l'analogie de l'être," *Les études philosophiques* 3/4 (1989): 291–304; Alain de Libera, "Les sources gréco-arabes de la théorie médiévale de l'analogie de l'être," *Les études philosophiques* 3/4 (1989): 319–45; and E. Jennifer Ashworth, "L'analogie de l'être et les homonymes: *Catégories*, 1 dans le *Guide de l'étudiant*" in *L'enseignement de la philosophie au xiiie siècle. Autour du «Guide de l'étudiant» du ms. Ripoll 109*, ed. Claude Lafleur with the collaboration of Joanne Carrier (Studia Artistarum 5. Turnhout, Belgium: Brepols, 1997), pp. 281–95. For a general discussion of analogy, see E. Jennifer Ashworth, *Les théories de l'analogie du XIIe au XVIe siècle* (Paris: J. Vrin, 2008).

2. Silvia Donati, "La discussione sull'unità del concetto di ente nella tradizione di commento della *Fisica*: commenti parigini degli anni 1270–1315 ca." in *Die Logik des Transzendentalen. Festschrift für Jan A. Aertsen zum 65. Geburtstag*, ed. Martin Pickavé (Miscellanea Mediaevalia 30. Berlin, New York: Walter de Gruyter, 2003), pp. 60–139; and Giorgio Pini, *Scoto e l'analogia. Logica e metafisica nei commenti aristotelici* (Pisa: Scuola Normale Superiore, 2002).

3. For discussion of Aquinas see E. Jennifer Ashworth, "Signification and Modes of Signifying in Thirteenth-Century Logic: A Preface to Aquinas on Analogy," *Medieval Philosophy and Theology* 1 (1991): 39–67; E. Jennifer Ashworth, "Analogy and Equivocation in Thirteenth-Century Logic: Aquinas in Context," *Mediaeval Studies* 54 (1992): 94–135; Joël Lonfat, "Archéologie de la notion d'analogie d'Aristote à saint Thomas d'Aquin," *Archives d'histoire doctrinale et littéraire du moyen âge* 71 (2004): 35–107; and Seung-Chan Park, *Die Rezeption der mittelalterlichen Sprachphilosophie in der Theologie des Thomas von Aquin. Mit besondere Berücksichtigung der Analogie* (Studien und Texte zur Geistesgeschichte des Mittalters 65. Leiden, Boston, Köln: Brill, 1999).

4. For more about modism see Costantino Marmo, *Semiotica e linguaggio nella scolastica: Parigi, Bologna, Erfurt 1270–1330. La semiotica dei Modisti* (Roma: Istituto Storico Italiano per il Medio Evo, 1994); Irène Rosier, *La grammaire spéculative des Modistes* (Lille: Presses Universitaires de Lille, 1983); and Irène Rosier, *La parole comme acte. Sur la grammaire et la sémantique au XIIIe siècle* (Paris: J. Vrin, 1994).

5. Lambert of Auxerre [or of Lagny], *Logica (Summa Lamberti)*, ed. Franco Alessio (Florence: La Nuova Italia Editrice, 1971), pp. 205–6: "[. . .] ad hoc quod vox sit significativa quatuor exiguntur: res, intellectus rei, vox et unio vocis cum intellectu rei. Res dicitur illud quod extra animam existens per sui speciem ab anima apprehenditur, ut homo vel lapis; intellectus rei dicitur

species vel similitudo rei que est in anima. [. . .] Sic ergo vox primo et per se et immediate est signum intellectus rei; ulterius vero mediate est signum rei. [. . .] significatio hominis solum extenditur ad hominem, non ad contempta sub homine: 'homo' enim significat hominem, non Sortem nec Platonem."

6. See Giorgio Pini, "Species, Concept, and Thing: Theories of Signification in the Second Half of the Thirteenth Century," *Medieval Philosophy and Theology* 8 (1999): 21–52; Giorgio Pini, "Signification of Names in Duns Scotus and Some of His Contemporaries," *Vivarium* 39 (2001): 20–51.

7. See for example Thomas Aquinas, *Summa Contra Gentiles* I, cap. 32.

8. See E. Jennifer Ashworth, "Metaphor and the Logicians from Aristotle to Cajetan," *Vivarium* 45 (2007): 311–27.

9. Irène Rosier-Catach, "Prata Rident" in *Langages et Philosophie: Hommage à Jean Jolivet*, ed. Alain de Libera, Abdelali Elamrani-Jamal, and Alain Galonnier (Études de philosophie médiévale 74. Paris: J. Vrin, 1997), pp. 155–76. On p. 155 she writes: "Trope ou figure de sens pour les grammairiens et les rhéteurs, variation de signification constituant un mode de l'équivocité pour les dialecticiens, déplacement sémantique intervenant dans tout discours sur Dieu pour les théologiens, le notion de transfert sémantique (*translatio, transumptio*), est au carrefour des arts du langage et de la théologie." See also Irène Rosier-Catach, "La notion de *translatio*, le principe de compositionalité et l'analyse de la prédication accidentelle chez Abélard" in *Langage, Sciences, Philosophie au XIIe siècle*, ed. Joël Biard (Paris, J. Vrin, 1999), pp. 125–64; Luisa Valente, "Langage et théologie pendant la seconde moitié du XIIe siècle" in *Sprachtheorien in Spätantike und Mittelalter*, ed. Sten Ebbesen (Tübingen: Gunter Narr Verlag, 1995), pp. 33–54.

10. For discussion and further references see Louis Holtz, *Donat et la tradition de l'enseignement grammatical. Étude sur l'Ars Donati et sa diffusion (ive–ixe siècle) et édition critique* (Paris: Centre National de la Recherche Scientifique, 1981), p. 200.

11. Quintilian, *M. Fabi Qvintiliani Institvtionis Oratoriae libri dvodecim*, ed. M. Winterbottom (Oxford: Clarendon Press, 1970), 8.6.1, p. 462:11–12. Luisa Valente, *Logique et théologie. Les écoles parisiennes entre 1150 et 1220* (Paris: J. Vrin, 2008), p. 70, suggests "légitimé par des motifs déterminés" as a translation of "cum virtute," thus contrasting a virtuous usage with the vice (*vitium*) of unjustified impropriety.

12. Quintilian, *Inst.Orat.*, 8.6.5, p. 463: 3–5. Later Quintilian, (*Inst.Orat.*, 8.6.34–5, p. 469) says that catachresis or *abusio* gives a name to things that have no name, and that it differs from metaphor because in metaphor there was a different word (*abusio est ubi nomen defuit, tralatio ubi aliud fuit*).

13. Donatus, *Ars Maior* III.6 in Holtz, *Donat et la tradition*, p. 667: 2–3. For metaphor, see lines 6–7.

14. Thomas Aquinas, *Summa theologiae* [cited as *ST*], Ia.13.3.

15. William of Ockham, *Expositio super libros Elenchorum*, ed. Francesco del Punta (Opera Philosophica III. St. Bonaventure, N.Y.: St. Bonaventure, 1979), p. 22: "[. . .] iste est quando dictio est primo imposita unica impositione ad significandum unum vel multa, postea propter aliquam certam rationem [. . .] imponitur ad significandum aliquid aliud, ita quod nisi esset primo imposita ad significandum suum primarium significatum, vel primaria significata, non imponeretur postea secundario." Note that he speaks of the primary significates in the plural since they are individuals rather than natures. Cf. William of Ockham, *Summa Logicae*, ed. P. Boehner, G. Gál, S. Brown (Opera Philosophica I. St. Bonaventure, N.Y.: St. Bonaventure University, 1974), p. 756, where he speaks of the attribution of another thing to the first significate.

16. Walter Burley, *Super tractatum fallaciarum*, p. 202, in Sten Ebbesen, "Burley on Equivocation in his Companion to a *Tractatus Fallaciarum* and in his Questions on the *Elenchi*," *Cahiers de l'institut du moyen-âge grec et latin* 74 (2003): 151–207; Thomas de Wyk, pp. 142–43, in Sten Ebbesen, "Texts on Equivocation. Part II. Ca. 1250–1310," *Cahiers de l'institut du moyen-âge grec et latin* 68 (1998): 99–307.

17. Aquinas, *ST* IIaIIae.57.1 ad 1: "consuetum est quod nomina a sui prima impositione detorqueantur ad alia significanda."

18. See for example Aquinas, *ST* Ia.29.3 ad 2 for *persona*; Thomas Aquinas, *In Quattuor Libros Sententiarum* in *Opera Omnia* I, ed. Roberto Busa (Stuttgart-Bad Cannstatt: Frommann-Holzboog, 1980), I.10.1.4 for *spiritus*; *ST* IIIa.2.1 for *natura*.

19. Aquinas, *ST* Ia.34.1.

20. Aquinas, *ST* Ia.67.1.

21. Aquinas, *ST* Ia.13.3 ad 1, ad 3; Thomas Aquinas, *De Potentia* in *Quaestiones Disputatae II*, ed. P. Bazzi et al. (Taurini, Romae: Marietti, 1965), 7.5 ad 8; *Sent.* I. 22.1.2. Gilbert Dahan, "Saint Thomas d'Aquin et la métaphore. Rhétorique et herméneutique," *Medioevo* 18 (1992): 85–117. On pp. 101–2 he argues that "lion" used of God is not an example of *translatio* properly so-called, and that the only true metaphor is *pratum ridet.*

22. Aquinas, *ST* Ia.1.10 ad 3.

23. Thomas Aquinas, *Super Epistolam ad Galatas Lectura* in *Super Epistolas S. Pauli Lectura I*, ed. P. Raphaelis Cai (Taurini, Romae: Marietti, 1953), cap. 4, lect. 7, n. 254: "Per litteralem autem sensum potest aliquid significari dupliciter, scilicet secundum proprietatem locutionis, sicut cum dico *homo ridet*; vel secundum similitudinem seu metaphoram, sicut cum dico *pratum ridet.*"

24. Aquinas, *Sent.* III. 38.1.3 ad 4: "[. . .] qui dicit, quod pratum ridet, sub quadam rei similitudine intendit significare prati floritionem."

25. Thomas Aquinas, *Quaestiones Quodlibetales*, ed. R. Spiazzi (Taurini, Romae: Marietti, 1949), 7.6.1 ad 4. He is speaking here of the spiritual sense, but his words are applicable to the literal sense.

26. See E. Jennifer Ashworth, "Equivocation and Divine Language in Some Theology Texts from the Twelfth and Early Thirteenth Centuries" in *30 Years Logica Modernorum. Acts of the Symposium in Honor of Professor L. M. de Rijk*, ed. C.H. Kneepkens and H.A.G. Braakhuis (Studia Artistarum 13. Turnhout: Brepols, forthcoming); Valente, "*Langage et théologie*"; and Valente, *Logique et théologie*.

27. Translation by Boethius in *Aristoteles Latinus I 1–5. Categoriae vel Praedicamenta*, ed. L. Minio-Paluello (Bruges, Paris: Desclée de Brouwer, 1961), p. 5: "Aequivoca dicuntur quorum nomen solum commune est, secundum nomen vero substantiae ratio diversa, ut animal homo et quod pingitur."

28. Boethius, *In Categorias Aristotelis libri quatuor* in *Patrologiae Cursus Completus. Series latina 64*, ed. J.-P. Migne (Paris, 1891), 166B-C.

29. Aristotle had used the example of *zoon* which is a chance equivocal in Greek, meaning both an animal and a picture of some sort. Medievals were unaware of this, and frequently used *homo* in place of *animal*. For further discussion of *homo pictus*, see Ashworth, *Les théories*, pp. 85–86.

30. For further discussion of Greek analogy in medieval logic, see Ashworth, *Les théories*, pp. 44–54.

31. Averroes, Commentary on *Metaphysics* in *Aristotelis Opera cum Averrois Commentariis* (Venice, 1562–74, facsimile reprint Frankfurt: Minerva, 1962), vol. 8, fol. 65 va.

32. Thomas Aquinas, *De principiis naturae* in *Opuscula IV* (Leonine edition, vol. 43. Romae, 1976), 6, pp. 46:42–47:57; Thomas Aquinas, *In Duodecim Libros Metaphysicorum Aristotelis Expositio*, ed. M.-R. Cathala and R. Spiazzi (Taurini, Romae: Marietti, 1950), 4, lect. 1, nn. 537–39.

33. Boethius, *In Cat.*, 166D–167A.

34. This phrase can be read in various ways, and it might also say that *translatio* is not a property of things.

35. Simplicius, *Commentaire sur les Catégories d'Aristote. Traduction de Guillaume de Moerbeke*, ed. Adrien Pattin (Louvain: Publications Universitaires de Louvain; Paris: Béatrice-Nauwelaerts, 1971), p. 43.

36. *Aristoteles Latinus VI 1–3. De Sophisticis Elenchis*, ed. B.G. Dod (Leiden: E.J. Brill; Bruxelles: Desclée de Brouwer, 1975), p. 9: "Sunt autem tres modi secundum aequivocationem et amphiboliam: unus quidem quando vel oratio vel nomen principaliter significat plura, ut piscis et canis; alius autem quando soliti sumus sic dicere; tertius vero quando compositum plura significat, separatum vero simpliciter, ut 'scit saeculum' [. . .]."

37. Walter Burley in Sten Ebbesen, "Gualterus Burleus, *Quaestiones super Sophisticos Elenchos* 4–12. A revised edition," *Cahiers de l'institut du moyen-âge grec et latin* 76 (2005): 239–82 [cited as *In SE*]. On p. 282 he writes: "[. . .] Aristoteles in libro Praedicamentorum solum facit mentionem de vocibus ut sunt proprie significativae; huiusmodi sunt aequivocae, univocae et

denominativae. Analogum enim illud quod <per posterius> significat transumptive significat et non proprie [...]."

38. For discussion, see Ashworth, *Les théories*, pp. 95–99.

39. Peter of Spain [Petrus Hispanus], *Tractatus called afterwards Summule Logicales*, ed. L. M. de Rijk (Assen: Van Gorcum, 1972), p. 100:18–20: "Secunda species sive secundus modus equivocationis est quando eadem dictio secundum prius et posterius significat diversa [...]."; p. 101:11–12: "Ad hanc secundam speciem reducitur equivocatio ex transsumptione"; p. 101:20–23 "hec verba 'currit' et 'ridet' per prius significant *ridere* vel *currere* et per posterius *florere* vel *labi,* quia hec significant ex propria impositione, illa vero ex assuetudine." See also Lambert, *Logica,* pp. 149–50.

40. [Thomas Aquinas], *De fallaciis* in *Opuscula IV* (Leonine edition, vol. 43. Romae, 1976), p. 406:38–42: "Secunda species est quando unum nomen principaliter unum significat, et aliud methaphorice siue transsumptiue: sicut hoc uerbum 'ridet' principaliter significat actum proprium hominis, methaphorice siue transsumptiue significat prati floritionem [...]." He then says: "Ad hanc speciem reducitur multiplicitas nominum analogorum que dicuntur secundum prius et posterius, sicut sanum dicitur de animali, urina et dieta" (p. 406:53–55).

41. Peter of Spain, *Tractatus,* p. 113:12–26: "In secundo autem modo non exemplificat de equivocatione nec de amphibolia, quia, licet transsumptio fiat apud omnes, non tamen fit eadem in eodem apud omnes. Et ideo de neutra illarum exemplificat, quia non debent determinari in scientia nisi ea que eadem sunt apud omnes. ¶ Vel dicendum, ut melius, quod propria significatio dicitur dictionis quam recipit usus communiter. Unde quod modo per aliquam dictionem significatur transsumptive, cum usus inoleverit, significabitur proprie; et tunc erit dictio equivoca quoad primum modum. Et ideo quia contingit sic significationem que non est modo propria, sed transsumptiva, fieri postea propriam per frequentem usum, ideo non debuit ponere exempla aliqua in secundo modo, quia non debet determinari in arte nisi quod semper manet idem."

42. *Aristoteles Latinus XXV 2: Metaphysica Lib.I–X, XII–XIV. Translatio Anonyma sive "Media",* ed. G. Vuillemin-Diem (Leiden: E.J. Brill, 1976), p. 60: "Ens autem multis quidem dicitur modis, sed ad unum et unam aliquam naturam et non equivoce, sed quemadmodum salubre omne ad sanitatem [...]." This is the *translatio media.* Cf. Lonfat, "Archéologie de la notion," pp. 48–49.

43. Harry Austryn Wolfson, "The Amphibolous Terms in Aristotle, Arabic Philosophy and Maimonides," *Harvard Theological Review* 31 (1938): 151–73; reprinted in *Studies in the History of Philosophy and Religion,* ed. I. Twersky and G.H. Williams (Cambridge, MA, London: Harvard University Press, 1973), vol. 1, pp. 455–77.

44. Al-Ghazâlî in Charles H. Lohr, "*Logica Algazelis*: Introduction and Critical Text," *Traditio* 21 (1965): 223–90. See §5, p. 246.

45. Avicenna, *Liber de Philosophia Prima, sive Scientia Divina I–IV: Édition critique de la traduction latine médiévale*, ed. S. Van Riet (Louvain: E. Peeters; Leiden: E.J. Brill, 1977), I. 5, p. 40: "Dicemus igitur nunc quod quamvis ens, sicut scisti, non sit genus nec praedicatum aequaliter de his quae sub eo sunt, tamen est intentio in qua conveniunt secundum prius et posterius [. . .]"

46. Averroes, *In Met.*, fol. 65 rb.

47. Ashworth, *Les théories*, pp. 28–31; Philip L. Reynolds, "Analogy of Names in Bonaventure," *Mediaeval Studies* 65 (2003): 117–62.

48. For the problem of analogical concepts, see E. Jennifer Ashworth, "Analogical Concepts: The Fourteenth-Century Background to Cajetan," *Dialogue* 31 (1992): 399–413.

49. For discussion see Ashworth, *Les théories*, pp. 80–88.

50. Donati, "La discussione sull'unità," p. 75: "Particolarmente interessante nella tradizione di commento inglese di questo periodo è l'ampia influenza esercitata nel dibattito da Tommaso d'Aquino; esse è storicamente significativa in quanto non ha un corrispettivo nella contemporanea tradizione parigina." In particular, she cites a passage taken from the commentary on the *Sentences*. See also Pini, *Scoto e l'analogia*, pp. 46–47.

51. Aquinas, *Sent.* I.19.5. 2, ad 1: "Ad primum igitur dicendum, quod aliquid dicitur secundum analogiam tripliciter: vel secundum intentionem tantum, et non secundum esse; et hoc est quando una intentio refertur ad plura per prius et posterius, quae tamen non habet esse nisi in uno; sicut intentio sanitatis refertur ad animal, urinam et dietam diversimode, secundum prius et posterius; non tamen secundum diversum esse, quia esse sanitatis non est nisi in animali. Vel secundum esse et non secundum intentionem; et hoc contingit quando plura parificantur in intentione alicuius communis, sed illud commune non habet esse unius rationis in omnibus, sicut omnia corpora parificantur in intentione corporeitatis. Unde logicus, qui considerat intentiones tantum, dicit, hoc nomen 'corpus' de omnibus corporibus univoce praedicari. Sed esse huius naturae non est eiusdem rationis in corporibus corruptibilibus et incorruptibilibus, unde quantum ad metaphysicum et naturalem, qui considerant res secundum suum esse, nec hoc nomen 'corpus', nec aliquid aliud dicitur de corruptibilibus et incorruptibilibus, ut patet 10 *Metaphysicorum*, ex Philosopho et Commentatore. Vel secundum intentionem et secundum esse; et hoc est quando neque parificatur in intentione communi, neque in esse; sicut ens dicitur de substantia et accidente; et de talibus oportet quod natura communis habeat aliquod esse in unoquoque eorum de quibus dicitur, sed differens secundum rationem maioris vel minoris perfectionis. Et similiter dico, quod veritas et bonitas et omnia huiusmodi dicuntur analogice de deo et creaturis."

52. *Physics* VII, 4, 249a22–23. This claim takes various forms. One version reads: "[. . .] in genere latent multae aequivocationes." See Walter Burley, *In Physicam Aristotelis Expositio et Quaestiones* (Venice, 1501; facsimile reprint Hildesheim, New York: Georg Olms 1972), fol. 13 ra; William of Ockham,

Quaestiones in librum Tertium Sententiarum (Reportatio), ed. F.E. Kelley and G.I. Etzkorn (Opera Theologica VI. St. Bonaventure, N.Y.: St. Bonaventure University, 1982), p. 338:5–6.

53. Thomas de Wyk in Ebbesen, "Texts on Equivocation," p. 142: "[. . .] hic enim est analogia quantum ad naturalem, quia hic est attributio et ordo inter res significatas ut inter substantiam et accidens, non autem in actu significandi [. . .]." See also William of Chelvestun quoted by Donati, "La discussione sull'unità," p. 76, n. 28: "[. . .] ista analogia non est ex parte significationis ipsius entis nec ex parte modi significandi [. . .]."

54. Aquinas, *ST* Ia.13.5: "Neque enim in his quae analogice dicuntur, est una ratio, sicut est in univocis; nec totaliter diversa, sicut in aequivocis [. . .]." Cf. Aquinas, *De principiis naturae*, 6, p. 46:19–41; Aquinas, *In Met.*, 4, lect. 1, n. 535: "Quandoque vero secundum rationes quae partim sunt diversae et partim non diversae [. . .]."

55. John Duns Scotus on the *Sophistici Elenchi* [cited as *In SE*] in *Quaestiones in Libros Perihermenias Aristotelis; Quaestiones Super Librum Elenchorum Aristotelis; Theoremata*, ed. R. Andrews et al. (Opera Philosophica II. St. Bonaventure, N.Y.: Franciscan Institute; Washington, DC: The Catholic University of America, 2004), q. 16, p. 344.

56. Burley, *In SE*, p. 281. He recognizes the real relations: "[. . .] vox significans aliquid ex impositione ipsam rem repraesentat absolute et sub ratione propria et non in comparatione ad aliud; ex transumptione autem significat rem non absolute et sub ratione propria sed sub similitudine vel proportione ad alterum, et ita non sub ratione propria."

57. For details of Oxford views, see Donati, "La discussione sull'unità."

58. Incerti Auctores, *Quaestiones super Sophisticos Elenchos*, ed. Sten Ebbesen (Corpus Philosophorum Danicorum Medii Aevi 7. Copenhagen: Gad, 1977), Anonymus SF, q. 57, pp. 133–34; Anonymus C, q. 823, pp. 315–17. For discussion, see Ashworth, "Aquinas in Context," pp. 119–20; Marmo, *Semiotica e linguaggio*, pp. 320–25.

59. Anonymus (SE 83) in Ebbesen, "Texts on Equivocation," p. 287, pp. 289–90. I indicate the number of the commentary given on p. 173 of the list established in Sten Ebbesen, "Medieval Latin Glosses and Commentaries on Aristotelian Logic Texts of the Twelfth and Thirteenth Centuries" in *Glosses and Commentaries on Aristotelian Logical Texts: The Syriac, Arabic and Medieval Latin Traditions*, ed. Charles Burnett (London: The Warburg Institute, 1993), pp. 129–77. See also Thomas de Wyk in Ebbesen, "Texts on Equivocation," p. 142, and Peter Bradlay, p. 182, in E.A. Synan, "Master Peter Bradlay on the 'Categories'," *Mediaeval Studies* 29 (1967): 273–327. They drop the genus case.

60. Anonymus (SE 83) in Ebbesen, "Texts on Equivocation," p. 290: "Unde prima analogia [corr. ex *analoga*] non impedit univocationem, nec etiam secunda, eo quod illa analogia principaliter est ex parte unius rei quae prius convenit uni quam alteri, et ideo vox significans illam rem habet unum significatum primo,

et ideo talis analogia quae est in primo modo et secundo non facit aliquam aequivocationem in termino nec tales termini sunt aequivoci secundo modo. Loquendo tamen de analogia tertio modo dicta, illa facit aequivocationem in termino, quia ibi vox est una et multa sunt significata, et ideo ista analogia principaliter est in voce."

61. Burley, *Super tractatum fallaciarum*, p. 202: "[. . .] sciendum quod analogia est triplex ad praesens, sc. a parte conceptus, et a parte rei, et ex transumptione. Primo modo est ens analogum ad substantiam et accidens quia ens importat unum conceptum qui prius reperitur in substantia quam in accidente. Secundo modo est animal analogum ad hominem et asinum, et quodlibet genus isto modo est analogum ad speciem magis perfectam et ad speciem minus perfectam; sed haec analogia non pertinet ad logicum sed ad naturalem—logicus enim non ponit analogiam in genere, sed naturalis. Tertio modo est 'pes' analogum, et vox quae unum significat ex impositione et aliud ex transumptione."

62. Walter Burley on the *Categories* in *Burlei super artem veterem Porphirii et Aristoteli* (Venetiis, 1497), sig. c 5 ra–rb; *In Phys.*, fols. 12 vb–13 ra and fol. 220 vb. For his first and second commentaries on the *Physics*, see Donati, "La discussione sull'unità," p. 79, especially the quotation from the second commentary in n. 36, pp. 79–80. For fuller discussion, see E. Jennifer Ashworth, "Being and analogy" in *A Companion to Walter Burley*, ed. Alessandro Conti (Leiden: Brill, forthcoming).

63. Donati, "La discussione sull'unità," p. 78.

64. John Duns Scotus on the *Categories* [cited as *In Cat.*] in *Quaestiones in Librum Porphyrii Isagoge et Quaestiones super Praedicamenta Aristotelis*, ed. R. Andrews et al. (Opera Philosophica I. St. Bonaventure University, St. Bonaventure, N.Y.: The Franciscan Institute, 1999), q. 4, pp. 280–81: "Ponitur autem analogia in vocibus tripliciter: vel quia significant unam rationem primo, quae in exsistendo diversimode convenit duobus vel pluribus, quae dicuntur analogata. [. . .] Alio modo ponitur analogia in vocibus, quia unum significatur per prius per vocem, et reliquum per posterius. [. . .] Tertio modo: quod vox uni imponitur proprie, et propter aliquam similitudinem ad illud cui primo imponitur, transfertur vox ad significandum aliud, sicut est in secundo modo aequivocationis, ubi etiam est quodammodo ordo in significando, quia numquam vox transfertur ad significandum aliquid nisi supponatur illam impositam esse ad significandum aliquid proprie, et hoc secundum significat solum propter aliquam similitudinem eius ad illud cui primo imponitur."

65. See Olivier Boulnois, "Représentation et noms divins selon Duns Scot." *Documenti e Studi sulla Tradizione Filosofica Medievale* 6 (1995): 255–80, especially pp. 270–71. Cf. Pini, *Scoto e l'analogia*, p. 60. See also E. Jennifer Ashworth, " 'Can I Speak More Clearly than I Understand?' A problem of religious language in Henry of Ghent, Duns Scotus, and Ockham," *Historiographia Linguistica* 7 (1980): 29–38, especially pp. 35–36.

66. Scotus, *In Cat.*, q. 4, p. 284.

67. Scotus, *In SE*, q. 15, p. 331.

68. Scotus, *In Cat.*, q. 4, p. 282.

69. Scotus, *In SE*, q. 15, p. 336: "Ad quaestionem dicendum quod quantum est ex parte vocis significantis, non est possibile vocem significare unum per prius et reliquum per posterius. Nam significare est aliquid intellectui repraesentare. Quod ergo significatur, prius ab intellectu concipitur. Sed omne quod ab intellectu concipitur, sub distincta et determinata ratione concipitur, quia intellectus est quidam actus, et ideo quod intelligit ab alio distinguit. Omne ergo quod significatur, sub distincta ratione et determinata significatur." Cf. *In SE*, q. 15, p. 334, *In Cat.*, q. 4, p. 284.

70. Boulnois, "Représentation et noms divins," p. 256, underlines "le caractère autonome de la signification, qui ne repose pas sur un concept."

71. Scotus, *In Cat.*, q. 4, p. 282–83: "Secundus modus analogiae supra dictus videtur impossibilis. Quia contingit ignorare simpliciter prius, quando nomen imponitur posteriori, quia posterius simpliciter potest esse nobis prius, et ita prius intelligi et prius significari. Si ergo secundo vox ista imponatur priori simpliciter, manifestum est quod <non> significabit per posterius illud cui primo imponitur, quia illud semel significavit primo, igitur semper. Vox enim postquam imposita est, non mutatur in significando illud cui imponitur, igitur ordo rerum non concludit ordinem in significatione vocum." The addition is taken from the apparatus. See also *In SE*, q. 15, p. 332.

72. Scotus, *In SE*, q. 15, p. 331–32. Cf. *In Cat.*, q. 4, pp. 283, 285.

73. Scotus, *In SE*, q. 15, p. 332.

74. Scotus, *In SE*, q. 15, pp. 337–38. Cf. Thomas de Wyk in Ebbesen, "Texts on Equivocation," p. 142: "[. . .] analogia duplex est: una pertine<n>s ad naturalem, et est quando aliqua duo vel multa significantur per aliquam vocem unam quae habent attributionem ad invicem sicut se habet ens respectu substantiae et accidentis, hic enim est analogia quantum ad naturalem, quia hic est attributio et ordo inter res significatas ut inter substantiam et accidens, non autem in actu significandi." Ebbesen writes of this text, "Probably an English product from the last quarter of the thirteenth century" (p. 102).

75. Scotus, *In SE*, q. 15, pp. 338–39.

76. Scotus, *In Cat.*, q. 4, p. 281.

CONTRIBUTORS

E. JENNIFER ASHWORTH is Distinguished Professor Emerita of Philosophy at the University of Waterloo, Ontario. Her many publications include *Language and Logic in the Post-Medieval Period* (Reidel, 1974) and *Les théories de l'analogie du xiie au xvie siècle* (Vrin, 2008).

CHARLES BOLYARD is Associate Professor of Philosophy at James Madison University. He has published in such forums as the *Journal of the History of Philosophy*, *Vivarium*, and the *Stanford Encyclopedia of Philosophy*, with a focus on medieval epistemology and metaphysics.

SUSAN BROWER-TOLAND is Associate Professor of Philosophy at Saint Louis University. Her publications in medieval philosophy include "Medieval Approaches to Consciousness: Ockham and Chatton," "Aquinas on Mental Representation: Concepts and Intentionality," and "Intuition, Externalism, and Direct Reference in Ockham."

BRIAN FRANCIS CONOLLY is Associate Professor of Philosophy at Bard College at Simon's Rock, where he teaches a range of courses in the history of philosophy. He is the author of "Averroes, Thomas Aquinas, and Giles of Rome on How 'This Man' Understands," an article discussing late thirteenth century theories of the intellect.

RONDO KEELE is Associate Professor of Philosophy at the Louisiana Scholars' College and is the author of *Ockham Explained*, and numerous articles on William of Ockham and his contemporaries.

GYULA KLIMA is Professor of Philosophy at Fordham University, Director of the *Society for Medieval Logic and Metaphysics*, and Editor of its annual *Proceedings* (ten volumes, published by Cambridge Scholars Publishing). His books include *John Buridan* (Oxford, 2008), *Medieval Philosophy: Essential Readings with Commentary* (Blackwell Publishers, 2007), *Summulae de Dialectica* by John Buridan (Yale, 2001), and *ArsArtium: Essays in Philosophical Semantics, Medieval and Modern* (Hungarian Academy, 1988).

TERENCE PARSONS is Professor of Philosophy and of Linguistics at the University of California at Los Angeles. He is the author of several papers on medieval semantics and logic, including "Supposition Theory in the Later 12th through 14th Centuries," in volume 2 of the *Handbook of the History of Logic: Medieval and Renaissance Logic*.

MARTIN TWEEDALE is Professor Emeritus of Philosophy at the University of Alberta. He has written extensively on medieval philosophy, especially Abelard, Ockham and Duns Scotus, and is the author of *Scotus vs. Ockham: A Medieval Dispute Over Universals*, published by the Edwin Mellen Press in 1999.

REGA WOOD is Professor of Philosophy at Indiana University, Emerita at Stanford University. She has prepared NEH funded critical editions of works by John Duns Scotus, William Ockham, Adam Wodeham, and Richard Rufus of Cornwall. Her numerous studies of scholasticism include the *Cambridge History of Medieval Philosophy*'s "The Subject of the Science of Metaphysics."

JACK ZUPKO is Professor of Philosophy at the University of Winnipeg. He is the author of *John Buridan: Portrait of a Fourteenth-Century Arts Master* (Notre Dame, 2003) and numerous articles on later medieval philosophy.

INDEX

abstraction, 139, 269n5
accidents: absolute, 87–88; accidental beings, 96; Aristotle on, 5, 84–87, 88, 208; causation and, 90–91, 92, 264n29; change and, 89–90; directedness of, 97–98; epistemological aspects of, 95–99; Eucharist and, 88, 97; John Duns Scotus on, 84–99; metaphysical aspects of, 88–95, 97; multiplicity of, 93–94, 265n40, 265n49; overview, 5, 84–85, 87–88, 97–99, 262n1, 262n3; perfection and, 90–91; Porphyry on, 86–87; in *Questions on the Metaphysics of Aristotle*, 5, 84–85, 87–99; relational accidents, 87; simplicity of, 89–90; subject and, 88–93, 95–99, 266n55; substance and, 84, 87, 88–92, 96–99, 264n14, 266nn54–55; unity as accidental, 113–14; unity of, 89, 91, 92; unity of subject and, 92–93; universals and, 84
Adam Wodeham, 284n50, 286n65, 287n66
Adams, Marilyn McCord, 168, 263n12, 264n16, 265n30, 265n42, 266n49, 280n4, 281n20, 281nn19–20, 286n65
Aegidius of Feno, 150–51, 276n45
Albert of Saxony, 288n8, 289n21
Alessio, Franco, 291n5
Alexander of Aphrodisias, 267n2, 267n8; Avicenna and, 105, 109, 110, 112,

117–18, 123; tokens and, 103–5; on universality, 103–5, 108–10, 112
Al-Ghazâlî (Algazel), 231, 295n44
analogy: *analogia*, 231; of being, 238; concepts and, 223, 231, 237, 238; *ens* and, 232, 233, 234, 236, 237; equivocals and, 232–36; equivocation and, 7, 223, 229–30, 234–35; *esse* and, 231–32, 233; Greek sense of, 229; imposition and, 231, 234; intention and, 231–32; John Duns Scotus on, 7, 234, 236–48; language and, 223, 231, 236–37; metaphor and, 7, 223, 227, 229–30; metaphysical, 223; overview, 231–36; *ratio* and, 232–36; semantic, 223–31; signification of, 242, 245–47; terms, 223, 231, 233; Thomas Aquinas on, 231–33; univocals and, 232–36; univocation and, 234; utterances, 238–42, 245–47; Walter Burley on, 235; of words, 236–38
Andrews, Robert, 298n64
anti-razor, 290n3; causation relations and, 208, 290n4; iterated analysis rule and, 211–15; overview, 207–11; in Walter Chatton's metaphysics, 207–15
aptitudinal being: actual being and, 66; Dietrich von Freiberg on, 49, 66, 258nn41–42; form and, 66; potential being and, 49, 66; privation and form and, 66, 258nn41–42
Aquinas, Thomas. *See* Thomas Aquinas

303

Aristotle, 2, 3, 11, 13, 21, 33, 35, 36, 51, 66, 77, 80, 92, 147, 150, 158, 209, 227, 247, 249*n*2, 250*n*10–11, 251*n*38, 251*n*40, 254*n*11, 257*n*39, 258*n*42, 261*n*70, 261*nn*62–63, 262*n*4, 263*n*5, 265*n*21, 268*n*13, 269*n*7, 270*n*19, 273*n*31, 274*nn*36–37, 284*n*51, 287*n*1, 288*n*7, 289*n*18, 292*n*8, 294*n*29, 295*n*43; on accidents, 5, 84–87, 88, 208; *Categories* of, 7, 85, 86, 228–30, 232, 235, 236, 238–41, 246; *De Anima* of, 138–41, 143, 145, 146, 149, 154, 273*n*30; on equivocation, 228, 229, 230, 231; on intellectual cognition, 146; logic of, 6, 188–94, 196, 198, 202; metaphysics of, 223–24; *Metaphysics* of, 5, 24–25, 85–87, 138, 139, 140, 230–31, 243, 245; *Nicomachean Ethics* of, 138; *Physics* of, 138–41, 236; *Sophistical Refutations* of, 230, 234, 235, 237, 241–48; on soul, 273*n*30; on spoken, written and mental terms, 141; *Topics* of, 85–86, 87; on universal cognition, 143; on universals, 112, 142, 271*n*17

Ashworth, E. Jennifer, 7, 286*n*64, 291*n*1, 291*n*3, 292*n*8, 294*n*26, 294*nn*29–30, 295*n*38, 296*nn*47–49, 297*n*58, 298*n*62, 298*n*65

Aubenque, Pierre, 291*n*1

Augustine, 2, 88, 263*n*10

Averroes, 3, 11, 14, 77, 229, 231, 261*n*64, 294*n*31, 296*n*46; unity of science of metaphysics and, 24–25; on universal cognition, 143

Avicenna, 3, 11, 231, 266–67, 267*nn*3–5, 268*nn*12–13, 268*nn*15–16, 296*n*45; Alexander of Aphrodisias and, 105, 109, 110, 112, 117–18, 123; on essence, 117–24, 267*n*9; on genus, 114–17, 119–20; idealism and, 108–9; on individual rational animals,

115–16, 117; *Logica* of, 115–16, 119–20; on ontology of types and tokens, 103–36, 267*n*6; overview, 5; *Prima Philosophia* of, 116, 122–24; on rational animals, 115–16, 117; on species, 114–17; on tokens as enmattered types, 105–8; on universality, 110–17

Avicenna Latinus, 266–67

Barnes, Jonathan, 262*n*4, 263*n*5

being, 208, 209; accidental beings, 96; actual, 66; analogy of, 238; conditions for arrangement under genus, 49, 68–72, 258*n*49, 258*n*52; Dietrich von Freiberg on, 67–70, 258*n*54; *ens* form of, 225, 231, 234; *esse* form of, 225; generation stages and, 67; God and, 225; incomplete beings, 70–71; metaphysics subject as concept of, 12; potential, 49, 66; principles of, 70; *ratio* of, 68–69; unity and, 89. *See also* aptitudinal being

belief: objects and, 179; objects of belief, 170, 173, 175–76, 182, 283*n*46

Bochenski, I. M., 288*n*5

body: body in potency to soul essentially, 58–60; Dietrich von Freiberg on, 56–64, 256*nn*34–36, 257*n*38; Thomas Aquinas on, 57, 256*n*28, 264*n*16; as univocal, 232. *See also* numerical identity; soul

Boehner, Philotheus, 293*n*15

Boethius, 84, 91, 227, 232, 262*n*1, 294*n*32, 294*n*34, 294*nn*27–28; on *Categories*, 228, 229, 230, 246; on equivocals, 228

Bogen, James, 274*n*38

Bolyard, Charles, 5, 253, 291*n*15

Bos, Egbert, 288*n*9, 289*n*20

Bosley, Richard, 263*n*12

Boulnois, Olivier, 262n3, 298n65, 299n70
Braakhuis, Henk A. G., 294n26
Bradlay, Peter, 297n59
Brower, Jeffrey, 287n67
Brower-Toland, Susan, 6, 282n25, 284n47, 284n50, 287n66
Brown, Stephen, 293n15
Brunellus, 144, 156, 157, 272n25, 279n65
Buridan, John. See John Buridan
Burley, Walter. See Walter Burley
Burnett, Charles, 297n59
Burr, David, 263n12
Busa, Roberto, 293n18
Busse, Adolfus, 263n7
Butler, Ronald J., 283n45

Cai, P. Raphaelis, 293n23
Cajetan, 252n11, 292n8, 296n48
Carrier, Joanne, 291n1
Cartwright, Richard, 283n45
Categories (Aristotle), 7, 85, 86, 232, 235; Boethius on, 228, 229, 230, 246; John Duns Scotus on, 236, 238–41, 246; Simplicius on, 229–30
Cathala, M.-R., 294n32
causation: accidents and, 90–91, 92, 264n29; perfection and, 90–91; relations and anti-razor, 208, 290n4; of supposition modes, 196
change, 169; accidents and, 89–90; in nature and privative opposition, 64–68; simplicity and, 89–90
Chatton, Walter. See Walter Chatton
Christ, Jesus. See Jesus Christ
Cicero, 2
Clement VI, 276n45
cognition: John Buridan on singular, 139, 145, 158, 279n68; knowledge as, 163–64, 280n7; sentence signifiers and propositional, 282n27; singular,

139, 145, 158, 279n68. See also intellectual cognition
common nature, 125–26, 131–33
concepts, 12; analogy and, 223, 231, 237, 238; equivocal terms and, 235–36; John Buridan on, 138–39; ratio as, 234; signification and, 225; singular, 150, 276n43; Thomas Aquinas on, 156, 278n63; universal, 150, 276n43; univocal term and, 235–36
conditionals, 288n8
Conolly, Brian Francis, 4
Conti, Alessandro, 298n62
Copenhaver, Brian, 287n4
Copi, Irving M., 262n4
Côté, Antoine, 279n69
Courtenay, Archbishop, 276n45
Courtenay, William, 281n14
Cross, Richard, 263n11, 264n14

Dahan, Gilbert, 293n21
De Anima (Aristotle), 146, 273n30; John Buridan on, 138–41, 143, 145, 149, 154
De corpore Christi in mortuo (Dietrich von Freiberg), 56, 59
de Libera, Alain, 291n1, 292n9
De Morgan, Augustus, 289n16
De origine rerum praedicamentalium (Dietrich von Freiberg), 56, 58–59, 68
De Rijk, L. M., 287n4, 288n5, 288n9, 294n26, 295n39
de Wulf, Maurice, 253n8
del Punta, Francesco, 293n15
Demange, Dominique, 12–15, 24, 26, 249n3, 249n5, 249n8, 250n13, 250n25, 250n31, 250nn18–19, 250nn21–22, 251n48, 251n51
Democritus, 98
Demorgan, 198
Dietrich von Freiberg, 4, 53, 253n4, 253n7, 253nn1–2, 255nn23–24,

Dietrich von Freiberg (cont.)
256*n*32, 256*nn*28–30, 257*n*37,
257*n*39, 258*n*40, 258*n*44, 258*n*52,
260*nn*57–58, 261*n*61, 261*n*65,
261*n*68, 261*n*71; on aptitudinal
being, 49, 66, 258*nn*41–42; on being
in potency, 67–70, 258*n*54; on body
and soul, 56–64, 256*nn*34–36,
257*n*38; *De corpore Christi in
mortuo* of, 56, 59; *De origine rerum
praedicamentalium* of, 56, 58–59, 68;
on generation and corruption, 49, 56,
64–74, 255*n*26, 258*n*43, 259*n*56,
260*n*59–60; homonymy of, 80–81;
on numerical identity, 48–50, 55–64,
74–83, 261*n*62, 261*n*67, 261*n*69;
overview, 47; on privation and form,
64–74, 257*n*39; Thomas Aquinas
and, 48; on unity of substantial form,
47–50, 55–83
divine names, 227; God and, 225, 226;
translatio and problem of, 226,
228
divinity, of Christ, 48–49, 53–55,
254*nn*17–18
Dod, Bernard G., 294*n*36
Donati, Silvia, 223, 291*n*2, 296*n*50,
297*n*53, 297*n*57, 298*nn*62–63
Donatus, 226, 292*n*13
Düring, I., 284*n*51

Ebbesen, Sten, 286*n*65, 293*n*16, 294*n*37,
297*n*53, 297*nn*58–60, 299*n*74
Ebert, Theodor, 86, 87, 262*n*4, 263*n*6
Elamrani-Jamal, Abdelali, 292*n*9
ens, 11, 229; analogy and, 232, 233, 234,
236, 237; as equivocal, 234, 236, 241;
form of being, 225, 231, 234; John
Duns Scotus on, 225; as univocal,
225, 234, 236, 238, 239
entity, 12, 16–18; anti-razor and
relational, 208, 209; *ratio* and, 14
Epicurus, 98

equivocation: analogy and, 7, 223,
229–30, 232–36; Aristotle on, 228,
229, 230, 231; Boethius on, 228;
chance, 228–29, 230, 238, 294*n*29;
deliberate, 228, 229, 230, 231, 233;
ens as, 234, 236, 241; homonymy as,
223; John Duns Scotus on, 7, 238;
metaphor and, 7, 223, 229–30; modes
of, 230; overview, 228; in *Sophistical
Refutations*, 235; terms and concepts,
235–36; *translatio* and, 230; univocals
and, 231, 232, 234, 235–36
esse: analogy and, 231–32, 233; form of
being, 225
essence: Avicenna on, 117–24, 267*n*9;
in creatures, 30–33; in God, 30–32;
as indeterminate, 129; intellect in,
118–19; logic in, 118–20; as multiple,
127; nature in, 122–23; nominal
and real, 32, 252*n*4; of thing and
quidditative definition, 37, 252*n*9;
Thomas Aquinas on, 30–44, 252*n*9;
types and tokens and, 117–24, 267*n*9
Etzkorn, Girard J., 250*n*9, 262*n*2,
282*n*21, 290*nn*1–2, 296*n*52
Eucharist: accidents and, 88, 97; John
Duns Scotus on, 88, 263*n*12; Pini on,
263*n*12
existence, 129–30; essence and, 30–44,
252*n*9

fictum-theory: *intellectio*-theory and,
137; John Buridan and, 269*n*3; of
William of Ockham, 137, 138, 148,
269*n*3
Fitzgerald, Michael J., 289*n*21
Fitzpatrick, Mary, 254*n*10
Flasch, Kurt, 253*n*4
form: aptitudinal being and, 66; matter
and, 4; universality and, 103–5, 108,
109. *See also* accidents; privation and
form
Führer, Markus, 253*n*1

Gabbay, Dov M., 288*n10*
Gál, Gideon, 293*n15*
Galonnier, Alain, 292*n9*
generation, 48, 257n38; being in potency and, 67; Dietrich von Freiberg on, 49, 56, 64–74, 255*n26*, 258*n43*, 259*n56*, 260*n59*–60; privation and form and, 49, 64–74, 258*n43*, 259*n56*, 260*n59*–60; Thomas Aquinas theory of, 253*n6*; in unity of substantial form, 50–52, 56, 64, 255*n26*
genus: Avicenna on, 114–17, 119–20; conditions for being arranged under, 49, 68–72, 258*n49*, 258*n52*; logical, 119–20; natural, 119–23; species relation to, 239; as universal, 114–15
Giles of Lessines, 53, 253*nn8–9*, 256*n28*
Giles of Rome, 4, 263*n12*, 265*n42*
God, 13, 14, 16, 22, 23, 251*n47*; being and, 225; divine names and, 225, 226; essence and existence in, 30–32; as God, 17; John Buridan on, 143, 271*n22*; language and, 224; metaphor and, 228; Neoplatonists on, 224; perfection of, 91; referential objects of, 179; sentence signifiers and, 170; truth and, 163, 165, 167, 169–71, 174–83, 282*n29*, 285*n55*, 285*n57*, 285*n61*
Godfrey of Fontaines, 265*n30*
Goichon, Amélie-Marie, 268*nn16–18*
Gonsalvus of Spain, 54
Grabmann, Martin, 287*n4*, 288*n5*
Gracia, Jorge 7
Grassi, Onorato, 286*n65*

Hankinson, R. J., 262*n4*
Heinaman, Robert, 262*n4*
Henninger, Mark G., 263*n8*
Henry of Ghent, 298*n65*
Hill, Benjamin, 279*n69*
Holcot, Robert. *See* Robert Holcot

Holtz, Louis, 292*n10*
homonymy: of Dietrich von Freiberg, 80–81; equivocation as, 223
Honnefelder, Ludger, 15, 250*n20*
Hubien, Hubert, 288*n6*

idealism: Avicenna and, 108–9; overview, 5
identity: logic with, 197, 289*n14*. *See also* numerical identity
Imbach, Ruedi, 253*n5*, 253*n7*
imposition, 224–25; analogy and, 223, 231, 234; language and, 227; metaphor and, 226
individuals, 115–16, 117, 129–30; tokens as, 106, 267*n6*
infinite regress: modern philosophy and, 222; overview, 207; in Walter Chatton's metaphysics, 207, 211, 216, 222
intellect: essence and, 118–19; logic and, 118–19; species and, 146, 273*n32*
intellectio-theory: *fictum*-theory and, 137; of John Buridan, 137–58; of William of Ockham, 137, 148, 268*n2*
intellectual cognition: Aristotle on, 146; John Buridan on, 145–49, 273*n23*, 273*n29*, 274*n38*; soul and, 143, 148, 149; universal cognition and, 145
intention: analogy and, 231–32; first- and second-intentional concepts, 156, 278*n63*
Isagoge (Porphyry), 86–87
iteration, 207, 210, 215, 216, 219, 221, 222

Jesus Christ: divinity of, 48–49, 53–55, 254*nn17–18*. *See also* Eucharist; numerical identity
John Buridan, 1, 4, 194, 252*nn5–7*, 268, 268*n4*, 269*nn6–9*, 270*n10*, 270*n18*, 270*n21*, 272*n26*, 272*n28*, 276*n43*, 279*n67*, 288*n6*, 288*n9*, 289*n12*,

John Buridan (cont.)
289n15; on abstraction process, 139,
269n5; *appellatio rationis* theory of,
36; on beatific vision, 271n22; on
concepts, 138–39; on *De Anima*,
138–41, 143, 145, 149, 154; on
dialectic, 141, 270n14; *fictum*-theory
and, 269n3; on God, 143, 271n22;
intellectio-theory of, 137–58; on
intellectual cognition, 145–49,
273n23, 273n29, 274n38; on John
of Mirecourt, 149, 275n40; on
Metaphysics, 138, 139, 140; on mind,
151–54; on *Nicomachean Ethics*,
138; overview, 5, 137–38, 157–58; on
Physics, 138–41; on singulars,
139–42, 145, 151, 154–55, 158,
269n5, 279n68; on soul, 148, 150,
151–52, 155, 276n45; *Summulae de
Dialectica* of, 138, 141; Thomas
Aquinas and, 30, 34–44; *Treatise
on the Difference between the
Universal and the Individual* of,
150–51, 157; on universals, 5,
138–45, 148, 150–58, 269n5,
276nn44–45, 278nn62–63; Walter
Chatton and, 5; William of Ockham
and, 5, 137–38, 148, 269n3
John Duns Scotus, 5, 14, 24–28, 223,
231, 249n4, 250n9, 250n21, 250n31,
251n47, 251n53, 251nn34–35,
263nn8–9, 265nn29–30, 266n55,
266n58, 291, 292n6, 297n55,
298nn64–65, 299nn66–69,
299nn71–76; on accidents, 84–99;
on analogy, 7, 234, 236–48; on
Categories, 236, 238–41, 246; on *ens*,
225; on equivocation, 7, 238; on
Eucharist, 88, 263n12; on metaphor,
238; on metaphysics, 11–13, 29; on
Metaphysics, 243; *Ordinatio* of,
263nn11–12, 264n14; overview, 4;
Paris prologue of, 12, 15–23, 29; on

Physics, 236; *Questions on the
Metaphysics of Aristotle* of, 5,
84–85, 87–99, 262n2; *Reportata
Parisiensia* of, 12; on signification,
236–48; on *Sophistical Refutations*,
237, 241–48; on substantial form, 87,
91; on universals, 278n62
John of Mirecourt, 140, 149, 275n40
John Peckham, 54
John Wyclif, 276n45

Karger, Elizabeth, 262n3, 286n65,
287n66
Keele, Rondo, 6, 7, 253, 263n8, 266n58,
286nn64–65, 287n66, 290n13
Kelley, F. E., 296n52
Kenny, Anthony, 4, 7, 30–34, 252nn2–3
Kieras, Timothy, 252n13
King, Peter, 279n69, 288n6
Klima, Gyula, 4, 252n1, 252n5, 279n69,
282n25, 290
Kneepkens, C. H., 294n26
knowledge: as cognition, 163–64, 280n7;
as propositional attitude, 164, 280n7;
true sentences signifying, 169,
282n23
Knuuttila, Simo, 286n65
Kretzmann, Norman, 7, 167–68, 280n4,
281n17, 281n20, 286n64, 287n4,
288n5, 289nn12–13

Lafleur, Claude, 291n1
Lambert of Auxerre (Lagny), 225,
291n5, 295n39
Landini, Gregory, 270n14
language: analogy and, 223, 231,
236–37; created natures and, 225;
God and, 224; imposition and, 227;
metaphor and, 228, 230; Thomas
Aquinas on, 227; univocation and,
225
Lectura (Walter Chatton), 207, 209,
212

logic: applied, 6–7; argument strategies, reasoning patterns and, 207; of Aristotle, 6, 188–94, 196, 198, 202; ascent and descent, 194–95, 288*n*10; causes of modes of supposition, 196; on concepts, 225; contradictories and equipollences, 189–92; contraposition, 220; conversion and syllogisms, 188–92, 196–97; essence and, 118–20; excluded middle principle, 268*n*15; exposition and expository syllogisms, 192–93; on imposition, 224–25; intellect and, 118–19; on language, 224–25; monadic propositional logic with identity, 197, 289*n*14; overview, 188; Peano's Postulates, 202–3; reductio, 189–91; on signification, 224–25; transitivity, 193–94, 204–5; truth-functional, 194; of William of Ockham, 206
Logica (Avicenna), 115–16, 119–20
Lohr, Charles H., 295*n*44
Lombard, Peter. *See* Peter Lombard
Lonfat, Joel, 295*n*42
Loux, Michael J., 289*n*21

Marenbon, John, 263*n*11
Marmo, Costantino, 291*n*4
Marmura, Michael E., 266
Marsilius of Inghen, 288*n*9, 289*n*20
matter: form and, 4; tokens as enmattered types, 103–8
Matthew of Aquasparta, 254*n*13
Maurer, Armand, 253*n*5
McGrade, A. S., 7
McGuire, James E., 274*n*38
metaphor: analogy and, 7, 223–31; equivocation and, 7, 223, 229–30; God and, 228; imposition and, 226; John Duns Scotus on, 238; language and, 228, 230; Thomas Aquinas on, 227–28, 293*n*25; *translatio* as, 226; tropes, 226

Metaphysics (Aristotle), 5, 85–87, 230–31, 245; Averroes and, 24–25; John Buridan on, 138, 139, 140; John Duns Scotus on, 243. *See also* *Questions on the Metaphysics of Aristotle*
Michael, Bernd, 140, 269*n*8, 276*n*45
Middleton, Richard. *See* Richard Middleton
mind: John Buridan on, 151–54; universals, 151–54
Minio-Paluello, L., 294*n*27
Mirecourt, John of. *See* John of Mirecourt
Mojsisch, Burkhard, 253*n*4
monism: Avicenna and, 108, 124–35; overview, 5; species, 125; types and tokens and, 124–35, 268*n*14
Moody, Ernest A., 168, 281*n*18, 281*n*20, 288*n*8

nature, 72–74, 260*n*57, 260*n*59–60; essence and, 122–23; language and created, 225; natural genus as, 122–23; opposition and change in, 64–68; *per se*, 131–33; *ratio* as, 228, 234
Nicomachean Ethics (Aristotle), 138
nominal essence, 32, 252*n*4
Noone, Timothy, 7, 279*n*69
Normore, Calvin, 274*n*38, 279*n*69, 287
Nuchelmans, Gabriele, 286*n*65, 287*n*66
numerical identity, 254*n*13; Christ's divinity and, 48–49, 53–55, 254*nn*17–18; Dietrich von Freiberg on, 48–50, 55–64, 74–83, 261*n*62, 261*n*67, 261*n*69; soul and, 56–64; Thomas Aquinas on, 48–49, 53–55, 254*nn*17–18, 255*n*22; unity of substantial form and, 48, 49–64, 254*n*10, 254*n*12
Núñez, Martin Carbajo, 249*n*3

objects of propositional attitudes: as
content objects, 177–78, 181; objects
of belief and, 170, 182; overview, 161,
186, 279n1; as referential objects, 179,
182; Robert Holcot on, 6, 162, 167–68,
171–76, 181–87, 283n37, 283n46,
285nn60–61, 287n66; sentences as,
166–67, 285n60; Walter Chatton on,
162, 169–72, 178–81, 185–87,
284nn49–50, 287n66; William of
Ockham on, 6, 163–79, 185–87,
283n38, 284nn47–48, 287n66
Ockham, William of. *See* William of
Ockham
Oliver, W. Donald, 262n4
Ordinatio (John Duns Scotus),
263nn11–12, 264n14
Owen, G. E. L., 284n51

Pagnoni-Sturlese, Maria Rita, 253n2,
253n7, 255nn24–25, 261n67
Panaccio, Claude, 268n2, 279n69
Park, Seung-Chan, 291n3
Parsons, Terence, 6, 288n10, 289n23
Pasnau, Robert, 7, 249n3, 266n54,
266n58, 281n14
Pattin, Adrien, 294n35
Paul of Venice, 288n6, 288n8
Peano mathematics, 6; Peano's
Postulates, 202–3
perfection: accidents and, 90–91;
causation and, 90–91; of God, 91;
simplicity and, 90
Perreiah, Alan, 288n6
Peter Aureol, 11, 23, 162
Peter John Olivi, 54
Peter Lombard, 162, 280nn3–4
Peter of Spain, 230, 287n4, 288n5,
288n8, 289n20, 295n39, 295n41
Philosophia Prima (Avicenna), 116
Physics (Aristotle): John Buridan on,
138–41; John Duns Scotus on, 236
Pickavé, Martin, 291n2

Pinborg, Jan, 7
Pini, Giorgio, 84, 223, 262n3, 263n9,
263n12, 264n14, 291n2, 292n6,
296n50, 298n65
Plato, 2, 3, 124, 127, 135, 140, 142–45,
151–55, 208, 270n10, 270n16,
270n18, 271n18, 272n25, 277n54,
277n56, 277nn51–52, 279n68,
284n51
Platonism, 128, 224, 268n13
Porphyry, 85–87, 230, 263n7
potential being: actual being and, 66;
aptitudinal being and, 49, 66;
overview, 49, 66
Prima Philosophia (Avicenna), 122–24
privation and form: aptitudinal being
and, 66, 258nn41–42; Dietrich
von Freiberg on, 64–74, 257n39;
generation and, 49, 64–74, 258n43,
259n56, 260n59–60; genus and,
68–72, 258n49, 258n52; opposition
and change, 64–68; ordering of,
72–74, 260n57, 260n59–60; Thomas
Aquinas on, 257n39
Proclus, 47
propositional attitudes: judgment as,
280n7; knowledge as, 164, 280n7.
See also objects of propositional
attitudes
propositions, 162–85; Aristotle's logic
and forms of, 189; contemporary,
161, 279n1; monadic propositional
logic with identity, 197, 289n14;
overview, 279n1; token-sententialism
about, 168, 175, 283n45. *See also*
objects of propositional attitudes
propter quid science: metaphysics as, 12,
13; overview, 11; *quia* science and,
251n40

*Questions on the Metaphysics of
Aristotle* (John Duns Scotus), 5,
84–85, 87–99, 262n2

quia science: metaphysics as, 12; overview, 11; *propter quid* science and, 251*n*40

Quintilian, 226, 292*nn*11–12

ratio: analogy and, 232–36; of being, 68–69; as concept, 234; entity and, 14; as nature, 228, 234; *ratio substantiae*, 228, 232

rational animals, 115–16, 117

rational soul, 52; in doctrine of unity of substantial form, 47, 50–51, 53

real essence, 32, 252*n*4

relations, and reasoning, 197–201, 289*nn*17–19

Reportata Parisiensia (John Duns Scotus), 12

Reportatio (Walter Chatton), 207, 216

Reynolds, Philip L., 296*n*47

Richard Middleton, 49, 54–55

Robert Holcot, 163, 281*n*18, 281*nn*14–15, 283*nn*38–41, 285*nn*54–55, 285*nn*57–58, 286*n*62, 286*n*64; on objects of knowledge, 181–85; on objects of propositional attitudes, 6, 162, 167–68, 171–76, 181–87, 283*n*37, 283*n*46, 285*nn*60–61, 287*n*66; Walter Chatton and, 172, 173, 176, 182, 186–87, 283*n*37, 287*n*66; William of Ockham and, 6, 162, 167–68, 172–76, 186–87, 283*n*37, 287*n*66

Rodler, Klaus, 249*n*7

Roger Bacon, 224

Rosier, Irène, 291*n*4

Rosier-Catach, Irène, 292*n*9

Russell, Bertrand, 222

science: of entity, 12; first entity as subject of, 18–22; of metaphysics, 24–29

Scotus, John Duns. *See* John Duns Scotus

sentences: cognition and, 282*n*27; as content objects, 181, 182; God's knowledge and, 170; mental, 178, 284*n*48; as objects of belief, 173; as objects of knowledge, 181; as objects of propositional attitudes, 166–67, 285*n*60; overview, 279*n*1; as referential objects, 182; tokens, 168; truth, 166–68, 173–75; as universals, 168; Walter Chatton on, 169–70, 180, 282*n*27; William of Ockham and, 168, 281*n*20

Sentences (Peter Lombard), 162, 280*n*3; Thomas Aquinas on, 231; Walter Chatton on, 170

signification, 224; of analogical utterances, 242, 245–47; concepts and, 225; John Duns Scotus on, 236–48; priority and posteriority, 237–38; of univocals, 225

simplicity: of accidents, 89–90; change and, 89–90; perfection and, 90

Simplicius, 229–30, 294*n*35

singulars: concepts, 150, 276*n*43; John Buridan on, 139–42, 151, 154–55, 269*n*5; singular animals, 114–17, 130–33; universals and, 139–42, 151, 154–55, 269*n*5

Smith, J. A., 273*n*30

Solère, Jean-Luc, 262*n*3

Sondag, Gérard, 262*n*3

Sophistical Refutations (Aristotle), 234; equivocation in, 235; John Duns Scotus on, 237, 241–48; *translatio* and, 230

soul: Aristotle on, 273*n*30; intellectual cognition and, 143, 148, 149; John Buridan on, 148, 150, 151–52, 155, 276*n*45; numerical identity and, 56–64; rational, 47, 50–53; in unity of substantial form, 47, 50–51, 53, 56–64; universals and, 142, 150, 151–52, 276*n*45. *See also* body

Spade, Paul Vincent, 2, 7, 11, 137,
249n1, 251n50, 262n1, 263n7,
265n40, 268n1, 287, 289n21
species: Avicenna on, 114–17; intellect
and, 146, 273n32; monism, 125;
as rational animals, 115–16, 117;
relation to genus, 239; tokens and,
108; as types, 117; as universal,
114–15
Spiazzi, Raimondo, 293n25, 294n32
Stump, Eleonore, 289n12
Sturlese, Loris, 253n2, 255n23
substance, and accidents, 84, 87, 88–92,
96–99, 264n14, 266nn54–55
Summulae de Dialectica (John Buridan),
138, 141
supposition: causes of, 196; determinate,
194–95; distributive, 195; merely
confused, 195, 288n10; overview, 194
syllogisms: Barbara, 196–97; Celarent,
196–97; conversions and, 188–89,
196–97; expository, 192–93
Synan, E. A., 297n59
Szyller, Slawomir, 150, 276n44

Tatarzynski, Ryszard, 279n68
Taylor, C. C. W., 262n4
terms: analogical, 223, 231, 233; Aristotle
on, 141; equivocal, 235–36; singular,
140–42; universal, 141–42, 150;
univocal, 235–36
Thomas Aquinas, 4, 5, 7, 16, 223, 225,
226, 229, 230, 250n26, 250n30,
252n1, 252nn11–12, 254n10,
254n15, 255n21, 255n27, 256n31,
257n38, 263n12, 291n3, 292n7,
292n14, 293nn17–24, 294n32,
295n40, 296n51, 297n54, 297n58; on
analogy, 231–33; on body and soul,
57, 256n28, 264n16; Dietrich von
Freiberg and, 48; on essence and
existence, 30–44, 252n9; on first- and
second-intentional concepts, 156,

278n63; generation theory of, 253n6;
John Buridan and, 30, 34–44; Kenny
and, 30–34; on language, 227; on
metaphor, 227–28, 293n25; on
numerical identity, 48–49, 53–55,
254nn17–18, 255n22; on privation
and form, 257n39; on Sentences,
231; unity of substantial form of,
47–48
Thomas de Wyk, 226, 293n16, 297n53,
297n59, 299n74
tokens: Alexander of Aphrodisias and,
103–5; Avicenna on, 105–8; as
individuals, 106, 267n6; as objects
of belief, 175–76, 283n46; about
propositions, 168, 175, 283n45;
species and, 108; about truth-bearers,
167, 173, 176; types distinguished
from, 106–8
Topics (Aristotle), 85–86, 87
transitivity: of consequence, 193–94;
stated, 204–5
translatio: Boethius on, 229, 294n34;
divine names problem and, 226, 228;
equivocation and, 230; as metaphor,
226; overview, 226; Sophistical
Refutations and, 230; Thomas
Aquinas on, 228; in tropes, 226;
Walter Burley on, 230
Treatise on the Difference between
the Universal and the Individual
[Tractatus de differentia universalis
ad individuum] (John Buridan),
150–51, 157
tropes, 226
truth, 173–74, 283n38; God's
knowledge and, 163, 165, 167,
169–71, 174–83, 282n29, 285n55,
285n57, 285n61; knowledge and,
163–64, 169, 280n7, 282n23;
mutability of, 163–66; overview,
279n1; quantity of, 163–66, 173, 177,
181; sentence tokens as, 167, 173;

sentence types as, 168; sentences as, 166–67; signifiers and, 169, 170, 180, 282n23, 284n53; William of Ockham on, 167, 174, 176
Tweedale, Martin, 5, 263n12, 267n2, 267n8
Twersky, Isadore, 295n43
Tyorinoja, Reijo, 286n65
types: sentence, 168, 281n20; species as, 117; tokens and, 103–8; universality of, 267n6

unity, 87; of accidents, 89, 91, 92, 113–14; being and, 89; Dietrich von Freiberg on, 47–50, 55–83; generation and corruption in, 50–52, 56, 255n26; in man and theology problems, 50–55, 253n8; of metaphysics as first philosophy, 11, 23–29; overview, 47; pluralists' theory compared to, 47–48, 51–52; of science of metaphysics, 24–25; soul in, 47, 50–51, 53, 56–64; of subject and accident, 92–93; of Thomas Aquinas, 47–48
universals: accidents and, 84, 109; Alexander of Aphrodisias on, 108–10, 112; Aristotle on, 112, 142, 143, 271n17; Averroes on, 143; Avicenna on, 110–17; common, 125–26; concepts, 150, 276n43; of form, 103–5, 108, 109; formal, 152, 156, 278n62; genus as, 114–15; intellectual cognition and, 145; John Buridan on, 5, 138–45, 148, 150–58, 269n5, 276nn44–45, 278nn62–63; John Duns Scotus on, 278n62; mind and, 151–54; overview, 5; Plato on, 142–43, 271n18; sentence types as, 168; singulars and, 139–42, 151, 154–55, 269n5; soul and, 142, 150, 151–52, 276n45; species as, 114–15; subjective, 152–53, 155, 156, 278n62;

types and tokens and, 108–17, 267n6; universals as, 141; William of Ockham on, 168
univocals: ambiguous words and, 231; analogy and, 232–36, 239; body as, 232; ens as, 225, 234, 236, 238, 239; equivocals and, 231, 232, 234, 235–36; language and, 225; levels of, 235; signification of, 225; term and concept, 235–36; Walter Burley on, 235
utterances: analogical, 238–42, 245–47; signification of, 242, 245–47

Valente, Luisa, 292n9, 292n11
Van Dyke, Christina, 249n3
Van Riet, Simone, 267nn3–4, 296n45
Vuillemin-Diem, Gudrun, 295n42

Wald, Berthold, 263nn11–12, 265n28
Wallace, William A., 253n3
Walter Burley, 7, 150, 194, 204, 226, 230, 231, 233, 289n12, 289n21, 289n22, 291, 293n16, 294n37, 296n52, 297n56, 298nn61–62; on analogy, 235; on univocation, 235
Walter Chatton, 163, 263n8, 282n21, 282n23–25, 284n53, 286nn64–65, 289, 290n4, 290n13; on anti-razor, 207–15; applied logic and, 6–7; infinite regress and iteration in, 207, 211–22, 290n10; John Buridan and, 5; Lectura of, 207, 209, 212; on objects of knowledge, 171, 178–81; on objects of propositional attitudes, 162, 169–72, 178–81, 185–87, 284nn49–50, 287n66; overview, 206–7, 221–22; Reportatio of, 207, 216; Robert Holcot and, 172, 173, 176, 182, 186–87, 283n37, 287n66; on sentence signifiers, 169–70, 180, 282n27; on Sentences, 170; William of Ockham and, 5, 6–7, 137, 162,

Walter Chatton (cont.)
    169–72, 186–87, 282n23, 282n29,
    283n38, 287n66
Wasserman, Roger, 263n11
Wedin, Michael V., 262n4
Wellmuth, John James, 254n10
Wettstein, Howard, 283n45
Wey, Joseph C., 282n21, 282n25, 290n2
William de la Mare, 54
William of Champeaux, 84, 262n1
William of Chelvestun, 297n53
William of Moerbeke, 229
William of Ockham, 2, 4, 95, 150, 157,
    161, 194, 206, 226, 263n8, 263n12,
    268n1, 279, 280n7, 280nn4–5,
    281n11, 281n19, 281nn8–9, 282n25,
    286nn64–65, 288n10, 289n21,
    293n15, 296n52, 298n65; fictum-
    theory of, 137, 138, 148, 269n3;
    intellectio-theory of, 137, 148,
    268n2; John Buridan and, 5, 137–38,
    148, 269n3; objections to anti-razor,
    207, 209–15, 290n3; on objects of
    knowledge, 176–78; on objects of
    propositional attitudes, 6, 163–79,
    185–87, 283n38, 284nn47–48,
    287n66; overview, 5; Robert Holcot
    and, 6, 162, 167–68, 172–76, 186–87,
    283n37, 287n66; sentence types and,
    168, 281n20; on truth-bearers, 167,
    174, 176; on universals, 168; Walter
    Chatton and, 5, 6–7, 137, 162,
    169–72, 186–87, 282n23, 282n29,
    283n38, 287n66
William of Sherwood, 191, 287n4,
    288n5, 289n13
Williams, George H., 295n43
Winterbottom, Michael, 292n11
Wippel, John F., 265n30
Wodeham, Adam. See Adam Wodeham
Wolfson, Harry Austryn, 295n43
Wolter, Allan, 262n2
Wood, Rega, 4, 249n3
Woods, John, 288n10

Zalta, Edward N., 253n1, 290n13
Zavalloni, Roberto, 254n13, 254nn15–16,
    255n19
Zupko, Jack, 5, 269n7, 274n38, 286n65,
    290, 290n11

MEDIEVAL PHILOSOPHY: TEXTS AND STUDIES

The Vatican Mythographers
Ronald E. Pepin

The Logic of the Trinity:
Augustine to Ockham
Paul Thom

Later Medieval Metaphysics:
Ontology, Language, and Logic
Charles Bolyard and Rondo Keele, eds.

Ens rationis *from Suárez to Caramuel:*
A Study in Scholasticism of
the Baroque Era
Daniel D. Novotný